MEMOIR OF DEHRA DOON

BY

G.R.C. Williams, B.A.,
Bengal Civil Service

Foreword

S.K. Das, IAS
Commissioner, Garhwal Division

NATRAJ PUBLISHERS
DEHRA DUN

First Published 1874
Reprinted 1985
Reprinted 1992
Reprinted 1998

Published by Mrs. Veena Arora for Natraj Publishers
(Publication Division) Dehra Dun and printed at Gayatri
Offset Press, New Delhi.

This book
is dedicated to
the memory of our
Late Prime Minister
MRS. INDIRA GANDHI
who in cognition of the history
and natural splendour of the
Doon Valley, always held it dear.

S.K.Das
I.A.S

Commissioner
Garhwal Division

FOREWORD

The Doon valley has a rich and colourful history. It is also endowed with a salubrious climate and some of the most enchanting natural springs and forests. In a world of strife and turbulence, it still offers a haven of tranquility to the visitor.

Since the last two hundred years, the Valley has been the home or resting place to some of the leading figures in our national life-Jawaharlal Nehru, Sardar Patel, K.D. Malaviya, M.N. Roy & Indira Gandhi to name only a few. It has also been a place of cultural ferment and some of our leading artists and writers have lived or have come here to rest and recuperate.

This book fills in a long felt void because there has been, as yet, no better or more comprehensive history of this Valley. It is a product of meticulous research and will be of enormous appeal to all those who love this Valley and would like to know more about its settlement.

Dehra Dun
October 2, 1992

(S.K.DAS)

PUBLISHER'S NOTE

The splendours of the verdant Doon Valley have provided attractive themes for writers down the years. By and large however, the prohibitive cost of publications has prevented many a potential reader from savouring the interesting history and charms of the famed Doon Valley in print. Inspired both by his love and a keen sense of public interest, Mr. P.K. Mohanty, IAS, District Magistrate, Dehra Dun has now come forward with a thoughtful and generous support that will enable far greater numbers to acquire this acclaimed book.

PREFACE.

ON being appointed Assistant Superintendel of Dehra Doon in 1871, I began to collect materials for the compilation of a Historical and Statistical Memoir of that District, in compliance with a Resolution of the Government, N. W. Provinces, dated June 1868, but my transfer to Mozuffernugger in the following year compelled me to discontinue the work, and at one time I almost despaired of ever being in a position to bring it to a satisfactory conclusion.

When, however, a partial relief from my current duties in the beginning of 1873, enabled me to turn my attention to the Gazetteers of the Doon and the two neighbouring districts, it struck me that my information was already sufficient to warrant my making the attempt.

I therefore commenced the present report on the 6th May, and finished it on the 14th August.

The interval since the latter date has been occupied with obtaining the sanction of Government to its publication, and putting it through the Press.

I would plead by way of excuse for its manifold imperfections, he disadvantage at which my transfer placed me with reference to such an undertaking, and the official pre-occupations which limited my sphere of enquiry even before I left the Doon.

Among the authorities consulted or directly referred to in the following pages are—

(1). MSS. Records of the Doon and Seharunpore.

(2). Mr. J. B. Fraser's Himalayan Mountains.

(3). Asiatic Researches, Vols. VI., XI., &c., &c.

(4). Hamilton's Description of Hindoostan.

(5). Historical Record of the 53rd Regiment.

(6). Dr. Royle on the Productive Resources of India, and Botany of the Himalaya Mountains.

(7). Falconer's Palæontological Memoirs.

(8). Law of the Extra-Regulation Tracts, by Mr. Whalley, C.S.

(9). Thornton's Gazetteer.

(10). General Cunningham's Archæological Survey Report.

(11). Raj Tarangini.

(12). Briggs' and Dow's Ferishta.

(13). Elliott's Mahommedan Historians.

(14). Forster's Travels.

G. R. C. WILLIAMS,
Asst. Magistrate, Meerut.

24th April, 1874.

CONTENTS.

PART I.—DESCRIPTIVE AND GENERAL.

PART II.—HISTORICAL.

Section I.   From the Earliest Times down to the Goorkha War.

PARA.

Section II.—*From the outbreak of the Goorkha War to the Present Time.*

PARA.

PART. III.—STATISTICAL AND MISCELLANEOUS.

Section I. *Fiscal History of the District. Dehra Doon Settlements.*

Section II. *Fiscal History of the District* (Continued). *Jounsar Bawur Settlements.*

Section III. Fiscal History of the District (Concluded).

Section IV. *Miscellaneous*, (Conclusion.)

APPENDICES.

PART I.—DESCRIPTIVE AND GENERAL

1. DEHRA* DOON, the most northerly district in the Meerut Division, comprises two distinct tracts, the Doon Proper or Valley of Dehra, and Jounsar Bawur, a more remote subdivision originally unconnected with the former.

The District comprises two distinct tracts.

2. The Doon is really composed of two valleys; the one sloping down to the Jumna on the North-West, the other, to the Ganges on the South-East. Their North-Eastern and South-Western boundaries are the Himalaya mountains and the Sewalik hills, respectively. Their united area is about 673 square miles, and they lie between lat. 30°—30° 32′, long, 77° 43′—78° 24′.†. The whole may be roughly described as a parallelogram forty-five miles long, from the N W. to the S. E., by fifteen broad, from the N. E. to the S. W‡

Geographical position of the Doon.

3. The beauty of this region is proverbial, and takes the visitor from the plains by surprise. It is well-wooded, undulating, and intersected with streams, some of which

---

* Written in the vernacular with a final *h*. The word Doon means " a valley " or " lowlands at the foot of a mountain range."

† So Thornton's Gazetteer ; corrected by Mr. E. T. Atkinson, C.S., to lat. 29° 57′ —30° 59′, long. 77° 37′ 15″—78° 22′ 45″.

‡ The Honorable Mr. Shore's calculations were as follows :—

Average length (sc. breadth),...   ...   .   45 }
     „   breadth (sc. length),...   ...   .   11 } = 495 Sq. miles.
to which add for the Sewalik forests, 50 × 4 = ...   200   „
besides a strip of the Himalayas containing 70 villages =   ...   60   „

Total square miles,   ...   755

The census report of 1865 gives 677·43

have a perennial flow of water throughout the whole of
their course. The ridges between, are,
except in places where shingle crops up,
covered with rich mould, nourishing a luxuriant vegetation.
The trees and shrubs have all the green freshness of the European forests, whilst the mountains on the north, the hills on
the south, give a charming variety to the landscape. When
describing the scenery, the French traveller Jacquemont,
hesitates between Haití and the Oberlands of Berne, in the
choice of an appropriate comparison for this lovely district.

*Beauty of the scen-
ery.*

4. On the North-East the horizon is bounded by the
lower, or Mussooree,* range of the Himalaya, which, opposite the town of Dehra,
bends back and encloses a portion of the
valley in an immense amphitheatre. The lower spurs of
chain are covered with dense forests; the loftier crests are,
except in shady clefts and gorges, comparatively bare, but
often support the rhododendron and the oak (*quercus inca-
na*), besides other rare trees belonging to the temperate
zone. Some of the peaks rise to a great height; the Great
Trigonometrical Survey Office at Dehra is no less than
5,136 feet below the highest point of the sanitarium of
Landour,† being itself 2,323 feet above the level of the sea,
and a few miles due east of Landour, on the road to Teeree,
one peak attains an elevation of 8,565 feet.

*Mountains. The
Himalayas.*

5. Running parallel with the Himalaya, the Sewaliks
slope gently into the Doon, having a softness of outline
strongly contrasting with their abruptness on the side
facing the plains. Owing to the elevation of the valley,

---

* More correctly, "Munsooree."
† Properly, "Landhaur."

they seem mere hillocks by comparison with the range in
the back ground. They are clothed with
The Sewaliks.
a thick forest, chiefly composed of *sál* and
sain, above which, on the higher crests, the pine (*pinus longi-folia*) frequently raises its head, indicating the proximity
of a cooler climate.

6. The only insulated hill is Nuwádá or Nágsidh, a
slight eminence about five miles South-East
Nuwádá.
of Dehra, where the Viceroys of the Gurh-wál Rájás had their residence in the olden time. It lies
parallel to the Sewaliks, and is unmistakeably an offshoot
from them.

7. The principal passes from the plains are—the Timlee,
seven miles East of the Jumna, and the
Passes from the
plains into the Doon.
The Timlee and Mo-hun.
Kheree or Mohun (Mohund) pass, al-most equidistant from that river and the
Ganges.

8. A ridge commencing a little to the West of Rajpore
and connecting the Himalayas with the lower
Watershed line.
hills at the entrance of the Kheree pass, de-cides the direction of the drainage; the valley sloping down
to the great rivers on either side, as already explained.

9. The Ganges, entering the Doon at Tupobun, 165
miles from its source, pours rapidly over
Rivers. The Gan-ges and Jumna, &c.
beds of boulders, between steep banks,
with an average descent of twenty-three
feet per mile, through several channels encircling islands
covered with thick jungle, and reaches Hurdwar, fifteen
miles below, at an elevation of 1,024 feet above the level
of the sea, with a discharge of from 7,000 to 8,000 cubic
feet per second in the dry season. The Jumna, sweeping

round Budráj mountain, enters the valley 110 miles from its source, flows over a succession of rapids with a descent of about 19 feet per mile,* likewise forming islands here and there in its passage, and debouches upon the plains twenty-one miles away, some three miles above Bádsháh Mahal, in the Seharunpore District, an old hunting seat of the Kings of Delhi, with a discharge of 4,000 cubic feet per second in the dry weather. Its banks in general shelve much more gently than those of the Ganges. Their tri-

Their tributaries. butaries, although a marked feature in the varied landscape, and turned to good account for agricultural purposes, are geographically insig-nificant, being in the upper part of their course, rather mountain torrents than rivers. Their direction is deter-mined by the ridge connecting Rajpore with the Mohun pass at Asaroree. They are two in number, the Sooswa and the Asun. These streams, rising near Bheem Tál, about

The Sooswá. half way between Dehra and Asaroree, flow eastward and westward, respectively, re-ceiving the whole of the mountain drainage from both sides, as they run along. The source of the Sooswa is 2,148 feet above the level of the sea, and its fall to the Ganges, 948. Six miles or so from that river it meets the Song, a

The Song. stream rising in the heart of the moun-tains behind Kalunga, a hill, or rather spur of the Himalaya, celebrated in Indian history. After their confluence, the united rivers flow onward under the name of the minor tributary.

10. The spring heads of the Asun are 2,121 feet above

---

* The distance from its confluence with the Tonse, 1,686 feet above the sea, to its confluence with the Asun, 1,470 feet, being 11 or 12 miles.

the sea, and the fall thence to the Jumna is 652 feet. It
receives only one tributary worth noticing;

The Asun.

the Tonse, which rises in the Southern
slopes of the Mussooree range, West of Rajpore, and

The Tonse, not a perennial stream.

joins the Asun a few miles beyond Bheem
Tál, but in the dry season has no water in
the lower past of its course, a fact incidental to a phenomenon common to the Doon and the

A fact connected with a curious phenomenon peculiar to the mountain drainage in the Doon and Seharunpore.

northern part of Seharunpore. Close under
the hills, the water lies near the surface,
appearing either in isolated pools, or rivulets, which, after flowing a short distance,
then vanish. Beyond the line of disappearance, it can only
be reached at extraordinary depths in the centre of the district. The well in the old Goorkha lines at Dehra, for instance, is 175 feet deep, and the Honorable

Great depth of the wells along the backbone of the Doon.

Mr. Shore's famous well near the Kutcherry, constructed at an expense of some
Rs. 11,000, is 228 feet deep. Hence there has always been

Whence the absence of well irrigation.

a total absence of irrigation from wells,
which are only used for drinking purposes.* In the palmy days of the Doon, however, the

* The list given by Mr. Shore in April 1827 is :—

Situation of well.					Depth, ft.	Date of construction.
Dehra,	..	..	..	..	88	1786.
Sutee Bágh,	..	..	..	..	75	1823.
Jhájhrá,	..	..	..	..	30	Many years ago.
Hureepore,	..	..	..	..	15	
Suhespore (two),	..	..	..	Shallow	
Dhákee,	..	..	..	..	do.	
Rámpore, on road to Hurdwar		..	..	45	

Besides the two above-mentioned, three others in different villages, and one in progress of construction ; in all 13. There are now altogether 29.

people had recourse to irrigation not only from dams and canals, but also from large tanks, the remains of which are to be found everywhere. The expediency of reviving these works of utility early arrested the attention of our officers. Among their advocates may be mentioned Mr. Calvert, Assistant Collector, who made the first settlement, Mr. Moore, Collector of Seharunpore, Mr. Shore*, and Colonel Young, whose recommendations finally determined Government to move in the matter.

11.   At the end of 1837 Colonel (then Captain) Cautley

Canals.   Captain Cautley's deputation to the Doon in 1837.

was deputed to the Doon to make an estimate of the expense of opening a Canal from the Tonse under the village of Beejapore, intended to irrigate the triangular tract between that stream, the Asun, and the Bindal ravine close to Dehra. He soon completed his task, and the works, commenced in October 1839, were finished in a year.

Beejapore Canal 1839-41.

12.   The next irrigation work undertaken was the restoration of an old canal of doubtful origin, called the Rajpore aqueduct, which had from time immemorial supplied the people of Dehra with drinking water drawn from the head of the Raspunah torrent at the foot of the Himalayas. This was commenced in the cold weather of 1841, and finished in the rains of 1844.

Rajpore Canal, 1841-44.

13.   The third was the Kutha Puthur Canal, leaving the Jumna, under the Himalayas, near a village of the same name, intended to irrigate the farthest extremity of the

* First Joint Magistrate of the Doon.

Western Doon between the Asun and the mountains. Kutha Puthur Ca- nal, 1840-41 and 1847. This water-course, designed by Captain Cautley in 1840-41, was not constructed for several years afterwards.

14. Since then, the execution of two other similar works has been carried out; the one, the Kalunga Canal, Kalunga Canal, 1859-60. drawn from the upper part of the Song at the village of Raepore, and the other, the Jákhun canal, so called from a Himalayan torrent in the Jákhun Canal, 1863-64. Eastern Doon, fifteen miles from Dehra, whence it takes its rise near the village of Bhogpore.

15. Compared with the more magnificent irrigation works in the plains, the Doon canals are Diminutive size of the Doon Canals. mere rivulets, though they yield returns forming no contemptible item in the revenue of the District.

16. Besides these helps to industry afforded by Government, the people further avail themselves Dam irrigation. of the natural advantages of the country for irrigation, by damming up the streams, and so obtaining an additional supply of water.

They also use them extensively for the purpose of turning corn-mills. Another source of profit Water-mills, &c. is the limestone boulders found in great abundance among the shingle of the torrents.

17. Owing to the depth of the ravines and their rapid No inundations or cases of alluvion and diluvion. slope, inundations never occur, in spite of heavy and sudden falls of rain, which often render water-courses, previously dry, completely impass-

able, in an incredibly short time. From the same causes, added to the stony character of the river beds, cases of alluvion or diluvion are almost unknown, although there are 122 villages hypothetically subject to fluvial action.*

18. In the rains and during the melting of the snow, immense volumes of water pass down the Ganges and the Jumna, which are then nowhere fordable. Such slight navigation as exists—principally consisting in floating timber rafts down the current—often becomes dangerous in the rainy season, and the single ferry boat that plies across the Jumna, at Rájghát Mundee, is worked with some difficulty. There is now no ferry on the Ganges, although there used to be at least two. The same river is spanned by a bridge of ropes at Tupobun, while the Jumna, opposite Kálsee, boasts an iron suspension bridge 383 feet long, with a roadway of ten feet, over which laden tattoes and even horses, as well as men, can pass.

Floods in the Ganges and Jumna.

Only one ferry.

Bridges.

19. A comparative absence of forest and swamp characterises the Western Doon. In the Eastern Doon on the other hand, traversed as it is by two perennial streams, the Song and the Sooswa, receiving numerous small tributaries in their course, the great excess of water nourishes a rank vegetation, and the forests contain large tracts of swamps. These begin close to the confluence of the above mentioned rivers, at the lower extremity of the Jákhan Ráo. The largest marsh in this

Difference between the Eastern and Western Doon.

Swamps.

* *Vide* Mr. Daniell's Settlement Report, dated 25th April, 1867, para. 68.

neighbourhood, named the Jogeewálá Jheel, is about two
miles long by half a mile in width. Its
Jogeewálá Jheel.
waters, covered with clumps of a gigantic
reed, called '*nul*,' and quite inaccessible in the inner portions, are apparently stagnant. Yet their proximity to a
river running on a rapid slope, proves that it might be
easily drained. Parallel with the Jogeewálá *Jheel*, on
the higher ground between the Ganges *Khádur* and the
Himalaya, is another large marsh containing about three
square miles of swamp—the Gosáinwálá *Jheel*. Beyond this
again is a third smaller marsh about one-
Gosáinwálá Jheel.
and-a-half miles long by a quarter of a mile
broad. Both are nourished by a stream named the Ram-
buha, the existence of which at the same time demonstrates
the great facilities for drainage,* for it passes through them
into the Ganges. How much these facilities have been
Facilities for neglected is illustrated by the history of
drainage neglected.
The Endeavour the Endeavour Farm, belonging to Mr.
Farm.
Vaughan, one of the old grantees, who
selected this locality as a field for enterprise, and settled with his family on the edge of the Ganges *Khádur*.
All succumbed after a few years to the malaria of the
neighbouring marshes. Their melancholy fate has gone
far towards deterring others from making similar attempts. In these parts the natives themselves are not
Prevalence of fe- fever proof, and the Police have to be
ver.
removed from Kánsrao during the sum-
mer monsoon. A few miles to the West, the climate
improves, and Col. Thelwall has a farm at Lachhiwálá,

---

* Since writing the above, I have been informed by Capt. Willcocks, that a survey
of the swamps in the Eastern Doon is now in hand.

carried on under European management, which promises to be a marked success.

20. The only marsh worth noticing in the Western Doon is one that formerly existed near Suhespore. The Zemindars began drain-ing it themselves years ago, and the land has been nearly all reclaimed, but future experiments of the sort are not likely to succeed without the aid of Government, for the' apathy of the people is even greater than that of the low-landers.

Suhespore Jheel.

21. Not to speak of the swamps, much of the district is absolutely barren, owing to the size of the shingle beds over which the moun-tain torrents flow, and elsewhere exten-sive tracts are covered with forests of natural growth, either belonging to Government or in the possession of private individuals. The cultivated area is therefore small.

Large tracts either barren or waste.

22. The General statement in Acres attached to Mr. A. Ross' report on the settlement of 1848, distributes the land (exclusive of the Government forests), as follows :—

Cultivated and culturable area.

CULTIVATED.	UNCULTIVATED.		
		CULTURABLE.	
34,327	Barren.	Waste.	Lately abandoned.
	1,19,895	48,157	5,833
		53,990	

We thus see that nearly fifty-four thousand acres of land, charmingly situated and all capable of yielding a good return, were then lying waste for want of labor, capital, and enterprise. Ten years before, the lamentable neglect of the productive resources of the Doon had attracted the serious attention of Government, who threw open the valley to European speculators on apparently favorable terms, subsequently modified : "the land was to be held rent-free for three years, and was not to reach the maximum of three annas a beegah till after 20 years, and then this rate was only to be laid on three-fourths of the whole culturable area, one-fourth being left unassessed." Many grantees came forward, and thousands of acres were given away to eager competitors. Their speculations failed. The causes of failure have been concisely summed up by a writer in the Calcutta review,* who has evidently drawn his conclusions from local experience :—

Plans for reclamation of waste.

Their failure—and causes.

"1st.—The large size of the grants.

"2nd.—The flight and death of cultivators.

"3rd.—The inexperience of the grantees, and

"4th.—But connected with the preceding. The illusory nature of the expectations, and of the supposed advantages, held out by Government."

To all this may be added an order issued from the Home Government prohibiting officials from holding land, which compelled several to sell their farms in a hurry, and, consequently, at a loss. This rule has since been relaxed, and at the present time more than one of the disqualified class are turning the resources of the valley to profit, for experience

* No. LXII. This subject will be afterwards more fully considered.

has at length taught what agricultural experiments are likely to be successful. Lord Canning's Grants,* too, have given
Lord Canning's grants.
an additional impetus to European enterprise by permitting the purchase of estates in fee simple, an immense boon to those whose prejudices render them averse to the theory of the Indian land tax.

23. Since the period of Mr. Ross' settlement, agricul-
Progress of agriculture.
ture has made considerable progress, but the estimate of the cultivated area in the year 1859 given by the writer above-mentioned is excessive :—

UNASSESSED OR GOVERNMENT LAND.			ZEMINDAREE, &c.	
Forest.	Lately abandoned.	Other culturable waste.	Forest.	Cultivated.
1,89,130	13,133	28,673	1,19,895	75,285

A statement lately prepared in the Superintendent's Office distributes the area included in the present settlement thus :—

Total Area measured†.	Lákhiráj.	Barren and village site.	Culturable waste.	Cultivated irrigated.	Cultivated unirrigated.
2,08,835	17,617	96,789	51,973	12,513	29,943

The last four columns of this table agree exactly with a return submitted by Kidár Narain, Tuhseeldar of Dehra ;

* Under orders of 1861, No. 1358A., dated 11th December ; cf. G. O., 4206, dated 15th August, 1862 ; 1042A., dated 17th September, 1862.

† The same report gives the area excluded from measurement as 2,24,715 acres.

Malgoozaree or Assessed Land, ...	Unculturable,... ...		96,789
	Culturable, ...	46,160	51,973
	Ditto lately abandoned,	5,813	
	Cultivated, ...	42,456	12,513 / 29,943
		Total,	1,91,218
Lákhiráj, ...	Unculturable, ...		13,512
	Culturable, ...		22,763
	Lately abandoned, ...		222
	Cultivated, ...		6,698
			43,195
Excluded from Settlement in possession of Government. (Sc. Forest Land), ...	Culturable, ...		7,784
	Unculturable, ...		183,919
			1,91,703

Assuming this calculation* to be approximately correct, and there is every reason for believing it to be not far wrong, the cultivated area is now about 49,000 acres or, roughly, one-fifth of the whole, exclusive of Government forests.

24.   The fertility of the soil has been sometimes over-rated, as will appear from the fiscal history of the District.   Soils are divided accord-

Classification of soils.

ing to a classification well known in the Upper Doáb; that of *meesun* (manured loam), *roslee* (un-manured loam), and *dákur* (clay-rice land), to which is added a fourth class, peculiar to the Doon; *Sankruh*, so called from the presence of gravel or pebbles and sand, representing the *bhoor* of the plains.   A return procured from the same source as that just now cited, professes to

---

* Another return gives—

Barren,	.. ..		2,94,220
Cultivable,	Jageer not paying revenue, ..	8,566	
	Cultivable, ...	76,313	
	Fallow, ...	5,813	
	Cultivated, ...	41,204	
			1,31,896
	Total,	..	4,26,116

show the various proportions of each, whether irrigated or unirrigated.

	ROSLEE.				DAKUR.				SANGAR.				MEESUN.		
Well irrigated.	Canal irrigated.	Irrigated from muddies, &c.	Dependent on rain.	Well irrigated.	Canal irrigated.	Irrigated from muddies, &c.	Dependent on rain.	Well irrigated.	Canal irrigated.	Irrigated from muddies, &c.	Dependent on rain.	Well irrigated.	Canal irrigated.	Irrigated from muddies, &c.	Dependent on rain.
..	4,151	2,344	11,295	..	1,067	894	1,879	..	177	124	4,881	..	1,936	112	586
..	385	1,467	2,764	..	207	529	926	..	16	298	3,744	..	100	444	368

It will be observed that the totals do not tally with the former statements, giving

40,694 acres $\begin{cases} \text{Unirrigated,} & \dots \quad \dots \quad \dots \quad 26,443 \\ \text{Irrigated,} \quad \dots & \dots \quad \dots \quad \dots \quad 14,251 \end{cases}$

25. The climate bears some points of resemblance to that of Lower Bengal, being moist and not so
Climate moist and mild. liable to extremes of heat and cold as other Districts in the North-West. Another peculiarity is the immunity of the valley from the blasts that scorch the less favored regions below during the hot weather. As might be expected from its altitude and close proximity to the Himalaya, it is also generally cooler, and snow has been known to fall. In February 1814, it lay on the ground for two whole days at Dehra itself, but this was an extraordinary phenomenon. The cold weather commences earlier and lasts longer than in the plains, while the rains of the summer monsoon are much heavier and more continuous. The winter showers too are plenteous, and in April the coming heat is generally tempered by thunderstorms. Even in May and the beginning of June, an occasional shower

refreshes the country.* In the same sultry season a breeze from the hills after sunset often enables Europeans to dispense with the punkha at night. During a hot weather storm, Mr. Shore once noticed a fall of 23° in the thermometer within an hour. The temperature fluctuates between 37° and 101°, as may be seen from the following register :—

	March.	April.	May.	June.	July.	August.	September.	October.	November.	December.	January.	February.
Maximum, ...	86	93	98	101	94	90	91	86	70	71	68	73
Minimum, ...	48	53	64	71	72	72	66	61	44	42	37·75	45
Difference,	38	40	34	30	22	18	25	25	26	29	30·25	28
Mean, ...	67	73	81	86	83	81	78·5	73·5	57	56·5	52·8	59·5

Mean Temperature, 70·65 †

26. At the Sanitarium of Mussooree, 6,000 or 7,000 feet above the level of the sea, the thermometer has a range of from 27° to 80°. In the winter months of November, December, January and February, the mean temperature is 50°, 45°, 42° and 45°, the thermometer rarely sinking below freezing point. The mean temperature of March, April, May and June is 53°, 59°, 66°, and 67°, and of July, August, September and October, 67°, 66°, 64° and 57°. Falls of snow in the cold weather are common. During the rains, which are exceedingly heavy, continual clouds obscure the atmosphere, and the climate of the hills can then

Climate of Mussooree.

---

* The average annual rainfall is about 80 inches.

† Nearly the same as that of Canton, *vide* Dr. Royle on the " Productive Resources of India," page 303.

be hardly called healthy, but it is bracing during the rest of
the year, particularly after the end of the summer monsoon.

27.   In common with the whole of Gurhwál, the Doon
is subject to occasional shocks from earth-
Earthquakes.
quakes.   These disturbances are rarely seri-
ous.   Indeed the only one at all severe on record, happened
in 1803.

28.   Notwithstanding the almost wholesale destruction
of game continually going on, the District
Animal Kingdom.
teems with animal life, and its Fauna pre-
sents a very wide field for enquiry, but the substance of a
few general remarks by Captain Bailey, late Deputy Conservator of Forests, will be quite sufficient to give the
general reader an adequate idea of the creatures met with :
" The Sewalik range abounds with wild elephants, which
do considerable damage to the crops, and
Elephants.
occasionally kill men.   In former years
trapping by means of pit falls (ogees) was extensively
carried on, and the old pits are constantly met with in the
forests, but of late years few attempts have been made to
take elephants in this manner."

29.   " The Maharajah of Bulrampore has several times
had permission* to catch them, which he
Their capture by
the Bulrampore Ra-   does by driving them into a " cul de sac"
jah.
and then noosing them.   This year (1872)

---

* I may here remark that unless Government places some restriction on such
permissions, not a single head of large game will be left in the Doon before many
years, and even small game will become very scarce.   I have heard that Jung Bahader
is about to make a raid upon the District similar to that undertaken by the Bulrampore Rajah last year, but on a much *larger* scale !   A fuller account of the former's
operations would be extremely interesting and instructive in connection with the
question of the expediency of permitting the frequent recurrence of these big hunts.
I cannot, however, pause to discuss the subject further.

he caught a herd of twelve in this way. He uses some sixty or seventy tame elephants for this purpose.

30. "Under the new rules, persons catching elephants give up one in four to Government, and pay 100 Rs. each for those they take away.

Rules for catching them.

31. "In the Sewaliks are also found tigers (*shere dhári-dár*), sloth bears (*jhábur*), leopards (*shere guldár*), hyenas (*lukar bugha**), the jerow mahá or *sámbar*), spotted deer (*chital*), four-horned deer (*chowsinghá*), the goorul, barking deer (*khákur*), pigs, porcupines, monkeys, among others the langoor of the Himalaya, and several sorts of wild cats, &c., &c.

Tigers, bears, &c., &c.
Hyenas, jerow, chital.
Chowsinghá, goorul, khákur, &c. &c.

32. "Elephants only come down into the valley to feed, nor does either the sloth bear, the gerow, the gooral, or the barking deer, live in the lowlands, where however all the other animals mentioned, besides hog deer (*párhá*), and huge pythons,† are found in abundance. *Nilgae* have also occasionally been seen in the Doon—but very rarely.

Habitat of certain animals.

Hogdeer, pythons, nilgáe.

"On the lower Himalayan slopes nearly every animal found elsewhere is met with, as well as others peculiar to the locality, such as the black bear (*bháloo*) and the serow.

Black bear, serow.

33. "There are traditions about the existence of the lion in the Sewaliks, but they are not authenticated, and it seems doubtful whether wolves or wild dogs live there."

Lions, wolves, wild dogs.

* A name also generally applied to the smaller species of leopard.
† Boas twenty feet long are not uncommon.

34. The scale of rewards for killing wild animals is as follows :—

Tiger,......... Rs. 10.	Bear,......... Rs. 5.
Leopard,..... ,, 5.	Hyena, ... ,, 3.
Cub-Leopard, ,, 2-8.	

Rewards varying in amount are also offered for the destruction of rogue elephants in case of necessity. The leopards are on the whole more dangerous and mischievous than the tigers. If not so fatal to human life, they certainly do greater damage to cattle and beasts of burden.

35. The Police returns give the following list of casualties for one year :—

Men killed by wild beasts,............................	3
,, ,, snake bites,...........................	1
Cattle lost from either cause, ...	33
Men and cattle injured ,, ...	25

This account is however beyond all doubt inaccurate, and does not represent the real amount of mischief done.

36. The birds are innumerable. Among them may be

noticed of game, the black partridge, the grey partridge, the peafowl, florikan, snipe (four kinds, the common or "full," the jack, the painted, and the solitary), quail (several kinds, as the bush, button, rain or black breasted), woodcock, bittern, jungle fowl, kalege pheasant,

duck, teal and goose. Woodcocks are not common, and according to Mr. Shore, only visit the valley from the hills after a heavy fall of

snow. Among other birds may be mentioned the black, brown, and fish eagle, the common vulture and several other varieties, kites, hawks, pelicans, and adjutants, cranes, &c., &c. One of

Forest king.

the most curious is a species of hornbill called the *Bunráo* or forest king, from the crown on its head and the size of its beak.

37. Nothing deserving the name of a skin trade exists, although the natives frequently sell skins,

No skin trade to speak of.

both of birds and beasts, to individual collectors, and the hides of the *sámbar*, &c., when converted into slippers, gaiters, and so forth, meet a ready sale.

38. The District is badly off for cattle, not to speak of horses. Neither oxen nor buffaloes ordin-

The breed of cattle and horses is inferior.

arily thrive there. Of the former there are two sorts: the "*puháree*," not peculiar in color, but stunted in size, with small crooked horns, bred at the foot of the Himalaya, and costing from 8 to 20 Rs.; and a superior kind, bought in the plains when yearlings, and reared in the mountains of Gurhwál. These fetch from 25 to 50 Rs. and upwards; still they are far inferior to those of the lowlands. In this respect matters do not seem to have materially improved since the year 1827. Yet the people of the plains have been always in the habit of feeding their livestock in the Sewalik pastures. The inhabitants of the Doon attribute their own want of success in cattle breeding to a sort of grass called *dholoo*, said to be injurious to any animal that eats it. All attempts to improve the breed of cattle and horses have proved abortive.

39. In a climate apparently so favorable to the development of animal life, this fact seems strange, and were proper care taken to keep the animals from rank fodder and protect them from the effects of excessive moisture, there

is no reason to doubt that they would thrive as well, if
not better, than elsewhere.   At present

This is chiefly due to defective management.

cattle plague is endemic in the valley,
like fever amid the malaria of the forests.

40.   The rivers abound in fish. *Mahaseer,*[*] a species of
carp generally, frequent the large rivers,

Fish.   The Mahaseer.

being commonly from 20 to 30 seers in
weight, often exceeding that limit, sometimes attaining the almost incredible weight of 90 ℔s.
They are also occasionally found in the smaller streams,
which swarm with trout.   To these may

Trout, soul, ro-hoo, &c., &c., fresh water shark.

be added the *soul,* the *chál,* the *giree,* the
rohoo, the *kálábáns,* and the *goonch,* or
fresh water shark, a repulsive brute of
great size, with capacious jaws displaying several rows of
saw-like teeth.   The native authorities enumerate in all
twenty-four species of fish, but there are certainly many
more.   The Ganges and Jumna moreover

Alligators.

breed alligators, both snub-nosed (*magur*),
and bottle-nosed (*guriál*).

41.   The natives catch fish in two ways, with nets and
by damming up the streams.   Successful

Native method of catching fish.   Efforts to prevent reckless destruction.

efforts have been made to prevent unnecessary waste and destruction of small
fry, by inducing them to desist from the
latter practice, and to employ nets with large meshes.   As
the law at present stands, everything here depends upon
the personal influence of the District officers.

42.   All true Doonites, whether Rajpoots or Brahmans,
eagerly consume fish whenever they can procure it, and

---

[*] Properly, I believe, " Mahashahr."

although immigrants from the plains deny doing so, they,
in all probability, adopt the custom of
their neighbours after a very short time.

<Fondness of the people for fish.>

The former consider the consumption of
fish necessary to the preservation of their health.

43. The vegetable is as prolific as the animal kingdom,
and the forests furnish a long list of plants,
shrubs and timber trees. Among the latter may be enumerated the *sál*, the *toon*
(scarce), the *sheeshum* (scarce), the *cheer* (*pinus longifolia*),
the *khyr* (*acacia katechu*), the *siris* (*acacia serissa*), the *sain*
(*pentaptera tomentosa*), and in the Himalaya, the oak and
the walnut. Gigantic creepers climbing about in every
direction, lend a tropical air to the forest scenery which
would otherwise appear semi-European. Of fruits, the
pear, the fig, the blackberry, the lemon, and strawberry, all
grow wild. When cultivated, those of almost every description, whether European or not, flourish; except the
peach, grape, strawberry, and mango. The humidity in-
jures the three first, and the heat is hardly great enough
for the fourth. European vegetables naturally grow better
than in the plains, and also flowers, for the violet and
primrose are common, while the abundance of roses, is one
of the first things that strikes the stranger from the lowlands. The rhea plant grows wild,* and promises, together
with tea, to be soon a valuable staple.

- Vegetable King-dom.

* This statement, though not incorrect, needs qualification. Dr. Jameson, (Superintendent, Botanical Gardens, Seharunpore), remarks : " There is a species of *Böh-
meria* met with in the Dhoon and Lower Himálaya under the name of Pooee and
Pooah, which is nearly identical with the Rhea, *B. nivea.* It is described by Don
under the name of *B. puza* or *putescens.* But it differs so little from the Rhea of
China as to form a variety only. Good fibre is prepared from it."

44. As elsewhere in the North-West, there are two crops, the *Khureef* and the *Rubbee*. The principal is the *khureef*, or *saonee*, of which *dhan*, rice, is the staple. There are three kinds of rice—two inferior, *chaitroo* and *hultyoo*, and one superior, *kyáree*. *Chaitroo* is sown in the month of *Chait* (March-April), and after being transplanted, is cut in *Bhádon* (August-September). It is sometimes called *Chumboo* or *Anjuná*, and is sown in land dependent for irrigation on rain. Neither does *hultyoo*, also cut in *Bhádon*, but sown in *Jeth** and *Asárh* (May-June), require artificial irrigation, when the rains are seasonable. Its other more popular names are *anjunnee* and *nuká*. *Kyaree*, the first class rice, is likewise sown in *Jeth*, and then transplanted in *Asárh* and *Sáwun* to slopes cut into terraces (*kyáree*), possessing the advantage of canal or *nuddee* irrigation†. It has to be carefully weeded, and is cut in *Bhádon*. This rice is also commonly called *rámjuwáin* and *básmutee*. Next to rice, *mundwa* is sown in the greatest quantity. The other khureef crops are *oorud*, *juwár*, *sánvuck*, *til*, *koolhut*, *mukee*, *lobyá*, *torya*, *arvee*, potatoes, ginger, turmeric (*huldee*) *poundá* (sugar-cane eaten in its natural state), sugar-cane (ordinary, *eekh*), red pepper, and *churree*. The rubbee is very much inferior in quantity to the khureef. Its staples are wheat and barley. Not much else is sown. Little or none of the ordinary produce is exported. On the contrary, importation has al-

Marginal notes:

Two crops—Khureef and Rubbee—as in the plains.

Khureef staples chiefly rice and mundwá.

The Rubbee staples wheat and barley.

---

* *i. e.*, if rain falls in that month—otherwise in Asárh.

† Excellent, perhaps the very best, *kyáree dhán* is grown in the hills ; *c. g.*, at Tapobun—it is also sown in the *khádir* lands where rain collects.

ways been necessary to meet the consumption, particularly since the hill stations of Mussooree and Landour have grown into large towns, and the establishment of the new sanitarium of Chukrata. Wheat, *oorud*, *moong*, gram, *arhur*, *bajra*, cotton, *moth*, barley, *alsee*, *sirson*, *torya*, and sugar in various shapes (*goor*, *shukkur*, *khánd*,) have all to be imported in large quantities, besides oil and ghee, and also Indian corn, of which hardly any is sown.

45. On the other hand, the Doon, in addition to timber, Products peculiar *bhábur* grass, *moonj*, and other forest produce, supplies the plains with tea and rhea, two products peculiar to it, though recently introduced.

46. The mineral kingdom has not yet been thoroughly explored. The Sewaliks, however, contain carbonate of lime, selenite, and pyrites. The minerals hitherto found in the Mussooree range are ; " calcareous tufa, frequently iron shot, calcareous sinter, white, brown and yellow calcareous spar in the primitive form, and sulphate of barytes, nodules of noble serpentine associated with hornblende slate, glassy actynolite, and earthy gypsum."*

47. The Sewaliks are an alluvial formation of the newer tertiary or upper miocene period, and are Geology of the regarded as débris swept down from the Sewaliks and Himalaya. Himalaya, over-lying an upheaved portion of the plains at the foot of the higher range. Their axis is parallel to that of the Himalaya. The strata of both chains have the same direction, from the N. W. to the S. E., and agree generally in dip†, being inclined towards the

---

* *Vide* Journal Asiatic Society, Vol., I., page 194.
† *Vide* Palœontological Memoirs, page 789, Vol. I.

North at an angle of 30° more or less, except where faults occur. Doctor Falconer divides the Sewalik strata into two classes; "1st, and lowermost, sandstone and conglomerate, containing subordinate beds of clay; 2nd, and uppermost, gravel." The sandstone is a whitish grey arenaceous rock with a fine quartz basis. Its consistency varies from extreme friability to crystalline hardness, according to the proportion of carbonate of lime cementing it together, but its leading characteristic is friability, so that it cannot be utilised to any extent for building purposes. The conglomerate consists of fragments of all the rocks entering into the composition of the higher range, viz., quartz, greywacke, hornblende, limestone, &c., resting on a clayey and arenaceous basis. It alternates with the sandstone. The beds of clay occur in both, and modify their character according to circumstances. Uppermost comes the gravel or shingle, which gradually develops from small pebbles, abundantly intermingled with sand where it is in contact with the sandstone, into boulders increasing in size as the proportion of sand decreases, until at length we find a deposit differing little from that seen at the bottom of the passes. The breadth of the inclined beds is from six to eight miles, and, as their inclination is northward, while their abutment to the south is steep, the hills rise abruptly from the plains and slope gently into the Doon. Dr. Royle's apt illustration* will render the general effect of their geological formation more intelligible. Let the reader imagine a series of parallel ridges in the form of right-angled triangles with bases resting on the passes, perpendiculars facing the S. W. and hypothenuses sloping towards the N.

* Botany of the Himalaya Mountains, Vol. I., Introduction, page xxvii.

E., succeeding one another like the teeth of a saw. Looking from the North, we see the gradual hypothenusal inclination from the crest forming the southern boundary of the District; looking from the opposite side, we are confronted by the perpendicular walls of weather-worn precipices. The same general description applies to the outline of the Himalayas, though the peculiar effect is not so striking, because the firmer consistency of the strata render them less liable to that process of detrition strongly perceptible in the case of the lower sandstone hills, which, it may be added, contain rich stores of fossil remains, popularly believed to be *exuviæ* of Titans killed in the war between the gods and the giants. The formation of the higher range is primary, chiefly consisting of limestone* alternating with clay-slate strata. Nearly half way down hill, about two miles west of Mussooree, below the Hatipaun peak, a bluish black slate is found, hard enough to be used for roofing houses, but it is generally soft and crumbling. About a quarter of a mile below Jurápánee, "large beds of primitive gypsum with earthy sulphate of lime occur." At Mussooree limestone predominates; on the ridge stretching away from Landour, N. N. E., clay-slate alternating with beds of quartz sandstone. Dr. Falconer briefly describes the whole formation as consisting of "vast strata of limestone, lying on clay-slate, crowned by slate, greywacke or sandstone. Beyond the limestone tract, gneiss, clay-slate, and other schistose rocks occur—granite, so far as I know, is not found."

48. The remains of iron mines exist near the village of Kutha Puthur at the debouche of the Jumna from the

* *Vide* Palæontological Memoirs, Vol. I., page 11, cf. Journal of the Asiatic Society, Vol. I., page 104, and Vol. 4, page 690.

E

mountains, but they have never yielded revenue to Govern-

Mines near Kutha Puthur. ment, although the people of the village used to work them from time to time.

49. The hills, as we have seen, afford little or no stone

Little stone fit for building,* and no kunkur. that can be utilised in architecture, and the geological formation of the valley itself, a vast shingle bed, interspersed with sand, having a partial covering of loam, forbids the existence of *kunkur*, the substitute for which is stone metalling, procured by breaking up the boulders found in the mountain torrents.

50. The population is thin. The two castes who take

Castes—two broad division of. the lead, in numbers and influence, are Brahmans and Rajpoots. Both are class- ified generally according to the broad divi- sion of highlanders and lowlanders. As a rule, the latter repudiate all connection with the former, and always lose caste by intermarriage with them.

51. The two principal sub-divisions of the hill Brah-

Hill Brahmans— Suroulé and Gingáré. mans are the Suroulé and Gingáré. Both have almost altogether lost sight of strict caste obligations, if indeed they ever really observed them at all, and will eat any sort of flesh except beef. Still the former affect a superiority over the latter, and will not take food from their hands, whereas even the Pamar Rajpoots of the Gurhwál Rájá's family, will break bread prepared by the Suroule, who fall in the social scale from intermarriage with their inferior brethren. These on

Inferiority of the Gingáré. the contrary not only intermarry with the meaner *soi-disant* Rajpoots, but follow a practice abominable to the pure Hindoo, marriage with

* *Vide* Appendix I.

widows. more particularly those of a deceased brother (*kurao*).
This, be it observed, is the essential point of difference between the high caste and low caste code throughout these
provinces. The Gingáré again drink spirits freely, which
the true Suroulé will not. Of the latter not more than ten
or twenty families remain. The others are numerous.

52. The hill Brahmans have a number of local nick-
names, on no account to be confounded
Brahminical nick-
names. with names of *Gotes;* such as Noútál, Dubhál, Dungwál, Boogáne, Unyále, Kukraitee, Kále, Thup-
lyál, Ghílyál, Bákoee, Joshee, Ramwán, Silánee, Poojáre,
&c., &c. Some of these are applied to all indifferently, for
instance, Noutál; but they chiefly belong to the Gingáré.

53. The Levites of the plains regard the hill Brahmans
as the illegitimate offspring of the pure
Lowland Brah-
mans, chiefly Gour Brahmans. They themselves are for the
and Sárusut. most part Gour and Sárusut. The former
will have nothing to do with those of the hills; the latter
are not averse to intercourse with them, and even eat the
flesh of game. Both are diligent cultivators.

54. The three principal tribes of Rajpoots, are Ránghurs, Ráwuts and Bishts. Ránghurs (a
Rajpoots—Rán-
ghurs of the Poon- name sometimes improperly alleged to be
deer clan. inapplicable to true Rajpoots) are the
descendants of strangers of Poondeer extraction from Seharunpore, who gained a footing in the Doon during the
decline of Gurhwál Ráj. There are very few of them, and
these are being gradually absorbed by intermarriage with
the hill women, a thing destructive to the purity of their
caste. Some live at Dhurmpore, Májrá, Kaunlí, Hureepore,
Ránghurwálá, Jhájrá, Meetheebheree and Jusoowálá (all in

the Western Doon).   A branch of the Mahomedan Poondeers, or Raos, of Kheree, zillah Seharunpore, also settled
near Nuwáda and still exists there, while Mahomedan
Chauháns from Raepore, whose ancestors came in the same
manner, live at Khooshálpore and Majra close to Suhespore.

55.   The Ráwuts are highlanders, though they pretend
that 1,200 or 1,300 years ago their ancestors, coming from Shaurajpore, Ráwut-
pore, Musanpore, and Chuchendee near
Cawnpore, took service with the Raja of
Almorah.   The former Raja having died childless, his
widow adopted a son of the Shaurajpore Rajá, who sent
four of his relations with the boy to Kumaon.   One of
these, named Kour Jámee Bhán, taking offence at something, left Almorah and emigrated to Sreenugur, where
he gained favor in the eyes of the Gurhwál monarch.
His descendants therefore prospered exceedingly, so that,
when in later days the legendary Ajbá Kour and Ránee
Kurnaotee took up their abode in the valley, as deputies of
the reigning prince, and founded the old palace at Nuwáda,
they settled the Rawuts at Ajbápore, Kurnpore and Oodee-
wala, where alone they are to be found.   This tribe inter-
marries with all the other hill Rájpoots, without losing
caste, a fact clearly distinguishing them from the Ránghur
Poondeers.   Their *gote* is " Angrah. "

56.   Mr. Traill* calls them Rajís.   He considers them
to be aborigines, and adds that in his
time they were, in Kumaon, reduced to
about twenty families wandering about
" in the rude freedom of savage life" among the sub-Hima-

_Ráwuts—Hill Raj-
poots claiming con-
nection with those of
the plains._

_Mr. Traill's ac-
count of them._

* Statistical Sketch of Kumaon, Asiatic Researches, Vol. XVI, pages 160, 200.

layan forests. According to him, they represented themselves to be descendants of an aboriginal prince of Kumaon,
who fled with his family to the jungle to escape the
violence of an usurper, and the outcasts called Dooms or
Dhooms are supposed to be their poor relations.

57. Another class claiming superiority over the ordinary Puháree Rajpoot, although belonging
to the hills, is the Bisht. The word really
appears to be a territorial title equivalent
to *Thokdoor*, or *Talookdár*. Negí, a term usually placed in
juxtaposition with it, and strongly resembling the name
of Nága, seems to be their true appellation, a fact striking
in connection with the habitat of these *soi-disant* Rajpoots,
and the universally received tradition of a Scythian or
" Chinese" supremacy in former ages.

*Bisht Rajpoots—
probably descended
from Tartar invaders.*

58. The other *Puháree* Rajpoots may be generally included in the term Khusia, a name of
which no satisfactory explanation has been
hitherto offered, though it is familiar to everybody through
the well-known ' Kossya hills.' They never wear the
Juneo, and their claims to relationship with the warrior
class do not even rest upon a foundation of plausible tradition.

Khusia Rajpoots.

59. There is one family of Rajpoots at Suhespore who
call themselves Tuars.

Túars (?).

60. Next come the Goojurs; like the Poondeers, they
immigrated from Seharunpore, as invaders,
in the last century, and settled near the
mouth of the Timlee pass, then the great
thoroughfare to and fro. They retain land at Timlee,
Kalyánpore, Soḷnáwálá opposite Suhespore, Tipurwálá,

*Goojurs; came
from Seharunpore,*

Játonwálá, Sháhapore, Dhurmáwálá and Purtálpore, &c.
Bhároowálá and Mothronwálá were formerly prosperous
Goojur villages. Now the community is there solely repre-
sented by an impoverished widow.

61. Besides the Chouháns of Khooshálpore and Májrá,
there are other people, likewise styling
themselves Chouháns, who have no right
whatsoever to the name, in spite of their
pretentions to Rajpoot ancestry, known as Khágee. This
tribe is common throughout the Ganges *khádur* in the Seharunpore and Mozuffernugger Districts, and it is exceedingly probable that they followed in the train of their betters,
with whom they claim relationship.

*Khágee Chou-
háns.*

62. Another more interesting tribe of low caste, is that
of the Mehrahs, numerous in the Eastern
Doon, and bearing a marked resemblance
to the Bhoksás of Bijnour. The Meh-
rah is a great eater of fish and drinker of spirits, whenever
he can get either. He is of inferior intelligence and physique, and has few traditions except that his ancestors were
Rájpoots. It is more likely that they were the aboriginal
inhabitants of the country. Raewálá, Kurkshámpore and
Jogeewálá may be indicated among their haunts. They
are also to be found in the forest belt south of the Sewaliks,
but are timid and averse to intercourse with strangers.

*Mehrahs, probably
aborigines.*

63. The same remarks apply to the Heries. They
however are much less numerous.

Heries.

64. A third similar community of outcasts is that of
the Dhooms, a tribe common at the foot of the Himalayas.
Mr Traill describes them as black, with
curly hair inclining to wool, and living in a state of almost

Dhooms.

universal slavery, probably arising from the fact that the
Hindoo settlers from the plains seized some of the aborigines and reduced them to bondage.   Traces of the ancient
régime still exist, and to this day, the Dhooms are hewers
of wood, and drawers of water.   Can they be the troglodytes
noticed by Hamilton?*

65.   The Mahommedan element in the population is
very slight.   Most of the Mahommedans
are chance visitors from the plains.   As
to conversions, they have secured few pro-
selytes, except among the wretched Dhooms, and even these
prefer Christianity to Islám.   So late as 1827, there was
not a single mosque in the whole valley.   Now, however,
there are some at Dehra and Rájpore, for example.

*Mahommedan ele-
ment, small.*

66.   Brahmoism has been occasionally represented by a
few enthusiatic Bengalees.

Brahmoism.

67.   The writer is indebted to that energetic minister,
the Rev. J. S. Woodside, for some information about the progress of our purer
religious system.

Christianity.

68.   The Dehra Mission, a branch of the American Mission of Loodianah, was established in the
year 1853.   Mr. Woodside himself commenced the work, with the assistance of
Gilbert MacMaster, then a scripture reader, now pastor
of the native Church of Dehra, a man educated at the
Seharunpore orphanage, under the care of the late Dr.
Campbell.   Gilbert was at the time the sole native representative of Christianity in the Doon.   The community of
native Christians at present numbers upwards of 500

*Dehra American
Mission, 1853.*

* Description of India, Vol. II., p. 641.

souls, including the agricultural colony at Annfield, belonging to the Church Mission, which consists of about 300 persons, some originally baptized at Dehra, others being part of a band of 40, whom Mr. Woodside brought with him from Rohilkhund in 1859.

69. The new mission at first met with much opposition. The Missionaries had many things laid to their charge, and were accused before the Superintendent, of resorting to illegitimate means of gaining converts, among others, of kidnapping children, and sending them *carefully nailed down in boxes*, to the establishment at Seharunpore. Then there was much difficulty about procuring a site for a schoolhouse, as the Oodásee Mohunt of Guroo Rám Ráe's temple, the principal landed proprietor in the Doon, was not inclined to encourage interlopers, by parting with his land to them. The Superintendent of the period remained *neutral*. At length this obstacle was removed. Mr. Colvin, the Lieutenant-Governor, happening to visit the District in the spring of 1854, gave Mr. Woodside's grievances a patient hearing, and, without further delay, ordered a portion of the Tuhseelee compound to be placed at his disposal. Such open countenance on the part of an official in high authority, would have been in itself sufficient to ensure success, but before the proposed arrangement could be carried out, a new Superintendent, Mr. Dunlop, came into office, and he, objecting to interference with the Tuhseelee compound, generously bought the site now occupied by a large schoolhouse in the town, and gave it to the Mission as a free gift.

The new Mission opposed.

Mr. Colvin the Lieut.-Govr. interferes, 1854.

Also Mr. Dunlop.

70. Mr. Woodside had previously made an attempt to open a school in a hired building situated

Previous attempts to establish a school frustrated.

unfortunately within the Cantonment boundary, whence the Commanding Officer had the intruders ejected, because the place might be possibly required on an emergency to serve as a Small Pox Hospital.*

71. Gradually all opposition died away, and the Mission henceforth became deservedly popular,

The educational field is eventually left almost altogether to the Mission.

except during one inauspicious period, when a Government school is said to have been deliberately brought into competition with it. This rival institution has never flourished, leaving the educational field almost altogether to the Mission.

72. In the year 1859, the Dehra Christian Girls' Boarding School was started under the Super-

Female Education.

intendence of the Rev. D. Herron. The need of a School of a superior character for the daughters of Native Christians had been long felt. There were many fairly educated men in the Christian community, but no educated women. Strange to say, moreover, experience showed that after marriage, the husbands, far from raising the wives to their own level, sank to that of their less cultivated helpmates. The sound common sense of the gentlemen connected with the Mission rendered them keenly alive to this fact, and they determined to strike at the root of the evil. The establishment in question was therefore opened on the 1st of April, 1859, commencing with fourteen pupils. By the end of 1863, their numbers increased to forty-four; by January 1869, to fifty-seven; and in

---

* A use, to which, by the way, it was never put.

F

1872, to upwards of one hundred. The institution is undoubtedly one of the most praiseworthy results of Missionary efforts in these provinces. A fine building has been erected on an admirably chosen site, for the accommodation of both teachers and pupils, at a cost of more than 40,000 Rs., and the advantages offered have been so thoroughly appreciated, that the present premises will, there is good reason to believe, soon be found unable to contain the whole number of candidates for admission.

73. Another interesting Christian institution is the *Orphanage for Girls.* Orphanage for Girls, established at Loodianah in the year 1836. Owing to an extraordinary mortality among the pupils, lasting several years in succession, it was removed to this more genial climate in April 1871. Of 37 girls, however, no less than seven died before the end of September. This unexpected coincidence must be attributed to pre-contracted disease, and had not the removal been effected, the mortality would unquestionably have been much greater.

74. The main feature in the policy of the Dehra Mission, is the prominence given to education *Policy of the Dehra Mission.* as a means of spreading the Gospel, and the Missionaries have thus won the good will of those whom they have been unable to convert.

75. The Statistics of the Mission[*] for the year ending *Statistics of the Mission.* September 30th 1871, were :—

AGENTS EMPLOYED.

Foreigners.—Ordained Missionaries,...   2
Female Teachers, ...:   3
Carried forward, ...   5

---

[*] According to the report for 1871-72, the number of girls at school is 105, (15 of these boarders)—of b vs, (including every denomination,) 275.

	Brought forward,	...			5
Natives.—Scripture Readers,	...	...	...	...	3
Male Teachers,	...	...	...	...	4
Female Teachers,	...	...	...	...	4
				Total,	16
Number of boys in the Schools.—Hindoos,		...	...		149
	Mahomedans,	...		...	17
	Others,		...	...	16
				Total,	182
Teachers of the same.—Christians,	...	...	...		4
Hindoos,	...	...	...		3
Mahomedans,	...	...	...		2
				Total,	9

Net cost of the above, Rs. 3,600.

CHRISTIAN COMMUNITY,

Number of souls,	...	...	...	...	215
Converts during the year, ... { Hindoos,		...	...		6
{ Others,...		...	...		1
Native Pastors, ...	...	...	...	...	1
Children at School, ... { Boys,		...	...		16
{ Girls,		...	...		109
				Grand Total, ...	348

Net cost of purely Christian Schools, Rs. 5,300.
Contributions of Native Christians, Rs. 50.

The Mission, though mainly dependent upon contributions from America, receives much valuable aid in this country. It presents the pleasing spectacle of a religious fraternity that has discovered the secret of carrying on its work without offending the prejudices of any class or denomination.

76. The Agricultural Colony at Annfield was esta-
Annfield Agricultural Christian Colony. blished by the Church Missionary Society in the year 1857. At first it consisted of only a few families, but the number of the colonists rose to 150 in the year 1859, and is now 302; men, women, and children. Most came originally from Meerug-

pore, and other villages between the old and new branches of the Ganges in the Meerut District.   They live entirely by agriculture, and to judge from the nature of their crops, (rice, bajra, cotton, sugar-cane, wheat and barley,) are diligent cultivators.   The estate, (belonging to a Major Rind,) measured 500 acres when first taken over, and to this 50 or 100 acres have since been added.   The colony is an outstation of the Mission at Meerut.   The secular affairs of the converts are managed on the *puncháyut* system.   They have a substantially built church, besides a school with an attendance of 80 scholars, and support themselves, receiving no grants except in aid of the church and school.*

77.   The inhabitants of the Doon are exceedingly simple-minded, albeit cunning after their own fashion, and that ill-disguised hostility to foreign religious systems, characteristic of the lowlanders, probably due to the influence of Mahomedan fanaticism, is here seldom perceptible.   Hence the district offers an unusually favorable field to Missionary enterprise.   Still the words of Mr. Shore, spoken in 1827, are no longer true: " from not having seen much of the English, they (the people) have no ridiculous affectation, that doing such and such things is against their caste, but will generally do what they are told, as is always the case where the English are little known."   In the present day, their affectation of caste is ridiculous, all the more so, because so few of them have

The Doon, a favorable field for Missionary enterprise, in spite of some caste affectation.

---

* Information furnished by the Rev. Mr. Hœrnle.   The printed report for 1872, gives 284 colonists + 42 baptized during the year (of whom 39 children, 3 adults) = 326.

any right to be considered genuine Hindoos of the four *burns* at all; yet they tolerate Christianity.

78. The principal heathen religious establishments of any antiquity are those of Rikheekesh and Tupobun, both

Heathen endow-
ments. sacred to Vishnoo, whose officiating priests are of the Rámánoojee Bairágee sect. They possess endowments of land, the villages of Rikheekesh and Tupobun being held rent free for their support. The foundation of the temple at the former place is attributed to Shunkur Achárj; at the latter, Guláb Singh, Rájá of Cashmeer, built another recently.

79. The modern temple, or Gooroodwárá of the Oodá-

Gooroo Rám Rae's
Temple. see Gooroo, Rám Rae, founded in 1756S., is more noted. The centre building, a handsome structure, designed in the style of the Emperor Jehángeer's tomb, contains the Gooroo's bed. At the corners, are four smaller monuments, erected in memory of his four wives. The material is brick plastered over, and painted in imitation of mosaic. Owing to the model, the whole has a Mahommedan air, curious in an Oodáseé place of worship. Close by, are two tanks providided with water from the Rajpore canal. One is a fine reservoir of great depth, 230 feet long by 184 feet wide. The other is small, and there is a third still smaller, filled with rain water, used to boil pulses, which cannot be softened in the canal water. The institution is supported by seven villages held rent-free from the British Government, and six held rent free from the Teeree Rájá. In 1827 Mr. Shore calculated the income derived from the former at Rs. 1,600, that derived from the latter at only Rs. 35, and the yearly.offerings to the temple at three or four thousand rupees a year. The revenue of the Mohunt has since in-creased enormously, owing to the immense rise in the value of land. In fact the present incumbent is reputed to be the richest man in the Doon. This functionary used for-merly to be elected by the Sikh chiefs in punchayut from among the chelas of the high priest last deceased.

80. A large crowd of people collect and receive food at

Installation of the Mohunt—manner of his dress.

each fresh installation. The old custom was to present Government with a *nuzrana* of Rs. 500 on these occasions, a pair of shawls being bestowed upon the new high priest in return. Both he and his *chelás* wear a distinctive head dress, a sugar loaf shaped cap of red broad cloth, with a black silk fringe round the bottom, worked all over with party colored thread.

81. All Oodasees of course acknowledge the sainthood

Gooroo Rám Rae's followers.

of Gooroo Rám Rae, and he has numerous devotees among almost every Hindoo sect. The inhabitants of the Doon regard them-selves as his chosen people, not without reason, since he came to end his days in their midst. His most enthusias-tic worshippers however have always been the Cis-Sutlej Sikhs. The Akálee Sikhs on the contrary refuse to recog-nise him, for his legitimacy was questionable, and his peaceful tenets were opposed to the stern code of the terrible Sri Gooroo Gobind Singh. Yet Runjeet Singh, being sick unto death, sent an offering of Rs. 500 to the temple in the Holee of 1826.

82. This popular festival has been chosen for the cele-

His Mela.

bration of the annual ceremonies in honor of the saint. On the first of Chait, the fair or *Mela* (called Sungat), commences. It lasts till the tenth.

On the 6th a new flag is hoisted upon an enormous flag staff standing between the temple and the large tank. Hundreds of pilgrims lend a hand to heave the huge standard up and down. The Mohunt supplies each with one day's food. The average attendance is from 3,000 to 4,000, but it sometimes amounts to 10,000, depending mainly on the size of the Hurdwar fair, whither the pilgrims flock immediately after. The majority of them come from the Punjáb. Many visitors from Bareilly and Moradabad also attend. There is also a small fair at Rikhee-

Fair at Rikhee-kesh. kesh in Magh, called *Mukr kee Sunkrânt,* and another in Baisakh, called *Sutwáteej,*

but there are never any great gatherings there, except on the occasion of a large fair at Hurdwar, when the crowd on this side of the bathing *ghat* is considerable, and trains of pilgrims afterwards come pouring through the Doon on their way to Budreenáth, Kidárnáth, Jumnotree and Gungotree.

83. The only other holy spot worthy of special notice is

The Suhusra Dhara. the Suhusra Dhara (सहस्र धारा), the Place of the Thousand Drippings. Which a very simple phenomenon has invested with peculiar sanctity in the eyes of the people. From the side of a charming valley to the east of Rájpore, oozes a mountain stream, distilling its waters over a precipice thirty feet high, and leaving a crust of lime on every thing it touches. Particles thus accumulating for centuries, have made a projecting ledge forming a sort of cave, from the roof of which falls a perpetual rain that turns every blade of grass coming in contact with it into a petrifaction. From above hang stalactites innumerable. Stalagmite covers the ground beneath. In a smaller cave of similar formation, lies a lump of stalagmite not unlike the popular figure of the Maha Deo (the Lingum). Two Brahmans, living in the neighbouring village of Nágul, eke out a scanty subsistence, as priests to this Divinity, nor do they disdain to accept alms from European visitors. Opposite, there is a sulphur spring, also possessing powers of petrifaction.*

84. The inhabitants of the Doon are exceedingly superstitious. Their belief in ghosts, spirits, demons, and witches, is implicit. This may be, because the grander

Superstitions.   phenomena of nature have overawed their mind and excited their imagination. Mr. Shore long ago described the great popular bugbears.†

---

* The following description of the place, extracted from the *Delhi Gazette* (1868), and already re-published in the *Calcutta Review* (No. XCVI., p. 82) will bear repetition :—

"In the commencement of this day's march, we enjoyed a sight of uncommon beauty, which was rendered more striking by being concealed by a jutting point of rock till we approached very near and ascended a little bank, when it suddenly burst on our view. It was a fall of water from an excavated bank with a cave or grotto at each extremity, forming together an arch of about 100 feet in perpendicular height, with a subtended base of 80 or 100 yards. Through every part of the impending summit the water oozed out in drops, which fell in showers into a basin, whence it was carried by a small stream into the river below. The lofty trees and luxuriant shrubs which overhung the brow threw a partial shade over the picture, while the sun striking full upon the cascade ; was reflected in the sparkling globules, giving a richness and brilliancy to the scene, which words are incompetent to express. Upon an inspection of the grotto to the right, we were struck with new and more singular appearances. It is a cavern, about six feet in height, ten in depth, and fourteen or sixteen in length, and is a natural excavation, the walls and roof of which are rock. The water filters through the top, from which pendent shoots like icicles are disposed in all the different stages of petrifaction : the small ramifications form variegated beds of moss serving as conductors for the water when it first begins to crystallize ; and from a tube or pipe, they become, by repeated incrustations, a firm consolidated mass. The various colors produced by the vegetation and changing with the different shades of light, give to the outer surface the appearance of mother o'pearl ; but when the petrifaction is complete, the inside has a great resemblance to alabaster."

† Report of 1st May, 1827.

First comes the Perchásan, (feminine—Choorel), like a human being in shape, with its feet *turned backwards*, a sign of evil omen, for those who see it soon die. This supernatural being is evidently nothing more nor less than the " fetch " of the British isles. Then there is the Dhág—our witch —a hag who, through long study and consequent familiarity with the devil, has acquired the fell power of making human life gradually waste away under the influence of her incantations. In the days of yore, many an old woman expiated some such imaginary offence with the loss of her own life. Several complaints of witchcraft were laid before Mr. Shore, when he first took charge. " He found an electrifying machine a grand specific. A rupee being placed on the Leyden jar, the suspected witch was desired to take it off with one hand, holding the chain in the other; her failure proved her to have no power; and a few shocks were given to the complainant as a specific against it." The cases were thus decided to the perfect satisfaction of all parties concerned. At one time men frequently died off suddenly, after having built houses inside fairy circles, and Bhungies had to bury their dead head downwards, feet upwards, lest the unclean spirits of the departed should wander about and annoy the neighbours.

85. Although the mountaineers are tough, well made, active and wiry, the peasantry generally are apathetic, averse to manual labour, and far inferior in physique to the lowlanders. This is undoubtedly due in a great measure to defective sanitation. We have seen how fatal the malarious jungles of the Eastern Doon may prove to Europeans, and among the natives, rheumatism, dysentery, fever, and their

Other characteristics of the peasantry. Their inferior physique and its probable cause.

G

concomitants, work such mischief that of those who survive the continual attacks of disease in the unhealthy tracts, a man fifty years old already appears to have run the allotted course of three score and ten. Were not the Police removed every year from Kánsrao to Bhogpore at the foot of the Himalaya, not a man would stand three rainy seasons, and the hardy faquirs themselves fly from Rikheekesh at the same time. The climate of the Western Doon is better, and the elevated ridges in the middle of the District, where the new cantonments, the town of Dehra, and the village of Rajpore are situated, are, comparatively speaking, very healthy.*

86. The humidity of the climate, in all probability, accounts for the inordinate love of liquor characteristic of the Doonites, who, feeling the want of stimulants, freely

Their intemperance.

consume spirits and intoxicating drugs, a circumstance perceptibly affecting the proportion of the excise returns to other items of revenue.

87. The dress of the immigrants or their descendants

Their dress.

in no wise differs from that of the lowlanders. The true local costume is a blanket skilfully wrapped round the body, so as to leave the arms and legs free, and ingeniously secured with a curious arrangement of wooden skewers.

88. In the valley the dwellings of the poorer classes

Habitations.

are chiefly grass huts—mud huts are very rare. Higher up, on the slopes of the Himalayas, stones and mud are used to build the walls. The great number of good brick masonry houses in the occupation of well-to-do natives is remarkable, because only

---

* I have so little faith in our mortuary statistics, that I think it useless to analyse those given in the Sanitary Commissioner's Annual Reports.

forty-five years ago there were not more than eight or nine such commodious residences (exclusive of European houses) in the whole District; three at Dehra, one at Rajpore, three or four at Rikheckesh, and one at the north end of Hurdwar, which can hardly be counted, for it was built by a *Zemindár*, who had the good fortune to marry the daughter of a rich Sikh *Sirdár*, and the building was only intended to be used during fair-time.

89. The food most commonly eaten is rice, with vegetable curry, and bread, or chupaties, sometimes made of wheat, generally of *mundwa, toour, oorud*, &c. The *Puhárees*, besides rice and *mundwa*, extensively consume barley and *musoor*. Their predilection for strong drink, fish, and other forbidden things, has been commented upon.

Their Food.

90. The most noticeable feature in their system of *Puncháyuts* is, that it is ordinarily resorted to among the lower orders, such as *Dhobies, Chumars, Bhungies*, &c., for the decision of questions connected with *caste*. Pending the jury's decision, both parties have to contribute towards the payment of the tobacco and so forth consumed. When a conclusion has been arrived at, the person to whom it is unfavorable, suffers excommunication, until he complies with the order of the jury, whatever it may be. Any fine realized from him is devoted to the purchase of country spirits and sweetmeats, to be fairly distributed among all concerned.

System of Puncháyuts.

91. Marriage wholly depends upon pecuniary considerations. The bride always receives a dower of from 10 to 500 Rs., according to the father's means, partly in cash, the rest in clothes,

Marriages.

furniture, and ornaments, &c. In fact the bridegroom is paid to marry her. This is the custom of the valley. In the hills, on the contrary, the bridegroom buys her from the father, and she sometimes fetches a good round sum.

92. The language is perceptibly different from the dialect of the plains, being purer Nágree, with peculiar local turns and inflections, which the writer has not had a fair opportunity of mastering.*

Language.

93. Beyond the sphere of the Dehra Mission, education cannot be said to have made much general progress since the days of Major Young, who, on opening a school at his own expense in the Goorkha lines, found he could induce no one to attend except soldiers' children, and one of these, having mastered Hindee, when invited to commence the study of Persian, replied by asking what on earth he could possibly want with a Mahomedan language?†

Education.

94. Heinous crime never has been rife in the Doon, nor have the people ever been wealthy enough to indulge much in civil litigation.‡

Crime and litigation.

95. The principal lines of communication in the Western Doon are:—

Communications— forms Asaroree to Rajpore.

(1). From Asaroree to Rajpore, fourteen miles; along this road passes the traffic from the plains through the Mohun pass, (which is

---

* During the short period of my residence in the Doon, the peculiar nature of my duties prevented my going out into Camp, and I never even once visited Jounsar Bawur.

† A sketch of the actual state of education is reserved.

‡ For Criminal and Civil Returns, *see* Conclusion.

pierced by a causeway seven miles long, practicable for carts and carriages), to Dehra, and beyond that town, to the hill station of Mussooree. Captain Willcocks, the District Engineer, remarks: "This (or rather a portion of it) is the only first class (*i. e.*, metalled and bridged) road in the Doon. Until 1872, with the exception of a piece three miles in length, bujree (gravel), from the rivers and torrents, was the only material used as metal. On comparatively level ground, bujree, although a very dusty material in the hot season, answers admirably, and is obtainable at the cost of labor and carriage only. But as the traffic has increased enormously, broken stone has become a necessity for most portions of the road."

(2). From Dehra to Rájghát on the Jumna, twenty-three miles; a second class (raised and bridged kutcha) road; next in importance to the former, for along *From Dehra to Rájghát.* a portion of it, as far as the village of Ghumowálá, 7½ miles on this side of the Jumna, passes most of the traffic to the military cantonment of Chukrata beyond that river.

(3). From the head of the Timlee pass (where there is now a road almost as good as that *From Timlee to Umbáree.* through Mohun) to Suhespore, six miles, and then from Ghumowálá to Umbáree on the Jumna opposite Kálsee, nine miles, important for the reason just assigned; the latter part of this line is of the same class, as that last mentioned; the first part is of the third class, *i. e.*, raised and unbridged kutcha. An estimate has already been submitted for metalling the road from Dehra to Rájghát as far as its junction with this,* and

* Since the above was written, some 4,000 Rs. have been sanctioned for the purpose.

one for metalling the line between Ghumowala and Um-
baree is probably by this time ready.

96.   In the Eastern Doon there is only one line of any
importance ; a third class road, thirty-one miles long, from

Only one road of
any importance in
the Eastern Doon,
from Dehra to Hur-
dwar.

Dehra to Hurdwar.   The District Engineer observes : " This *was* a very good
road, but during the floods of the past
few years in the Song river, portions of it
have been cut out, until it has become almost useless for
traffic.   Measures are in hand either to carry it much
further into the Northern face of the Motee Chor hill, or,
if this is not found practicable, to open out and improve an
old road which runs from Kansrao across a low portion of
the Motee Chor Rao to its junction with the present road."

97.   Another, however, deserves to be mentioned, al-

From Hurdwar to
Tupobun.

though it is rather a path or track than
a road ; that along the Ganges from Tupobun to Hurdwar, a distance of seven-
teen miles.   This during certain seasons of the year is
much frequented by pilgrims.

98.   From Rajpore to Mussooree and Landour, the tra-

From Rajpore to
Mussooree.

veller ascends by a path along which one
can ride with comfort.   The distance to
the post office at Landour is seven miles.
A similar path follows the crest of the mountains for thirty-
eight miles, to Chukrata.   There is a lower road from
Rajpore to Mussooree, about fourteen miles long, which

Administrative
divisions.

used to be practicable for country carts,
but was lately impassable on account of
landslips.

99.   The administrative divisions, together with various

particulars relating to each, are exhibited in the following tabular statement.*

Tuhseel.	Pergun-nah.	Number of estates.	Land revenue for 1872-73.	Area in acres.	Population.	In the Civil jurisdiction of	In the Police jurisdiction of	Remarks.
		INCLUDES						
DEHRA.	Western Doon.	222	28,610	219,520	60,134	Subordinate Judge and Judge of the Small Cause Court of Dehra and Mussooree, and Judge of Seharunpore.	Suhespore	1st Class Station—jurisdiction from Jumna to the Tonse.
	Eastern Doon.	165	8,116	213,760	16,279		Dehra.	1st Class Station—jurisdiction from Tonse to the Ganges.
							Rajpore.	2nd Class Station—includes a small strip of both under the hills. The first class station of Mussooree in the hills above, cannot, properly speaking, be said to be in the Doon at all. Its jurisdiction extends along the mountains right away to the Jumna, and a short distance east, towards Teeree.
Total,	2	387	36,717	433,280	76,413			

Formerly there were five pergunnahs in the District; two in the Western, or Puchhwá, Doon—Kalyanpore and Suntour; three in the Eastern, or Purwa Doon—Busuntpore, Souree (or Soree) and Suhjpore. The present fiscal divisions were fixed in the last settlement (from 1863 to 1893)†. The boundary line between them passes along the Ruspunah, a mountain torrent two miles east of Dehra, the chief town.

* This return excludes from column 3 a tract given to Major Rind not shown in the Settlement papers, also 18 grants of various descriptions. The Census report of 1865 gives a different estimate of the area in acres.

Western Doon, ... 2,26,122
Eastern Doon, ... 2,07,428 } A third return says 4,26,116.

Total, ... 4,33,550

† *Vide* Mr. C. A. Daniell's Settlement Report, dated 22nd February, 1864.

100.   The administrative staff at various periods appears
Administrative   to have been :—
staff.

	1822-23.	1850-51.	1860-61.	1870-71.
Number of Magisterial Courts,	1	3	3	3
Number of Civil Courts, including Revenue Courts and Deputy Collectors, empowered to hear rent suits, ...	2	6	6	5
Number of Covenanted Officers at work, ...	1	3	3	3

101.   It is necessary to explain that of late years the
How constituted   staff has generally consisted of a Super-
both at present and   intendent, with the powers of a District
formerly.
Magistrate and Collector, and two Assist-
ant Superintendents, both having Magisterial powers as
well as those of a Deputy Collector, one being also *ex-officio*
Sudder Ameen and Moonsiff, now Subordinate Judge and
Judge of the Small Cause Court. This, strictly speaking,
gives three Magisterial, three Revenue, and two Civil
Courts, but, in practice, the duties of the Subordinate
Judge are at present confined to Civil work. In 1860-61,
the Superintendent was Principal Sudder Ameen, and thus
represented an additional Court. In 1850-51, he represented three Judges, being at once Principal Sudder Ameen,
Sudder Ameen, and Moonsiff. Hence the number of courts
appears greater on paper than it is or ever has been in
reality. Moreover it is very questionable whether any functionary in the Doon legally had powers to hear rent suits
as a Deputy Collector before the year 1871. All are sub-

ordinate to the Civil and Sessions Judge of Seharunpore. In 1822-23, and for several years after, the whole work of the District devolved upon one officer, the Hon'ble Mr. F. J. Shore, who, as Joint Magistrate and "Register" (Registrar) of the Civil Court of Seharunpore, was subordinate to the Judge and Magistrate of that District, and also had charge of the Revenue, (*vide* Resolution of Government, dated 24th October, 1822.) *

102. Previously to this, the Doon, annexed to Seha-

The Doon once annexed to Seharunpore.

runpore by Regulation IV. of 1817,† had no separate staff at all.

103. Regulation XXI. of 1825‡ trans-

ferred it to the jurisdiction of Mr. Traill, the Commissioner

Territorial changes; the District transferred to Kumaon together with part of Chandee.

of Kumaon, together with a part of the pergunnah of Chandee, a wild tract situated in the north-western extremity of Bijnour (then included in Moradabad), between the Ganges and the lower hills, attached to Seharunpore in May 1818, and afterwards placed under Mr. Shore's charge as well as the Doon.

104. The proceedings of the Governor-General in Coun-

Result of this arrangement, the Doon a non-regulation District. Position of Mr. Shore.

cil, dated the 8th December, 1825,§ explain that gentleman's position under the new system, which suspended the operation of the regulations within the boundaries of the District. He became Assistant to the Commissioner of Kumaon, subject to whose control he was to exercise the powers of a Magistrate, Collector, and Zillah Judge.

* *Vide* Appendix II.
† *Vide* Appendix III.
‡ *Vide* Appendix IV.
§ *Vide* Appendix V.

105. The Ruwasun, a mountain torrent running

Ruwásun, the Eastern boundary of his jurisdiction.

through pergunnah Chandee into the Ganges, was fixed upon as the boundary between his jurisdiction and that of the Magistrate of Moradabad (March 1826). He had charge of several pergunnahs in Kumaon; not of Jounsar Bawur, as Mr. Whalley suggests.*

106. But this arrangement also was only temporary, as

Further changes; the Doon removed from the Kumaon Commission.

Regulation V. of 1829 removed the Doon from the Kumaon Commissionership, without, however, defining its legal relation to the Regulation Provinces, an omission that gave rise to a good deal of quibbling, of which an

Consequent legal difficulties.

account will be found in the law of Extra-regulation Provinces subordinate to the Government of the N. W. Provinces, by Mr. P. Whalley, Under Secretary to the Government, N. W. P., (page 192 sq.) Simultaneously with this ambi-

Appointment of a Superintendent.

guous enactment, orders were passed (12th May, 1829),† placing the District under a Superintendent subordinate in his treble capacity of Judge, Magistrate, and Collector, to the Commissioner of Revenue and Circuit of the 1st or Meerut Division. It followed that the Resident at Delhi possessed the powers of the Courts of Sudder Diwánee and Nizámut Adawlut, and of the Sudder Board of Revenue, with reference to the Doon, under Clause II., Section IX., Regulation I., of 1829, while appeals in civil suits lay to the Commissioner, who also discharged the function of a Sessions Judge, as a Court

* Law of the Extra-regulation tracts, page 191.
† Vide Appendix VI.

of Circuit. The subsequent well-known modifications in the law, placed the District in a very anomalous position. Animated discussion and "some blundering" ensued.

107. Act XXI. of 1871,* at length put the Doon on

Legal doubts removed by Act XXI. of 1871. exactly the same footing as other Districts in these Provinces.

108. Major F. Young, of the 68th Regiment Native Infantry, commanding the Sirmore Battalion, was appointed

Major Young the first Superintendent; his jurisdiction, from the Ganges into Jounsar Bawur. the first Superintendent, on a consolidated salary of Rs. 500 a month. The Ganges again became the eastern boundary. On the other side, Major Young's jurisdiction extended beyond the Jumna into Jounsar Bawur, a tract already under his management, and his functions included our political relations with the Rájá of Gurhwal, to whom the valley had once belonged. In the year 1842, the office of Political Agent of the Doon was abolished, and his duties were entrusted to the Commissioner of Kumaon. In the same year, the salary of the Superintendent was fixed at Rs. 1000 a month.†

109. Jounsar Bawur is the *Ultima Thule* of the North-

Jounsar Bawur; its boundaries. West Provinces, and unfortunately no complete maps are at hand upon which a perfectly accurate description of its boundaries and geography might be based. Its area comprises a triangular tract of mountain, measuring about 343 square miles, nearly all wedged in between the Tonse‡ on the west,

---

* *Vide* Appendix VII.

† He was at first subordinate to the Magistrate of Seharunpore, as Joint Magistrate and Deputy Collector in charge of a sub-division.

‡ *i. e.* The Western Tonse, not to be confounded with its smaller namesake in the Doon valley.

dividing it from Sirmore and Joobul, and the Jumna on the east and south, dividing it from Gurhwál and the Doon. On the north, the boundary line runs up the Tonse for about ten miles in a north-easterly direction, from its confluence with the Pábhurn to its confluence with the Kunigád, a small stream rising in the Kidár Kántá mountains. It thence passes almost due south, partly along the Kunigád, partly along the main ridge running down from Kidár Kántá and separating the Tonse and Jumna watersheds, as far as the source of the Riknál nuddee near the Jako pass. Then turning eastward, it follows the course of that stream down to its junction with the Jumna. One[*] strip of debatable land, called Khág Deoghár, is situated west of the Tonse and Pábhurn.

110. Jounsar Bawur is really the name of two pergunnahs, once distinct, and includes three
Natural sub-divi-
sions.   natural sub-divisions ; *first,* Jounsar,
bounded on the north by the Kándah, or
Kánthá, mountains; *second,* Kándah, the still more mountainous region north of Jounsar; and *third,* Bawur, in the very interior. Major Young, whom I follow, in the absence of a more trustworthy authority, thus describes the boundaries of each : " Jounsar is bounded on the north by an elevated belt of mountains, called Loha Kandy, on the

---

* Mr. C. Bagshaw, Assistant Conservator of Forests, Jounsar Division, to whom I am chiefly indebted for information about the geography of the pergunnah, explains that : "There are *three* detached portions of Jounsar Bawur on the right (or western) bank of the Tonse. Two of these, Jitár and Sunsoq, are a little way up the Pabur river. The third, Mundhole, is partly bounded on the west by the Chachpúr ridge which divides the watershed of the Tonse and Shállú rivers, and by lines of pillars running thence to the Tonse and Shállú (a tributary of the former). ....It will be noted that the *main block* is surrounded by Dehra Doon, native Gurhwál, the Mandhole block, Joobul, and Sirmore.......Jitár, Sunsoq, and Mandhole are surrounded by Raingurh, Taroch, Joobul, and Jounsar Bawur on the left bank of the Tonse."

SKETCH OF JOUNSAR BAWUR DISTRICT.

Scale, 8 British miles = 1 inch.

Furlongs

16 Miles

east by the river Jumna, west by the river Tonse; and on the south by the junction of these two rivers, thus forming a triangle, the greatest length of which is six and a half miles, and its greatest breadth eighteen miles........Loha Kandy is bounded on the north by Bawur, on the south by Jounsar, on the east by the Jumna, on the west by the Tonse. Its length (Q. breadth?) is twenty miles, and its breadth (Q. length?) five miles........Bawur is to the north of Loha Kandy, is (*sic*) bounded on the east by the Riknál nuddee, on the north by the Darmee, and on the west by a very undefined line ranging from three to five miles on the west of the river Tonse from the Pubber (*i. e.* Pábhurn), to the Sarun river, its length from east to west being about 18 miles, and its breadth, from north to south about 10 miles." The small tract west of the Tonse is the holy land, where the worship of the Mahásoo Devtá, of whom more will be heard in due course, originated.*

111. Thornton places the whole be-
Geographical position. tween lat. 30° 30′ and 30° 57′, long. 77° 46′ and 78° 9.

112. Jounsar Bawur is entirely composed of a succession of hills and mountains, so that, to quote Major Young's words: "There is not a single spot of
Description of the country. Mountains innumerable. one hundred yards of level ground in the whole country." Starting from the confluence of the western Tonse and the Jumna, 1,686 feet above the level of the sea, we ascend steadily, as we approach Kálsee, the chief town of the sub-division, situated about

* *Vide* Hamilton's Description of India, Vol. II., page 631. "Bhawur.—The section of this pergunnah situated to the west of the Tonse was formerly named Bucan, but now Dewgur, from being the spot where the sect and tenets of the Mahásoo Devtá religion originated, since which period, the division of Dewgur has been considered holy land."

two miles north-east. Beyond that point, we enter the
Himalaya proper. To the right, Bairáth, some six miles
off in a direct line, rears his head to an
Bairáth and Deo-
bund. elevation of 7,423 feet, while Deobund,
one of the Kándah mountains, fourteen
or fifteen miles away in the interior, attains the imposing
height of 9,347 feet. Less than half a century ago, the
whole of this region was covered with
Forests.* noble forests, for the most part *deodár*,
the remains of which yield a considerable revenue to the
State. At Deobund itself there is still some *deodár*, but
its majestic sides are chiefly clothed with the oak, the
spruce fir, and silver fir. Eight miles due west of Deobund, close to the Tonse, the limestone
The Bodya forest. cliffs of the Lokundee spur enclose a valley about two miles wide by one deep, containing a rich
loam, where the *deodár* flourishes so vigorously that,
"thousands upon thousands of young seedlings may be
seen coming up, literally as thick as corn in a field."
North of Lokundee comes the Mushuk
The Mushuk for-
est. forest, containing firs on the lower ridges,
patches of *deodár* and cypress higher up,
besides oaks and rhododendrons. East of Mushuk is the
Kotee forest, growing in a lovely glen
The Kotee forest. around a temple, small in size, but wholly
composed of splendid *deodár*. In the hills above, there is a
magnificent growth of silver and spruce fir. Some *deodár*,
oaks, maples, and firs, shade the road from
Kyolo forest. Deobund north-eastwards to the Karámá
peak, and the neighbouring forest of Kyolo contains

several thousands of fine *deodárs*. Farther north still, beyond the Karámá peak and the Silgád river, are two extensive *deodar* forests interspersed with fir, called the Totwá and Lokwá, considered by Major Pearson to be the very finest in the District.

Totwá and Lokwá forests.

Other forests fill up the interval between the Jako pass on the one side and the Tonse on the other. Those in the immediate vicinity of Bastil, the residence of the Mahásoo Devtá's *vizier*, seem to be in the most perfect state of preservation, although the trees are stunted.

113. The Jumna reaches the sub-division called Khut Bondur twelve and a half miles due east of Deobund, there receiving the small stream named the Riknál or Riknálgád, which divides Bawur from Ráma Sarai, the Happy Valley, in the Rawain pergunnah, the finest piece of land in the whole of the old Gurhwál Ráj, except the Doon, a place much frequented by the Court in former days.[*] Eight miles lower down, it receives another similar stream, the Kutno or Kutnogád, which flows through the Mohná and Bawur *Khuts*, being at this point ninety feet wide, four or five deep, rapid, and not fordable. After a southerly course of about twenty miles from its confluence with the Riknál, the Jumna turns due west and meets the Tonse below Hureepore, nine and a half miles off, in lat 30° 3′, long. 77° 53′, at an elevation of 1,686 feet above the level of the sea.

Rivers—Jumna.

Biknál.

Kutno.

The Amláwáh.

Two and a half miles east of its confluence with the Tonse, it receives another small tributary, the Amláwáh, rising at the southern base of

[*] *Vide* Mr. J. B. Fraser's Himalaya Mountains, p. 402.

the Deobund mountain, and watering a triangular valley formed by two lofty ridges, the one running N. W. from Bairath, the other N. E. from the Naga peak (6,743 feet high), a few miles West of Bairáth, and both meeting in a point at

Watershed line. Deobund itself. The Naga peak chain separates the Jumna from the Tonse drainage in Jounsar Proper. Higher up, in Bawur, the water-shed line seems to be a ridge stretching away from Deobund north-east to the Jako pass, a continuation of the chains culminating in

The Pábhurn. a point between Chukrata and Deobund. The Pábhurn, commonly called the Pábur, a large and rapid stream, after a course of some fifty-eight miles through Busáhir, falls into the Tonse between the villages of Raegee and Kotee in *Khut* Bawur, lat. 30° 56′, long. 77° 54. The Tonse reaches Bawur near the village of Hanolee, a few miles West of its confluence with the Páphurn, and falls into the Jumna, to which it is here superior in volume, after a tortuous and rapid course of about fifty-three miles. Its tributaries, like those of the Jumna, are insignificant mountain torrents; viz., the Daragad, Bunálgád, both

Dárágád, Bunál-gád, &c. in *Khut* Bawur, and others of less note. The ordinary discharge of the Tonse has been estimated at 2,827 cubic feet a second, and of the Jumna at 1,045, close to their confluence.

114. The mountainous nature of the country is an in-

Irrigation. surmountable obstacle to the construction of regular canals, but the villagers themselves largely utilise the water of the numerous minor streams for the purpose of irrigating the fields cut in terraces, one above the other, along the sides of the mountains, according to the system of cultivation locally termed *kheel*.

The water power also serves to turn innumerable mills. The deep limestone ravines forming the banks of the Tonse prevent irrigation from that river, and there is not much from the Jumna either.

115. The Tonse has three wooden bridges—at Mendrát

Bridges.

and Bastil in *Khut* Bawur, and Singotá in *Khut* Burhm. The Pábhurn is nowhere bridged, and has to be crossed during the rains by means of a rope (*tún*). There are three iron bridges across the Jumna; at Juláwutá in *Khut* Lukhwaree, Punaha in *Khut* Punchgawn, and Goolur Ghat in *Khut* Hureepore Biás

116. Notwithstanding the great depth of the river

Floods.

and their rapid slope, such floods come down from the mountains during the monsoon, that the water frequently rises high enough to seriously damage the crops growing along the banks— owing to the height and rocky nature of which, however, cases of alluvion or diluvion are impossible.

117. Putting aside the tracts now included in the

Very little land under cultivation.

Government forests, very little of the country is either cultivated or culturable. The census report of 1865 distributes the area thus :—

Total area in acres.	Cultivated Mal- goozaree in acres.	Culturable Mal- goozaree in acres.	Lákhiráj.	Barren.
2,19,721†	21,450	1,096	174	197,001

* *Vide* Supra., page 8.
† Another return gives—Total area, 216,926 ; cultivated, 21,603.

I

According to more recent calculations, the cultivated area is only 18,724 acres, out of a total of 2,19,520, and the culturable area 620.

Classifications of soils,   118. The culturable area is thus classified :—

Irrigated from artificial water-courses.	First class soils dependent on rain.	Second class soils dependent on rain.	Total.
Acres. 1,682	Acres. 3,930	Acres. 7,112	Acres. 18,724

The first class soil is the manured clay rice land. The reddish clay is considered the best, that of a darker color inferior. All other unirrigated land comes under the third heading. The worst sort containing gravel and shingle, is popularly called *sankránee*.

119. The climate of Kálsee does not differ materially

Climate.   from that of Dehra. That of the heights above, is the same as at Mussooree or Landour. The cold becomes more intense on the loftier ranges in the interior. Chukrata, immediately south of Deobund, has been pronounced a more eligible sight for a Cantonment than any at a more convenient distance from the plains.

120. The *Fauna* is pretty much the same as that of

Fauna.   the Mussooree range, including the *goorul, mahá,* black bear, and leopard.*

---

* It should be noted that the *tiger* also has been shot in the hills of Jounsar Bawur, and along the Mussooree range.

121. The horned cattle are inferior even to those of the Doon, and the use of horses was absolutely unknown to the natives before the conquest. Sheep and goats are abundant.

Cattle even inferior to those of the Doon.

122. Besides the timber of the forests, the characteristic vegetable products are rice, turmeric, ginger, red pepper, tobacco, potatoes, opium, and walnuts. In 1827 the little grain in the country was more than sufficient to meet the wants of the people. Now it has to be imported in considerable quantities, as well as other articles of consumption. This must be chiefly due to the growth of the cantonments at Chukrata.

Vegetable Products.

123. The metals found are lead, antimony, and copper, but the mines of Kándah have not yet been explored, still less worked, an anticipation fondly cherished half a century ago by Major Young. Neither is a copper mine near Kálsee on the banks of the Amláwáh worked.

Mines.

124. The population is, roughly, about one half that of the Doon, and the remarks already made about caste are, in a general way, applicable to the sub-division, except as regards the foreign immigrants whose descendants dwell in the valley of Dehra.

Population; castes.

The majority of the Rajpoots belong to the Khusiá tribe. The Brahmans are generally called Bháts—Dhooms predominate—indeed so few of the indigenous inhabitants have any plausible pretentions to high caste, that till the year 1830 there was only one family of Mahájuns at Kálsee.

The Mahomedan element may be said to be wholly wanting. There are of course a few Mussulman residents at
Kálsee and Chukrata.

125. The manners and customs of the people are of a
Manners and cus-   simplicity verging upon absolute barbar-
toms of the people.   ism. Some have received semi-judicial
Polyandry.
sanction by being embodied in the famous
*dustoor ul aml,** or Code of Common Law, drawn up under
the superintendence of Mr. A. Ross, in the Settlement of
1848. The most remarkable is polyandry, a practice declared by Major Young in 1827 to be on the decline, yet
unquestionably common to this very day.

Indeed, a bachelor without brothers, it is alleged, experiences some difficulty about getting a wife.

The marriage ceremony is conducted without much for-
mality. The father of the bridegroom sends, or himself
brings, one rupee to the father of the bride elect on the
part of his eldest son, who has afterwards to share her favors with his younger brothers, and the recipient of the
money gives the bearer a feed of *poories*. Afterwards the
girl, being arrayed in a *chola* (a sort of bridal garment),
a *ghághrá* (petticoat), and a *dhuntoo* (head dress), is escorted
by a procession of her relatives and friends to the house of
her intended father-in-law, who makes her parent a present
of 8 or 10 Rs., called *Jeeo-dhun*, which is distributed among
all the guests. Nothing then remains except to consummate
the marriage. Women are free to choose their first husbands, nay to leave them, if dissatisfied with them, on
condition of the second husband's defraying the expenses

of the previous wedding. Younger brothers legally have only the usufruct of their senior's wife, for she and her children are held to be the exclusive property of the eldest brothers. Hence he keeps both woman and children, in the event of the household being broken up and the rest of the fraternity going to live elsewhere. The custom of polyandry is supposed to promote good fellowship among brothers, and is (or used to be) observed so consistently that if a mother-in-law dies leaving an infant son, the daughter-in-law is, properly speaking, bound to rear the boy and marry him herself when he attains the age of puberty. A married woman is called *Mámee*, possibly a sarcastic allusion to her maternal duties.

It is almost needless to add that there is a considerable amount of freedom between the sexes. Another very marked peculiarity in the habits of the people is their extreme uncleanliness, all the more conspicuous on account of the comparative fairness of their complexion, and scantiness of their clothing, the nature of which is familiar to every one who has ever had occasion to make a journey to a hill station.

126. The superstition of these mountaineers is as gross as their filth and immorality. The Mahasoo Devtá, a deity whose eccentricities will again demand attention, exercises a most pernicious influence over their minds, and he is only one of the many spirits, demons, and devils, constituting their religious scarecrow. If one man falls out with another, all he has to do is to take a stone out of the wall of his enemy's house or a clod of earth out of his field, and dedicate it to Mahásoo. Henceforth no one dare live in

Their superstition.

the house or till the field.   Both are avoided as though
haunted.   This is a very convenient method of settling
any dispute about property likely to go against one, and
many a deserted house, or fallow field, in Bawur particularly, shows how frequently the plan has been resorted to.

127.   The *puncháyut* system is in full force.   Until very

Puncháyuts.

recently, *puncháyuts* were officially acknowledged as a valuable administrative agency,
and in practice they still govern the country.   Each member of a jury receives a regular fee of 2 Rs. and upwards,
called *bishtárá* or *bishárá*, from the parties concerned.

128.   *Sutoo* (parched gram made into a paste), *chauláee*

Food.

(a sort of vegetable), *gágtee* (ditto), and
mundwa, constitute the principal articles
of diet.   Rice is too costly to be generally used.   Fish and
goat's flesh—probably every kind of flesh—are greedily
devoured—whenever they can be procured.

129.   The language* is a dialect of Hindee, quite or

Language.

almost unintelligible to the Lowlanders.
A few words may be cited by way of example :—

> *Cheeskia,*—burnt.
> *Handná,*—to walk.
> *Dená,*—ditto.
> *Kodwá,*—bread made of coarse grain.
> *Cháprá,*—ditto.
> *Pohit,*—dál.
> *Pujhár,*—wood.
> *Daroo,*—ditto.

* Circumstances already alluded to prevent my touching upon this subject in any but
the most superficial manner.

Nyár.—grass (green on which cattle are fed).

Gád.—too appears to be the equivalent of *Nuddee.*

130. Education is simply *nil.* To counterbalance this
disadvantage, there is a pleasing absence
of heinous crime as well as of civil litigation.

Education—nil.

131. The communications have not been properly opened up, nor is there much necessity for
roads ; one goes from the Jumna at Hureepore to Kálsee, a distance of two miles ;
it is twenty-seven feet broad, with stone metalling nine feet
wide and nine inches thick. The ruling gradient here is 3
in 100. From Kálsee commences the hill cart road, which
is sub-divided into two sections, viz., (1) from Kálsee to
Saiáh, eleven miles, and (2), from Saiáh to Chukrata
parade ground, seventeen miles. These sections have an
average width of eighteen feet, but are not metalled. The
ruling gradient is 5 in 100. There is also a bridle-path
from Saiáh to Chukrata, about eight feet wide, with a
ruling gradient of 10 in 100 more or less. The distance
this way, to the cart road, a mile short of the parade
ground, is only nine miles The bridges and also the road
across the mountains from Mussooree to Chukrata have
been already mentioned.

*Communica-
tions; from Huree-
pore to Kálsee.*

132. The administrative divisions of
Jounsar Bawur are altogether peculiar,
as may be seen from the following
table :†—

Administrative
divisions of Jounsar
Bawur.

* Information supplied by Lieut. G. Hildebrand, R.E., Offg. Ex. Engineer.

† The number of the *Khuts* will be increased under the new settlement. The
census report of 1865 gives the area as 2,19,721 acres.

Tehseel.	Pergunnah.	Number of Mahâls.	Jamma.	Area in acres.	Population.	In the Civil jurisdiction of	In the Police jurisdiction of	Remarks.
		INCLUDES						
KALSEE.	Jounsar Bawur.	35 *Khats*, containing many villages.	19,695	2,19,520	40,533	The Superintendent Dehra Doon, as Judge; of Naib Tuhseeldár of Kálsee as Moonsiff; and of the Cantonment Magistrate at Chukrata, with powers of a Small Cause Court within limits of Cantonment.	No Thânah.	The Police system of Jounsar Bawur is almost unique. There are no Thannah jurisdictions, only a few outposts, as at Chukrata and Kálsee, The Naib Tuhseeldár of Kálsee is apparently a sort of *ex officio* Police Superintendent or Daroghá for the whole sub-division.

133. The more minute peculiarities of the Jounsar

Administrative system of Jounsar Bawur.

Bawur administrative system will gradually unfold themselves farther on. Here I need only note a few leading points. From the year 1815 to the year 1829, the sub-division remained in charge of one officer, immediately subordinate, it would appear, to the Governor General's Agent at Delhi. In his criminal jurisdiction he was guided by the provisions

At first subject to the criminal provisions of Regulation X., 1817.

of Regulation X. of 1817,* implicatively empowering the Superintendent to try minor felonies of his own authority, and directing the appointment of a Special Commissioner for the trial of more heinous crimes. Had the necessity for such a procedure arisen, the Superintendent himself would have been the only officer available, but, it does not seem to have ever arisen, and all or nearly all

* *Vide* Appendix IX.

the criminal judicial business was transacted with the help of a singular subordinate agency of which an account is reserved. The civil judicial work was disposed of in the

Civil suits dispos-
ed of according to
local custom.

same way. Had such things as heavy civil suits been known, it is not obvious how they would have been settled. When regulation V. of 1829 rescinded Regulation XXI. of 1825, Jounsar Bawur was consigned to the same state of general outlawry as the Doon.

134. Years after, the concluding sections of Act XXIV.

Act XXIV. of
1864.

of 1864,* vested the administration of justice and the collection of the revenue in such officers as the Lieutenant-Governor might appoint, who were to be guided by the rules framed for the Terai District under Act. XIV. of 1861, and

Introduction of the
Terai Rules.

promulgated in Resolution of Government No. 2264A., dated 10th October, 1861. Notification No. 1170½A. dated 29th April, 1864, supplemented the Act, investing the Superintendent with the general administration of the sub-division, and empowering him to assign to his assistants, such executive, fiscal, or judicial duties as they might be qualified to discharge, in subordination to the Commissioner of Meerut. The functionaries to be employed in the administration of Civil justice were the Assistants to the Superintendent, the Superintendent himself, and the Commissioner of Meerut; in the administration of the Revenue and Criminal Justice, the Tuhseeldar of Kálsee, the Assistants, the Superintendent, and the Commissioner. The previous Resolution defined the powers of these officers and the procedure to be

* *Vide* Appendix X.

K

observed by them.   The Superintendent received authority
to try original suits without limit of value,
Administration of and hear regular appeals from the deci-
civil justice.
sion of the Assistant, who had power to try
original suits not exceeding Rs. 1000 in value, while a
regular appeal lay from the Superintendent to the Commissioner, and where the two latter differed, Government had
the option, if petitioned, of referring the point at issue to
the decision of the Sudder Court.   A special appeal might
also be made to the Commissioner from the decision of
the Superintendent in regular appeal.   The Tuhseeldar
could only try petty criminal cases made over to him by
the Superintendent, nor did his powers
Administration of extend beyond the infliction of Rs. 50
criminal justice.
fine, or a sentence to six months' imprison-
ment.   The Assistant likewise, unless specially empowered,
was restricted to the trial of cases so referred, and his
powers only extended to the infliction of a fine of Rs. 100,
or a sentence of twelve months' imprisonment.   The orders
of both were appealable to the Superintendent, who had the
ordinary full powers of a Magistrate of a District.   Appeals lay from him to the Commissioner of Meerut, who
was also empowered to revise the proceedings of any subordinate authority, and to whom all cases of a more heinous
nature were to be committed for trial, but in those of
murder and all others demanding a more severe punishment
than fourteen years' imprisonment, his sentence could not
be carried out without the concurrence of the Judge of
Meerut, or in the event of a sentence of death, without the
confirmation of the Nizámut Adawlut.

135.   The suits cognizable in the Revenue Courts were

divided under two heads—summary and regular. The
summary suits were thus classified—(1),
suits by *malgoozars*, &c., against tenants,
or of tenants against sub-tenants, for ar-
rears of rents; (2), by *lumberdars*, against under-sharers for
arrears of revenue; (3), by *malgoozars*, &c., against agents
for production of accounts and recovery of money due; (4),
by farmers of excise duties, against licensed manufacturers
and vendors, for recovery of arrears due on sub-contracts;
(5), by cultivators and tenants, against *malgoozars*, &c., and
of under-sharers against *lumberdars*, for undue exaction of
rent or revenue; (6), of the same against the same, for illegal
dispossession, actual or attempted. The period of limitation fixed for the institution of suits under Cl. I., II., III.,
IV., was twelve months, and for the institution of those
under Cl. V., VI., sixty days. The regular suits were
defined to be—(1), suits about the *malgoozaree* right in land,
the right to registered *maafee* land, or land held on a
quit rent, or claims to share in the profits or rent of such
land, or in manorial privileges not reserved to Government; (2), summary suits (as classified above) where from
lapse of time, or on other grounds, they cannot be tried
in the ordinary way; (3), suits by *malgoozars*, &c., for rent of
land held in excess of or contrary to lease; (4), suits by the
same to oust tenants-at-will, not in default, at the end of the
year, or at the expiration of a lease; (5), suits by the same
for enhancement of rent. Regular appeals from the Revenue Courts under the Terai Rules lie solely to the Commissioner, and in the case of summary suits, only on the
question whether the issues raised are fit to be tried summarily or not. His decision on the latter point is final.

Revenue adminis-
tration.

In regular suits a special appeal lies from his order to the Board of Revenue.

136. A regularly organised Police under Act V. of 1861 was not introduced. The people Police administra- themselves were, as heretofore, to extem- tion. porise a rude constabulary, in case of necessity, and the Superintendent, being immediate head of the Police, was to be guided by the spirit of the old Regulation XX. of 1817 ; by its provisions, wherever applicable.*

137. The appointment of a Cantonment Magistrate to Chukrata, under Government Order Subsequent modi- No. 415, Judicial Criminal Department, fication in the judi- cial system. dated 2nd April, 1869, subsequently suggested some modifications in the judicial system. By Notification No. 1393A, dated 19th September, 1872, the Lieutenant-Governor, in virtue of the authority vested in him under Section 2, Act I. of 1865, (the Acts and Regulations Extension Act), extended the operation of the Code of Criminal Procedure, Act. XXV. of 1861, to Jounsar Bawur, and under Section 3, of the same Act, the Superintendent of Dehra was invested with the powers of Zillah Magistrate in the pergunnah, the Cantonment Magistrate of Chukrata, with the local jurisdiction of a Sub-divisional Magistrate under Section 23D, Code of Criminal Procedure, and the powers of a Magistrate as defined in Section 132, under Section 23H, Jounsur Bawur being declared a sub-division under Section 18 ; the Judge of Seharunpore, with the powers of a District and Sessions Judge within the pergunnah under Section 2, Act XIX. of 1871

---

* In matters not specially provided for, the local authorities were required to adhere to the *spirit* of Act. XLV. of 1861. *Vide* Appendix XI.

(the Bengal Sessions Court Act). A Resolution of the same date, No. 427A, extended to the sub-division the operation of the Code of Civil Procedure (Act VIII. of 1859, as amended by Acts XXIII. of 1867 and IX. of 1863). Under Section II. of the said Act, the administration of Civil Justice was vested in the Naib Tuhseeldar of Kalsee, with powers of a Moonsiff for the trial of suits up to Rs. 300, the Superintendent of the Doon, with powers to hear appeals from the Moonsiff, and decide suits above Rs. 300 in value, and the Commissioner of Meerut with final appellate powers from the decision of both.

138. In his capacity of *ex officio* Assistant Superintendent, the Cantonment Magistrate is the Chief Police Officer of Jounsar Bawur, and all offences are reported directly to him, while the Naib Tuhseeldar is the subordinate through whom cases are worked. He is also Sub-Registrar of the pergunnah as well as Small Cause Court Judge, with power to try cases where the cause of action does not exceed Rs. 200, within the limits of the Cantonments.

Position of the Cantonment Magistrate.

139. There are no large towns either in Dehra Doon or Jounsar Bawur, and the principal places have been all casually mentioned. Such as require further notice will be afterwards described.

Towns.

140. I shall now attempt to patch together such shreds of history as my opportunities have enabled me to collect.

NOTE.—Victor Jacquemont visited the Doon in April, 1830. A reference to his observations (vide *Voyage dans l'Inde*, Vol ii. page 11, *sq.*), of which some further account will be given in the Historical and Statistical Memoir of the Seharunpore district, would repay the reader. His comparison of the valley to the Oberland of Berne and to Haiti, has been already noticed. He distinguishes the climate from that of the plains—*firstly*, by its invariably greater humidity, *secondly*, by the '*partial*' suppression of the hot winds, (besides the general mildness of the temperature,) but marks the connecting link between both of the " solstitial rains............one of the most striking features of intertropical meteorology............the cause why tropical and Alpine forms of vegetation are found mixed together at an elevation of several thousand feet" (page 14). There he remarked *gôitre*, for the first time during his travels in India. Had he, however, extended his enquiries to the sub-Sewalik forest-belt of North Seharunpore, in the direction of the Jumna and Ganges, he would have certainly noticed the disease there also. His observations about the geology of the Mussooree range are too discursive for repetition, and all the information practically necessary on the subject of Sewalik geology (and Palæontology) will be found in the Seharunpore Memoir, a more elaborate compilation than the present work. He divides the Doon Flora into four categories (page 34); plants common in the plains; others, peculiar to the place, met with on entering the Kheree pass, such as *Boswellia*, *Semecarpus*, *Bauhinia racemosa*, &c., &c.; others again, found on the lower slopes of the Himalaya, which cannot be exactly said to be peculiar to the hills ; and, finally, those which vegetate vigorously at a somewhat greater height, but, having been transported to the valley, may be occasionally seen below. Of grasses, he observed, among others, the *Saccharum spontaneum* and *Panicum dactylon*, as having a remarkably European look. At the Suhunsruh Dhârâ he secured a *Primula*, and here, by the way, his eyes were at length gratified with the sight of bold magnesian limestone rocks. Ascending to Mussooree, he first noticed the oak; then "a middling-sized tree, (name unknown,) the leaves of which are deadly to goats;" next, the Rhododendron; after that, the *Grislea tomentosa*, already found in the Kheree pass, *Indigofera*, &c., &c., a nut tree (*Juglans regia*), the *Pyrus* and *Prunus persica* (Himalayan greengage and wild pear, *Prunus ovalifolia*, *aloocha*, and *Pyrus variolosa*, *mehul ?*); and, lastly, a vine (*vitis*), the first plant of the kind he had seen. It may be added that he indicates Jurâpânee as the boundary line between the Doon and hill Flora, properly so called.

PART II.—HISTORICAL.

SECTION I. FROM THE EARLIEST TIMES DOWN TO THE GOORKHA WAR.

141. The early history of the valley is lost in the mists of mythology, a wide field, which it is impossible to explore thoroughly in a brief practical essay. At a period far beyond the reach of human reckonings, the Doon was included in the mysterious region of the Kidárkhund, the abode of the great God Shiva, the Destroyer, whose memory is preserved in the name of the "Sewaliks" (शिवालय, the Habitation of Shiva), properly, and more correctly, called the *Shiv-Puhár*. In the Sutya, Treta and Dwapur ages, after the war between the Gods and the Titans,* the place remained desolate ; ascetics

Mythology.

The doon included in Kidárkhand.

---

* I have already noticed the fact that the fossil remains found in the Sewaliks are supposed to be the skeletons of the defeated giants, who are apparently believed to have been the original tenants of the Doon. A story republished from the *Delhi Gazette* in an article in the *Calcutta Review* quoted above (p. 40), refers to this tradition ; " not far from the place stood a village in ancient days, in which two brothers resided, *giants*. To show their feats of strength, one of them raised the upper stone before me upon the other ; the younger brother took it down ; and so they continued for hours, until at last the eldest came off victorious, as the younger brother left the stones as you see them. I remarked a hole close to the base of the large stone, and, on enquiring the cause was told that about three years ago, a little boy herding cattle, whilst sitting, resting himself on the big stone, remarking a crack in the ground,

alone frequented it.   Here, according to Brahminical lore,
Ráma and Luchman Jee, his brother, be-

Ráma and Luchman Jee do penance for the slaughter of Rávana. ing Kshatryas, came by the advice of the sage Vasishth to do penance and so atone for the death of the Brahman Ravana,

slain at the taking of Lanká.   In obedience to the words of the holy man, they lived in the wilderness apart from one another, Rama at Rikheekesh, and Luchman at Tupo-bun, until they had obtained remission of their sin.

142.   Again, in the Dwapur Yug, Drona Acharj, the Brahman preceptor of the Kauravas and

Coming of Drona Acharj.   Pandavas, came in search of a lonely spot to perform his devotions, and sojourned

for a season near the village of Dwârâ, in tne Deodar Par-but, a part of the lower Himalayan range, six koss east of Dehra.   Hence the valley was called Drona Asram, "the dwelling of Drona."

---

inserted a stick, which struck something that sounded like a metal pot, went home and told his father ; at night he came, dug, and found buried there an iron vessel full of money and jewellery.   The story got wind ; it reached the Teree Rajah's ears. The lucky, or rather unlucky, finder was immediately summoned to the capital, asked to give up the treasure, or submit to a fine of 500 Rupees.   He declared he had found nothing, but paid the fine in preference to being put into irons.   I recollect perfectly hearing the story from the puhárees of the treasure being found.   I now actually saw the spot from whence it had been dug.   Instead of the story related of the " Giant Brothers " being true, I should think it more probable that the stones piled upon each other must have been placed there as a mark by the party who con-cealed the treasure, and who probably died soon after, taking the secret of the hidden treasure with him to the grave.

" Money and jewels in silver and gold are frequently found by the hill men.   Here and there, along the banks of the River Aglor, may be seen terraces about fourteen or twenty feet square, built of enormous masses of rock, said to be where the head men of the villages used to collect and discuss any momentous affairs regarding themselves or of the nation.   There they are, and call f rth surprise to imagine how they could have raised such tremendous stones, weighing *tons*, without mechanical aid !   The hill men say they were only built by giants !   The present race could not do it."   The narrator missed the point of these legends.

143. Finally, in the Kul Yug, the five Pandava brothers,

The five Pandavas pass through on their way to the snowy range.

Yudhishthir, Bhima, Arjun, Nukul, and Sahadev, passed through, with Draupadi and their dog, on their way to the inner recesses of the snowy range, where they immolated themselves upon the peak of Mahá Panth behind Kidar.

144. One very holy spot, or Tirth, associated with the mythological period, is that named Bhimghora close to Hurdwar. There, some say, the mighty Bhim was posted when the Ganges descended from heaven, to guide her course. In proof of this, they point to a cavity in the rock, about twelve feet above the sacred pool beneath, produced by an accidental kick of the hero's horse; whence the name of the place is derived.

Bhímghora.

Perhaps about the same time, a curious incident occurred, the details of which are more generally known than the scene of action.

145. The sage Kashyapa once gave a great feast, to which all the gods were invited. Now Indra, the God of rain, a most disreputable deity, while on his way to the entertainment, happened to meet 60,000 pigmy (balkhil) Brahmans, endeavouring in vain to cross a cow's foot-print filled with water, to them a vast lake. Seeing this, he could not restrain his laughter, and scoffed at them. The indignant pigmies, determined to have their revenge, at once set to work about creating a second Indra, who should supplant him then reigning. This could only be accomplished by means of penance and mortifications, in which they steadily persevered, until the sweat flowing from their tiny bodies, made a river at first known as the Subhan

Indra and the 60,000 pigmy Brahmans. The origin of the Sooswa.

L

(सूम), "the pleasant waters"—now as the Sooswá. The irreverent God, being greatly surprised and alarmed at the preliminary effect of their religious exercises, besought the intercession of Brahma, through whose good offices he succeeded in retaining the throne.

146. The Sooswa flows under Nágsidh or Nágachal Parbut, which another legend connects with traditions of a Scythian supremacy, for it was on the top of this hill that the snake (nág) Bámun, or Bamní, did penance, and thereby became lord of the Doon.

The Nág Bámun becomes supreme. Nágsidh.

147. The belief in the Nágá ascendency here typified is universal, and natives generally attribute the construction of the Baráhát trident in Gurhwál (described in the Asiatic Researches, Vol. XI., &c.,) to the Chinese or Tartars, while the famous Kálsee stone, near Hureepore on the right bank of the Jumna, inscribed with the edicts of Asoka, is considered to be an ancient boundary mark between Hindoostan and China. General Cunningham has given an excellent description of this interesting monument:*
" Between Kálsee and the Jumna the land on the western bank of the river is formed in two successive ledges or level steppes, each about 100 feet in height. Near the foot of the upper steppe stands the large quartz boulder which has preserved the edicts of Asoka for upwards of 2,000 years. The block is 10 feet long and 10 feet high, and about 8 feet thick at bottom. The south-eastern face has been smoothed, but rather unevenly, as it

Belief in a Nágá ascendency. Traditions about the Baráhát trident and Kálsee stone.

General Cunningham's description of the Kálsee stone.

* Archæological Survey Report, Vol I., p. 246.

follows the undulations of the original surface, which measures 5 feet in height with a breadth of $5\frac{1}{2}$ feet at top, which
increases towards the bottom to 7 feet $10\frac{1}{2}$ inches. The
deeper hollows and cracks have been left uninscribed, and
the lines of letters are undulating and uneven. Towards
the bottom the letters increase in size until they become
about thrice as large as those of the upper part. Owing
either to this enlargement of the letters, or perhaps to the
latter part of the inscription being of later date, the prepared surface was too small for the whole record, which was,
therefore, completed on the left hand side of the rock.

148. "On the right hand side an elephant is traced in
Figure of an ele-
phant. outline, with the words 'Gajatame' inscribed between his legs in the same characters
as those of the inscription. The exact meaning of these
words I do not know; but as the Junagirí rock inscription
closes with a paragraph stating that the place is called
Sweta-Hastí, or the " white elephant," I think it probable
that Gajatame may mean the " dark or black elephant,"
and may therefore, be the name of the rock itself. Amongst
the people, however, the rock is known by the name of
Chhatr Silá, or " Canopy-stone," which would seem to
show that the inscribed block had formerly been covered
over by some kind of canopy, or perhaps only by an umbrella, as the name imports. There are a number of squared
stones lying about close to the rock, as well as several fragments of octagonal pillars and half pillars or pilasters, which
are hollowed out or fluted on the shorter faces, after the
common fashion of the pillars of Buddhist railings. There
is also a large carved stone, 7 feet long, $1\frac{1}{2}$ feet broad and
1 foot in height, which from its upper mouldings I judged

to have formed the entrance step to some kind of open porch in front of the inscription stone.

149. "When found by Mr. Forrest early in 1860, the

First brought to notice by Captain Forrest, in 1860.

letters of the inscription were hardly visible, the whole surface being encrusted with the dark moss of ages; but on removing this black film, the surface becomes nearly as white as marble. At first sight the inscription looks as if it was imperfect in many places, but this is owing to the engraver having purposely left all the cracked and rougher portions uninscribed. On comparing the different edicts with those of the Kapurdagiri, Junagiri, and Dhauli versions, I find the Kálsee text to be in a more perfect state than any one of them, and more specially in that part of the 13th edict, which contains the names of the five Greek kings— Antiochus, Ptolemy, Antigonus, Magas, and Alexander."

150. The supposition that an old city once existed in

Probability of existence of old city near Kalsee, Raja Risáloo. Hwen Thsang is silent on the subject.

this locality, receives countenance from the legend of a king, Raja Risaloo,* whose stronghold is buried beneath a mound, (*tibree*) near Hureepore. When, however, in the year 635-36 A.D., the Chinese pilgrim, Hwen Thsang, visited the kingdom of Srughna, which included the whole of the Doon and Seharunpore, together with a portion of the Umballa District, the only place in the neighbourhood noticed by him, was the capital itself, a town situated on

---

* The fact of "Rája Risáloo kee Tibree" being found almost in juxtaposition with the Kálsee stone, opens out a tempting field for speculation, which, however, I dare not venture upon without making minute local enquiries, the opportunity for which have unfortunately been denied me. But it may be as well to remind the reader that Raja Risáloo is the same as the Rásáloo of Syalkote, the son of Sáliváhana, the slayer of the seven cannibal Rakhshasas of Manikyála. *Vide* General Cunningham's Archæological Survey of India, Vol. II., pages 21, and 153.

the right bank of the Jumna south of the Sewaliks, at no
great distance from Kálsee. Had a large city existed in the
vicinity, he would most probably have mentioned it, and
his silence justifies the inference that Hureepore was not a
town of any magnitude in the seventh century, although,
it may have been at some earlier period.*

151.   After leaving Mundáwur (in Bijnour), the Chinese
traveller advanced fifty miles northward.
We must consequently look for Polokimo-
pulo, or Brahmapura, "the dwelling of
Brahmans," in the sacred region extending from Tupobun
to Deoprág, or perhaps still nearer Sreenugur.   Under any
circumstances, his wanderings evidently brought him close
to the eastern Doon, if not actually through it, but no place
on that side presented features worthy of his attention,
except Hurdwar.   Tradition corroborates his testimony to
the absence of cities.

Brahmapura near Tupobun.

152.   In those days the valley, it is said, was desolate,
and remained so until about seven or
eight hundred years ago, when a caravan
of Bunjárás travelling from the west, attracted by the beauty of the country, permanently settled there.   The Doon, though
neglected, was, according to this popular account, already a
part of the dominions of the Gurhwal Rájá, who, however,
did not hear of the encroachment upon his territories for
several years.   At length an expedition was organized to
expel the intruders, but the king first sent an ultimatum to
the Bunjárá chief, giving him the choice between imme-

The Doon desolate for many years, until colonised by Bunjáras, although included in the kingdom of Gurhwál.

---

* Had it subsequently grown into a place of importance, we should most probably
have heard something of it from the Mahomedan historians.

diate submission and a trial of arms. The stranger accepted the first alternative, did homage to the Mahárajah, and submitted to the regular payment of an annual tribute.

153. In proof of the truth of this story, the people cite the number of Bunjárás still living in the Doon and the country at the foot of the Sewaliks, likewise the wells, groves and villages called after the Bunjárá chieftain; for instance, Bunjáráwálá close to Dehra. Futehpore Tándá, on the banks of the Song is, they add, the very place where he used to keep his flocks and herds, as the name denotes.

Bunjárá element in the population.

154. Whether this tale is founded on fact or not, the belief in the enterprise of Bunjaras, as pioneers of primitive civilisation, is very general in this part of the country. They attended, it is alleged, to the commissariat of the Pandavas during their exile in the woods of the neighbouring kingdom of Hastinapore, and besides other towns, the ancient city of Deobund (*zillah* Seharunpore) sprang up in consequence of their efforts.

Similar traditions of Bunjárá colonisation current elsewhere.

155. Under the management of these early colonists, such was the fertility of the soil and the excellence of the cultivation, that (to use the hyperbolical language of the natives), no one dared drive a loose bullock through a single village between the Jumna and the Ganges, lest irreparable damage should be done to the crops.

Early fertility of the country.

156. After the death of their leader, the first settlers ceased to prosper and almost died out. From time to time the Gurhwál Rájá endeavoured to replace them by other colonists, but

Decline of the Bunjárá colony.

all his attempts failed, and the Doon, relapsing into its previous condition, did not recover itself till about the seventeenth century, when the Sreenugur Rájás take their places in authentic history.

157.   The origin of this dynasty is plunged in the usual mist and obscurity surrounding Indian royal pedigrees.

Origin of the Gurhwál Ráj.

158.   According to the account given to Captain Hardwicke* in 1796 A.D., the whole country had been, 3774 years before the accession of the reigning prince Purdooman Sáh, divided into twenty-two pergunnahs, each under the sway of an independent chieftain.   This anarchy continued, until a Pamar Rajpoot from Ahmedabad in Goojurat, called Bhog Dhunt, appeared upon the scene.   He was a man combining genius with ambition, and having emigrated with his brother Suhj Dhunt to seek his fortune, entered the services of the Chandpore† Rájá, the most powerful of the rival chieftains.   He soon acquired considerable influence, and rose to a military appointment of high trust.   At this period, a *jogee* appearing to him in a dream, suggested a design which he at once proceeded to put into execution with perfect faith in the divine inspiration.   He first of all deposed his master, and then turning his arms against the surrounding chiefs, reduced the whole of the neighbouring districts beneath his sway in a few months.   The usurper governed his do-

Captain Hardwicke's account.

That the Ráj was founded by a Pamar Rajpoot from Ahmedabad in Goojurat, named Bhog Dhunt.

* Asiatic Researches, Vol. VI.

† A mountainous tract in the very centre of British Gurhwál, on the left bank of the Alukminda.

minions under the title of Rájá of Gurhwál, the region of fortresses, the ancient name of the country.

159.   Personal enquiries have elicited another version of the story, which there is some reason to regard with greater confidence. In it the founder of the Gurhwál dynasty bears a name famous in Indian Archæology—

Other account, that it was founded by Kunk Pál of Dharanugur.

Kunuk, Kunk or Kank Pál, possibly the same personage to whom a sister legend ascribes the foundation of the old town of Gungoh in Seharunpore, viz., Gung (identical with Kunk), a prince celebrated in local romance. This Kunk did not come from Ahmedabad, a comparatively modern town, but from Dháránugur or Dhár, in Malwa; and the principalities welded together by him instead of twenty-two, were fifty-two in number, being to this day remembered among the people as the " *Bawun Thakurae.*" They con-

The Bawun Thukurae.

stituted in fact a "*laonee,*" one of the most common federal systems of the old Indian communities. The Thukuraes of the hills had their exact parallels in the plains, for folk-lore represents each district south of the Sewaliks to have been similarly split up into petty principalities, under eponymous heroes, each affecting independence and giving his name to his seat of Government. One of these potentates was the very Gung in question, whose legendary existence may be a reflection from that of his more celebrated namesake.

160.   Besides the difference in the title and birthplace of the rival claimants to the honor of heading the line of Gurhwál kings, another more serious discrepancy in the accounts

Serious discrepancy in the two accounts.

submitted to Capt. Hardwicke and the writer is, that in the

lists of their successors hardly any names in the one tally
with those in the other.*

Were this inconvenience confined to the earlier kings, it
might warrant the suspicion that each list was invented *ex-
tempore* to suit the occasion, but as it extends down to

*

Number.	Hardwicke's List.	No. of years reigned.	Number.	My List.
1	*Bohg-dunt,* the first R á j á, between whose reign and *Adjey-Pall,* (an i n t e r v a l embracing fourteen genera- tions), 900 years passed of which no records exists,	900	1	*Kunk Pál,* came from Dhárá- nugur.
	Adjey Pall, ...	50		*Bisheshvur Pál.*
	His son, *Bejey Pall,*	60		*Sumát Pál,* had a younger broth- er, *Som* or *Somá Pál,* (the same as Ism or Soma Singh who colonised, Hurdwar, &c. ?)
	Laak Pall, ...	55		*Poorun Pál.*
5	*Dherm Pall,.*	65	5	*Amee Gut Pál.*
	Kerrem Pall,.	70		*Shuktee Pál* (the Sukwanti king of Kumaon, who seized on Indraprasth, a. 57 B.C. ?)
	Narrain Deo,.	72		*Retee Pál.*
	Hur Deo,.	45		*Sáliváhun Pál* (opponent of Vik- ram ?)
	Govin Deo, ...	49		*Mudun Pál.*
10	*Ram Deo,*	51	10	*Bidhee Pál.*
	Runjeet Deo, ...	53		*Bhugdut Pál.*
	Inder Sain, ...	35		*Bhog Pál,* or *Vibhog Pál.*
	Chunder Sain, ...	39		*Jeychunder Pál* (No. 2 of Hard- wicke ?)
	Mungul Sain, ...	32		*Heerut Pál.*
15	*Choora Mun,*	29	15	*Mudun Suháee.*
	Chinta Mun, ...	33		*Abergut Pál.*
	Pooren Mun,.	27		*Sooruj Pál.*
	Birk-e-Baan, ...	79		*Jeyut* (Jugut ?) *Pál.*
	Bir Baan, ...	81		*Aneerudo Pál.*

M

modern times (though in a less degree), the more rational
inference is, that anarchy was chronic in Gurhwál, and different versions of oral tradition have preserved the names of
various chiefs, who severally pretended to supremacy over
their fellows from time to time.   These discrepancies render
the main point of agreement all the more striking.

Number.	Hardwicke's List.	No. of years reigned.	Number.	My List.
20	Soorey Baan, ...	79	20	Vibhog Pál II.
	Kerreg Singh, ...	60		Gugyan Pál.
	Sooret Singh, ...	72		Bikram Pál, came from Amwán Kot (in Gurhwál ?)
	Mahah Singh, ...	75		Vichitr Pál.
	Anoop Singh, ...	59		Huns Pál.
25	Pertab Singh, ...	29	25	Suvern Pál, came from Bilung (query Tilung?)
	Hurree Singh, ...	39		Kánteekripápál from Chandpore.
	Jaggen Naat, ...	55		Kámdeopál.
	Byjee Naat,.	65		Sulukshun Deo.
	Gookul Naat, ...	54		Mahálukshun Deo.
30	Ram Naat, ...	75	30	Sut Pál.
	Goopee Naat, ...	82		Apoorub Deo.
	Lechme Naat, ...	69		Jey Deo (from whom the Khoobur Goojurs?)
	Preeim Naat, ...	71		Jitáng Pal.
	Saada Nund, ...	65		Kulyan Pál.
35	Perma Nund, ...	62	35	Ajay Pál.
	Maha Nund, ...	63		Anunt or Arunt Pál.
	Sooka Nund, ...	61		Sunder Pál.
	Suba Chund, ...	59		Sehj Pál.
	Tárá Chund, ...	44		Vijey Pál.
40	Maha Chund, ...	52	40	Baháder Páh.

It should be borne in mind that the writer's list does not profess, like Hardwicke's,
to give a *lineal* succession of kings, each name is only supposed to represent the
power paramount in the country for the time being. The names of others will be
given as the narrative proceeds.

161. Bhog Dhunt was a native of Goojurat. So also

Main point of agreement between both, that the founder came from Goojurat.

was Kunk, for he came from Dharanugur, the Dhara of Sauráshtra, the ancient name of Goojurat. The two legends then really agree about the origin of the dynasty, differing only in nomenclature. This point will be again referred to in the Memoir of Seharunpore, in connection with:—

(1). The discovery of coins of the Kanerki, Kanishka, or Kanak series in that district.

(2). The origin of the Goojurs, more particularly that of the Khooburs, the principal clan in Seharunpore, where they had a *chourasee*, who say they came from Dháránugur itself, and claim relationship moreover with a certain Jugdeo "Puár of Sreenugur."*

(3). And finally the identity of the title of the Gurhwál and old Saurashtra kings, viz., Sáh.

162. Another point of resemblance, minor indeed, yet

Other point of agreement.

worth noticing, is, that in both lists the names of the founders are followed by a series of kings bearing the title of Pál.

163. On the whole, assuming Kunk to be identical with

Probable date of the foundation of the kingdom of Gurhwál; about the first century B.C. Irruption of hill men into the plains. Sakwanti of Kumaon.

Kanerki or Kanishka, we may fairly carry back the foundation of the kingdom of Gurhwál to the era of the Scythian supremacy, in the first or second century before Christ, but having arrived at this conclusion, we are cast adrift for hundreds of years, with the exception of one brief interval. The Ráj Tarangini tells us how Ráj Pál of Indraprastha lost his life in battle with

* *Vide* preceding foot note.

Shakaditya or Sakwanti, king of Kumaon, who occupied the metropolis (71 B.C.), and held it fourteen years, at the expiration of which the great Vikram immortalized himself by the expulsion of the invaders (57 B.C.) Soon after, however, the victor lost his life in battle with the Sácá Sáliváhana, and *princes from the Sewaliks*, again pouring down upon the plains, seized Delhi, which long remained desolate.

164. The Ráj Tarangini is precise about where the invaders came from, and there can be little

The invaders were Indo-Scythians. doubt as to their nationality. They were unquestionably Indo-Scythians from the mountains of Gurhwál, a mongrel race still largely represented there, and sixth on the writer's list of the Gurhwál kings appears the name of Shaktí Pál, who may safely be identified with Shakaditya.   Moreover, by a coincidence which can hardly be accidental, the next name but one after his, is that of Sálivahan Pál, Vikram's Scythian conqueror.   The latter, it is true, has been represented as a king of Southern India, but if his nationality be taken into consideration together with the fact that Vikram's death was followed by the complete ascendancy of the Trans-Sewalik invaders in northern Hindoostan, it appears far more probable that he was a barbarian from beyond the hills.   The suggestion is at least as plausible as most others that have been hitherto offered about this obscure period.

165.   The foundation of Sreenugur, the former residence of the Gurhwál Kings, has been variously

Foundation of Sreenugur. ascribed to Rájá Ajay Pál, who, in Mr. J. B. Fraser's[*] opinion, cannot have lived more than four hundred and eighty years ago, and to Mahi-

---

[*] Himalaya Mountains, page 383.

put Sáh, whose name is not to be found in Captain Hardwicke's list. Mahiput was a prince of much more modern date than Ajay Pál. According to Hamilton,[*] he was the first independent Rájá.

166. In spite of a well known passage in Ferishta,[†]
which has been more than once discussed,
it is very doubtful whether the Mahomedans ever penetrated the Sewaliks north of the Seharunpore District, before the time of the celebrated Nujeeb u' Douluh. It is there related that in the
year 472 A.H., 1079 A.D., Sultán Ibraheem Bin Musáood I. of Ghuznee, after capturing Rood Pál, which, from the name and description of the place, appears to have been Roopur in the Punjab, marched on to a town called Dera or Derapoor, inhabited by exiles from Khurasan. A belt of mountains, nearly impassable, cut them off from all intercourse with their neighbours, and the inaccessibility of their position had hitherto guarded them against invasion, but Ibraheem having cleared a road through the hills, succeeded in reducing their capital after a siege of three months, during which his troops suffered severely from the heavy rains. Near the town was a large reservoir of water of inexhaustible capacity.

Mahomedan invasions before the the time of Nujeeb u' Douluh doubtful.

Expedition of 1079 A.D. (?)

167. Elliott observes,[‡] "it is possible that the Dehra of
Dehra Doon may be meant, but though
the belt of mountains, the inaccessible jungle, the seclusion of the inhabitants, and the identity of the

Elliott's opinion.

* Description of India, Vol II., page 636.
† *Vide* Briggs, Vol. I., page 139.
‡ Mahomedan Historians, page 207.

name, are in favor of the supposition, we are at a loss for the inexhaustible lake and the impregnability of the position."*
On the other hand, the exiles of Khurásán can hardly fail to remind the reader of the Bunjárá strangers, and although lakes are natural features wanting in the Sub-Himalayan Valleys or Doons, the presence of an immense artificial reservoir near Dehra in former times is not improbable. The direction of Ibraheem's march also must have brought him in close contact with the district, if not actually into it.

168.   Yet the following extract from Táreekh-i-Budaunee,† seems to show that all this part of the country was a *terra incognita* to the Mohomedan Historians five centuries later. "In A.H. 996, the son of the Rájá of Kumaon arrived at Lahore from the Sewalik hills, for the purpose of paying his respects.   Neither he, nor his ancestors (the curse of God on them!) could ever have expected to speak face to face with an Emperor.   He brought several rare presents, and amongst them a Tibet cow, and a musk-deer, which latter died on the road from the effect of the heat.   I saw it with my own eyes, and it had the appearance of a fox.   Two small tusks projected from the mouth, and, instead of horns, it had a slight elevation, or bump. As the hind quarters of the animal were enveloped in a cloth, I could not examine the whole body.   They said that there were men in those hills, all hairy, and men who fly with wings, and they pointed out a tree which yields fruit all the year round.   God knows whether all this is true."

(marginal note: Gurhwál a terra incognita to the Mahomedan historians.)

* I do not consider General Cunningham's identification of the place with Dara-poor on the Jhelum, by any means conclusive, (Archæological Survey, Vol. II., page 24).   I shall recur to the point in my Memoir of Scharunpore.

† Mahomedan Historians, page 252.

169. A fleeting ray of light breaks forth from the dark-
Ray of light at Aur-
rungzebe's accession.
ness at the end of the civil war which seated
Aurungzebe upon the throne of Delhi.

170. After the mutiny of his troops near Allahabad,
prince Solimán resolved to make a forc-
Flight of Prince
Solimán.
ed march with the shattered and undis-
ciplined remains of his army, along the
foot of the hills, for the purpose of joining his father Dárá
at Lahore,* (1658 A.D.) The usurper, receiving intelligence of this movement, at once despatched Fidae Khán
with a detachment to Hurdwar, to intercept the fugitive,
who therefore turned into the hills, and took refuge with
Who takes refuge
with Prithee Singh
of Sreenugur.
Prithee Singh, Rájá of Sreenugur. The
Rájá received his guest hospitably, and
announcing his determination to defy the
Emperor, sent troops to guard the Sewalik passes. Bernier
states that an unsuccessful expedition was undertaken to
compel Solimán's surrender. If so, the border warfare
that ensued may have been the real origin of a system of
interplundering between the Doon and Seharunpore, which
lasted with little intermission down to the second Goorkha
invasion, and in which the unhappy people of the valley
eventually got much the worse of the game. A wild legend, susceptible of association with the events of the time,
still lingers in the memory of the people of Seharunpore.†

171. In spite of Prithee Singh's good intentions, he
betrayed the refugee. Either the latter
Solimán's betrayal.
gave offence to his protector (perhaps,
as is sometimes said, by violating the privacy of the royal

* *Vide* Dow. III., pages 245, *sq.*
† *Vide* Memoir of that District.

harem), or Aurungzebe worked upon Prithee Singh's cupidity. However this may be, the youth, feeling no longer safe, tried to make good his escape to Thibet with a few faithful followers, but losing his way in the mountains, wandered round and round, till at last he found himself back at Sreenugur, the point from which he had started. A shepherd discovered the party taking shelter under a rock, and informed the Rájá, who seized the wretched Soliman and delivered him into the hands of his inexorable uncle (1660-61 A.D.)

172.   It has been stated that Prithee Singh received a grant of the Doon from the Emperor as a reward for his so called loyalty. A copy of the imperial *sunud* is even said to have existed among the records of Chandee in 1845. If this be so, it is strange that the document should have escaped Mr. Shore's researches. At all events, Aurungzebe cannot have really granted what was already in the possession of the grantee, although, to gratify his own vanity, he may have issued a *firman* formally recognizing Prithee Singh's title to the district.

Statement that the Doon was granted by the Emperor to Prithee Singh as a reward for this service, incorrect.

173.   There is a still older story invented to place the Gurhwál Rájás in the light of the Emperor's vassals. During the progress of Akbar's famous settlement, the reigning prince is supposed to have been dancing attendance at the Delhi court. Being in due course desired to submit a map of his dominions, together with an account of the revenue, he solicted an audience, and, on coming into the royal presence, exhibited the requisite ca-

Older story representing the Gurhwál Rájá as a vassal of the Emperor.

counts, but, in place of a map, produced a lean camel, symbolic of the bare rugged character of his territory. Akbar took the hint, and generously excluded Gurhwál from the general assessment.

174. There are strong grounds for believing that, after the endorsement of the alleged *firman*, the Sreenugur potentate was far from being the Emperor's humble and obedient servant. The annals of Seharunpore* contain references to border warfare towards the close of Aurungzebe's reign, and in the year 1103 h., one Futeh Singh led a raid from the Doon into the plains, whence he retreated to the Suhusrah pass in the western Sewaliks, holding his ground there until dislodged by Saiud Alee, the imperial general. The Poondeer Rajpoots of Seharunpore must have done good service against the intruders, for the keeping of the passes from the Doon into the plains was entrusted to one of their chieftains, Rana Gujé or Jugut Singh. Futeh Singh can have been no other than Futeh Sáh, Prithee Singh's grandson, a most enterprising prince, who penetrated through the Niti pass into Thibet, and exacted tribute from the Rájá of Deba.†

Submission of the Gurhwál Rájá to the Emperor nominal.

* Cf. Seharunpore Memoir.

† Cf. Hamilton, (Description of India, Vol. II., page 636,) who represents him to have been Solimán's betrayer, making him the successor of his cousin Syám Sáh, son of Mahiput Sáh. Prithee Singh's name does not appear in Hardwicke's list. The writer's gives after Beháder Sáh—(1), Sítal Sahae, *who conquered Sirmore ;* (2), Man Sáh; (3), Ram Sáh or Sám Sáh (Hardwicke's Rámrú and Hamilton's Syám Sáh); (4), Mahípatí Sáh; (5), Prithví or Prithvípatí Sáh, (Prithee Singh); (6), Medini Sáh; (7), and Fatah Sáh. Hardwicke places after Maha Chund—(1), Goolab Chund; (2), Ram Narrain; (3), Gobind Narrain; (3), Lechmen Narrain; (4), Jegget Narrain; (5), Mahant Narrain; (6), Sheetaub Narrain; (7), Annand Narrain; (8), Herry Narrain; (9), Mahah Narrain; (10), Renjeet Narrain; (11), Raamroo; (12), Chirsturoo; (13), Jeggeroo; (14), Herroo, and then Futteh Sáh. I have attempted to evolve a rational and connected narrative from the conflicting accounts.

N

175. The famous Sikh Gooroo Rám Ráe, took up

Gooroo Rám Ráe arrives in Futeh Sáh's reign.

his abode in the Doon in the reign of Futeh Sáh. He was a lineal descendant of Nanuk, being Hur Govind's great-grandson. His father Hur Ráe, a Gooroo of mild ministry, having taken part with Dara Shekoh in the late civil war, had been compelled to give him up as a hostage to the Emperor. The accident was fortunate, for when left an orphan at the age of fifteen (1661 A.D.), he found himself

His prosperity due to Aurungzebe's patronage, for the Sikhs disputed his legitimacy.

with few partisans except Aurungzebe, into whose favor he had ingratiated himself. His legitimacy was doubtful, so his claims to succeed his father were pronounced inferior to those of his infant brother Hurkishen. Again, when the latter died, the fierce Tegh Bahánder, Hur Govind's son, was elected ninth Gooroo, to the exclusion of the milder Ram Ráe (1664 A.D.), who left his father's home at Keerutpore* on the Sutlej, and betook himself first to Delhi, then to Agra, where some accuse him of having aided the machinations of his friend, the Emperor, against his rival. After Tegh Bahánder's cruel execution (1675), he cherished fresh hopes of succeeding to the Sikh apostleship, but the undeniable superiority of Govind Sing once more supplanted him. He therefore resigned himself to the less brilliant prospect of becoming the respectable head of a sect of dissenters, and retired to the Doon, bear-

His retirement to Dehra.

ing recommendations from his powerful protector Aurungzebe to the Raja of Gurhwál (1756 s., 1699 A.D.). After sojourning at Kándlee on the far side of the Tonse, where there

* Mr. Shore says "Kirtálpore."

is a jack-fruit tree* said to have been planted by him, he removed thence to Koorburah (now included in the modern town of Dehra), and built his temple at the neighbouring village of Dhamoowala, unless, as some allege, the edifice was constructed by his widow Punjáb Kour. His presence soon attracted numerous devotees, and a flourishing town, called Gooroodwárá, or Dehra, grew up around the Saint's

Gooroodwárá. dwelling. It is not certain whether Dehra is an old name, or like Gooroodwara, one of modern origin, meaning the resting place of the Saint. In the latter case, the ordinary spelling must be wrong, and the word ought to be written Dera.

176. Rájá Futeh Sáh endowed the temple with three villages, Koorburah, Rajpore and Cham-

Endowment of the Gooroo's temple by Rájá Futeh Sáh. asuree. His successor added to these four others, Dhamoowálá, Myanwala, Pundit-waree, and Dhurtawálá. The income from them, which has varied greatly at different times, is now considerable.

177. Many wonders are related of Gooroo Ram Rae. The Oodasee faqueers, his principal disci-

The Gooroo's su-pernatural powers. ples, are ready enough to tell stories of how he used to die of his own accord, and come to life again, whenever they find a willing listener. He tried the experiment, however, once too often, for having told his obedient wife not to come near him

And manner of his death. for three days, he shut himself up in his cell, where he was found lying stark dead, when she opened the door. The bed on which he died,

---

* Whence probably the present Mohunt's fondness for sending presents of jack-fruit.

stands within his cenotaph, and is an object of peculiar adoration with the devout.

178. After the Gooroo's death, his wife, Máta Punjab Kour, managed the affairs of the endow-

His wife manages the endowment. His successors.

Hur Purshad. .

ment with the assistance of an agent named Hur Purshad, subsequently elected Mohunt, for twenty-five years. The third

Hur Sewuk.

Mohunt was Hur Sewuk, a man of some ability and considerable influence, who died in 1818, when the revenue of seven *Maafee* villages was supposed not to exceed 1,300 or 1,400 Rs.*

179. Mr. Shore, writing in 1827, describes his successor,

Suroop Das.

Suroop Das, as "a very ignorant, stupid sort of person, who till the other day could not read." Neither is the present Mohunt, Preetum Das†—the fourth,

Preetum Das.

a man conspicuous for intelligence.

180. All Gooroo Rám Ráe's successors, in spite of, or

Their affectation of celibacy.

possibly owing to, their inferior sanctity, have affected celibacy.

181. The original construction of the Rajpore canal,

The Rajpore Canal.

which supplies the tanks attached to the temple with water, is sometimes attri-

buted to Máta Punjáb Kour,‡ more generally to a Raj-poot Princess "Ranee Kurnavutee," who

Its construction attributed to Panjáb Kour or Ranee Kurnavutee.

made it to fertilise the villages between Dehra and Rajpore, before the Gooroo-dwara was built, or the Gooroo himself had

---

* *Vide* Moore to Secretary Board Commissioners, 9th December, 1818. Cf. Latter to former, 3rd February, 1819.

† Deceased since the above was written.

‡ *Vide* Moore to Secretary Board Commissioners, 20th February, 1818. Latter to Murray, 22nd May, 1818.

come to the Doon. Afterwards its management became vested in the Mohunt, at whose expense it was annually repaired. He had a greater interest than any one else in its mainten- ance, because its water not only supplied his ornamental tanks, but also irrigated the rent-free lands on which the religious establishment was dependent. On the strength of this, Hur Sewuk, shortly before his death, attempted to establish claims to proprietary right in the water-course; without success, although the fact of his superintendence was acknowledged, and his right to a supply of water, in common with the rest of the landholders, admitted.

Its management originally vested in the Mohunt.

182. Ranee Kurnávutee's name is always coupled with that of Ajboo Kour, as Viceroy of the Doon. They may have been husband and wife. Their palace was at Nuwádá, the low serpentine hill clothed with *sál*, on the left bank of the Sooswa, five miles south east of Dehra, whose strange reptilian appearance probably originated the name of *Nág-sidh*, and traditionally associated the spot with the penance of the Nág Bámun. A supernatural being, in the form of a snake, still haunts its slopes, appearing now and then to receive the offerings of worshippers.

Ranee Kurnavutee and Ajooo Kour.

183. There the Ranee built her palace, a handsome edi- fice, judging from the foundations, which can be distinctly traced close to the village of Nuwádá, once a large town, and the capital of the Doon. Under her fostering care the valley smiled. Settlers, chiefly Rajpoots and Gocjurs, gladly immigrated from the plains, and many flourishing villages sprung up, such as

Their palace at Nuwádá once an im- portant place.

Prosperity of the Doon.

Ajubpore (so called from Ajboo Kour), Kurnpore (named after the Ranee), Kaulaghir, Kyarkoolee, Bhát Beer and Bhogpore. Suhunspore, Pritheepore, Kulyánpore, Nágul, Rajpore, Bhugwuntpore and Thano were then all large towns with busy marts, and the Gurhwál Rájá used to honor them with his presence, as well as Nuwádá. At Pritheepore especially, exist remains be-

Remains at Prith-
eepore.

speaking its former prosperity—an old fort, temples and *sutee* monuments, consi- dered to be relics of a once powerful family related to the Rájás of Gurhwál. Chunda or Jhunda Myán was a famous chieftain of the stock, but the particulars of his life have not been preserved.

184.　Futeh Sáh died soon after the arrival of Gooroo Rám Ráe, and was succeeded by his grand-

Death of F u t e h
Sáh about the year
1699 A.D. Accession
of Prudeep Sáh.

son Prudeep,[*] Pruteep, or Purteep, Sáh, an infant only five years old, whose reign lasted the best part of a century. The period of his accession was still one of peace and prosperity. The Doon was a happy valley where the inhabitants reap- ed fine harvests with little toil, paying, notwithstanding light assessments, a larger land revenue than they do now.

185.　There were no less than four hundred villages under cultivation, and the gross collec-

Continued p r o s-
perity of the Doon at
the beginning of his
reign. The land re-
venue.

tions of the year 1786 s., (1729 A.D.) amounted to 94,346 Rs. The easy going Rájá appropriated a comparatively small portion of this, for the deductions on ac- count of rent-free tenures were very large, and little more than half went to the State. In 1804 s., (1747 A.D.,) the

---

* Son of Duleep, who may perhaps have reigned himself for a short time.

five pergunnahs were assessed at 97,645 Rs., from which a deduction of 42,845 Rs. left a balance of Rs. 54,800. The schedule attached to the Resolution of Government deciding upon the annexation of the Doon to Seharunpore, dated 17th November 1815, exhibits the distribution of the whole amount.

Names of Pergunnahs.	Assessment on each.	Deduction for rent-free tenures.	Net assessment for each Pergunnah.
Suhjpore, ...	13,595	4,010	9,585
Busuntpore, ...	12,397	7,515	4,864
Suntaur, ...	29,715	12,350	17,365
Kulyánpore, ...	37,955	18,970	18,985
Sauree,*	4,001	...	4,001
Totals, ...	97,645	42,845	54,800

186. The prosperity of the district soon attracted the

Conquest of the Doon by the Rohillas, 1757 A.D.

attention of the energetic governor of Seharunpore, Nujeeb u' Douluh, Ameer ul Umra of the Empire. Considering the habits of the times, he cannot have experienced much difficulty in finding an excuse for hostilities. He crossed the Sewaliks and occupied the country without encountering any serious opposition (1757 A.D.) Pruteep Sáh offered a very feeble resistance to Nujeeb Khán's disciplined, yet impetuous, Afghans, the men who presently turned the scales of victory at Paneeput.

* Often called "Sowree;" sometimes also, "Soree" (with r hard). The sound of the word is uncertain.

187. Nothing is known of the details of the expedition,
but a tradition* about the siege of an old

Particulars of the expedition not known.

fort at Bhogpore by the Ameer ul Umra's son Zabitah Khán, who never entered the Doon, must refer to some incident either in this campaign or a later expedition undertaken by his grandson Ghulam Kádir.

188. A writer in the *Calcutta Review*, previously alluded to, places the event in the year 1744,

Doubts about the date of the expedition.

perhaps following the authority of the old Cánoongoe Soba Ram, quoted in the Census Report of 1865. This is an anachronism possibly originating in some recollection of a still earlier enterprise,† that of Allee Mahomed Khán, who planned the conquest of Kumaon, and entrusted the execution of the design to Háfiz Rehmut and three other less distinguished leaders. They took Almorah, and coming into collision with the Rájá of Sreenugur, routed his disorderly rabble without much trouble. Pruteep Sah prevented further encroachments by consenting to pay an annual tribute of Rs. 60,000 a year to the Rohilla government, and profited by the misfortune of his neighbour Kalián Chund Raja of Kumaon, to extend his own dominions, getting a lease of their conquest from the Rohillas for Rs. 300,000 a year (1741 A.D.‡)

189. Hamilton mentions " several wars " between Pruteep

---

* Mentioned in the Proceedings of the Asiatic Society (1865).

† *Vide* Memoir of Seharunpore.

‡ Mr. J. H. Batten places the event in 1744 A.D. He says," the irruption was arrested in the very heart of the hills on the downs of Ghyr Mundee, near the sources of the Ramgunga," close to the residence of the Kumaon Commissioner (Report on Kumaon and Gurhwál, p. 171).

Sáh and Nujuf Khán, whom he evidently confounds with

Mistake of Hamilton's. Nujeeb Khán or, as the poorer classes generally call him, "Nujeem Khán."

190.   Although, towards the close of his active career,

Nujeeb Khán's administration. Its excellence. the Ameer ul Umra must have been too busy guarding his original fief of Seharunpore against the fierce incursions of the Sikhs, to devote much time to the management of this remote district, his administration is most gratefully remembered on account of its benevolent and enlightened character. Mahomedan colonists were encouraged to settle in the valley, but he favored no one class to the prejudice of another, and the original occupants of the soil received that protection which their helplessness at the time rendered so necessary to them. Canals and wells were dug,

Agriculture. agriculture flourished, and the land revenue increased to Rs. 1,26,000.   The numerous mango topes and remains of tanks frequently found in the midst of what now seems a primeval forest, warrant the statement that at this happy period there were 500 estates in the Doon all under cultivation.

191.   Trade kept pace with agriculture, and the term

Trade. The Hatnálá. Hatnála (from *hat*, a shop or market, and *nálá* a pass or ravine), still applied to Nágul, Rajpore, Bhugwuntpore, Thano and Bhárápore, preserves the recollection of the course taken by the stream of traffic to and from the hills.

The prosperity of the country ceases with Nujeeb's death. 192.   These halcyon days suddenly ceased with the death of Nujeeb u' Doulah in October 1770 A.D.   Henceforth the people were harried by Rajpoots, Goojurs, Sikhs and Goorkhas, in succession, till from a fertile garden the district was converted into a barren waste.

193.   The feeble old Rájá of Gurhwal himself began the mischief, driving out the Mahomedan set-

Folly of the Gurh-wál Rájá.

tlers, and neglecting the real interests of his own co-religionists.   The influence of the Mohunt of Gooroo Rám Rae's temple became paramount in the royal counsels, and the seat of

Seat of Govern-ment transferred from Nuwádá to Dehra.

the local Government was transferred to Dhamoowála, within the boundaries of the Dehra township.   Nuwada declined and before long fell into absolute decay.   The date of Pruteep Sáh's death cannot be ascertained with per-

Pruteep Sáh's death.

fect certainty, but since, according to the most reliable accounts, his son and succes-sor, Lulut Sáh, reigned only seven years, dying in 1781 A.D., he most probably departed this life in the year 1774 A.D., after a brief interval of undisturbed apathy and self-indulgence.

194.   During the next three reigns, the Doon hardly ever knew the same master for six months

Subsequent Anar-chy.

running.   Irruptions from Seharunpore and the Punjab never ceased.

195.   The first well-authenticated Sikh invasion occurred in 1783 A.D., when Bughél Singh and his lawless com-panions, after devastating Seharunpore,

First Sikh inva-sion, 1783 A.D.

were checked at the Ganges by the troops of Asuf u' Douluh, the Nuwáb Vizier of Oude.   A large detachment of the marauders, turning northward, penetrated the Sewaliks and invaded the Doon. No one resisted them.   The inhabitants fled like sheep, and all who could, consigned their valuables to the sanctuary of the Gooroodwara. The device proved successful, for the Sikhs respected the temple, whereas the houses around it were sacked. The enemy did not remain long, retreating hurriedly after burning a few villages.

196. It was either in this or the year following that the unfortunate Purdooman Sah came to the throne. Lulut Sáh had, on his death-bed in 1781 A.D., bequeathed the kingdom of Sreenugur to his elder son, Jaikurt Sáh, and Kumaon* to the younger, Purdooman. The former died about two-and-a-half years after, and the latter succeeded him.

Purdooman Sáh's accession.

197. By that time, the decline of Zabitah Khan's power had removed the last barrier to further aggressions, and the spoilers roamed to and fro, as occasion required or inclination prompted, for the valley, though much exhausted,

The decline of Zábitah Khán's power injurious to the Doon.

* I confess my utter inability to unravel the politics of this period with any degree of satisfaction to myself. According to one account, Deep Chund, king of Kumaon, Kulyán Chund's successor, was treacherously murdered, (together with his Minister, Jey Kishen Joshee,) by his spuriously descended cousin, Mohun Singh, who himself ascended the throne of Kumaon. Then Lulut Sáh and the Rájá of Dotee, leaguing with the family of the unfortunate Jey Kishen and other malcontents, expelled the usurper, and placed Purdooman Sáh on the throne in his stead. The new king reigned in Kumaon for *nine* (?) years, one of his principal Ministers being Hurruk Deo, Jey Kishen's brother. *After that*, Lulut Sáh died, leaving Gurhwál to Jey Kurt Sáh. The latter, favoring Mohun Singh's pretentions, desired to depose Purdooman Sáh, who, reciprocating the feelings of his brother, was anxious to establish Prákurm Sáh, his own full and younger brother, at Sreenugur. Jey Kurt Sáh dying in the meantime, Purdooman Sáh therefore occupied Gurhwál, and entrusted Kumaon to Hurruk Deo's care. The Viceroy was soon driven out by Mohun Singh, but regained his footing, and put the usurper to death. Then again, Lall Singh, Mohun Singh's brother, once more drove him out, with the aid of Faiz Ullah Khán's Rohillas from Rampore. He soon, however, regained possession of Almorah with Purdooman Sáh's assistance, until Prákurm Sáh (!) took Lall Singh's part, when he was compelled to retreat to Sreenugur, where he ended his days in retirement (Report on Kumaon and Gurhwál, *ut suprá*, page 174-179). Hurruk Deo Joshee must have been a patriot with a very elastic conscience, for "he enjoyed a place of trust in the immediate household of Nujeeb u' Douluh."

still repaid the trouble of plundering, and Dehra itself, having supplanted Nuwada, was a populous well-built town.

198. The Sikh claims were perhaps the easiest to satisfy, for a compromise was effected by which the Maharajah agreed to pay certain *Sirdars* a fixed annual tribute of 4,000 Rs. in return for protection.

The Rájá pays tribute to the Sikhs.

199. An English traveller, Forster, happened to be at Suhnspore, when two truculent tax collectors came to receive the customary tribute. The quaint observation suggested to him by the event, sounds strange in the mouth of a Covenanted Civil Officer in the service of the great Company Bahádeŕ : "from the manner in which these men were treated, *or rather treated themselves,* I frequently wished for the power of migrating into the body of a Sicque for a few weeks.*" Their horses were foddered with green barley torn from the standing crop, and we may hence infer how well the riders themselves fared.

Forster's remarks.

200. The raids of the Rajpoots and Goojurs from Seharunpore did more mischief than the Sikh incursions. They were not petty enterprises of no greater dignity than common *dakoities,* but regular invasions on a small scale, organized by men of consequence, who were able to lead into the field miniature armies composed of horse and foot in due proportion. These were days when a Rajpoot or Goojur chieftain could, at a pinch, muster one thousand fighting men. Against such a force the people of the Doon were helpless, although they occasionally attempted reprisals.

Rajpoot and Goojur raids from Seharunpore.

* Forster, Travels, Vol. I., page 199.

201. Mr. Shore has been consequently induced to compare the interplundering between the Doon and Seharunpore to the border warfare between the counties on either side of the Cheviot hills in the middle ages. The comparison is hardly correct. At an earlier period, it is true, when the Doon maintained an abundant population, and the lowlanders were under the control of a vigorous Government, the hill men made dashes into the plains with a fair chance of success, meeting their neighbours on more equal terms, so that the expeditions undertaken by the latter in retaliation may be properly considered reprisals, and the comparison so far holds good. The excursions of the plains men in the second half of the eighteenth century cannot, however, be regarded in this light, being the acts of wanton aggressors, and the inhabitants of the Doon had no more chance against the Rajpoot or Goojur chiefs of Seharunpore than the latter themselves had against the more powerful *Sikh Sirdars.*

Mr. Shore's comparison.

incorrect.

202. The banditti plied their trade through the two passes most used in the present century for purposes of peaceful traffic—those of Timlee and Mohun. The defiles of Kánsrao and Hurdwar were at first less frequented, but when the Khoobur Goojurs gained strength at the expense of the Poondeers, Rája Ramdyal Singh of Landourah appropriated these two gorges to his own use, and began to exercise his hereditary profession of robbery in the intervals between his graver occupations in the capacity of *Talookdar.*

Passes most frequented by the marauders; the Timlee and Mohun.

203.   The Gurhwál Rájá, far too weak to attempt resistance, submitted to the necessity of
handing over a few villages to each of
the offending chiefs in *jagheer*, on condition of their guarding each pass against
marauders belonging to their own or other clans.   In this
manner Guláb Singh, the Poondeer Rana, obtained twelve
villages, together with the hand of Raja Lulut Sáh's daughter in marriage, and his son, Bahádar Singh, actually got
the fiscal management of the whole Doon in the year 1195
F., 1787 A.D.   Two *mouzahs* only, Peelion and Chuktun-
wala, remain in the possession of his descendant, young
Petumbur Singh, the present Rana.   Raja Ramdyal Singh
got five, and others were similarly distributed among the
Raos of Kheree, Sukroudah and Raepore.   The Goorkhas
dispossessed the Rana, but appear to have allowed the
other jagheerdars to retain possession of their fiefs, which
were of course resumed at the British conquest.*

The Gurhwál Rá-jú gives away Jag-heers in lieu of black-mail.

204.   In 1786 A.D., the notorious Ghulam Kádir, me-
ditating the reconstruction of his grand-
father's principality, determined to rean-
nex the Doon to Seharunpore.   Accompan-
ied by his Hindoo adviser, Raja Munyar Singh, he entered
the valley from Hurdwar about the middle of the year.
Fire and bloodshed marked his onward progress.   Not
content with sacking Dehra, he gutted the Gooroodwara.
Cow's blood profaned Ram Rae's holy shrine, and the con-

Second Rohilla Invasion, 1786 A.D.

* Rájá Rámdyál Singh at first had seven villages, but the Gurhwal Rájá resumed
one or two, on account of some misconduct of his followers.   Rájá Khoushál Singh
laid a claim to them, which was negatived in 1823. *Vide* Mr. Shore to Secretary
Board of Revenue, 24th October, 1823, and 22nd July, 1824.

queror, it is said, otherwise expressed his contempt for superstition in an extravagant fashion, smashing the Mohunt's cithern, and reclining disdainfully on the couch where the Saint had breathed his last. It is an article of faith with many orthodox Hindoos that God, as a punishment, smote the sacriligious Nuwab with the madness which drove him to destruction.

205. He nevertheless gave evidence of sound judgment, by entrusting the administration of his easy conquest to a Hindoo deputy, Umed Singh, who served him most faithfully to the very day of his death (1789).

Ghulám Kadir evinces sound judgment in the disposal of his conquest.

An example of fidelity so unusual at the time, shows that the Nuwab, however tyrannical, possessed some sterling good qualities, and at all events knew the secret of conciliating his followers.

206. After Ghulam Kádir's execution, Umed Singh courted the friendship of Purdooman Sáh, to whom the district once more became nominally subject, but about three years

Umed Singh's intrigues.

later, he betrayed his new master to the Raja of Sirmore, who proclaimed his own government in the Doon, and, it is alleged, deputed a representative to live at Pritheepore. The cause of the breach between Umed Singh and the Gurhwál Raja is unknown.

207. Purdooman Sah had recourse to an alliance with the Mahrattas, who, glad of an opportunity for plunder, hastened to his assistance, but retired after a few skirmishes

Purdooman Sáh's alliance with the Mahrattas.

with the Sirmore troops, without effecting anything decisive.

208. Umed Singh was thus enabled to maintain the authority of his new patron several years longer,[*] until the Gurhwal Rája again won him over to his side, giving him the hand of his daughter in marriage. Still the district belonged to anyone rather than to Purdooman Sah. It was the public property of every sturdy freebooter.

Umed- Singh betrays the Rájá of Sirmore.

209. The Sikh incursions continued, while the hungry Rajpoots and Goojurs of Seharunpore emulated the activity of the "Singhs." Whenever any delay occurred about the payment of blackmail, fifty or a hundred Punjabee troopers generally sufficed to sweep the country clear. The operations of the others were, as already noticed, sometimes conducted in a more ambitious style.

Continued incursions.

210. Whatever slipped through the fingers of the professional spoiler, fell into the hands of the official harpy. The *amil* for the time being, was his own master, and collected booty with all possible expedition, not knowing the moment when he might suddenly fall a prey to some other more influential or cunning than himself. The original owners retained few villages, and almost all records of right perished.

Corruption of the officials.

211. Among the more unscrupulous of the official spoliators beneath whose oppression the people were groaning, is counted one Huree Singh of Goolair,[†] son-in-law of Purdooman Sah,

Huree Singh.

---

[*] Mr. Shore's says for " eight or nine."

[†] He built a Shiwálá at Nuwádá. Is he the father of Mohun Singh, Deep Chund's assassin ? (*Vide supra* ; cf. Report on Kumaon and Gurhwál, page 174, *note*).

whose extortions are still notorious. Rajá Rámdyál Singh, his rival, vied with him in rapacity, as much to grudge him as to satisfy his own avarice. Both stripped the country bare, and the revenue fell at first to Rs. 12,000, then to Rs. 8,000, only double the sum hitherto paid to the Sikhs.

212. In 1800 or 1801 arrived a swarm of locusts, in the shape of a band of Mahrattas from Seha-

Mahratta inva- sion. runpore, who settled down, devoured all they could lay hands upon, and then departed. On this occasion there was little or no bloodshed, for the Sreenugur government was more feeble than ever, and resistance would have been vain.

213. A vague tradition about one Rughnáth Ráo, Mahratta, "who devoted the Doon to

Tradition about Rughnáth Rao, Mah- ratta. Budreenáth," must have some connection with this event. Another, about Futeh Sáh's (? *) having met them in battle, defeated them, and given the district to his brother, Ajey Singh, in recognition of his bravery, looks like a pure invention

214. After this, two brothers, Dubhál Brahmans, named Ráma and Durnee, are said to have

The Dubhál Brah- man brothers, and others. got power; then Poorun Singh, *Räezádáh* of Suhnspore; and, finally, Shib Rám of Sukneeana, where the Song takes its rise. This man's ancestors had obtained the *talook* so called, rent-free from one of the Gurhwal Rajas. After the British conquest, the grant was confirmed to him and his relative Kashee Rám, on account of services rendered in the Goorkha

---

* Q.—Is Futeh Sáh, after all, merely a title borne by more than one of the Gurhwál Rájás ? It seems very probable.

war.[*] It is hence evident that the family to which he belonged, had great influence from early times, and as an example of their importance, it is related that one of them,

Sees Ram tortures the Mohunt.

Sees Ram (grand-father of the late Cánoongo Soba Ram) did not scruple to have the hands of the Mohunt plunged into boiling hot sugar, when the holy man was strongly suspected of having committed a murder. The proceedings, though summary, were strictly judicial, being of the nature of a trial by ordeal. The Mohunt was severely burned, and therefore sentenced to pay a heavy fine.

215. Although many may have thus acquired a tempo-

Umed Singh Viceroy down to the Goorkha conquest.

rary ascendancy, Umed Singh continued to be the recognized Viceroy of the Sreenugur Rájá down to the time of the Goorkha conquest, which interrupted a design he had formed of making himself independent.

216. So little being known about the history of the

Little really known about the country in the last century.

country north of the Sewaliks in the last century, the impressions of a contemporary writer who penetrated to Sreenugur, are fraught with special interest.

217. When Captain T. Hardwicke[†] visited Gurhwál

Capt. Hardwicke's impressions.

in 1796, the journey to the capital was considered an ardous undertaking. The direct road through the Doon, too, was more difficult than the more circuitous route *viá* Kotdwara on the opposite side of the Ganges. His journal, therefore, gives no direct information about the condition of the

---

[*] *Vide* Young to Delhi Resident, 15th December, 1829.
[†] Asiatic Researches, VI., 322 cf. 333, *sq.*

valley, but he bears strong testimony to the nakedness of the land in the vicinity of Sreenugur itself: "to sum up the whole in one general conclusion—depopulation and misery are striking features throughout, and a greater share of the country seems in the undisturbed possession of the birds and beasts of the forest than appropriated to the residence of man."

The nakedness of the land.

218. The royal family, consisting of the Raja and his two brothers, Prakurm Sáh and Preetum Sáh, did not stand on ceremony, and visited the traveller in company with a miscellaneous following.

Simplicity of the royal family.

219. The king himself appeared to be about twenty-seven years of age, a man of low stature, slender make, regular features, an effeminate air, nervous in speech, and altogether, judging from his exterior, not made of the metal fit for coping with the hardy Goorkhas, who had already made decided advances in this direction.

Description of Pardooman Sáh.

220. The manners of the brothers denoted great simplicity. Their apparel had none of that ostentatious tawdriness conspicuous in the costume of the Hindoostanee nobility, and the dress of the Raja differed in no respect from that of the other princes. He seemed to be a man of fair intelligence, possessing some knowledge of contemporary politics, and taking an interest in them. He conversed about British progress in the East, about the late Rohilla war, and expressed much admiration of European proficiency in the military art.

Their manners unaffected.

221.   He knew nothing however of the tactics of civil-
ised warfare, and was for the first time in
his life indulged with the sight of the
movements of a disciplined soldiery by
the party of sepoys guarding Capt. Hardwicke's camp.

. The King's igno-
rance of military
tactics.

222.   The capital was about three quarters of a mile
long, and not nearly so broad, disposed in an elliptic
form without much attention to order or
convenience.   The houses were built of
rough stone masonry, with slated roofs,
being generally two stories high.   The streets were so
narrow that two people walking from opposite directions
could hardly pass one another abreast anywhere except
in the bazaar.   The palace, situated in the centre of the
town, was very old and dilapidated.

Sreenugur; i t s
description.

223.   The revenue of the whole kingdom, comprising
the Doon, Gurhwal, and Kumaon, barely exceeded five
lakhs, including the income from all
sources ; exports, imports, land revenue,
mines, and gold-washing.

Revenue of the
kingdom.

224.   The land revenue was paid partly in kind, partly
in money, generally in the proportion of
one-half of the produce of the soil or its
value.

Land revenue,
how paid.

225.   Very little money reached the royal coffers, after
the deductions necessary to meet the local
expenditure.   Most of the land-tax went
in the payment of the troops quartered
upon the several districts, and even the soldiers on duty in
or about the metropolis, particular employés, musicians, and
dancing girls, were paid by money orders on the zemindars.

Mostly spent in
payment of troops.

Capt. Hardwicke met several persons belonging to the classes last-mentioned, going on a journey of some thirty koss to have the cheques for their arrears of pay cashed. A further alienation of the land revenue arose from constant donations to Brahmans and endowments of temples in successive reigns.

226. The fiscal management of the gold washing was extremely simple. Each gold washer paid

Revenue from gold-washing.

Rs. 100 a year to government for the privilege of search, without reference to the quantity of gold dust found. The localities where the precious metal used to be sought, were Kurmprag, three days' journey east of Kidarnath, at the confluence of the Pindur and the Alaknunda; Painkunda on the Ganges; Deoprág at the junction of that river with the Bhageera-thee; and, finally, Rikheekesh and Lukhurghat, two well-known places in this district on the same river.

227. At Nagpore, forty koss north-east, and Dhanpore fifty koss north of Sreenugur, were cop-

From mines. Copper mines at Nágpore and Dhanpore.

per mines, worked only eight months in the year. The ore yielded on an average 50 per cent. of pure metal, one half of which went to the Rájá, the rest to defray the expense of working, smelting, and supervision.

228. At Dusoulee fifty or fifty-five koss east of Sree-nugur, was a lead mine, the whole pro-

Lead mine at Du-soulee.

duce of which went to the State, the miners being maintained by plots of rent-free land. The Raja called their labor into requis-ition from time to time, according to the quantity of ore wanted.

229. Iron, found at Chandpore and several other places, was left to any one who chose to extract it, for the mines did not repay the expense of working them.

Iron mines at Chandpore, &c.

230. The principal imports were rock-salt and borax from Bhootan; musk in pods, *chouries,* hawks, and, according to Hamilton, slaves from the country bordering on Budreenath; sheep's wool blankets from Painkunda, called *punckee,* resembling the *loee* of the Doab in texture, but stronger and finer; cotton cloths of every description from Rohilkhund, and Lahore salt, exported again by the Bhootan people in exchange for the merchandize they themselves brought. Duties averaging six per cent of the value of the merchandize were levied at the passes, on all imports, and certain exports. The Kotdwara pass was farmed for 12,000 Rs. a year. Mr. Traill, Commissioner of Kumaon, mentions another peculiar source of revenue, indeed "the principal source of the ordinary revenue of the sovereign," viz., offerings presented by subjects at the Hindoo festivals. On extraordinary occasions, moreover, such as the marriage of any of the royal family, a general impost was levied from all the assigned lands. Yet the Rajas were miserably poor, being latterly sometimes reduced to absolute want.

Imports.

Duties on imports and exports.

Peculiar source of revenue.

231. The standing army consisted of not more than five thousand infantry, a motley force armed after the fashion of the place to which each division belonged; with matchlocks, bows and arrows, or swords and bucklers. But the sword was the peculiar wea-

The Army.

pon of the hill warrior. One thousand men were quartered
at the capital. The rest were scattered in various directions
to assist in collecting the revenue. Dress, discipline, and re-
gularity in paying them, were all treated with equal disregard
by the government, who soon suffered for their neglect.

232. The forces were maintained much on the same
principle as in the plains. Certain lands

Maintained by as-
signments of land.
were assigned* for their payment, under
the management of the commanders (*Fouj-
dárs*), who conducted the civil as well as military administration of each district, superintending the collections,
dispensing justice in civil and petty criminal cases, and
referring those of importance to the Di-

Administration of
justice.
wan of the Sreenugur Court. This official
also superintended the proceedings in any
case where the cause of action arose at or near the capital.

233. Fines and confiscations were the ordinary punish-
ments for almost every degree of crime.

Method of punish-
ment.
Even murder was seldom punished with
death; the convict, if a Rajpoot, was severely fined, if a Brahman, banished; but treason was
generally punished capitally, as well as cow-killing, and

Cow murder and
certain violations of
caste laws punishable
with death.
the violation of caste laws by a Dhoom;
for instance, smoking a Rajpoot's pipe
&c. &c. The methods of execution, a
rare event, principally confined to the unhappy Dhooms,
were either beheading or hanging. The Goorkhas afterwards introduced the novelty of impalement. The sentence of mutilation of the hand or nose was occasionally

---

* Cf. Mr. Traill's Report on Kumaon.

passed in cases of heavy theft. Adultery with a woman of the lower classes was a petty misdemeanour punishable by fine, but if the adulteress happened to be a lady of rank, the rule was to cut off her nose and kill her lover. To make the punishment more signal, its infliction was left to the injured husband.

234. Although the Government was a simple monarchy, the sovereign's power was not absolute, being controlled by an aristocracy chiefly composed of officials; Diwáns, Dufturees, Viziers, Foujdárs and Negis. These titles were hereditary in certain families, and the last clearly points to the period when the dominant race was of the Scythian (Nágá) stock, still largely represented in the remoter parts of Gurhwál, where the dissimilar features of two distinct sections of the population mark the difference between the Caucasian and Mongolian types.

Constitution; a limited monarchy.

235. When Hardwicke visited Sreenugur, Purdooman Sáh paid an annual tribute of Rs. 25,000 to the Goorkhas, the history of whose aggressions now claims attention.

Tribute to the Goorkhas.

236. They are Nepalese, and consequently of Thibetan origin, but their pure Tartar blood is mingled with that of Hindoo colonists, to whose energy and superior intelligence the foundation of several principalities in Nepal under Rajpoot chiefs is attributed. One of these was Goorkha,* a petty state situated west of the Trisul-Gunga, the pretentions of whose later chiefs to true Rajpoot descent, in

Origin of the Goorkhas.

* Cf. Asiatic Researches, Vol. II., p. 307 *sq.*, and Hamilton, Vol. II., p. 681-695.

spite of the rigid observance of Hindoo customs, is extremely questionable, for their ancestors are said to have been men of a heretical mountaineer tribe called Mugurs. About the year 1765, Prithee Naráin, an ambitious scion

Prithee Naráin. of this pseudo-Rajpoot family, the first of the Nepalese to appreciate the advantages of fire-arms and European discipline, became formidable to his neighbours of Katmandoo, Lalitapatun, and Bhatgáon in Nepal proper, and ultimately overpowered them. The failure of an expedition sent against

Capt. Kinloch's
expedition, 1767 A.D.
him in 1767 under Capt. Kinloch, at the application of the Katmandoo Rájá, confirmed his success, and the inhabitants of the whole country accepted the designation of the conquerors.

237. Prithee Narain's son, Purtap Singh, succeeded

Purtap Singh. him in 1771 A.D. and died fourt† years after, leaving an infant son, Ráná or Run

Run Baháder.
The regency.
Baháder, under the guardianship of his widow Rajendrá Lakshmee, and brother Baháder Sáh. 1775 A.D.

238. The regents were ambitious, and devoted them-

Ambition of the
regents.
selves, in the intervals between their private disputes, to schemes of conquest.

239. The progress of the Goorkhas was westward, and

Fall of Almorah. they advanced rapidly. In 1790 the fall of Almorah made them masters of the whole country east of the Ramgunga. They next invaded Gurhwál

---

† Fraser (Himalaya Mountains, p. 5) says only eighteen months after, cf. p. 383. *Vide* also Ham., Vol. II., p. 608-636, 652-682, &c., As. Res., XI., p. 499 *sq.*

at the invitation of Hursha Dev, a turbulent Brahman,* in 1791 A.D., when they were unexpectedly stopped before a strong fortress named Langoor,† close to Sreenugur. The intelligence of a Chinese invasion raised the siege, after it had lasted twelve months, 1792 A.D.

Invasion of Gurh-wál and siege of Lan-goor 1771 A.D.

240. Two years before, a Goorkha army, crossing the Himalaya, had impiously plundered the holy temples of Teshu Lumbu, the residence of a sacred Lama. The Em-peror of China, in his capacity of defen-der of the Buddhist faith, was therefore compelled to send a force of 70,000 men into Nepal for the purpose of pun-ishing this horrid outrage. The avenging army marched almost up to the gates of Katmandoo, and the Nepalese consented to pay tribute to the Emperor, besides disgorg-ing their plunder.

Chinese invasion provoked by sacrili-gious conduct of the Goorkhas.

241. The Rájá of Gurhwál, however, ignorant most probably of the predicament of his assailants, was glad enough to buy them off at an annual out-lay of 25,000‡ Rs., but the nominal peace did not preserve the country from incur-sions or prevent the Court from being fre-quently treated with contumely. Another inconvenience arising from the Raja's relations with the Nepalese Govern-

The Rájá of Gurh-wál ignorant of their difficulties, submits to the exaction of the Goorkhas.

---

* Evidently the same as Hurruk Deo, " the Earl Warwick, or King-maker of Ku-maon." (*Vide* Report on Kumaon and Gurhwál, *ut supra*, p. 177, *note*).

† In the Gunga Sulán pergunnah, north of talooka Chandee, betwen the Ganges and the Koh river (*idem*, p. 157).

‡ Raper says the tribute was at first only 3,000 Rs., afterwards raised to 9,000 Rs., a sum trebled again by various exactions.

ment was, that he had to endure the presence of a Goorkha Resident, whose demands were in themselves costly, and whose friends continually came to sponge upon the Court under pretence of going on pilgrimages.

242. The queen regent of the kingdom of Nepal died in 1786 A.D. In 1795, Rana Bahader, then nineteen years old, vindicated his manhood and capacity to govern, by casting his old uncle into prison, where Bahader Sah died a miserable death, from starvation and general maltreatment. The new administration, thus horribly inaugurated, proved so detestable, not only to his humbler subjects but even to his own favorite wife, that the king was soon forced to abdicate in favour of his illegitimate infant son, Girván Godh Bheer Bikram Sáh, and take refuge under the wing of the British at Benares (May 1800.)

Ráná Bahader's majority, 1795 A.D.

243. There followed another regency under a previously neglected Ranee, during which the conquest of Gurhwal and the Doon was completed. Umr Sing Thapa, and Hustee Dhul Chautra, uncle to the infant king of Nepal, led an army of 8,000 or 10,000 men against Sreenugur, (February 1803). Purdooman Sáh abandoning the capital, according to Raper, made a stand at Barahat, whence he was driven into the Doon, which the invaders occupied in the following October, after a very brief struggle. He then fled into Seharunpore, and pawning his family throne for Rs. 1,50,000, besides the jewels and plate of Budreenath for 50,000 Rs., succeeded in raising a new army of about 12,000 men with the assist-

Second regency. Conquest of Gurh-wál completed.

Flight of Purdoo-man Sáh. Occupation of the Doon 1803 A.D.

He renews the struggle.

ance of Rajá Rámdyál Singh. Thus reinforced, he returned to the Doon, and encamping at Kurburah, a sub-
urb of Dehra, once more gave battle to the enemy. During the engagement a musket ball cut
His death, January   short his career, while he was standing
1804.
in front of his tent by the side of Dulail
Singh Myán of Pritheepore (January, 1804.)

244. The famous earthquake of 1803, which, in the
opinion of the vulgar, announced the
Earthquake o f   British supremacy in the Upper Doab,
1803.
is also considered to have been the har-
binger of the Goorkha conquest. It almost shook Sreenugur to pieces, and left its mark on Gooroo Rám Ráe's
temple.

245. Mr. J. B. Fraser* mentions, incredulously, the
belief that the Brahmans of Palia Gurh, a
Prophesy of the   terrific and most holy glen in the bosom
Palia Ghur Brah-
mans.   of the mountains on the road to Jumnoo-
tree, prophesied the misfortunes of Purdooman Sáh, the
rise of the Goorkha power, and its decline before that of
the British. Although Mr. Fraser smiled at this, we need
not doubt the truth of the report, for the priests of Palia,
men not devoid of intelligence, were re-
Occupation of the
Doon by the Goor-   cipients of many a suggestive traveller's
khas coincident with
that of Seharunpore tale about events then taking place in
by the British.   different parts of India, and as to the latter part of the alleged prophesy, they can hardly have
failed to be struck by the fact that we reached the Sewaliks from the south-east, just as the Goorkhas were ap-

---

* Himalaya Mountains, p. 409.

proaching them from the north east. Col. Burn marched into Seharunpore only a few days before Umr Singh Thápá occupied Dehra in October 1803.

246. Upon Purdooman Sáh's defeat and death, his younger brother Preetum Sáh being made prisoner, was sent to Nepal, where he remained in cap-

Capture of Preetúm Sáh. Flight of Soodurshun Sáh and Prákurm Sáh. tivity till 1815. His son, Soodurshun Sáh, fled to Jooalapore (two miles below Hurdwar,) whither the victors courteously sent the king's corpse, with all due respect, to be solemnly burned. His second brother Prákurm Sáh, escaping in the opposite direction, found an asylum with Rájá Rám Surn of Hindoor.

247. In the same year, Run Baháder returned to Kat-

Return and assassination of Run Baháder. mandoo, and at once recommenced a system of indiscriminate persecution. This provoked a conspiracy that ended in his assassination. According to good authority, Sher Baháder his younger brother, happened to pick up a stray proscription-list, and having read his own name in it, promptly stabbed the Rájá. He himself fell in turn beneath the dagger of Bulrám Sáh, or of Bheem Singh Thápá, another faithful follower of the late king, Umr Singh Thápá's son, under whose vigorous administration the Goorkha sway was extended through all the hill states as far as the Sutlej.

248. At first the Goorkhas ruled unmercifully, with

Tyranny of the Goorkhas. a rod of iron, so that the Doon threatened to become literally a desert. Most of the inhabitants emigrated, and the little cultivation that still lingered, began to disappear rapidly. But

when Mohunt Hur Sewuk Ram was reinstated in his
possessions, a perceptible improvement took place.   He
was the only land-owner left, possessing any real local
influence, and he used it judiciously, inducing the peasantry to return to their deserted hold-

Efforts of Hur Se-
wuk for the improve-
ment of agriculture.
ings and giving every encouragement that
lay in his power to agriculture.   Still,
for some time the district could only afford an insignificant
revenue of Rs. 9,000 a year.   Presently, this increased to
Rs. 16,000, and then again to Rs. 18,000

Gradual rise in
revenue.
from all sources ; land-tax, transit duties,
escheat of property of persons dying with-
out heirs (*muro*), confiscation of property of emigrants
(*ruhta*), appropriation of unclaimed property (*buhta*), fines
for offences against caste (*punch khut*), and treasure trove
(*kuliandhun*).*

249.   *Ruhta* and *buhta*, be it observed, are two most
significant items, speaking volumes about

Significant items
in the revenue.
the real state of the country.

250.   The official returns for the year 1870 s.† (1220
F., 1812-13 A.D.), exhibit a marked im-

Maximum of
revenue under the
Goorkhas about Rs.
25,000.
provement in the resources of the district, which may be in great measure
ascribed to the determined character of
the Goorkha Governors, who, though themselves prone
to oppression, did not suffer others to molest their subjects.

251.   Raids from Seharunpore and the Punjab had been

---

* Mr. Shore's Report of 1st May, 1827.

† *Vide* Resolution of Government, dated 17th November, 1815.

Pergunnahs.	Assessment.		Sair duties.	Collector's present or Seeburjey.	Fines or Dand.	Totals.	
	RS.	A.	RS.	RS.	RS.	RS.	A.
Suntaur, ...	7,095	0	2,800	708	1,100	11,703	0
Kulyánpore, ...	1,163	8	1,280	118	200	2,761	8
Busuntpore, ...	2,169	8	650	224	91	3,134	8
Sauree, ...	939	8	4,200	96	100	5,335	8
Suhjpore, ...	1,379	0	571	94	25	2,069	0
	12,746	8	9,501	1,240	1,516	25,003	8*

brought to an abrupt termination by the fulfilment of a
threat to burn one village for every plun-

Improvement due to protection. dering party that entered the Doon.   A
band of Sikhs once had the temerity to set
the new government at defiance, and, as in the days of
yore, sacked a village, carrying away several women and
driving off the cattle.   The Nepalese commandant, receiving intelligence of the outrage, sent two hundred men in
pursuit of the marauders, whose own dwellings were surrounded and set on fire.   Every man,

A terrible example made of a Sikh village. woman, or child attempting to escape,
was massacred in cold blood, except a few
of the handsomest females, whose beauty purchased them
their life.   This signal example had the desired effect.

252.   Such summary methods of securing life and pro-

---

* Hamilton's figures do not differ materially from these.   According to him the
revenue of the Doon in 1811-12 was Rs. 22,264.   (Vol. II., page 634).

perty were indeed barbarous. Still, several of the Goorkha governors were capable of a more
enlightened policy. The Dehra Doon
records have preserved the names of a
few.

253.   The first to check the excesses of the domineering
soldiery, and so stay the tide of emigra-
tion that would soon have left the valley
desolate, was Amrit Káji,*·but the administration of Hustee
Dhul Chautra is extolled above that of
all others. He put a high premium upon
agriculture, making liberal advances and
giving away whole villages at nominal rents (5 Rs. or
so), to various Zemindars who were thus enabled to grant
leases to cultivators at one-twelfth and even one-sixteenth
of the produce.†   According to Mr. Shore, 1867 s. (1810
A.D.) was a year famous for his efforts in the cause of
progress, the results of which were most striking in the
Kulyánpore pergunnah, a tract much less prosperous under the English system.   The same authority states that
he was unfortunately removed from office in 1869 s.,
(1812 A.D.).   Captain Raper,‡ however, alleges that, having
been recalled from the siege of Kangra
about the year 1805, he was then appointed Governor of Sreenugur, while his
brother Rudravír Sáh took his place before Kangra.   Soon

Doubts about the
period of his admi-
nistration.

---

* Q.—The same as Raper's Amr Singh Cadzi ; and, therefore, identical with Amr
Singh Thápá ?

† *Vide* Mr. Shore's Settlement Report, 15th December, 1825, cf. Letter to Mr.
Traill, 30th March, 1828.

‡ Asiatic Researches, XI.. p. 501, 460-493. He calls him brother of Bum Sáh,
Governor of Almorah.

after, the Thápá party (low-born men of the agricultural caste) got the upper hand of the Chautrás (aristocrats of the blood royal), so the brothers lost their appointments. When Captain Raper visited Hustee Dhul, at Kurkuree, close to Bhímghora, on the 8th of April 1808, the Chautrá had been already superseded in the Government of the Doon by Bhairo Thápá, who returned the

Bhairo Thápá succeeds him in 1808.

English traveller's visit a few days after in company with his predecessor. The new Governor, a man of very different temperament from Hustee Dhul, appeared suspicious and obstructive, endeavouring to throw difficulties, both imaginary and real, in the way of Captain Raper's further progress. The Doon was then bustling with warlike preparations, for troops were marching backwards and forwards, to and from Rájá Sunsár Chund's impregnable fortress, which defied all the efforts of the Goorkhas to capture it. Bhairo Thá-

Siege of Kangra.

pá himself soon proceeded thither, leaving his son, Shista Thápá, to manage affairs during his absence.

254. Raper describes Dehra as an "extensive village."

Dehra in 1808.

Not many years before, it had been a populous town. His estimate of the Doon revenues, Rs. 35,000, is certainly excessive, especially since

Raper's estimate of the Doon revenues excessive.

the heavy duties on imports levied under the Goorkha government (one anna in the rupee), had materially checked the commerce previously carried on with Thibet.

Goorkha system of administration, not very different in form from that which had preceded it.

255. The Goorkha conquest does not appear to have made much difference in the administrative system, except that the chief governors exercised powers formerly vested in the

R

Gurhwal Rájá's Deewan. The conquered territory was divided into three *puttees* or provinces, sub-divided into eighty-four pergunnahs, each under a military governor, one of whom was Bhairo Thapa. As the siege of Kangra fully occupied all of them, they exercised their unlimited judicial powers through deputies, who, by all accounts, transacted business in a very summary manner.

256. The various commandants holding districts assigned for the payment of troops, administered

Functions of the
Foujdárs.

justice in most civil and all petty criminal cases where the cause of action arose within their jurisdiction, heavy cases or those originating close to head quarters being decided by the principal military governor or his deputies. But the commandants also generally delegated their powers to deputies, called Becháries, who, as a rule, farmed the dues on all law proceedings. Their method of procedure, too, was summary, and they were prone to get rid of intricate suits by having recourse to ordeals of different kinds, sometimes " by tossing up."

257. The system of assignments did not work satisfactorily with the Nepalese. The govern-

The system of as-
signments works
badly under the new
government.

ment had a tendency to overrate the value of each, and regulate the assessments rather from a calculation of the supposed means of the inhabitants than of the actual capabilities of the land. The *Foujdárs* on their part were inclined to regard the *talooks* as a means of personal emolument, instead of tenures held in trust. Balances, therefore, frequently accrued, to liquidate which the effects or even the families of the defaulters used to be sold, for the Goorkhas had a sovereign contempt for life, and thought less of a human being than of a cow or bullock, animals whose sacrilegious slaughter could only be expiated by the offender's death.

258. It cannot then be wondered at that slavery flourished. While the revenue system recruited the slave market, the ordinary procedure of the courts condemned defaulters in cases where sentence of fine had been passed, to life-long bondage, together with their families. Besides, parents sold their children and, under certain circumstances, uncles, their nephews, or nieces; elder brothers, their younger brothers or sisters; and so on.* It need hardly be added that many were reduced to slavery for no better reason than the right of the stronger, and Mr. J. B. Fraser computes the number of Gurhwálies sold by auction during the brief period of the Goorkha supremacy, at 200,000. But if the notorious sparseness of the population be considered, this will be surely pronounced to be an exaggeration.

Slavery prevalent.

259. Just above the Hur kee Pairee or Bathing Ghat, at Hurdwar, within a stone's throw of a British Police station, stood a Goorkha outpost, where hundreds of unhappy persons, varying in age from three years old to thirty, were annually brought down and exposed for sale during the fair time. They only fetched from ten to a hundred and fifty rupees a head, whereas the average price of a camel was seventy-five; of a common horse, from two hundred and fifty to three hundred. Such was the thraldom from which it was our destiny to rescue a feeble and degraded people.

Goorkha slave-market at Hurdwar.

* Shore to Magistrate, Morádábád, 3rd May, 1828.

SECTION II. FROM THE OUTBREAK OF THE GOORKHA WAR TO THE PRESENT TIME.

260. A full account of the Goorkha aggressions along
our frontier in Purneea, Tirhoot, Sárun,
Goruckpore and Bareilly, as well as in
the protected territory between the Sutlej and the Jumna, may be dispensed with. Suffice it to say, they rendered war sooner or later inevitable. The Goorkhas, essentially a military people, eager to try their strength with us, let slip no opportunity of provoking hostilities, and it was most probably only because they were busy guarding their more recent conquests beyond the Jumna, that they refrained from making raids upon our possessions in the Doab.

Goorkha encroachments on our frontier.

261. The Goorkha soldier is a short, thick-built man,
of great strength and activity in proportion to his size. He prefers fighting at close quarters, sword in hand, but his national weapon is a heavy crooked knife, something like a chopper, called a *kukree*, with which a skilful practitioner will strike off a man's head at one blow. The officers formerly used bows and arrows as well.

Peculiarities of the Goorkha soldier.

262. Just before hostilities commenced in 1814, the standing force of Nepal amounted to thirty or thirty-five

thousand men, in addition to the army of occupation west of the Gograh. The men were provided

Strength of the Nepalese army. with fire-arms, drilled, dressed, and equipped in imitation of the European fashion, their officers bearing commissions of captains, colonels, &c., as in the British service.

263. The immediate cause* of the Goorkha war was a wanton attack upon the principal police

Immediate cause of the Goorkha war. Attack upon the Bhootwál police station. station in the disputed frontier territory of Bhootwál, in which eighteen of our constabulary were killed and six wounded, (29th May, 1814). Munraj Foujdár, the hero of this exploit, himself superintended the Police Darogha's barbarous murder, although the latter had surrendered himself a prisoner. A comment upon the cruelty of the Goorkhas generally may here be not out of place.

264. We are too prone to overlook this defect in consideration of their pluck, a quality which, if once formidable to ourselves, as it might indeed again

Cruelty of the Goorkhas. be, we have known how to turn to good account in the hour of danger. The history of Kirtheepore affords an excellent example of this grievous blemish in their character. When its inhabitants, after gallantly holding out for several months against Surooparatna, Prithee Narain's brother, at last surrendered on the faith of a promise that their lives would be spared, the principal men of the place were at once put to death, while those of an inferior order were shockingly mutilated. Their noses and lips enabled the Rájá to take

* *Vide* Proclamation of the British Government. dated Lucknow, 1st November, 1814.

a census of the town, the name of which was changed to Naskatapur, "cut nose town." Compared to this achievement the murder of the Bhootwál Darogha was a very tame affair.

265. The capture of another police station with more

The capture of another police station.

loss of life followed, but as the unhealthiness of the season precluded the adoption of active measures to check these encroachments, the Governor-General was fain to write a letter of remonstrance to the young Rájá, whose aggravating answer rendered reasoning no longer

Declaration of war.

possible, and war was formally declared on the 1st November, 1814. Before this, however, our troops had taken the field.

✓266. Our army consisted of four divisions—one formed

Disposition of the British forces. The third division.

at Dinapore, another at Benares, a third at Meerut and a fourth at Loodianah. It is only necessary to watch the operations of the third, under the command of Major-General Gillespie, which originally consisted of—

Artillery, ...	247 men.
H. M.'s 53rd Regiment, ...	785 „
Native Infantry, (1st Battalion 6th, 1st Battalion 17th, and 1st Battalion 7th), ...	2,348 „
Pioneers, ...	133 „
Total, ...	3,513 „

Ordnance—Two 12-pounders;
Eight 6-pounders;
and Four howitzers.

This division had afterwards to be re-inforced.

267.   Its first duty was to penetrate the Sewaliks and occupy Dehra Doon.   It was next to act, as circumstances might dictate,   either against Umr Singh Thapa's troops, who held Sreenugur, or against his son Runjore Singh, commanding at Nahun, so as to co-operate with the fourth division under General Ochterlony.

Duties of Third Division.

268.   Meanwhile Mr. Metcalfe, the Resident at Delhi, had received instructions* to institute enquiries of a political nature about Soodurshun Sáh, the exiled heir to the kingdom of Gurhwál.   He deputed the duty to his assistant Mr. Fraser, who, after visiting Hurdwar, joined the third division, which marched on the 14th October, before the General's arrival, under the command of Lieut.-Col. Mawby of the 53rd regiment (quartered at Meerut during the preceding year), and reached Seharunpore in four days.   On the 19th, Lieut.-Col. Carpenter of the 17th N. I., advanced with a small column including two companies of the 53rd under Lieut. Young, towards Timlee, and entered the pass next day.   Col. Mawby, following with another column, felt his way through the Mohun pass with the assistance of the Kheree Zemindars.   Ráná Jeewun Singh, Baháder Singh's son, also joined the invading army, hoping to recover his possessions beyond the Sewaliks.   Both officers met at Dehra on the night of the 24th October.

Mr, Fraser's deputation.

Advance of the Third Divison.

Occupation of Dehra by the British.

269.   The enemy, a mere handful of men commanded

---

* *Vide* Auber's Rise and Progress of the British Power in India, Vol. I., 504.

by Capt. Bulbhudr Singh, nephew of Umr Singh, had

Bulbhudr Singh. taken up their position in a rude fort hastily constructed on the highest point of a low Himalayan spur projecting into the Doon valley south-east of Rajpore. The site of the fort is about three and a half miles north-east of Dehra. The hill itself is very steep, except to the south, and a thick sál forest now covers its sides. It has become celebrated in Indian

Kalunga. history under the name of Kalunga, but is better known to the people as Nalapanee. The works, built of boulders strengthened with stockades, were still incomplete, and the garrison was busy raising them.

270. That same night Bulbhudr received a written

Bulbhudr refuses to surrender. summons to surrender from Col. Mawby. He tore it up, sending back word that the Colonel would see him soon enough. This act of defiance excited much astonishment in the British camp, for so little had anyone reckoned upon encountering serious opposition in the Doon, that General Gillespie evidently considered his presence there quite unnecessary.

271. The day after, Colonel Mawby reconnoitred the

Colonel Mawby reconnoitres Kalunga. place, and having had some light field pieces carried up the hill on the backs of elephants, fired a few rounds. The idea of taking the fort by a " *coup de main*" proved quite impracticable. He therefore sent a report to that effect to the General, who came up with the remainder of the division on the 26th.

272. After another reconnaissance, preparations for

an assault on a grander scale were commenced. They

Preparations for a
regular assault. proceeded without the slightest interference from the enemy. Batteries presently sprang up on a piece of level ground opposite the fort, at a distance of six hundred yards, and by the morning of the 31st October, two twelve-pounders, four

Strength of storm-
ing party. five-and-a-half-inch-howitzers, and four six-pounders, lay ready to cover the advance of a storming party divided into four columns of:—

611 Officers and Men under Colonel Carpenter.
363   ,,   ,,   ,,   Captain Fast.
541   ,,   ,,   ,,   Major Kelly.
283   ,,   ,,   ,,   Captain Campbell.

besides a reserve of 939 men under Major Ludlow, making a total of 2,737.

273. General Gillespie's plan was simple in theory; the

General Gillespie's
plan. various columns were to advance simultaneously from opposite directions at a given signal, so as to distract the enemy's attention. In practice it was not so easy; this the General would have understood, had he made himself acquainted with the difficult nature of the ground, and known the calm resolution of his antagonists.

274. Boulders piled up steep ascents, netted together

Difficulties of the
attack. by jungle almost impenetrable to men encumbered with accoutrements, opposed the progress of the assailants, except in a few places not leading directly to the point of attack. Nor had the defenders of Kalunga been idle. No part of the wall could now be scaled without ladders, and that system of stockades, with which our subsequent experience of moun-

s

tain warfare, has since rendered us familiar, secured the whole. Guns also swept the easiest approaches, and one especially, served with grape, commanded the way along the wall to a wicket gate flanking it, the only entrance which would have been otherwise practicable.

275. When the batteries opened fire, the guns proved too light to produce much effect, and the General, unable to control his impatience, ordered the signal gun to be fired long before the appointed time. The officers in command of the second, third, and fourth columns, either did not hear the report, or hearing did not understand it, and remained inactive. There is also a strong probability of their having been absolutely unable to act in perfect unison with the others. The first column and the reserve moved forward about 9 A.M., and made their way bravely across the stockades up to the very walls of the fort, under a heavy fire, beneath which numbers fell. There the want of ladders brought the survivors to a stand still. At length ladders came, but Lieut. Ellis of the Pioneers was shot dead, while in the act of putting the first against the wall, and the rest were burned in a village of grass huts, to which the Pioneers retreated, followed by the whole of the storming party. Two companies of the 53rd were present on this occasion.

Failure of Gillespie's plan.

276. As they retreated, three others arrived after a distressing march, under the command of Capt. Wheeler Coultman.* With these and one hundred dismounted men of the 8th Royal Irish Dragoons, his own old regiment, the General resolved to make one desperate effort. A

* *Vide* Historical Record of the 53rd, page 19.

party of the 53rd dragged two six-pounders up the ascent willingly enough, but on getting within thirty yards of the wicket, the men sulked and refused to stir a step farther.* There they stood doggedly, stubbornly allowing themselves to be shot down, while the brave Gillespie cheered them on, sword in hand, until he fell shot through the heart. His aide-de-camp, Lieutenant O'Hara, died by his side. Colonel Carpenter then ordered a retreat.

His death.

277. On that unfortunate day, the gun enfilading the wall of the fort from the wicket gate, did great execution, pouring showers of grape on our men. Of the reserve alone, every single soldier in the front rank was either killed or wounded at the very first discharge. The few who did reach the gate, were received with volleys of arrows, and even stones, as well as bullets, the Goorkha women being conspicuous among the defenders of the passage.

Execution done by the gun commanding the approach to the wicket gate.

278. This inglorious repulse must be mainly attributed to General Gillespie's impatience. Success would not have added much to his reputation, and his death only prevented such a failure from being disgraceful. Overlooking the strength of the enemy's position, he apparently expected a repetition of his brilliant *coup de main* at Vellore. One moment's reflection would have made him change his plan, for with the resources at his command, he might have easily blockaded Kalunga and starved out the garrison in a few days, with little or no loss to his own forces.

Gillespie's impatience.

* A fact omitted from the Historical Record of the Regiment. They were not afraid, but, it is said, hated their Commanding Officer.

279. The net result of his imprudence was—a General

Our loss.

and four officers killed, besides fifteen others wounded, of whom several died afterwards; twenty-seven non-commissioned officers and men killed, and 213 wounded. Of the hundred dismounted troopers engaged, more than half were either killed or wounded, because "there was not one among them who would not have stayed by his commander to the last, although certain death were in his view."

280. Colonel Mawby, being senior officer on the spot, succeeded to the command of the division.

Col. Mawby succeeds to the command; his excessive caution.

His caution was as excessive as his predecessor's rashness. Abandoning his position, he retired to Dehra with the intention of awaiting the arrival of a battering train and other reinforcements from Delhi. It is difficult to imagine what possible advantage could have arisen from this retrograde movement. It served to discourage our own troops, and to inspirit the enemy, enabling them at the same time to procure supplies and repair their fortress. Nearly a month passed in purposeless inactivity.

281. The battering train arrived on the 24th November, and the siege recommenced the day

Renewal of the siege.

after. The place was shelled, while a battery of eighteen-pounders erected within 300 yards of the fort, pounded the wall, effecting a breach pronounced practicable early in the afternoon of the 26th. The fire of the besieged did not do much harm in return, and galled by the incessant cannonade, they made a fruitless sally. Another assault was immediately ordered.

282. Major W. Ingleby of the 53rd led the storming

party, viz., the flank companies and one battalion company
of his own regiment, together with all
Second assault; its failure. the grenadiers of the native corps. Being
wounded, he retired to the rear. Capt.
Coultman, who took his place, never got beyond the breach,
which Lieut. Harrington alone ascended, at the expense
of his life. According to the annalist of the 53rd, some
of the men followed his example, but although the remaining companies of the regiment were brought up to support
the attack, no advantage was gained. The breach was not
sufficiently large, most resolute warriors defended it, and our
troops, refusing to make a dash, were compelled to retreat.

283. The men of the 53rd displayed the same dogged
apathy that had previously distinguished
Apathy of the men of the 53rd, and gallantry of our officers. them, whereas their antagonists fought
like demons. Sullenness, not cowardice,
held them back; "no one turned to fly; but none went onwards; they stood to be slaughtered." The conduct of
the British officers was on the contrary conspicuous for
devoted gallantry. Lieut. Harrington, we have seen, died
upon the breach. Lieut. Luxford of the horse artillery
was shot near him in the act of attempting to clear the way
with a gun. Two other officers also lost their lives; Capt.
Campbell of the 6th N. I. and Lieut.
Loss of the British. Cunningham of the 13th N. I. Seven more
(six of the 53rd, Major Ingleby, Capt.
Stone, Lieutenants Horsley, Green, and Brodie, and Ensign
Aufrere), were wounded. Of the men, 33 were killed, and
636, including twelve sergeants, three drummers, and 184
privates of the 53rd, were either wounded or missing.

284. Each Goorkha must have given an account of

some four of the attacking party, for when a well sustained
bombardment compelled the survivors of
the garrison to evacuate the fort three
days after, they barely numbered 70, and
more than 80 or 100 can hardly have been put *hors de com-
bat* in the interval. This miserable remnant fought their
way through 'the besiegers' lines on the night of the 30th
November. Major Ludlow went in pursuit with a detachment 400 strong, and Major Kelly occupied the fort. The
place bore hideous testimony to the valour
of its defenders ; " the whole area was a
slaughter-house strewed with the bodies of the dead and
wounded, and the dissevered limbs of those who had been
torn to pieces by the bursting of the shells." The groans
of the wounded lingering in an agony of thirst, intensified
the misery of the scene, for during the last few days the
garrison had been debarred access to the only spring from
which water was procurable. But for this, the defence
would certainly have been still longer protracted. The
stench from the putrifying bodies was intolerable, and the
mangled remains of women and children completed the
horrors of this Golgotha.

Evacuation of the fort.

Its horrible state.

285. Such was the conclusion of the defence of Kalunga, a feat of arms worthy of the best
days of chivalry, conducted with a heroism
almost sufficient to palliate the disgrace
of our own reverses. A curious episode illustrates the
spirit with which the Goorkhas met the British in this
memorable fight. One suddenly appeared advancing towards our lines, right under the fire of the batteries, waving
his hand as he approached. The firing ceased, and he was

Chivalry of the Goorkhas.

welcomed into our camp. It then turned out that a shot had shattered his lower jaw, so he had come with the most perfect *naïveté*, to put himself under the treatment of the English Surgeons. When discharged from hospital, he ingenuously asked permission to rejoin his corps and fight the British again. Several similar instances of Goorkha frankness occurred.

286. Two modest white obelisks standing side by side, crown the left bank of the Raspunah ravine opposite Kalunga; the one is sacred to the memory of Sir Rollo Gillespie, and those who perished with him; the other is a tribute of respect to our "gallant adversary Bulbudhr" and his brave followers, who survived the siege to die a soldier's death elsewhere.* We may credit the tradition which says, that on abandoning his stronghold, the Goorkha Leonidas triumphantly exclaimed in a loud voice; "to capture the fort was a thing forbidden, but now I leave it of my own accord."

Monuments near Kalunga.

Bulbhudr's boast.

---

* The following is a facsimile of the inscription on the monuments :—

(1). (WEST SIDE).	(EAST SIDE).
To the Memory of	*Troops engaged.*
MAJOR-GENERAL SIR ROBERT ROLLO GILLESPIE, K.C.B., LIEUT. O'HARA, 6TH N. I., LIEUT. GOSLING, LIGHT BATTALION., ENSIGN FOTHERGILL, 17TH N. I., ENSIGN ELLIS, PIONEERS, KILLED ON THE 31ST OCTOBER, 1814. CAPTAIN CAMPBELL, 6TH N. I., LIEUT. LUXFORD, HORSE ARTILLERY., LIEUT. HARRINGTON, H. M. 53RD REGT., LIEUT. CUNNINGHAM, 13TH N. I., KILLED ON THE 27TH NOVEMBER. AND OF THE NON-COMMISSIONED OFFICERS AND MEN WHO FELL AT THE ASSAULT.	DETACHMENTS HORSE AND FOOT ARTILLERY. 100 MEN OF THE 8TH ROYAL IRISH LIGHT DRAGOONS, WHO WERE DISMOUNTED, AND LED TO THE ASSAULT, BY SIR R. R. GILLESPIE. H. M. 53RD REGT. 5 LIGHT COMPANIES FROM CORPS IN MEERUT. 1ST BATTALION 6TH N. I. Do. 7TH DO. Do. 13TH DO. Do. 17TH DO. 7TH NATIVE CAVALRY. 1 RISSALAH OF SKINNER'S HORSE.

287. Issuing forth with the seventy, he first halted

His retreat.   near the source of Nalapanee, the stream
whence the hill derives its popular name, for
his men were faint with thirst. Careless from fatigue, or

Discrepancy be-   indifferent to danger, the fugitives kept
tween tradition and   no watch. Spies brought word of this
written authority.
to the British camp the same night, and
Bulbhudr, being surprised, was again compelled to fly. Such
is the oral account. Written authority is either silent about
this incident, or gives a different version of the same
event. Before Kalunga fell, three hundred men had been
lingering about in the neighbourhood, watching their opportunity to make a dash in and reinforce the beleaguered
garrison. These Bulbhudr joined at a hill several miles
off, and Major Ludlow did not, according to Mr. Fraser,
follow in pursuit, until the day after (1st December). A
harassing march brought our force in sight of the enemy

(2). (WEST SIDE).	(EAST SIDE).
ON THE HIGHEST POINT OF THE HILL, ABOVE THIS TOMB, STOOD THE FORT OF KALUNGA. AFTER TWO ASSAULTS, ON THE 31ST OCTOBER AND 27TH NOVEMBER, IT WAS CAPTURED BY THE BRITISH TROOPS, ON THE 30TH OF NOVEMBER, 1814, AND COMPLETELY RAZED TO THE GROUND.	THIS IS INSCRIBED AS A TRIBUTE OF RESPECT, FOR OUR GALLANT ADVERSARY, BULBUDDER, COMMANDER OF THE FORT, AND HIS BRAVE GOORKHAS, WHO WERE AFTERWARDS, WHILE IN THE SERVICE OF RUNJEET SINGH, SHOT DOWN IN THEIR RANKS, TO THE LAST MAN, BY AFGHAN ARTILLERY.

General Gillespie's body was removed to Meerut, where his tomb is. His monument is the most conspicuous in the cemetery, consisting of a high pillar surmounting a pedestal, in the western side of which is inserted a marble slab inscribed,

VELLORE CORNELLIS PALIMBAUG.
SIR R. R. GILLESPIE,
DJOEJOCARTA,
31ST OCTOBER,
1814,
KALUNGA.

To the east is another slab recording the fact that the whole was repaired in 1862, by his old Corps, the 8th K. R. I. Hussars.

by one o'clock on the morning of the 2nd, when Major
Ludlow, coming upon them suddenly, drove them to the
top of the hill with considerable loss.
Bulbhudr surpris-
ed by Major Ludlow, He could not however dislodge them, so
continues his flight they retreated in good order to Jountgurh,
to Jountgurh.
a mountain fortress on the left bank of the
Jumna, about eight miles north-east of Bairath, in Jounsar.

288. The fort of Kalunga was so completely demolish-
Kalunga razed to ed that little more than an inequality
the ground. in the surface of the ground distinguishes
its site.

289. Col. Mawby's instructions now were to co-operate
with General Ochterlony in the Kyarda
Col. Mawby's in- Doon, west of the Jumna, against Umr
structions. Singh Thapa and Runjore Singh.

290. Col. Carpenter had been already sent to Kálsee
between the Jumna and the Tonse, a posi-
Col. Carpenter oc- tion admirably adapted for cutting off the
cupies Kálsee. communication between the eastern and
western extremities of the Goorkha line of operations. Unexpected success attended his movements.

291. Capt. Fast occupied the heights above the town
without losing a man, and the fort of
Evacuation of Bairath, perched on a mountain upwards
Bairath. of 7,000 feet above the level of the sea,
apparently impregnable by comparison with Kalunga, was
immediately abandoned (4th December). The people of
Jounsar, long writhing beneath the yoke of Goorkha oppression, had declared for us, and starved the enemy out
of the stronghold, by intercepting their supplies. Its
evacuation completed the conquest of the Doon and Jounsar.

T

292. On the 5th December, Col. Mawby left Dehra,

Col. Mawby leaves Dehra and gives over command to General Martindale. and returning to Seharunpore by the Timlee pass, reached Moginund, near Nahun, on the 19th. He there gave over command to Major-General Martindale, who on the 24th occupied the town of Nahun, whence Runjore Singh retreated to Jaituk, a fortress that defied all our efforts to take it, until evacuated, together with, all the Nepalese strongholds between the Kálee and the Sutlej, under the terms of a convention concluded between Umr Singh Thápá and General Ochterlony at Malaun, on the 15th May 1815.

293. Among the valiant defenders of Jaituk was the brave Bulbhudr. When he threw himself

Bulbhudr Singh repulses an attack upon Jountgurh. into Jountgurh, Major Baldock had been detached with a force about 1,000 strong, partly composed of regulars, partly of irregulars, from Kálsee, with orders to dislodge him. The enterprise failed utterly. This failure has been attributed to " some misin-formation regarding the numbers opposed," and judging from the sample already seen of Bulbhudr's fighting, we must certainly admit that Major Baldock acted under some misconception, since the attacking force was not much more than double the number of the Jountgurh garrison. Hav-ing repulsed this attack, Bulbhudr left

And retreats to Jaituk. sixty men behind him to hold the place, and crossing the Jumna, reached Jaituk about the middle of February. After its surrender, he en-listed his handful of heroes in the service

His death. of Runjeet Singh, under whose standard they died to a man in battle with the Afghans.

294. Hustee Dhul Chautra, the humane and enlightened Governor of the Doon, played a less brilliant part in the campaign. To him the defence of Kumaon against a British force assembled at Moradabad under Col. Nicholls, in March 1815, had been entrusted. On the 12th April, a general salute from the enemy's guns announced his arrival at Almorah, while our troops were investing that town. Eleven days later, he was defeated in an engagement with a detachment commanded by Major Patton, and died, during the retreat, of a mortal wound in the temple.

Fate of Hustee Dhul Chautrá.

295. With the exception of the people of Jounsar, who not only cut off the Goorkha supplies, but harassed Bulbhudr's retreat from Jountgurh to Jaituk, and actually came to an engagement with him at the passage of the Western Tonse, the inhabitants of Gurhwál and Sirmore appeared, either from fear or apathy, quite indifferent to the result of the struggle upon which their fate depended. A letter from Prithee Singh of Koolee to Tooleram, an *employé* of our political agent, quoted by Mr J. B. Fraser, exactly expresses the popular feeling on the subject : " you talk to us to stand up in arms, and to come to Doon, as were this the time of the year sixty (*i. e.*, 1860 s.), before the Goorkha conquest, and we, as we then were, whereas we are worse off now than our servants were then. We were even before badly off, but for the last ten years we have got over the time in want of clothes and food. *I owe* 500 *Rupees........and three or four hundred men, who were in Nálapánee you have not been able to drive out.*" Badly off as the people were, they

Good behaviour of the people of Jounsar.

Apathy of others.

feared something worse if they aroused the suspicions
of the Goorkhas, whose confidence was
overweening at the commencement of the

Confidence of the Goorkhas.

campaign. Few are aware of the audacity of the Nepalese commanders. Some went so far as to contemplate the invasion of Seharunpore, even after our occupation of the Doon.

296. Elated with the advantages he had gained over General Martindale at Jaituk, Umr Singh Thapa* cherished hopes of worsting Ochterlony himself; in that case, he argued,

Umr Singh Thápá's views.

Runjeet Singh would surely join him ; then an allied Sikho-Goorkha army would cross the Jumna in two divisions, one of which was to make an immediate descent on the plains, while the other, after recovering the Doon, joined the Nuwáb of Lucknow, whose hearty co-operation might be relied upon, at Kunkhul on the right bank of the Ganges, near Hurdwar. Having in his mind's eye arrived so far, Umr Singh already saw the seat of the Government of Hindoostan transferred from Calcutta to Katmandoo, and however wild his schemes may at present seem, the facility with which the scene of the contest might have been shifted from the hills to the plains is unquestionable, particularly if we consider the very doubtful nature of our successes at the beginning of the war.

297. A Resolution of Government, dated 17th November, 1815, ordered the annexation of Dehra Doon to the District of Seharunpore.

Annexation of the Doon to Seharunpore.

Article V. of a treaty drawn up at Sugoulee on the 2nd of December, formally ceded their new

* *Vide* his letter to the Rájá of Nepal, intercepted during the advance to Almorah, dated 2nd March, 1815.

conquest to the British. The war party of Katmandoo, however, led by the enthusiastic Umr Singh Thapa, managed to delay the ratification of the treaty, by inducing the Raja of Nepal to withhold his signature. Hostilities were therefore resumed under the direction of General, now Sir David, Ochterlony, who eventually forced the delivery of the document duly signed and executed* (4th March, 1816).

298. The first definite instructions issued to the Magistrate of Seharunpore on the subject of the administration of the Doon, are contained in a letter from the Secretary to Government (Judicial Department,) to Mr. Grindall, dated the 20th January 1816, directing him to take over charge of the district from Mr. Fraser of the Delhi Residency, Commissioner for the Settlement of Gurhwal, and make arrangements for the organization of a Police, and the management of the revenue in concert with the Assistant Collector (Mr. Chamberlain). Pending the introduction of the Regulations, he was to act in accordance with their spirit.

Instructions to the Magistrate of Seharunpore.

299. At the suggestion of the Board of Commissioners, the Government subsequently entrusted the management of the collections to Mr. Calvert, Assistant Collector of North Seharunpore, (15th March), who was directed to proceed to the Doon and decide upon the Revenue subdivisions in consultation with the Magistrate, who was at the same time to fix upon the allocation of the Police (29th March).

Mr. Calvert undertakes the management of the revenue.

* *Vide* Aitchison's Treaties, Vol II., page 190.

300. Regulation IV. of 1817, passed on the 18th February, legalised the annexation of the Doon to Seharunpore, declaring the laws of the ceded and conquered provinces to be in force within its boundaries.

Regulation IV. of 1817.

301. In the following month (26th March,) the Registrar of the Court of the Circuit communicated the sanction of Government to the maintenance of a Police establishment on a very modest scale :—

Establishment of Police.

Name of Thannah.	Number of Officers.	Monthly Salary.		
		RS.	A.	P.
Dehra, ...	1 Darogha, ...	30	0	0
	1 Jummadár,...	10	0	0
	1 Mohurrur, ...	8	0	0
	16 Burkundazes, at Rs. 4 each,	64	0	0
	Stationery, &c., ...	5	0	0
	Total, ...	117	0	0
Kánhurwálá, ...	1 Darogha, ...	25	0	0
	1 Jummadár,...	8	0	0
	1 Mohurrir, ...	7	0	0
	12 Burkundazes, at Rs. 4 each,	48	0	0
	Stationery, &c., ...	3	0	0
	Total, ...	91	0	0
Suhnspore (or Suhespore),	Ditto, ...	91	0	0
	Total of all, 49 men at per month,	229	0	0

It is interesting to compare this return with the allocation statement of 1868, which gives a total of 224 men, on

Rs. 1768 a month, but then, in Mr. Grindall's time, the po-

Compared with more modern estab-lishment.

pulation was barely 17,000, and few of the inhabitants had the heart to commit crime. As to civil litigation, there was little of

that, as nothing was left them to litigate about, and had

they been inclined to cross the Sewaliks,

Absence of crime and litigation.

a course to which they were extremely averse, there was no Civil Court nearer

than Meerut. Arbitration, therefore, settled their rare dis-putes, and continued to do so, even after Regulation IV. of 1818 had re-established the *Deewanee Adawlut* of North Seharunpore.

302. The Doon was left completely to itself, except during the brief period of Mr. Calvert's deputation to

make the first settlement, until a Resolu-

The Doon is, after some years, entrusted to the management of Mr. Shore.

tion of the Governor General in Council in the Judicial Department, dated the 24th October 1822,* introduced an im-

portant administrative change, by appointing the Honora-ble Mr. Shore, Officiating Joint Magistrate of Bolundshuhr and Mr. Grindall the Judge's Registrar elect, to the Joint Magistracy and Superintendence of the Revenue of the dis-trict. His administration, which commenced on the 22nd February 1823, and lasted nearly six years, comprises two distinct periods: *the first*, and more eventful, when he was subordinate to Mr. Grindall; *the second*, when he was subordinate to Mr. G. W. Traill, the Commissioner of Kumaon, after Regulation XXI. of 1825 had annexed the valley to that province.

* *Vide* Appendix II.

303. To explain the leading incidents illustrating the first period of Mr. Shore's administration,

First period of Mr. Shore's administration.

a reference to the history of the neighbouring district of Seharunpore* about the same time is absolutely necessary. A hasty settlement imperfectly revised, followed by years of scarcity, had reduced it to a wretched condition.

Condition of Seharunpore.

The people were discontented; their leaders, with Ranee Dhun Kour, Rájá Ramdyal's widow, a woman of great cunning, some ability, and considerable hereditary influence, at their head, did their best to foster the discontent, and an impatient desire for a change of government became very general. With their minds thus unsettled, the sturdy Rajpoots and Goojurs, many of whom had seen better days, neglected agriculture, and went back to their ancient profession of brigandage, expecting what might come; for the idea had got abroad that our sway was as ephemeral as the systems which had preceded it. The outrages which followed, though at first isolated, and of no great outward significance, gradually assumed an alarming magnitude, and almost culminated in a serious insurrection.

304. Such a juncture was well calculated to display Mr. Shore's peculiar qualities to good advantage. Eccentric in his habits† and ideas, he at the same time possessed a vigorous, well-trained intellect, and his physical energy far surpassed his mental powers. An inclination to assert his

Mr. Shore's character.

---

* The incidents here noticed will be considered more fully in the Memoir of that District.

† For instance, his affectation of wearing an Oriental costume drew forth a general order from Government addressed to officers in the Western Provinces, prohibiting such practices. About his ideas, *see* Note at the end of this section.

own individuality made him somewhat impatient of control, but his new appointment gave him a rare opportunity of carrying out his own views without prejudice to himself and with benefit to others.

305.   Long before his arrival at Dehra, fiscal misman-
Kulwá.   agement coincident with a series of hard
                     seasons, had produced disastrous results
in Seharunpore, and when he came here, matters had reached a crisis, of which the first signs were dreadful stories about a certain Goojur named Kulloo or Kulwa, a cruel bandit, chief of an immense gang of disciplined robbers, who infested the pergunnahs on both sides of the Ganges, and lived by pillage.   No one seemed to know his history, and few of those who had seen him, dared confess the fact, lest they should compromise themselves.   Strange to say, no outrage proportionate to the terror his name inspired, or robbery planned upon a scale corresponding to the demands of an unusually large and daring band of marauders, had hitherto taken place.   This rendered his great reputation incomprehensible, and Mr. Shore was inclined at one time to regard Kulwa as the creature of an excited imagination. Still his fame went on increasing, and in the spring of
                     1823, Mr. Glyn, then Acting Magistrate,
A military force   was obliged to call in the aid of a detach-
called out.
                     ment of the Sirmore Battalion, to assist his
police in maintaining order.   On the 31st March, Mr. Shore, " having received information of different parties of armed thieves lying scattered about in the jungles between Dehrah and Hurdwar," confederates of the malefactors below the Sewaliks, made a similar application to Captain Young, Commandant of the Battalion, and obtained the help of

forty Goorkhas, before whom the freebooters vanished into Seharunpore. Half of them were therefore sent forward to support Mr. Glyn, May 11th, the rest went back into the cantonment. The services of all were again required seven days after.

306. Intelligence came that the Doon was threatened

The Doon threatened.

by several really formidable bodies of marauders, but Mr. Shore's confidence in himself remained unshaken : " I am sure we shall succeed in catching them," he wrote to Capt. Young (18th May). His hopes were doomed to disappointment, for he caught no one, and his inclination to regard the stories about Kulwá in the light of nursery tales became greater than ever. Mr. Ewer, Superintendent of Police, Western Provinces, on the contrary, was firmly convinced of their truth, and pressed the Government to adopt stringent measures for the purpose of rooting out the evil. Circumstances, meanwhile, forced the local authorities to anticipate the result of the deliberations of Government by themselves taking decisive action.

307. In May 1824,[*] the well authenticated appear-

Dacoity at Nuwadá.

ance of Mr. Shore's invisible foes at Nuwada close to Dehra, once more put him on the alert. A gang entered the Doon through the Káloowala pass, and, having plundered the village, retreated hurriedly the same night, without securing the whole of their booty. The Joint Magistrate followed in pursuit at 5 o'clock the next morning with twenty-four Goorkhas and some chuprassies. His follow-

* Letter to Ewer, 10th May.

ers had little to encumber them. Each carried, besides his weapons, a blanket and a meagre allowance of parched gram and sweatmeats. Their leader had no better fare himself.

308. Thus lightly equipped, they pursued the track of the fugitives right into Seharunpore, without out even once catching sight of them, and returned to Dehra much disheartened. Mr. Shore, in consequence of this fruitless expedition, officially announced his utter disbelief * in the existence of the great brigand chief; the Goorkhas, he argued, had scoured the jungles in every direction for months, and never come upon any large band of robbers, nor could a numerous body of professional thieves possibly subsist upon the proceeds of such robberies as had occurred; again, the victims were always either inhabitants of the Doon, or Buneeas, or travellers; whence he inferred that the real culprits were the people of the villages at the foot of the Sewaliks; their fathers had held jagheers in lieu of black mail, theft was their heir-loom, and Kulwa, he concluded, was a mere bugbear invented by them to throw the Police on the wrong scent.

Fruitless pursuit of the dacoits.

The real culprits.

309. His judgment was in one respect quite correct. His suspicions fell upon the right persons, without however penetrating beneath the surface. A naturally lawless people had partially reverted to their old ways of living, but the fact had a deeper meaning than he thought. The offenders were actuated by a spirit of rebellion, and

Mr. Shore's judgment how far correct.

* " I was always inclined to doubt it, and am more than ever so. " Letter to Ewer 10th May.

not merely forced into crime by the pressure of poverty, nor were their ranks recruited solely from the lower orders. The disaffection had taken a much more serious turn than highway robbery, and a bold leader had been found to guide it. For this reason, ordinary crime did not keep pace with the growth of Kulwa's fame, and also because, although the malcontents could not resist the temptation of making occasional onslaughts upon wealthy strangers, or raids into the Doon, as in the days of yore, they did not, like common outlaws, labour under the necessity of carrying on an indiscriminate system of plunder. The leaders of the movement had ample resources, and whenever these happened to fail, the reign of terror established rendered requisitions easy, and prevented sufferers from volunteering information against their oppressors.

310. In his ignorance of the real facts of the case, Mr.

His policy. Its advantage exemplified.

Shore could not have adopted a better line of policy than that chosen by him. He did his best to teach the friends of order the virtue of helping themselves. Thus, on the 30th May,* their own vigilance preserved the people of Raepore, near Dehra, from pillage and bloodshed. About sunset, Goojur after Goojur came dropping into the village, until a goodly company soon assembled. A few questions judiciously put to the strangers, proved their inability to give any satisfactory account of themselves, and all were captured before they had time to get their arms concealed in the neighbouring jungle. After this, Mr. Shore expected to hear nothing more of Kulwa. He was soon compelled to confess his mistake.

* *Vide* Letter to Ewer, 15th June, 1824.

311. By the autumn of 1824, Kulwa, with his lieutenants Kour and Bhoora, both Seharunpore
Goojurs, had levied a very respectable force,
recruited from amongst his own clans-
men and the more turbulent Ranghurs.

*Organization of
Kulwa's force; Kour,
Bhoora, and Bijé
Singh.*

They wielded swords, spears, and matchlocks, affecting a
sort of military discipline. Their head quarters were at
the fort of Kunjah, a village a few miles west of Roorkee,
belonging to Bijé Singh, a connection of the Landourah
family, *talookdar* of forty-four villages. He was in league
with other powerful landholders, and had confederates in
Meerut and Moradabad, if not in more remote districts.

312. Their first act of direct and open defiance to
Government* was an attack on the Police
out-post of Kutarpore (7th September);
their next, the sack of Bhugwanpore, a
town situated immediately to the north of

*First acts of open
defiance to Govern-
ment. Mr. Shore's
trying predicament.*

Kunjah, five days later. The news of this event forced
Mr. Shore to admit Kulwa's existence, though he persisted
(and rightly too) in doubting that the only resource of his
followers was plunder. The Doon, he now perceived, was
in a really perilous position; and even after making allowances for exaggeration in the number of the outlaws, he
saw the impossibilty of defending a frontier of nearly fifty
miles against a large and compact body of well armed des-
peradoes, with thirty-six badly equipped *burkundazes*.† To

---

* *Vide* Shore to Ewer, dated 16th September, 1824; of ditto to ditto, 11th October;
&c., &c.

† The whole Police establishment then consisted of one Thannah and six chowkies—
with one Darogha, seven Jummadárs and Duffadárs. Except a few who carried
spears, they had no weapons but swords. He occasionally got the help of the Tuhseelee chuprassies, 33 in number.

equalise the chances of a struggle, he solicited a supply of carbines. Before the fire-arms arrived, still more startling intelligence reached him from Seharunpore.

313. Mr. Grindall, having failed to realise the grave import of the attack upon Bhugwanpore, had directed the Police to investigate the case in the usual manner. The course of their enquiries led them to Bijé Singh's fort, from the walls of which they were saluted with a volley of bullets. They prudently retired and sent in a report to the Magistrate, who contented himself with issuing a summons to the refractory *talookdar* (24th September). Bijé Singh naturally paid no attention to the process, and Kulwá was encouraged to attempt fresh exploits.

Repulse of the Seharunpore Police from Kunjah.

Bijé Singh refuses to obey a summons.

314. On the 1st October, a Police guard of 200 men bringing in a large sum of money from the Jooalapore Tuhseelee to the Sudder Treasury, met an overwhelming force of insurgents at Kulálhutee, east of Bhugwanpore ; they were speedily routed, and forced to leave the treasure in the hands of the enemy.

Attack on Treasure escort at Kulál-hutee.

315. The Goojur adventurer had by this time exchanged the name of Kuloo for the title of Rájá Kulián Singh, and used to despatch messengers in various directions to exact tribute from the villages within his jurisdiction. His band numbered upwards of one thousand men, more than could be brought against him without great delay, and re-inforcements were on the point of coming to his assistance. He therefore plainly announced his intention of throwing

Kulwá assumes the title of Rájá Kulián Singh.

off the foreign yoke, and releasing the prisoners in the jails, part of a more modern programme. Many considered the threat no vain boast.

316. At Seharunpore, the alarm approached a panic,
and several officers in the station justly
apprehended a general rising. An attack
upon the city was at all events no remote
contingency.

Alarm at Seharunpore.

317. Mr. Grindall resolved to anticipate any such
event by striking a rapid and decisive
blow. He had but one company of Goorkhas (150 men), at his disposal, and foreseeing the disastrous consequence of a repulse, despatched an express to Capt. Young, requesting him to send a reinforcement to support the detachment at Seharunpore.

Mr. Grindall sends for help to Dehra.

318. Admirable promptitude was exhibited on the occasion. The fight at Kulalhutee, taking
place in the morning, was reported to Mr.
Grindall in a few hours, and the express
reached Dehra by the evening of the same day, just as Mr. Shore heard that Imrutgeer, *Zemindar* of Raewala, had received a requisition for the payment of Rs. 400 from Rájá

Promptitude displayed upon the occasion.

Kulián Singh. His information on the
subject of the events passing in the Seharunpore district being imperfect,* he was
then busy making arrangements to entrap Kulwá's messenger, intending, through his instrumentality, to trace out the rest of the gang, when Captain Young brought

Mr. Shore determines to accompany the expedition.

* " I had not then heard of their openly taking possession of the Garree of Kunjah, and defying the Government authority. " Letter to Ewer, dated 12th October, cf., letter of the 23rd.

him the more serious news. He at once determined to accompany the Goorkha Commandant in the expedition.

319. Taking with them two hundred rank and file,

Which leaves Dehra and helps to quell the rising.

besides native officers, they left Dehra early next morning, and joined Mr. Grindall at Sekundurpore, five miles north of Kunjah,* on the 3rd October. By the sunset of the same day, the rising insurrection was quelled. A full account of the conflict between the regulars and the rebels will be given in the Memoir of Seharunpore. Here it is sufficient to briefly notice the leading incidents of the engagement.

320. When the troops approached the fort, the enemy

Fight at Kunjah and death of Kulwá and Bijé Singh.

at first had the "incredible presumption" to await the attack outside, and challenged the Goorkhas to come on, with abusive language, calling them "mountain monkeys" (*ṛuharee† bundurs*). A fortunate accident, however, made them change their plan, and went far towards speedily deciding the event of the day. Kulwa fell at the very first discharge. Their leader's death made his followers lose heart. They retreated into the fort, with the exception of a few, who ran away. Only one sally was made, and this the Goorkhas repulsed vigorously. Success then encouraged the besiegers to attempt a *coup de main.* The walls were too high to escalade without ladders, and Mr. Grindall

Mr. Shore's valour

had no guns, but the soldiers managed to improvise a battering ram with which the gate was burst open. After they had

---

* The "Buhadoorpoor" of the Great Trigonometrical Survey map.

† There was some truth in this taunt. A large proportion of the 2nd Goorkhas (Capt. Young's regiment,) certainly *were* and would still appear to be simply *puhárees.*

thus effected an entrance, a desperate struggle ensued. Mr. Shore there found himself in his own element. He fought in the front rank with Capt. Young and Mr. Grindall by his side. The moon rose before the fight was over, and Mr. Shore nearly lost his life, escaping with a severe wound.

321. The insurgents were at last beaten with a loss of 122 men killed, and twenty-six prisoners,* twenty-two of whom were wounded. Of the soldiery, five only were killed, and thirty-eight wounded, but the casualties among the Police and other civilians engaged on our side are not recorded.

Loss on both sides.

322. Two small guns taken in the fort served to grace the triumph of the victors, who marched back to Dehra with their battering-ram —and a prize they valued immensely— Kulwá's head. Not long ago, the guns, the earliest trophies of the regiment, stood beside the battering-ram on the Dehra parade-ground, and Kulwá's head hung in an iron cage over the door of the jail.

Return of the expedition to Dehra.

323. The rising so suddenly suppressed, popularly termed the Kulwagirdee, was no petty disturbance. It was the commencement of a serious insurrection, the imminence of which Mr. Shore, one hard to convince of the presence of danger, could never look back to without emotion: "had Mr. Grindall," he subsequently assured Mr. Ewer, " delayed one day in writing to Capt. Young, Kulloo's gang would have amounted to at least three thousand men, and not only

Gravity of the rising.

* Their small number shows how little quarter was given.

X

the whole of Seharunpore but part of the neighbouring districts, would have been one scene of plunder and murder."

324. The Government fully endorsed his opinion, and gave him unqualified praise for his con-

Opinion of the Government.

duct in joining the expedition. Mr. Ewer, less clear-sighted than Mr. Shore, had ventured to express doubts as to the propriety of a Magistrate leaving his own immediate jurisdiction under the circumstances described, but, had not a simple reference to the orders defining the Joint Magistrate's position relatively to Mr. Grindall, been sufficient to settle the question, the decision of the Governor General in Council would have left no room for further discussion. His

Favorable to Mr. Shore.

Lordship held, that Mr. Shore " could not have adopted any other course so well calculated to secure the peace of his own immediate jurisdiction, or to promote the general interests of Government as that which he actually followed," (13th January, 1825).

325. The remains of Kulwá's band still continued to give trouble. A report that Kour had

The remains of Kulwá's band prowl about under the command of Kour and Bhoora.

been killed in the attack on the Jooallapore treasure party, and Bhoora slain, together with the two other chiefs, at Kunjah, proved false. Escaping from the fort with the other fugitives, the surviving leaders lurked about the jungles, while the wounded either recovered or died off, procuring food chiefly from Bunjárás, sometimes from sympathising villagers. They kept to the thick Sewalik forests, particularly the more deserted parts, in the region of the Doon.

326. Intelligence of their whereabouts was soon obtained, and on the 8th November, Mr. Shore
*Mr. Shore's fruit-
less expedition in
pursuit.* organised a fruitless expedition in search
of them, with the help of twenty-five
Goorkhas. During his wanderings through the wilderness,
he, in all probability, contracted the illness which carried
him, before many years, to a premature grave. Malarious
fever smote his powerful frame, temporarily incapacitating
him from leading the active life he loved so much. His
enforced absence at Seharunpore* left the district to Capt.
Young's care, and the outlaws recovered some of their former daring. Early in January 1825, they ventured to
show themselves, and made a swoop at
*The outlaws re-
gain courage and
invest Tháno.* Rikheekesh. Another hard season in Seharunpore had given them an accession of
new recruits, and on the night of the 12th† a dismayed
chowkeedar reported the investment of Tháno by 200 men,
to Capt. Young. He immediately sent four Jummadars'
parties to Lachhiwálá, ten miles east of Dehra, with instructions to wait there until he joined them next morning.

327. They did not obey orders. Getting information
that the enemy were in the neighbourhood,
*The Goorkhas at-
tempt a surprise.* and unable to restrain their ardour, they
followed a narrow track through the jungle
leading to Thano, in Indian file. Unluckily they forgot to
load their muskets, nor could they keep a good look out
ahead, owing to the nature of the ground. Toiling along la-
boriously all night, they passed Kánhurwala, and were approaching Tháno at early dawn, when they suddenly came

---

* *Tempora mutantur.* The Civil Surgeon sent him there for change of air.
† Shore to Ewer, 27th January, 1825.

upon a gang of about thirty-five men reposing under the
trees. The outlaw sentries gave the alarm,

Its failure.

firing upon our men and killing a *burkundáz.*
One Goorkha fell wounded, and before his companions had
time to load, the bandits scattered into the surrounding
forest. Several volleys were fired after them, but not a
single robber was ·taken dead or alive, although stains of
blood along the grass showed that some of the shots had
told.

328. This partial surprise had the good effect of cow-
ing the dacoits. Some villagers who met

Retreat of the ban-
ditti into Scharun-
pore.

them during their flight brought in good
news; Kour was wounded in the hand,
and two others had died of their injuries. A party of
Scharunpore Bunjaras met some of them issuing from the
Kansrao pass, " helter-skelter."

329. All clue to their movements was again lost, until
on the 27th February, a letter came from

Their presence in
Moradabad.

Mr. Halhed, Magistrate of Moradabad,
complaining about a band of freebooters—
some mounted, some on foot—who were giving trouble
in the district; and requesting the help of a company of
the ubiquitous Sirmore battalion. Kour had retreated
across the Ganges, whence he evidently received accurate
information of what was going on elsewhere, for before
the soldiers had time to start, he temporarily dispersed
his followers and returned to his former haunts.

330. The period of the annual Hurdwar fair was now
approaching, and the constant passage to

Dacoity at Bho-
putwálá.

and fro of timid pilgrims afforded the robbers tempting opportunities of performing new achieve-

ments. Two companies of the Goorkha battalion pat-
rolled the road between Lachhiwálá and Khuruk, but the
line from Kansrao to Hurdwar lay unprotected. Along
this some 300 pilgrims were listlessly plodding on the
morning of the 9th April,* laden with bottles wherein
to store away the precious Ganges water. At Bhoput-
wala, about six miles from Hurdwar, their pilgrimage was
rudely interrupted. Twenty or twenty-five dacöits, armed
for the most part with spears and swords, dashing in among
them, like wolves among a flock of sheep, began pointing
and slashing right and left. The cruelty and swiftness of
the attack paralysed the 300. Most of them fled, others
were struck down dead or grievously wounded, the rest stood
still, quietly allowing themselves to be fleeced. The wanton
malignity† of the outlaws must have arisen from pure des-
peration ; so far, their callousness was satisfactory.

331. Mr. Shore, being in camp at Hurdwar, heard of
the dacoity the same morning. The retreat of the bandits was understood to be
among the lower hills. He therefore sent
one party of the Goorkhas doing duty at
the fair, to patrol the road north of Hurdwar, and went
himself with another along the foot of the Sewaliks, past
Jooalapore, on the chance of the rascals making their exit
from the Doon through any of the neighbouring passes.
In the afternoon, he marched as far as the mouth of the

Mr. Shore endea-
vours to hunt the
offenders down, but
fails.

* Shore to Ewer, 10th April, 1825.

† Mr. Shore remarks : " The thieves were going to cut off the hands of one woman,
as her wrist rings were difficult to take off ; they did not however do so, but the vil-
lainous disposition shown by talking of such a thing, would almost induce me to suppose that they had killed and wounded the people out of malice."

Kansrao ravine, reached the middle of it at sunset, and re-entered his district in the morning. Meeting there several Bunjaras, he questioned them. They gave information of so vague and unsatisfactory a nature as to raise strong suspicions of their being in league with the malefactors. Baffled in his enquiries, the Joint Magistrate returned to Hurdwar. The only two facts ascertained with any degree of certainty were, that Kour had led the attack in person, and that it was premeditated, because their assailants had enquired from the pilgrims after one particular Buneea, the richest whom Dehra boasted. The *coup* is supposed to have been arranged at the fair.

332.   The atrocity of the Bhoputwálá tragedy occasion-ed much excitement, and its audacity seemed to necessitate some radical and extraordinary cure. During the recent disturbances, Captain Young's regiment had been increased to one thousand strong. A hundred and fifty were enough to garrison the fort at Seharunpore ; all the rest were in cantonments at Dehra. Mr. Shore therefore proposed* to establish a permanent line of Goor-kha out-posts bewteen Lachhiwala and the Motee Chor hill near Hurdwar, but the necessity for the measure had ceas-ed before the sanction to it came.

He recommends the employment of the Goorkhas as a permanent consta-bulary.

333.   The banditti possessed one great advantage over their pursuers. At Hurdwar several dis-tricts meet; Seharunpore, Bijnour (for-merly included in Moradabad), the Doon, and Kumaon. This circumstance rendered escape easy, on the one hand; the Police were glad enough to avail

Advantage pos-sessed by the out-laws.

* 13th April, 1825.

themselves of the excuse thus afforded to cloak their own negligence or want of detective ability, on the other. Mr. Shore, always indefatigable in devising ways and means, consequently suggested* the expediency of locating a Joint Magistrate at Jooalapore, having concurrent jurisdiction in all four districts, with a Soobahdar's party, besides a squadron of irregular cavalry, to support him. The scheme, a most judicious one, might have been carried out, had not his own activity supplied the place of many thief-takers.

334. Never once did he relax his efforts to extirpate the survivors of Kulwá's band, and avail-

Mr. Shore's activity.

ing himself of his position as Mr Grindall's Joint Magistrate, steadily pursued the policy of extending his operations beyond the border. Early in May he collected more evidence against them. Kour, falsely reported to have been killed by a tiger, was still alive, and under his command they skulked about the Sewaliks in the vicinity of Hurdwar. The number of his followers fluctuated considerably. Twenty or thirty men generally remained with the leader; the rest resided in

Death of Bhoora.

their own villages, only joining the main body occasionally. Bhoora was no longer living; his arm had been broken by a musket ball at Kunjah, the wound mortified, and he died.

335. The failure of the soldiery to apprehend him, had inspired the sole surviving chief with some

Proceedings of Kour.

of his former audacity. The Seharunpore peasantry, too, were averse to informing against him, as much through sympathy as fear. He was thus enabled to carry on the old system of requisitions,

* 16th April, 1825.

and would have continued it much longer with impunity, but for Mr. Shore's pertinacity in hunting him down. Like his predecessor Kulwá, he deliberately issued mandates to the village headmen, requesting supplies of food or money, according to his necessities. In spite of reverses, his influence was still so great that two or three of his satellites would constantly venture even among an unfriendly population, and sit hour after hour in the *choupál*, calmly smoking their *hukkás* by the side of the complaisant Zemindars, making methodical arrangements about their own requirements and those of their leader. In the rare cases where such demands met with a refusal, granaries were burned and cattle driven off.

His system of requisitions.

336. Kour's later exploits, however, were almost altogether confined to the Seharunpore district, whither Mr. Shore returned at the end of April,[*] and encamped at Sekundurpore. There receiving intelligence of a requisition which was to be satisfied by the Zemindar of Sohulpore near Roorkee, on the evening of the 11th May, he attempted to surprise the dacoits that very night, but only reached Sohulpore to find it burned to the ground, having in the meanwhile succeeded in capturing one solitary prisoner shot down at a neighbouring village. His movements had been anticipated, but he did not return to Sekundurpore, until he had, under, the guidance of clever spies, explored the favorite haunts of the robbers, which were situated in

Mr. Shore returns to Seharunpore.

And explores the haunts of the robbers.

---

[*] Cf. Letter of 29th April, 1825, requesting a reinforcement of 32 Goorkhas from Captain Young. Cf. letter of 12th May.

the wild and difficult country, intersected with **ravines**, and covered with jungle, at the foot of the Sewalik hills.*

337. From this date we hear little more of Kulwá's
Who give little
more trouble.
myrmidons. Mr. Shore's perseverance and indefatigable energy had at length done their work. The outlaws were completely demoralised and lost their prestige. The Doonites themselves, overcoming their natural cowardice, caught some of their protector's spirit, and a few days later we find the Joint Magistrate soliciting a reward of 100 Rs. for the Zemindars of Doeewálá and Hunsoowálá, in a tone akin to triumph (27th May). They had actually pursued some of the banditti and captured one. Thus hunted from place to place, Kour could no longer find a spot of ground, on which to rest the sole of his foot. He was
Capture and exe-
cution of Kour.
captured in 1828, and sentenced to death. After the execution, his body hung gibbetted at Sekundurpore, hard by the scene of his principal exploits.

338. In July 1825,† the connection between this dis-
Extension of Mr.
Shore's powers.
trict and Seharunpore was strengthened by the express investment of Mr. Shore with the powers of a Joint Magistrate in the Sub-Sewalik Police stations immediately adjoining those within his original jurisdiction. This measure was adopted for the purpose of removing all doubts about the Joint

---

* A ravine about two miles south-west of Rajpore, called "the Robber's Cave," a favorite place for pleasure parties, picnics, &c., is vulgarly supposed to have been one of their haunts. It is *not a cave*, but a sort of cañon, at the bottom of which runs a small tributary of the Tonse, between high walls of limestone and conglomerate.

† *Vide* Chief Secretary Government to Grindall, 7th July, 1825.

Y

Magistrate's legal competency to co-operate, on an emergency, with Mr. Grindall, and possibly also to allay a feeling of jealousy on the part of the latter at his junior's interference with the affairs of the larger district, which afterwards displayed itself in a most unmistakeable* manner.

339. Regulation XXI. of 1825 ushers in the less eventful period of Mr. Shore's administration as Assistant to the Commissioner of Kumaon. It was unchequered by any stirring incidents, but marked by a decided improvement in the condition of the district and the inhabitants themselves.

Second period of Mr. Shore's administration. Its character.

Improvement of the district.

340. The points he himself most frequently insisted upon in proof of the general progress, were ;† the fact that on his arrival in the District, the whole of the agricultural community could not muster among them much more than half-a-dozen carts, whereas, when he gave over charge to Capt. Young‡ on the 10th December 1828, they possessed upwards of one hundred ; again, in 1822 the Doon was absolutely without roads, but, before his departure, thirty-nine miles of road (valued at Rs. 300 a mile) had been made by convict labor, with little or no assistance from Government, while Government itself had, at his instance, expended from Rs. 50,000 to Rs. 60,000 in such improve-

Points upon which Mr. Shore chiefly prided himself.

Increase in the number of carts used for agricultural purposes.

Opening up of communication.

---

* Unfortunately, it seems to have had just the contrary effect.

† *Vide* Letter to Traill, dated 10th March and 30th November, 1828, and Dehra Doon Records, *passim.*

‡ Now Major.

ments as opening up the Hurdwar and Kheree passes, and other works of utility; finally, the people had, under his influence, shaken off some of their charac-

And improvement in the character of the people them-selves

teristic apathy. They, too, had actually made roads (in all some ten miles long) at their own expense ; Dehra, through which one used, during the rains, to wade along in gutters knee-deep with mud, might now be traversed with perfect comfort; the waste land was being gradually brought under cultivation ; and labourers, whom nothing could have once induced to work more than six hours in the twenty-four, and who often declined to work at all on a cloudy day, were willing to toil from sunrise to sunset.

341. Mr. Shore believed that had not the affairs of the

The general improvement might have been more marked, but for the neglect of Government in the first instance.

district been left almost completely to the guidance of chance for some years after the conquest, the improvement would have been much greater, and the revenues might have been in 1828 Rs. 39,000 a year, instead of about half the same amount. Of the justice of his views there can be little doubt. At all events, he himself declared officially that had not private considerations rendered his departure to England necessary, he would have consented to remain permanently in the Doon, without hope of preferment to a higher appointment, the increase of his salary being dependent on the increase of the revenue; such was his confidence in the correctness of his own judgment.

342. Mr. Shore belonged to a class of officers destined, some fear, to become extinct under a less sympathetic Government. His abilities have been often excelled, but

his official morality* commands our unqualified admiration. Eminently possessing what he himself defines as the essential qualification for a good district officer, "not so much great talent as a determination to submit to perpetual annoyance in various petty ways," he was full of physical energy, and unceasingly devoted the whole of that energy to the performance of his duty and the benefit of those around him. Frequently, his loyalty to his employers went beyond the strict performance of duty.† For instance, he advanced the money to build the Dehra jail out of his own pocket, and after the settlement of European residents at Mussooree and the establishment of the convalescent depôt at Landour in December 1827, had increased the influx of visitors from the plains, his generosity extended to such minute details as having Buneeas' shops set up along the high roads, for the convenience of travellers, by means of advances (hardly ever repaid) out of his own private purse, and paying a *chowdree* whose duty it was to supply labour, for which the demand had suddenly risen to a degree probably unprecedented in these provinces. Yet many misunderstood him, and some even accused him of vexatious interference.

Marginal notes:
Mr. Shore a representative officer; his "official morality."

Devotion to work.

Loyalty to his employers

and generosity.

His character misunderstood.

---

* There is undoubtedly a sort of "moral sense" peculiar to the official, as distinguished from the private individual.

† On his return from leave, he was rewarded with the Sessions Judgeship of Furkhabad, and in 1836 officiated as Civil Commissioner and Political Agent in the Sagur and Nerbudda territories, when he published his "Notes on Indian Affairs," a book of considerable merit.

343. Although a repetition of the disturbances of 1824

Recurrence of gang robberies in 1827.

seemed no longer possible, gang robberies were still not unknown, and in June 1827,* we hear of five villages being plundered in Seharunpore as well as three in the Doon. The employment of the Goorkhas as a constabulary (under orders† of Government, dated 21st July, 1825) appears to have been again necessary, but the banditti soon withdrew to the Sikh territory, whence they had made an irruption into this and the adjoining district.

344. As the jurisdiction of Mr. Shore's successor, Major Young, comprised Jounsar Bawur, some account of

Jounsar Bawur under Major Young's jurisdiction.

the history of that tract may be here properly introduced, though so little is known of it that not many years ago, a Superintendent of the Doon was called to account for being absent from his district without leave, when his duties rendered his presence at a distant corner of the sub-division necessary.

345. Sirmore, of which Jounsar Bawur is a part, re-

Early history of Sirmore unknown. Interesting monuments. The Kálsee stone.

mained, like Gurhwál, a *terra incognita*, down to a very recent period. Such monuments as the Kálsee stone, popularly known by the significant name of the *Chhatr Silá,* " or Umbrella stone," which seems to show that above it was once raised the Chaityá emblem of a Buddhist dynasty, and the " *Tibree* of Rájá Risáloo," the same as

---

* *Vide* letter of 7th June, 1827.

† Sanctioning the location of seventy men, with ten Havildars and two Jummadárs, in chowkies, along the road from Dehra to Hurdwar. Cf. letter of 12th January, 1827.

the Râsâloo celebrated in Punjáb tradition, render it probable that at a remote period the tract between the western Tonse and the Jumna was the scene of great events,
and the site of populous towns.   Another interesting monument of the olden time is the temple of
And temple of
Lákhmundul.   Lákhmundul in the Bondur Khut, at a
village of the same name, on the banks
of the Jumna, about forty miles north-east of Kálsee.
Ancient graven images are said to be lying about there
in hundreds, and in the month of Bhádon, the people assemble annually to worship the shrine.

346.   Never having been able to visit the place myself,
Mr. J. B. Fraser's   I transcribe Mr. J. B. Fraser's descrip-
description of Lákh-   tion of Lákhmundul, as it was in the
mundul.   year 1815 :*—"This village is situated
almost upon the banks of the river.   It is claimed by
Sirmore and Gurhwál.   It cultivates the land of each State,
and pays an assessment to both.   It is apparently wholly
appropriated to the maintenance of several temples and
their priests ; and there are some fine rich pieces of land,
both on the banks of the Jumna and of a nullah a little
farther on, set aside for this holy purpose ; for which the
village pays half tribute to each State.   There is a neat
temple to Seewa, and to the five brothers, called the Pundos,
viz. :—Joodisthul, Bheem Singh, Arjun, Sahadeo, Nircolo ;
one to Bhysram and to Purseram ; an old ruined place of
worship to Mahadeo, under the name of Kedar, and some
curiously carved stones, representing the Hindoo deities.
Two figures in stone, representing Arjun and Bheem Singh,
are remarkably well executed ; but their faces have been

* Himalaya Mountains, page 399.

mutilated, it is said by the Rohillas in an old incursion. There is also a curious stone, representing in relief a number of the Hindoo Divinities—Ganesh, Durgah, Bhawanee, &c. —which are very readily distinguishable. There is also at this place a narrow passage leading under ground through the rock to the river side, used it is said by the people of the country in time of danger, when pressed by their enemies.

347.   "Opposite to this village, Birnee-ke-gadh, a large ravine proceeding from the lofty peak, Bougee-ke-teeba, debouches into the Jumna.

And of the vicinity.

In this ravine there is a curiously situated house, on a small *teeba* rising from the nullah belonging to a Zemindar of some consequence, called Bhoop Singh. Our route now lay along some table land, just on the river bank. Passing Bundergurree, a ruined fort situated on a *teeba* 200 feet high above the road, we descend to Neekrall-ke-gadh. This is said to be the boundary here between Sirmore and Gurhwal, but there seems to be a tract of *debateable land* around Lak,ha Mundul, which contains some spots of level cultivation far richer than that we have generally met with in the hills. The stream in this nullah is very considerable, and is said to take its rise in T,hirar-ke-teeba, two days journey from hence: its immediate banks are steep, rocky, and woody; and much alder grows on the edges of the water."

348.   The traditions of such localities would doubtless well repay the trouble of collection, but with the exception of an occasional allusion in the Mahomedan historians to the Rájás of the Sirmore hills, nothing for certain can be ascertained about the history of the

First well ascertained fact in connection with the history of the sub-division.

country before the year 1775 A.D, when Rájá Kíneh Singh

Death of Rájá Kí-neh Singh in 1775. died.* He sprang from a stock of Jusul-meer Rajpoots, before whose arrival in Sirmore anarchy prevailed.

349. Kíneh Singh had four sons; the third, Kurm Prukásh, succeeded to the throne on the *Accession of Kurm Prukásh.* death of his two elder brothers. Owing to his tyrannical disposition, this eccentric potentate's reign was passed in alternate dethronement and restoration. His unpopularity reached a climax in 1803, *He becomes tri-butary to the Goor-khas.* when he excited the indignation of his more warlike neighbours, by making an alliance with the Goorkhas, to whom he became tributary. In consequence of this, Rájá Sunsár Chund of Kangra, and Rájá Rám Surn of Hindoor, toge-ther with other minor hill chiefs, sup-*His consequent expulsion.* ported by his rebellious subjects, expelled him from his dominions. He therefore had recourse to his friend Umr Singh Thápá (May 1804), whose operations were at first unsuccessful. A Goorkha expedition undertaken to crush the allies *His restoration by the Goorkhas.* in the following October being more fortunate, Kurm Prukásh was restored. But his restoration involved the observance of certain con-ditions, which he failed to fulfil. He *His final deposi-tion.* was consequently once more deposed, and never again re-instated.

His brutal charac-ter. 350. He is said to have been an utterly worthless person, whom Mr. J. B. Fraser,†

---

* Hamilton, Vol. II., p. 618. Cf. 608.
† Himalaya Mountains, p. 77.

most properly describes as "a man of violent passions, no judgment, and much cruelty." His misfortunes then claim no sympathy.

351. Before the conquest, and even long after, so far as the land revenue was concerned, the affairs of Jounsar Bawur* were managed by means of a curious system of representative government, requiring careful explanation to render it intelligible. The pergunnah was divided into sub-divisions (*Khuts*), over each of which presided a headman (*Siáná*), generally the most intelligent member of some leading family among whom the office was hereditary, and the four most influential *Siánás*, bearing the title of *Chauntra*, constituted a senate (*Chauntroo*) which exercised control over the whole. So long as the revenue was paid up regularly, the Government never interfered in their proceedings ; still, the occasional official visits that did occur, were dreaded exceedingly, and it was the policy of the Chauntrás to avoid them altogether, if possible.

The administration of Jounsar Bawur originally conducted by means of a peculiar system of representative Government.

The Siánás.

The Chauntroo or Senate.

352. The Government arbitrarily fixed the revenue on the whole pergunnah in a lump sum ; this the Chauntras distributed over the *Khuts*, and the Siánás again re-distributed it among individuals. All appear to have been jointly, as well as severally, responsible for the collections. Their system of payment was unique : "the united body of Siánás appointed at the commencement of each settlement their Mahájin (*sic*) who resided at Kálsee, and with whom alone

Method of assessment.

* *Vide* Mr. A. Ross' Settlement Report, dated 20th April 1849, paras. 17-18-19.

Z

the whole country till late years dealt, their *Málzámin* or
security for the due and regular payment
of the Government revenue. The Málzá-
min undertook to pay up the revenue punctually on the
day it became due, debiting each individual Zemindar on
certain fixed dates with the amount of the advance thus
made on his account. All such advances were regarded as
a personal debt of the Malgoozar's and were chargeable
with interest from the date fixed without reference to the
date on which the revenue may actually have been paid to
Government."

System of pay-
ment; the Málzámin.

353. The *Chauntras* were not only chief collectors of
land revenue, but also managed all inter-
nal affairs, being arbitrators and judges
in civil and criminal suits. They had
plenary power to flog, fine, imprison, mutilate and execute.
As revenue officers, they received a small salary of 40 Rs.,
60 Rs., or 100 Rs., a year,* besides fees in money and kind
for every case decided before them.

Duties of the
Chauntrás; their re-
muneration.

354. In the same way, the *Sianas* received various fees
for the performance of their specific du-
ties, and an allowance of 5 per cent. on the
collections.

And that of the
Siánás.

355. The emoluments attached to the office of *Málzamin*
were considerable, consisting of—(1) $\frac{1}{4}$ anna
per cent., or a month's interest, on the gross
revenue for which he was security, "this
perquisite was termed *Ghutkolai*, a name implying that it
was an earnest for the Málzámin's readiness 'to open his

Emoluments
of the Malzamin.

---

* Mr. A. Ross says in the report quoted above, Rs. 40 or Rs. 60, and Rs. 100 in a previous report dated the 1st November 1848.

purse strings' whenever required;" (2), interest on advances, which was charged as though each of the four annual instalments had been paid six months before they were due to Government, and calculated at the rate of Rs. 1-9-0 per cent. a-month, or Rs. 18-12-0 a-year. In theory, the *Málzamin* had no official existence, but practically he had, and his influence was paramount, for all were dependent on him.

356. The living representatives of the four Chauntrás are—Ram Das, Siana of *Khut* Koroo, Devee Singh, Siana of *Khut* Udpalta, Kooloo, Siana of Selee, and Jwala, Siana of *Khut* Sumalta.

Rural aristocracy of Jounsar Bawur.

The first has the rare and enviable reputation of being " a man who speaks the truth." Lala Shunkur Das, Cánoongo and Zemindár of *Khut* Hureepore Biás, is a descendant of *Lálá Deendyál Málzámin* at the time of the conquest, whose ancestors, the only wealthy *Mahájuns* in Kálsee, had held the office before him from time immemorial. These personages, together with Kurm Singh, the degenerate son of Mudun Singh, Vizier of the Mahasoo Devtá in *Khut* Bawur, constitute the aristocracy of this semi-barbarous tract.

357. The Mahasoo, formerly all-powerful, still retains much of his ancient influence. Major Young found him a great nuisance during the early settlement operations, and I extract some information about his proceedings in the year 1827, from one of that officer's old reports. This permanent residence is a temple at the village of Hunolee,* in *Khut* Bawur, sixty miles from Kálsee, said to have been built by Shunkur Achárj, which he shares

The Mahasoo Devtá. His pernicious influence and exactions.

* Major Young says, " Unonce, about 10 miles north of the District of Bawur."

with another mysterious divinity, who always remains stationary.   He himself used to visit Jounsar Bawur, and the neighbouring hill state of Joobul, alternately, sojourning for a space of twelve years in each, much to the annoyance of the inhabitants, because with him came a crowd of attendants, sixty or seventy men, besides dancing girls and others.   The deity always stood on ceremony, for his visits had to be preceded by a formal invitation through his Vizier, but such was the dread he inspired that he never remained long without one, although ruinous expenses attended his progress.   Whenever the god expressed a wish to go to any particular place, some mishap was sure to occur there, which might be made a pretext for calling a meeting of the neighbouring Zemindars, who submissively resolved to send the Devtá an invitation.   The latter was then, after the performance of certain ceremonies, brought to the village in great state, in a *pálkee* covered with silver.   An enormous concourse followed, consisting of all the idlers in the country and the inhabitants of the other villages through which the procession accompanying the idol had passed.   The amateur hierophants were only fed for one day, but the people attached to the Devtá's temple never stayed for less than six months, or as long as they could find entertainment at the expense of their hosts. To defray the cost of the entertainment, collections had to be made from the different *Khuts* in the division, at the rate of 8 annas a house, or more, according to the means of the proprietor.   Many other contributions were also exacted, such as *ghee*, goats, and supplies of various sorts, amounting altogether to a heavy tax upon the people, who attributed the occurrence of an accident in any village to the indignation of the unpropitiated deity. To check these exactions, Major Young passed summary order at Kálseé in the presence of the assembled Siánás, banishing the Devtá and his attendants from the district of Jounsar Bawur, and also commanded the Vizier to abstain from accepting any invitation on the part of Mahasoo without the sanction of Government. Yet I have heard from Mr. Cornwall, the late Settlement Officer of Jounsur Bawur, that he continues to give trouble to this day.

358. It would appear from the account given by Hamilton[*] of the origin of the worship of this eccentric deity, that he is of Scythian descent: "according to Brahminical traditions, at a remote era of time, a man ploughing in the pergunnah of Bucan saw a snake, which, erecting itself before him, said, "I am sent by the divinity, raise near this place an image to be worshipped, call it the Mahasoo Dewtah, and it will reveal to you laws that are to be obeyed." On learning this vision of the cultivator, some Brahmins made an image, and placed it in the field where the snake had appeared, and after some time had elapsed, it was inspired to give them the following instructions, the observance of which secures the devout from the evils of the present world, and insures their happiness in the next, viz. :—

The Mahasoo is probably a deity of Scythian origin. Hamilton's account of him.

" 1st. Never to sleep in a bed with four legs.

" 2nd. Never to drink pure milk.

"Butter milk is permitted, but it is meritorious to abstain from eating the butter, it being more praiseworthy to burn

[*] Vol. II., page 632.

it at the places appointed for the worship of the Mahasoo Dewtah, or demi-god.

" *3rd.* Always to sacrifice the finest goats at the demi-god's shrine, and if similar sacrifices elsewhere be abstained from—so much the better. "

359.   Mr. J. B. Fraser mentions a temple at the village of Bankowlee,* not far from Lákhmundal, sacred to Mahasoo, whom he considers to be identical with Mahadeo. He also says the shrine is built on a Chinese model.

Chinese shrine sacred to him at Bankowlee.

360.   The first vizier whose name is on record, was Roop Singh. He died at Bástil in 1826, leaving two sons by different mothers. Both pretended to succeed to the viziership.   Their conflicting claims caused two factions, and the dispute was referred to Major Young for decision.   He decided the case in favor of Ugur Sain, the elder brother, but the adherents of the younger, Rám Náth, on their return to Bástil, repudiating the judgment, sent an invitation to the Mahasoo, who made a visitation to the Kánde division, which materially interfered with the settlement recently concluded.   The fine and imprisonment of the principal offenders put a stop to their excesses.   The present vizier, Kurm Singh, having fallen into evil courses, is held in small respect, not being even entitled to the compliment of a chair, but it is said, that were he to reform, he would be like the older members of the family, " venerated as much as the deity himself. "

The Mahasoo's vizier, Roop Singh, disputes between his sons.

Kurm Singh.

---

* Himalaya Mountains, p. 400.

361.   The campaign resulting in the transfer of Joun-

Transfer of Joun-
sar Bawur to the
British.

sar to the British has been already related.   It has also been mentioned that
the inhabitants of the pergunnah were the
first to join us against the Goorkhas, harassing Bulbhudr's
troops during their retreat, and enlisting in an irregular
corps then raised, to the number of nearly 1000 men.*
When the army lay before Náhun, ten of the principal
men who were confined there, escaped to the British camp,
and were deputed to encourage the insurrection.

362.   Although this speaks well for the character of the

Habits of the peo-
ple immoral in the
extreme.

people, they were really barbarians plunged in superstition, who lived in a state
of promiscuous sexual intercourse, four
or five brothers marrying the one wife; among whom
the meaning of female chastity was absolutely unknown.
The conquest seems to have had a favorable effect upon
their habits, for Major Young, writing only twelve years
after, speaks of polyandry as being on the decline, and
of the people themselves as being ashamed of the custom.   That it actually prevails is, however, certain.

363.   No immediate change in the revenue system follow-

Our policy in
Jounsar Bawur con-
servative.

ed, except the introduction of four instead
of two annual *Kists*, and the management
of the Police was still left in the hands of
the Sianas and Chauntrás.   The general superintendence

Capt. Birch the
first Commissioner.

of the tract, now separated from Sirmore,
was entrusted to Capt. Birch, a Commissioner apparently subordinate to the Resident at Delhi.

364.   Kurm Prukásh at once put forward his claims to

* Q.—The Sirmore battalion ?

the remainder of his former dominions, but taking into consideration his abominable character, government determined to exclude him from the sovereignty, and placed his

Claims of Kurm Prukásh disallowed; his son Futeh Sing supersedes him.

son, Futeh Singh, upon the throne (15th September 1815), under the guardianship of his mother. A *sunud* dated the 21st September,* secured the whole of Sirmore proper to the young Rájá, with some trifling exceptions. The restored territory was calculated to yield him an income of about Rs. 40,000 a-year. Subsequently the Kyardah Doon was added to the Ráj

Shumshere Prukásh.

(5th September 1833). The present Rájá, Shumshere Prukásh, received a *Khillut* of Rs. 5,000 in recognition of services during the mutiny, and is entitled to a salute of seven guns. His revenues amount to at least a lakh. The nature of

His legal relations with us of a very peculiar nature.

his relations with us is unsatisfactory, for, while he holds property and trades in the Doon, it has been ruled that he is not liable through his agents to the jurisdiction of our courts, whereas he can avail himself of their action for the purpose of enforcing contracts with our subjects.†

365.   Until the end of 1828 Jounsar Bawur remained

Jounsar Bawur, at first a separate charge under a Superintendent subordinate to the Delhi Resident, was incorporated with the Doon in the year 1829.

a separate charge, at first under Captain Birch, then under Capt. Ross, and finally under Capt. Young, who, like his predecessors, was subordinate to the Governor General's Agent at Delhi. At all events, his earlier reports are addressed

* *Vide* Aitchison's Treaties, Vol. II., p. 315, *sq.*

† The late Mr. Justice Jardine (then Government Advocate) succeeded, I believe,

to that official. After the promulgation of Regulation V. of 1829 had made him independent of the Commissioner of Kumaon, the pergunnah became an integral portion of the Doon District, and the Superintendent was at the same time appointed political agent between the British Government and the Gurhwál Ráj, to the history of which I must return.*

366. At the termination of the Goorkha war, Soodur-shun Sáh was found lingering about Dehra in a state of abject poverty. His destitute condition claimed our sympathy, and although his apathy concerning the issue of the struggle, left the British Government free of all engagements about the disposal of their conquests, they decided upon restoring to him his territories west of the Aluknunda and Mundákinee, exclusive of Dehra Doon and Ram Gurh, or the Rawáin pergunnah (4th March, 1820).† Rawáin was afterwards also restored to him, and his dominions, with this addition, were calculated to yield an income of Rs. 40,000 a-year. At first the channel of communication between him and the British Government was the Governor General's Agent in Kumaon. The latter's duties were thus defined: "The Commissioner will watch over the affairs of the Ráj, and while he abstains from frequent and minute interference in the proceedings of the Government, will

Soodurshun Sáh's restoration.

The Governor General's Agent in Kumaon; his duties.

in carrying this point in the Court of the Sub-Judge of Dehra and Mussooree. If the ruling in question be correct, the circumstance merits the attention of Government.

* Young to J. Hawkins, Resident of Delhi, 4th December, 1829.

† The grant of that date is conditional on his preventing traffic in slaves, helping our troops with supplies, in case of necessity, and not alienating any of his possessions without our consent.

always be prepared to point out any capital errors that
may be committed, admonish and advise the Raja, and
afford him the aid of his experience and authority, he
will maintain that sort of communication with the Rájá
and his ministers, which shall keep him apprized of the
progress of affairs, and enable him to execute this part
of his duties with readiness and effect." The discussion
of questions connected with aggressions committed by
the people of Rawain, and the decision of disputes between the Raja and his uncle Preetam Sáh on the subject
of the latter's allowance, as well as with the *Maafeedars* of
Sukliana, or Sukliana, seem to have given the Political
Agent some occupation.

367. This *talook*, which I have had occasion to notice
once before, is situated on the north-east
frontier of the Doon, being bounded on the
north-west by the Bándul Nuddee and
on the south by the Song. At the close of the Goorkha
war, the government restored it to the hereditary *Jagheerdars*, Shiv Rám and Káshee Ram, on account of alleged
services* during the campaign, but after the former's death,

The Sukniana
talook.

---

* To which I can find no testimony anywhere, unless the following extract from
Fraser's Himalaya Mountains, Appendix XIII., page 547, can be construed into
circumstantial evidence of them :—

" *Letter of the assembled Zemindars of Seekhneánce to Seeb Rám, who had come
over thence to the British.*—Since you have joined the English you have taken no care
of us ; you have forsaken us. The Captain (Bhulbudder), having fled from Kalunga,
came to Doobra, and from Doobra came flying all night to Suckneanee. He plundered
a little in his retreat. Reendeep Qaree was also encamped at Suckneanee. Both united
and went next night to Chumoon. In all they are 400 men. Bewant Qazee is also
come. We are lost, if, in a day or two, troops do not reach us. We are looking out
anxiously on the road. Our eyes are day and night, towards you ; if troops come we
are saved, otherwise write to us, advise us what to do. We are rated rebels ; they
seized our people, and took them to Chumoon, but they fled. They send soldiers to
seize headmen of villages. If they come to take us, write to us, advise us what to do ,

the Raja of Gurhwál, " through some mistake or misunderstanding," took upon himself to resume the estate, which
was again restored to Káshee Rám and Huree Ram, the
deceased's heirs, by an order of Government dated July 31st
1824.   Subsequent disputes about the succession were left
as a legacy to Major Young.*   Kashee Rám dying without
issue, his nephew Devee Dut claimed to succeed him as his
adopted son and devisee by will.   His claim, however, was
violently contested, and the subsequent disagreements rose
to such a height that the property had to be attached, pending orders from higher authority.   Unluckily, the attachment was carried out through Nund Rám, Tuhseeldar of
Dehra, who proved to be Devee Dut's father, and therefore
had an interest in fostering the feud, but eventually an
order of the Delhi Resident, dated August 3rd 1830, settled
the affair, by putting Huree Rám and Devee Dut in possession.

368.   The administration of the talook was peculiar.
An order of the Governor General in
Its internal admin-
istration.
Council, dated 31st December 1828, ruled
that people guilty of crimes of the kind
specified in Section 2, Regulation X of 1817, should be
committed by the Assistant in charge of the Doon to
stand their trial before a Commissioner appointed under
that law, who was to hold his Sessions in the reserved Hill

unless you support us we are lost to one another. When they call on us for corn, and
assemblage of the people, as they certainly will do, we will write to you for advice.
We are on the look out for troops and assistance. Judgidolee has come from Sreenug-
gur and taken possession of the Teree jhoolas " (rope bridges over the Bhágeeruthee).
This letter shows how much the Goorkhas were still dreaded, even after the taking of
Kalunga.
   * *Vide* Letter of 15th December, 1829. Cf. letters of 17th December and of 28th
July, 1830.

Territory, whilst the ordinary management of the Police and cognizance of petty offences remained in the hands of the Talookdár.

369. Since the repeal of Regulation X of 1817 by Act X of 1838, I have been unable to ascertain to what law Sukniáná* is subject, as it· has ceased to have any connection with this District.

It no longer has any connection with the Doon.

370. After his restoration, Rájá Soodurshun Sáh fixed upon Teeree, a place on the left bank of the Bhágeeruthee, 2,328 feet above the level of the sea, as his residence. At that time there was not even a village on the spot,† and settlers were unwilling to come. He accordingly expended Rs. 700 in building thirty small houses, for which tenants were at length found, each paying a rent of Rs. 3 a-year. Such was the humble origin of the new capital of Gurhwál, which is now a respectable town.

Rájá Soodurshun Sáh settles at Teeree.

371. Soodurshun Sáh was in some respects an enlightened monarch. Mr Shore contrasts his efforts towards the improvement of his dominions, with the apparent indifference of our Government to the welfare of the Doon immediately after the conquest. It seems, indeed, that he had hopes of recovering the *Zemindaree* right over this district, or compensation in lieu of it, but success did not justify his pretensions. In 1857 the Rájá of Gurhwál rendered us valuable assistance, and, in consideration of his services,

Mr. Shore bears witness to his good character.

* The Maafeedars paid the Teeree Rájá a Nuzeranah of Rs. 200 (*kutcha*) a-month. *Vide* Traill to Young, 30th April, 1829.

† Shore to Traill, 30th March, 1828.

his eldest illegitimate son, Bhuwán Singh, was allowed to

Succession of Bhuwán Singh.

succeed him after his death in June 1859. Bhuwán Singh died not long ago. The name of his successor is Purtáp Sáh. The revenue of the

Purtáp Sáh.

country has at least doubled since the accession of Soodurshun Sáh.

372. A Resolution of Government, dated 26th December 1842, abolished the office of Political

Abolition of the Dehra Doon Political Agency.

Agent of the Doon, and transferred his functions in connection with the territory of the Gurhwál or Teeree Rájá, to the Kumaon Commissioner. Strange to say, when this Resolution was passed, no measures were taken to guard against legal difficulties which may at any moment be raised owing to the uncertain nature of our north-eastern boundary on the Mussooree and Landour range.

A noteworthy point of law; a part the of Doon District really within jurisdiction of the Teeree Rájá.

The fact is, a large portion of the hill stations, although practically included in the Doon, in reality belongs to Gurhwál, and the Teeree Rájá is an independent prince, so that a part of the district is beyond the jurisdiction of the ordinary courts.

373. The question of the true boundary line between British and foreign territory, was first

Boundary line between the Doon and Gurhwál; the crest of the Mussooree and Landour range.

discussed at the period of the establishment of the Convalescent Depôt at Landour in the year 1827 (24th December,) in the course of enquiries concerning encroachments made by certain English gentlemen upon the lands of the Kyárkoolee and other villagers. It appears from the correspondence on the subject that the acknowledged boundary line between the two States was the *crest dividing the south-western from the north-eastern water-shed of the lower Himalayan* range.*

* *Vide Shore to Colonel Fagan, Adjutant-General, dated 4th August,* 1828.— " The top of the ridge all along forms the boundary between the Doon and the territories of the Rájá of Gurhwál. " Cf. *Young to W. Ewer,* Commissioner of Revenue and Circuit, N. W. Provinces, dated 13th August, 1829.—" The boundary which separates the Doon from Jounpore (a pergunnah belonging to the Rájá of Gurhwál) is determined by the course of water which falls on the summit of the range." Major Young settled all disputes by making the following arrangements about the payment of rent for land occupied by private individuals, agreements being registered in the Superintendent's office :—

Pergunnah.	Amount of land occupied.	Annual rent.		
		RS.	A.	P.
Jounpore, ...	Beegahs, *pucca,* 271 18	52	8	0
Doon, ...	„ „ .. 246 7	62	8	0
Jagheer of Mohunt, ...	„ „ .. 23 5¾	19	0	0

And for land occupied by public bungalows at Landour and Rajpore :—

Pergunnah.	Amount of land occupied.	Annual rent.		
		RS.	A.	P.
Jounpore, ... • ..	Beegahs, *pucca,* 120 7 7½	35	0	0
Doon, ...	„ „ 3 0 0	1	0	0
Mohunt's ⎱ Landour, ...	„ „ 24 2 7½ ⎱	31	0	0
Jagheer, ⎰ Rajpore, ...	„ „ 25 0 0 ⎰			

This arrangement was sanctioned on the 3rd October 1829. An accurate survey of both the hill stations has since been made, which seems to establish the correctness of the boundary line as laid down by Mr. Shore and Major Young.

The Mussooree Municipality now pays to

	RS.	A.	P.
Teeree Rájá, ...	272	6	8
Mohunt, ...	134	7	0
Zemindars, ...	387	0	4

Government pays for Landour Depot, to

Teeree Rájá, ...	70	0	0
Mohunt, ...	42	0	0

And for the Bunog Observatory, to

Teeree Rájá, ...	2	12	8

374. Compensation was accordingly fixed for the land

Rent paid to the Teeree Rájá by Government. appropriated on the northern slope of the hills, and not only does the Mussooree Municipality pay rent to the Teeree Rájá for land in the occupation of private individuals, but Government also pays him rent for a part of the Landour Depôt, so that our tenure of what is generally considered an integral portion of the Dehra Doon District is, at best, that of mere tenants with rights of occupancy.

375. It is not generally known that the fact was pointed

Mr. Bohle argues the point with Col. Young. out years ago to Colonel Young by a certain Mr. Bohle, an adventurous merchant, who set up the first brewery at Mussooree in the 'Frost valley,' besides a distillery, and " commenced selling *a strong spirit, called whiskey,*" without a license. This gentleman, when called upon to account for his conduct,* defended it on the ground of his being " within " the jurisdiction of the Rájá of Teeree, and consequently " without the pale of British Jurisprudence. " He eventually waived the point, and similar questions have never since cropped up.

376. The Dehra records afford no further material for

Tranquility during the Mutiny. general narrative. The shock of the Mutiny itself was scarcely felt in the valley, and although a part of the Jullundur Mutineers, about 600 strong, crossed the Jumna at Rájghát, they passed through the District without stopping or coming into collision with a party sent in pursuit.

I therefore pass on to the Fiscal History of the Doon.

* Col. Young to Mr. Bohle, dated 21st April, 1831. Cf. Bohle to Col. Young, 25th April..

NOTE.—The Hon'ble F. J. Shore's name has been so often mentioned in the preceding, as it will again be in the following pages, that it seems proper to give some account of his private history. He was the second son of Mr. J. Shore of the Company's civil service, who distinguished himself by his opposition of Lord Cornwallis's famous permanent settlement, which, nevertheless, he himself superintended, being at the time the best authority in India on matters of revenue, and who, rewarded with a baronetcy, succeeded to the Governor-Generalship in his forty-third year (1793). Sir J. Shore's administration has been pronounced a failure, and he certainly appears to have lacked firmness in his dealings with the Mahrattas and the mutinous officers of the Indian army. But the difficulties with which he had to contend, were mainly the creation of his predecessor, who might not have been more successful than he in surmounting them, and it cannot be denied that it would have been hard to display the necessary sternness in the second instance without disobeying the dictates of justice. Finally, the fact remains that, in spite of his recall, the Court of Directors, whom we may fairly presume to have been the best judges of their own real interests, endorsed his views, nor did he show any want of resolution in settling the delicate question of the Oude succession. On the whole, in the face of adverse criticism, he is generally admitted to have been an officer of conspicuous merit, and it can hardly be doubted that his administration would have been reviewed more leniently, had he been born a member of the peerage, to which he himself was raised as Baron Teignmouth, in October 1797.

The son inherited the talents of the father, and would, there is reason to believe, have left a really great name behind him, had he lived a few years longer. He was not only a remarkably able and unusually well-informed official, but also, in private life, a true reformer, and a zealous "preacher of righteousness," in the highest sense of the word. Not to speak of reports innumerable, in which his style contrasts most favorably with that of his contemporaries, he has handed down his opinions, the result of fifteen years' hard work, not of an unthinking residence in the country, apathetic because compulsory—an accident too often passing muster for "Indian experience"—in a book now seldom read, though well worth perusal, entitled "Notes on Indian Affairs." The work consists of a series of essays, or letters, on every imaginable subject that could interest the Anglo-Indian politician, which first made their appearance, under the signature of "A Friend to India," in the "India Gazette," a Calcutta daily paper, and were afterwards published in 1836-7, when the author was Officiating as Civil Commissioner and Political Agent in the Saugor and Nerbudda territories, his substantive appointment being that of Civil and Sessions Judge of Furukhabad. Their tendency was decidedly radical, for they aimed at exposing the social and political abuses of the day and their effect upon our relations with the natives of the country. Many of these abuses have happily been remedied; still, Mr. Shore's reflections can hardly fail to supply the panegyrist of the past with much wholesome food for meditation, and even where his recommendations are no longer applicable to the present state of things, they carry with them many a suggestion of practical use, while his experiences lead us to the true method of understanding the alien people among whom we have been thrown, ascertaining their wants, and regulating our conduct towards them.

The first lesson we learn is, that the very circumstances popularly and fallaciously considered to be most unfavorable to the development of practical thought, are those which an energetic man, at once desirous of self-improvement, and inspired with an honorable ambition to do good beyond the narrow circle of official routine, may turn to the very best account. We read how the writer came to the country, a raw boy of seventeen years of age, naturally prone to receive superficial impressions from what he saw going on immediately about him in the capital of British India. His earliest impression* was indeed pleasant, a "quiet, comfortable, and settled conviction" of the unalloyed blessings the English had conferred upon the natives of India, and of their heart-felt gratitude for the favors received. The usual compulsory residence in Calcutta was not calculated to disabuse his mind of this idea, and discouraged him from extending his sphere of enquiry, nor did his appointment to a large station in the Mofussil tend to enlarge his views, which were in those days extremely limited. "Shooting, and other boyish recreations," occupied his spare moments, and as to an acquaintance with the people, he held " no more communication with them than the actual demand of business required." But an ordinary accident changed his whole way of life. His transfer to Boolundshuhr, then a very lonely out-station, and afterwards to Dehra, one still more lonely, threw him upon his intellectual resources. and before long, he had reason to congratulate himself upon a change which must, in the beginning, have been very distasteful to a man of his exuberant animal spirits. Instead of moping, or driving away *ennui* by indulging his passion for field-sports, or, as was formerly too often the case, falling into habits of vulgar dissipation, he availed himself of his isolation to study the feelings of those with whom his profession had brought him in contact, together with their past history. Reading, supplemented by intelligent intercourse with natives of every class, soon proved the falsehood of his preconceived ideas, and his opinions underwent a remarkable transformation. He began to perceive that, on the one hand, our own system of Government, however well intended, was far from being all that could be wished, still farther from what it has been described to be by its ardent admirers; on the other hand, the Hindustanee had been the subject of much ignorant, if not deliberate, mis-representation, and was not quite so black, in fact, as he had been painted; his faults were not so much innate as the inevitable result of surrounding circumstances; his good qualities had been wilfully ignored; and, lastly, he was by no means enamoured of his detractors. That he should have been, would be too much to expect from human nature.

Subsequent experience only confirmed Mr. Shore's faith in the correctness of these conclusions, which he, meanwhile, set about submitting to the test of public

* Vol. II., 516-18.

opinion through the medium of the press, and it must be confessed that, although enthusiasm for his subject occasionally carried him into vehemence of language, he was generally right. Justice as well as expediency, he now felt, demanded sweeping reforms. The calm, comfortable assurance, that a debased populace had gladly accepted the blessings of an unselfishly paternal government, yielded in his mind to a certainty of the direct contrary. Such an assumption obviously involved an absurd paradox; and truth compels us to confess that, at the period in question, "a strong feeling of disaffection towards the British Government" was accompanied by a violent "dislike to the English themselves as a nation." It is unnecessary to follow Mr. Shore in his analysis of the acknowledged faults of the Company's rule, but it may be well to urge something in justification of his views on the latter point. We have small reason to be proud of our predecessors in this country, for their conduct was ill-calculated to command either affection or esteem, and the native was not so purblind as he sometimes affected to be. Those were days* when gentlemen commonly sent their private letters 'on service' for the sake of saving a few pence; others made government pay for their domestic servants by entering them as court chuprassies; commanding officers turned a penny, not an honest one, by exacting annual tribute from the shopkeepers living within the cantonment boundary, a practice euphemistically termed 'making your bazaar.' But these were mere trifles. So low was the tone of Anglo-Indian society, that a certain Collector, having been turned out of the service for embezzling Rs. 2,00,000 or so, from the Treasury under his charge, a freak too much for the patience of a wonderfully tolerant government, was afterwards greeted by his friends and acquaintances in Cawnpore, rather like an enterprising man who had been unfortunate in a clever speculation, than a common swindler. He eventually became one of the leaders of fashion at Seetapore! Mr. Shore himself was an eye-witness of the fact. Society probably thought her behaviour excusable in this instance, from the example of her betters, because another unlucky member of the civil service, "after having been dismissed for malpractices, with a positive order from the Court of Directors against his future employment, was sent up to Lucknow with a recommendation from the Governor-General to the King, which the latter considered in the light of a command to give him an official post!!" One Commissioner was notoriously under pecuniary obligations to his native revenue officers, and Mr. Shore assures us that positive corruption was not unknown in equally high quarters. After that, we can hardly be surprised to read of a gentleman in the Public Works Department who used daily to congratulate himself, in the most open manner, among a circle of admiring friends, of 'having done John Company for so much this morning.' Again, people had curious ways of doing their work; "a crack collector" for example, would sometimes expedite his settlement operations by making a refractory *Zemindar* stand up to his neck in water, or incarcerating him without food until the pres-

---

* Notes on Indian Affairs, Vol. I., p. 88, 93, 94; Vol. II., p. 83, 258, 435, 457, 522, 528, 537.

sure of hunger compelled obedience, and in the intervals between their official occupations, some men used to go "on rajah-hunting tours," *i. e.*, "going on round of visits to native chiefs, in order to get as many valuable presents as possible." Meanwhile, it is carefully noted, their friends watched their progress with more curiosity than disgust. Religion of course was at a sad discount, and military officers, as a rule, preferred cock-fighting to divine service on Sundays. In short, the ordinary Anglo-Iudian of the period lived a most godless life, " as if there were neither a heaven nor hell." So Mr. Shore pithily remarks—and one natural consequence was—that Christianity, becoming unpopular, has never won its way to the hearts of the people to this day. Another equally natural consequence was, that they did not like the English. At any rate, Mr. Shore flatly refused to believe in their alleged affection for us, because the prevailing laxity of morals was unredeemed by flashes of wit or gentility of manners.* The English gentleman took his turn out of the native gentleman, even if he did not know him, by kindly borrowing his elephant, and then treated him with the greatest rudeness, when he came to pay a visit; as to calling him *áp*, instead of *tum*, that was a thing rarely thought of; sportsmen angled in Brahminical ponds, and beat the narrow-minded priesthood when the latter ventured to remonstrate ; nay, Magistrates themselves committed strange outrages against the feelings of those whom it was their bounden duty to protect ; " at the Hurdwar fair, there is of course, a great demand for sweetmeats of all kinds, and the street is lined with shops; at each of which the *hulwaee* (pastry-cook) is seated with a large pan of boiling butter before him, replacing his stock as fast as it is sold. Some years ago, the Magistrate of one of the neighbouring districts, mounted on his elephant, having provided himself with a large number of *bails* (a round, hard fruit, as big as a large orange) passed through the street, dashing one into each of the pans of boiling butter, splashing the poor *hulwaees*, and of course scalding them severely. He would not have dared to treat a set of booth-keepers so, at an English fair, &c." Our countrymen were, therefore, held to be an ill-bred, low-caste race, although they behaved with the most haughty insolence, giving themselves such extraordinary airs that even a *bagman*, having effected an entrance into the Civil Service, had the audacity to pass himself off as the intimate friend of the titled aristocrats from whom he had humbly solicited orders in England, under instructions from his father,† during his earlier career. If this picture of the times be somewhat highly colored, the reader should remember that it is of Mr. Shore's painting, not mine.

According to the same authority, the ignorance and incompetence‡ of his older contemporaries was as gross as their general misbehaviour. Their education had been of a most elementary nature, so it could hardly be expected that men whose knowledge of their mother tongue was extremely defective, should be

* *Notes, ut supra,* Vol. I., p. 4, 14; Vol. II., p. 345.
† Vol. I., p. 18, 19; Vol. II., p. 114 (*note*).
‡ Vol. I., p. 8, 24, 48, 82, 163 ; Vol. II., p. 111 (*note*).

skilful in the use of foreign languages. Yet so little pains were taken to supply this deficiency, that gang-robberies on a gigantic scale had been regularly perpetrated for two whole years in Lower Bengal, under the very noses of the Magistrates, without their ever hearing of them, and, on one occasion, the first intelligence received by Government of an insurrection going on within a few miles of the Magistrate's residence, at Baraset, was from a Calcutta merchant, who had got the news from an indigo planter. In the former case, moreover, when the truth did leak out, Government found their own highly paid executive so incompetent to deal with the emergencies, that they had to employ the agency of several planters, in a magisterial capacity, to aid in quelling the disturbances. In truth, if we are to believe Mr. Shore, a very high premium was paid on inefficiency ; "provided a man be not an absolute idiot, or notoriously corrupt, mere incapacity to perform the duties expected from him in an efficient manner, forms no bar to his promotion. I do not mean to say that the Local Government makes no difference between a stupid and an able person, no doubt some distinction is occasionally shown. The former may be twelve or fourteen years in attaining to the office of Collector or Judge, while the latter may receive the appointment in ten—but this is the whole !"* This uncompromising critic adds that it was easy enough to get a reputation for ability ; " a man has only to tax the people of his district at a higher rate than his predecessor, and his name is established," and unscrupulous persons, he assures us, did not shrink from acts of downright extortion, so as to retire from rack-rented districts with the name of "crack collectors," "first-rate collectors," leaving behind them a. splendid revenue on paper, for the non-realization of which their more conscientious successors were destined to suffer. I have been all the more careful in explaining the nature of Mr. Shore's subsequent impressions, because they here lead us up to a point having a direct bearing upon a striking episode in the history of the Doon, which narrowly escaped the infliction of a crack officer. The neighbouring district of Seharunpore *was actually* " cursed some years ago by a *first-rate collector*, who, to raise his own credit with Government, was the ruin of thousands." Whether this imputation against the character of the officer in question was justifiable or not, it is impossible to judge from a distance of so many years ; let us hope it was not, but the Doon may congratulate herself upon his not having extended his operations northward of the Sewaliks. That he did not, was a mere accident. It will be afterwards my duty to describe how injudicious settlements affected the larger district. At present it is sufficient to remind the reader that fiscal mismanagement† was one of the main causes of the disturbances of 1824.

* Vol. I., p. 131, 172, 203.

† The details of settlement work were frequently left to " a few natives, clerks and measurers, who were as ignorant as themselves " (*i. e.,* as the Settlement Officers). Yet the latter had a wonderful opinion of themselves. Mr. Shore " actually knew one young man who declared that he did not want any survey ; that he would gallop ten miles across country, and return with a perfect idea of what each field he had passed through was calculated to pay." Vol. I,, p 207, cf. p. 488.

In speaking of the dissatisfaction then leavening " the mass of the people, Mr. Shore modestly acknowledges administrative failures of his own, while he indicates the successes of others : " I could even particularise one province of the Hill tract, the Deyra Doon, conquered from the Goorkhas, who, in their distant and newly acquired territories were undoubtedly guilty of the most tyrannical conduct, by the people of which the change was notwithstanding regretted. In Kumaon proper I have been told that it is different; but this may easily be accounted for, by the character of the present able Commissioner of that district,* whose zeal in promoting the interest of the natives, and long experience of their habits and sentiments, has already been celebrated by an abler pen than mine."†
Farther on, he continues : " I will now give another instance to show the estimation in which our Government is held by the people. On the Goorkha conquest of the Himalaya mountains, their tyranny was such, that immense numbers of the people emigrated. From the Deyra Doon and parts adjacent, a few individuals settled in our neighbouring provinces; but the greater number crossed the Jumna, and fixed their abode in the independent Sikh territories. When the Goorkha government became a little settled, the chiefs endeavored to encourage the inhabitants to return to their homes, and partially succeeded; the majority still remaining in their new possessions. On the accession of the British government, the return of the expatriated population to their own land was fully anticipated; but no such event followed. On the contrary, the number already in some parts of the province was diminished by the partial emigration to the Sikh territories. Some years after, very great efforts were made by the civil functionary‡ to induce the old inhabitants to return, but without success. The strong local attachment of the natives of India is well known. In this case, there was no long journey through a perilous country to be undertaken, the generation that had been exiled still existed, and the distance from their own home was from fifteen to fifty miles, yet they preferred remaining in their newly-adopted country." He certainly undervalues his own work, and we can hardly believe that the inhabitants of the Doon sincerely regretted the days of the Goorkha supremacy.

The experiences of his first administration, however, powerfully influenced his political opinions : " it is universally acknowledged,"§ he says, " that the constant pressure of our troops alone prevents disturbances, or, in plain English, insurrection; and we have had proofs sufficient that on any opportunity a spirit of insubordination has immediately been manifested. The disturbances in most of the Upper Provinces in 1824, and there was scarcely a district in which the spirit of disaffection was not more or less manifested, arose from the same cause. I am aware that a different version was attempted to be given, and that it was asserted that the idea of our having sustained reverses in the operations against the

* Mr. Traill.
† Bishop Heber's. *Vide* Notes, Vol. I, p. 150-158.
‡ Mr. Shore himself.
§ Vol. I., p. 158-159.

Burmese, and of our troops being required in that quarter, was the cause of what happened; also, that many of the parties of insurgents were merely a few banditti who were on the look out for plunder. Certainly these were the proximate causes; but if the natives really enjoy such happiness under our government, how comes it that they are so ready to unite in opposition to our authority? How is it that in the whole of the Upper Provinces not one of the leading landholders was found to come forward in support of Government? It is also true that some of the insurgent parties originated in a gang of banditti formed merely with the hope of plunder; but what was the conduct of the people? On the first success of the robbers, numbers, even of the better sort of inhabitants, immediately joined them, and *then* insurrection, and not mere plunder, was the object. The rallying cry all over the country, repeated with the most enthusiastic exultation, was, the English reign is over! 'Down with the English!' It will not avail to say that it was foreign to the habits of the people to come forward, and that they stood aloof, leaving the business to our police and troops : the history of India abounds with instances in the Native States, where, in the event of a disturbance, those of influence called out their retainers and tenants, and boldly stood forth in defence of the Government. But it was very different at the period above-mentioned : they did not merely stand aloof: even those ordinarily in frequent attendance on the different Magistrates, separated immediately to their homes, under pretence of exerting their influence to preserve order in their own neighbourhood, and began raising men; but for what purpose? to be ready, if occasion proved favorable, to turn their whole weight and power against our Government; some of them did so; and it is not going too far to assert that had not the most prompt, and vigorous measures been adopted, and a fortunate issue not occurred at the first serious collision, or had a delay of a few days longer taken place, an insurrection would have broken out, which it would have required all the troops in the Upper Provinces to quell; and that it might have terminated in the utter subversion of our power. I have seen the official correspondence from most of the districts in that part of the country at the time. In that from Seharunpore it was stated that a gang of banditti was first formed for plunder; that on their success, they were joined by others, villagers, when further plunder was perpetrated; a few days after which their numbers amounted to about twelve hundred, joined by one of the principal landholders in the district, who received them into his fort, openly defied the Government, and supported one of the party in assuming the title of Rájá; and that had the collision with the troops who were called out been delayed a day, their numbers would have swelled to at least three thousand; it having been *ascertained* that several parties of from fifty to four hundred had been already formed, expressly to join the insurgents ; and that had our forces sustained a reverse, the whole of that country would have been one scene of rebellion and outrage. So far from being controverted, the truth of these statements was acknowledged by Government, and the exertions of those engaged received their due: to them a fortunate, and, let me observe, not very common occurrence; for it has generally been the practice of

Government to endeavor to show that the local functionaries have been precipitate, and have had recourse to harsher measures than were necessary ; being well aware of the tendency of an insurrection to excite suspicion, that all is not as it should be on the part of the Government."

The more modern enquirer may still contemplate with advantage his general summary* of the causes of impatience :—

"1st. The habitual and inordinate idea of our own superiority, and the equally strong impression of the corruption and inefficiency of the natives.

"2nd. Their consequent exclusion from all offices which it was possible to procure Englishmen to accept, and the attempt to conduct all affairs by European agency.

"3rd. The annihilation of almost all existing institutions, and the total inadequacy of those which have been substituted, for the administration of justice.

"4th. The gradual impoverishment of the country by a system of taxation and extortion, unparalleled in the annals of any country.

"5th. The ruin of the old aristocracy, and of all the respectable landholders, which has been systematically effected, in order to increase the Government revenue. "

We have seen what he thought of the privileged classes, and, he argued, the native was not the villain he was popularly supposed to be.† It is idle to expect every virtue under the sun for £20 a-year, though it is comparatively easy to be good on an annual income of £3,000 or £4,000. Men are, to a great extent, the creatures of circumstances. An English school-boy will often beat the cleverest Hindoo at lying, and as to bribery and corruption, there is no want of that at parliamentary elections in Great Britain, while, as regards illegal qualifications, commanding officers were 'making their bazaars' every day of their lives ; the English sergeants in the Calcutta Police had, 'previous to late improvements,' shown quite as much aptitude for extortion as the most astute Thannahdar, and the less said about some branches of the P. W. Department the better. He, therefore, boldly demanded that the people, who were then excluded from all except the minor offices, should be given a fair trial, on salaries sufficient to support them respectably without recourse to dishonest expedients, judiciously indicating the local corps as a proper field, among others, for the employment of the native gentry.‡ It is much to be regretted that he did not steadily face the difficult question of the advisability of employing them in his own service on *exactly the same conditions* as Europeans of the better class.§ He also fought for the emancipation of the East Indians,|| (*i. e.*, half-castes,) who were even worse off than their darker cousins, being debarred from almost every kind of public office. Had he lived a few years longer, he would have had the satisfaction of

* Vol. I., p. 356.
† Vol. I., p. 51, 54, 55, 85, 89, 92, 115.
‡ Vol. II., p. 428-9.
§ Most probably, the idea never occurred to him.
|| Vol. I., p. 104.

seeing much more than he claimed for them, granted to both, and might have refreshed himself with the spectacle of the ablest politicians exercising their minds in devising some means to fill the void caused by the annihilation of the time honored institutions, which collapsed with the downfall of an aristocracy who mainly owed their ruin to a defective system of taxation and laws. This pleasure was denied him, for he followed his father to the grave, at a short interval of three years, in 1837.

Mr. Shore, if judged by the light of the times and country in which he lived, must be admitted to have been one of the most remarkable men of his day, and his close connection with my subject (his name yet lives in the memory of the inhabitants of the Doon and Seharunpore) surely justifies this digression. He was, to use a common metaphor, at least half a century in advance of his age. The liberty of the press, education, nay, even municipal committees were all included in his programme of reform,* and, although the staunch champion of the oppressed native, he was at the same time the firm friend of the much-abused European interloper.† It is hard to find a single topic in which he has not, directly or indirectly, anticipated the most advanced thinkers of our own day. The press he valued as a harmless vent for hidden disloyalty and a sure signal of approaching danger. Education he considered to be the only means of improving the condition of the lower orders, by teaching them, through the medium of their own vernacular,‡ the necessity of imposing upon themselves those restraints which come into action in the higher forms of civilization; finally, he looked forward hopefully to municipal institutions as the first step towards self-government. One should bear in mind that these were not the sentiments of a *zealous* officer anxious for promotion, and only too ready to spur away at the official hobby of the moment, but those of a perfectly unbiassed man, calmly ventilating his own independent views. He believed in European colonization as a source of strength to our rule, and a wholesome check upon the arbitrary proceedings of practically irresponsible officers. With a keen insight into the proper bearing of the question, he invited the enterprise of men combining the possession of solid capital with sound experience, who could confine themselves to the *superinten-dence* of commercial or agricultural speculations, warning away needy settlers from the country, but he prayed heaven to defend us against the introduction of their laws along with the colonists.§ The false economy that saves a few half-pence and lavishes as many pounds, the legislative indecision that allows no man rest, the maze of " returns and statements, the Nuksha Ráj or government

* Vol. I., p. 428, 443; Vol. II., p. 44, 246.
† Vol. I., p. 39; Vol. II., p. 36.
‡ Vol. I., p. 25; Vol. II., p. 248.
§ He aptly quotes (Vol. I , p. 276-277) Fielding's observation : " That a stranger would suppose that English law was framed, not with the object of protecting the honest part of the community from the machinations of villains, but that thieves and rogues should be able to escape punishment." Again (p. 302), he remarks : " The scheme of introducing English law into India is just as unjust and impolitic as it would be to establish the Mahommedan or Híndoo law in England."

of forms," that invariably ends in dethroning honest work, the anomalous system of political agencies designed to regulate the intercourse between the Company and Native States ; all these, not to speak of many other errors, he unmercifully exposed.* On one solitary point he was decidedly mistaken. Disagreeing with his father, he advocated a permanent settlement all over India, assuming that taxation had reached its extreme limits, and denying that Government was head landlord of the country ;† " as well might a foreign conqueror of England in the present day assert that Government was the proprietor of the soil ; in proof of which he might quote the existence of the land-tax." The early settlements were, it is true, almost always much too severe, and the revenue used to be realised in a reckless manner, yet, subsequent experience has proved his assumption to be gratuitous, and the imaginary conqueror would not be far wrong in his assertion. Another point, on which most modern politicians will differ from him, is his defence of the internal government of Oude,‡ whose annexation he would assuredly have deplored. A third, about which many will be disposed to agree with him, is Russophobism,§ and he evidently foresaw the Mutiny.‖

---

* Vol. I., p 344-357 ; Vol. II., p. 259 239-73.
† Vol. II., p. 42-245.
‡ Vol. I., p. 152.
§ Vol. I., p. 166
‖ Vol. I., p. 22-9

PART III.—STATISTICAL AND MISCELLANEOUS.

SECTION I. FISCAL HISTORY OF THE DISTRICT.

DEHRA DOON SETTLEMENTS.

377. After the occupation of the Doon in 1814, the land revenue was held *kham* for two years.

The district at first held kham. The Government share of the produce was calculated at the time of harvest on an appraisement of the value of the crops, in the proportion of one-half or one-third, and, in some cases, one-fourth of the whole. This produced a very small revenue, yet more than the district could bear, for it was so unfairly distributed, that twenty villages were soon deserted.

378. When Mr. Calvert took over charge from Mr. Fraser of the Delhi Residency in the be-

Mr. Calvert's deputation in 1816. ginning of 1816, he computed the actual collections* on account of land revenue for the year 1222 F., at only Rs. 11,456-3-0, plus 9,134-9-3

---

* The demand was Rs. 13,214, *vide* Report to Secretary Board of Revenue, dated 29th July, 1816.

on account of miscellaneous income, or *sair ;* total Rs. 20,590-12-3; and the total collections of 1223 F, at Rs. 22,515-12-0, including Rs. 12,688-10-3 *sair.* The amount of land then lying waste was enormous, because there were no hands to till it, as the population did not exceed 17,000 souls.

379. Mr. Calvert made a settlement (the first) for four years with the headmen of the villages,
His settlement; the first; from 1224 F. to 1227 F. taking the average of the collections in the two former years as a basis. His proceedings were necessarily summary, for he had other work to do in Seharunpore. The assessments,* though their annual total was light, were in consequence inequitably distributed :—

1224 F. ...	...	...	...	Rs. 11,244	12 0
1225 F. ...	...	...	...	,, 12,020	12 0
1226 F. ...	...	...	...	,, 12,048	12 0
1227 F. ...	...	...	...	,, 12,050	12 0

380. Mr Moore, Collector of Seharunpore, who made the next, a quinquennial settlement, was
Second Settlement by Mr. Moore, from 1228 F. to 1232 F. more successful, raising the assessments in some of the best villages and thus providing for an abatement in others. The disadvantage of

---

* *Vide* Mr. Calvert's Report to Secretary Board of Commissioners, 5th September, 1817, which also gives the separate items for each pergunnah. His original establishment was very small, only consisting of

One Ameen, ...	...	...	...	...	...	... Rs. 50	a-month.
,, Mutsudee,	...	...	...	...	...	... ,, 15	,,
10 Chuprassies,	...	...	...	...	...	... ,, 30	,,
A Surishtadar, Darogha, and Mutsudees for *sair* collections, ,, 110	,,

Total, ... 205

He afterwards got 35 peons and a Canoongo on Rs. 15 a-month.

having no resident Magistrate at Dehra appears from his remarks on the *begaree* system, owing to the abuse of which several villages on either side of the main road through Dehra had been completely deserted; "the evil would not have been so great if confined to Euro-

Evil consequences of forced labor.

pean visitors as it is to be supposed they generally remunerated the people for their service but natives who passed through, considered it a matter of right to press a cooly to carry his bundle or his spear and payment for the amount was never thought of," (Settlement Report to Secretary Board of Commissioners, dated 13th December, 1821). The figures* of this settlement stood as follows:—

1228 F.,	...	...	...	Rs.	13,365
1229 F.,	...	...	...	„	13,438
1230 F.,	...	...	...	„	12,756
1231 F.,	...	...	...	„	12,805 (12,697?)
1232 F.,	...	...	...	„	12,966 (12,858?)

Engagements were again taken from the former *malgoozars*.

381. The third, also a quinquennial settlement, from

Third settlement, from 1233 F. to 1237 F.

1233 F., to 1237 F. was made by Mr. Shore, who had more time to devote to the work than his predecessors. It exhibited the following results:—

---

* That is, according to Mr. Shore (Report of 1st May, 1827), who gives for the preceding years:—

1222 F.,	..	..	..	..	..	Rs.	12,987
1223 F.,	..	..	..	..	..	„	9,643
1224 F.,	..	..	..	..	..	„	11,146
1225 F.,	..	..	..	..	..	„	12,020
1226 F.,	..	..	..	..	..	„	12,050
1227 F.,	..	..	..	..	..	„	12,050

The writer has no means of reconciling these discrepancies.

1233 F.,	...	...	...	...	Rs. 13,570
1234 F.,	...	...	...	...	„ 13,595
1235 F.,	...	...	...	...	„ 13,645
1236 F.,	...	...	...	...	„ 13,645
1237 F.,	...	...	...	...	„ 13,645

382. It should be borne in mind that the statistics of

Pergunnah Chandee.

these last two settlements include the revenue of a part of Chandee, from Anjunee *Ghát* upwards to Rikheekesh, annexed to the Doon under orders of the Board of Commissioners, dated 11th November 1817, and assessed in the second, at a *jumma* of from Rs. 297 to Rs. 1,113; in the third, at Rs. 259, a sum increased by Rs. 783 (?) when the Ruwasun was made the boundary between Mr. Shore's jurisdiction and that of the Collector of Moradabad in the year 1826. The portion[*] at first transferred to this district, was merely a strip of unhealthy jungle situated between the spurs of the eastern Sewaliks and the Ganges, containing seven inhabited and nine deserted villages. Mr. Shore estimated the land revenue from this tract to be—

1,228 F.,	...	...	...	...	Rs. 1,113
1,229 F.,	...	...	...	...	„ 1,113
1,230 F.,	...	...	...	...	„ 335
1,231 F.,	...	...	...	...	„ 297
1,232 F.,	...	...	...	...	„ 335

The assessment from 1233 F. to 1237 F., was Rs. 259 a

Seems to have once belonged to Major Hearsay, who sold his estate to the British Government.

year. There were besides, forest duties. The sixteen villages in question, together with twenty others in the pergunnah, had apparently been granted by the Raja of

[*] Cf. letter, without date, October 1823. Mr. Shore's Settlement Report, dated 15th December 1825. Letter to Mr. Halhed, Magistrate of Moradabad, dated 19th March 1824. From same to Shore, dated 24th March 1824, &c., &c.

Gurhwál to a certain Major Hearsay,* who used to take a tithe of every sort of produce in lieu of rent. He eventually sold his property to the British Government.   The new arrangement put fourteen more of the Chandee villages under Mr. Shore's management.   Five of these had been in the possession of the Nawab Vizier before the cession, the Rájá's *sunud* was therefore waste paper, so far as they were concerned, and their purchase a gratuitous concession to Major Hearsay on the part of the British Government. Five others had formed part of the *jagheer* of one Muduh Khan Heree, whom the Major had dispossessed on his own authority. Mr. Halhed, Collector of Moradabad, calculated the land revenue of the fourteen at Rs. 833 for 1233 F., and Rs. 858 for 1234 F.   The principal source of revenue, however, was the *duh-i-ek*, or tithe of forest

The duh-i-ek.

produce, which, when farmed in 1230 F., yielded Rs. 3,159-8-3; when kept under direct management in 1231 F., Rs. 4,649-8-3 (Rs. 3,159-8-3 net), and in 1232 F., Rs. 3,680-11-3 net.

383.   The third settlement is remarkable, because the position of the *malgoozars* was then, for the

Real position of the Malgoozar's first indicated in the third settlement.

first time, indicated to be identical with that of the Zemindars of the plains,† although they retained the name of *Thekadars*, or farmers (*vide* Mr. Shore's Settlement Report, dated 15th December 1825). Before the conquest, indeed, they had been often treated as tenants-at-will, rather than lessees.

---

* Father, I believe, of General Hearsay, whose son, Capt. Hearsay, still has property in the Doon.

† "I have entered all engagers as Thekadars; though they have as many priviledges (*sic*), and are as little likely to be turned out as the Zemindars of the plains."

384. The highest rate of assessment was only about 4 annas* per kutcha beegah, while the *Thekadar's* share of the produce in kind never exceeded one-fourth, averaged one-seventh or one-eighth, and some-

Rate of assessment in no case exceeded 4 annas per kutcha beegah. Wretched condition of the cultivators.

times fell so low as one-eighteenth. But such was the incredible laziness of the cultivating tenants, that they were in a most wretched condition, living from hand to mouth, and completely at the mercy of petty money lenders. Nothing else could be expected of men who thought it a grievance to work on a cloudy day, remained altogether idle on a rainy one, and never went through more than six or seven hours' honest toil, out of the twenty-four. The great demand for agricultural labor, due to the large proportion of waste lands, encouraged their indifference by keeping rents down, since nothing was easier than to emigrate to villages where the land was nearly all fallow and the rates merely nominal.

385. The number of villages included in the original

Number of villages.

settlement was :—

Pergunnah Suntaur, ...	...	...	...	64
,,	Kulyánpore,	...	...	...	54
,,	Busuntpore,	...	...	...	13
,,	Suhjpore,	...	...	...	16
,,	Sauree, ...	...	...	...	9
,,	Chandee, ...	...	...	...	6
	Total,		...	...	162

The half of pergunnah Chandee transferred from Morada-

---

* Mr Shore elsewhere (Report of 1st May) says 3 annas per kutcha, 9 annas per pukka, beegah, while in most villages it did not exceed 1½ anna or 2 annas per kutcha beegah, and in some the rates were merely nominal.

bad, was re-settled at Rs. 683 for 1235, 1236, 1237 and
Settlement of 1238 F., in the year 1828 (*vide* Mr. Shore's
Chandee.   report, dated the 24th April).*

386. It may be added, that about the same time,
another settlement was made of the
Settlement of various pergunnahs of Barasoo, Dewalgurh, Nag-
ous pergunnahs be-
longing to Kumaon.   pore, Chándkoth and Gungásulán, all belonging to the Sreenugur Tuhseeldaree
then included in jurisdiction of Mr. Shore as Assistant
to the Commissioner of Kumaon. The settlement, an account of which would be out of place, as the pergunnahs
referred to were soon detached from the Doon, was for five
years in the case of the three first, for four, in that of the
two last; the total amount of yearly revenue in 1825-6-7-8
being Rs. 35,252† Mr. Shore's Report dated 20th
November 1828).

387. Mr. Shore, a liberal conservative, was strongly in
favor of creating a rural aristocracy with
Mr. Shore advoca- a permanent interest in the improvement
tes the bestowal of
Zemindaree rights   of agriculture, by placing the so-called
upon the so-called
Thekadars.   farmers on the same footing as the Zemindars of the plains, and acknowledging their
claims to a transferable proprietary right in the land.‡
The good Hustee Dhul had actually promised this boon to
a number of petitioners, and procured "lal mohurs" from
Nepal, we may infer, to seal the title deeds. Again, in April

---

* Elsewhere, he gives Rs. 783 as the new *jumma* (*vide supra*), and Rs. 3,200 as
the revence derived from jungle produce (*vide* Report of 1st May).

† In 1827 the total collections of the Sreenugur Tuhseeldaree had been Rs. 33, 999.
Vide Statistical Report of 1st May, para. 179.

‡ *Vide* Report to Mr. Traill, dated 30th March 1828.

1822, Surjun Negi, a man of great influence, petitioned
Mr. Ross, Senior Member of the Board of
Commissioners, on the subject. as representative of the united body of landholders. That gentleman not only verbally
promised that their request should be granted, but had a
vernacular report expressing his views drawn up by the
Peshkar. It may be still lying among the records of the
Dehra Tuhseel, for the question was shelved, till Mr. Shore
revived the controversy. He justly argued that the Thekadars did not essentially differ in status from the zemindars
over the greater part of India at the time when we first
took the country, and there was no imaginable reason why
they should not receive the same privileges, with the *pro-
viso* that the farmer of a village newly formed, or deserted
and re-peopled, should not obtain *zemindaree* rights, until
the estate paid a revenue of Rs 50 a-year, and contained not
less than 500 standard beegahs of cultivated land. In such
cases, moreover, he proposed to make the boon conditional
upon the estate being entailed on one son (not necessarily
the eldest) to prevent the subdivision of property, and consequent impoverishment of families after a few generations.

A measure already contemplated by the Goorkha govern-ment, and again in 1822.

388. His successor, Major Young, having radical*
tendencies, held diametrically opposite
views, and dealt a severe blow to Mr.
Shore's *protégés.* Starting with the per-
fectly correct assumption that the proprietary right in the
land had been from time immemorial vested in the Government, he jumped to the conclusion that no one else had

Major Young holds different views.

* I mean, in the sense of being opposed to the creation of a local landed aristocracy,
for Mr. Shore was in some respects a violent radical himself.

any intermediate title at all. The farmers, he added, had been guilty of oppressions that had materially contributed to the apathetic and degraded condition of the cultivators ; they were, in fact, the bane of the district, and might legally, nay ought, in equity, to be altogether thrown over-board.

389. The next settlement should, therefore, be made direct with the cultivators, to whom " a grant of the proprietary right or zemindaree *huck*, of those lands which are now actually under cultivation, shall be presented by Government, as a mark of great favor and a proof of the great interest taken in their welfare........to them and their heirs for ever." He made one exception ; " the Thekadars of respectability and long standing, that is, whose ancestors have held the situation, and who are now Resident Landholders in the Doon, shall be selected, and as a matter of great favor and kindness, and in consideration of their former services, invested by Government with the rank and title of Mookuddum Zemindars of all the lands now under cultivation and over which they and their families held sway as Thekadars." Engagements, he proposed, should be taken from the cultivating tenants at a general rate of 3 annas per local beegah (1,008⅓ square yards)* of land under cultivation. The mookuddums would make the collections from the newly constituted zemindars, and pay the amount of each *kist* into the Treasury, *minus* 10 per cent. as a remuneration for their trouble. All land not under cultivation was to be considered the *bond*

His proposals for a fourth settlement with the cultivators.

At a general rate of 3 annas per kutcha beegah of cultivated land.

---

* The standard beegah being then 3,025 square yards.

fide property of Government, but might be let out under certain conditions, to people desirous of cultivating it, on application to the neighbouring mookuddum. The right
Appointment of
Mookuddums of succession to this office Major Young intended to be hereditary; " by entail to the next male heir without the power of selling, willing it
and Putwarees. away, or sequestrating it in any manner." Another feature in the new scheme was the appointment of an efficient staff of Putwarees.

390. Its immediate effect would, he calculated, be :—

<table>
<tr><td>Effect of new
scheme; to give a
net land revenue of
about Rs. 16,000.</td><td></td><td>RS.</td></tr>
<tr><td></td><td>100,000 local beegahs, at 3 annas each
beegah, ...</td><td>18,750</td></tr>
<tr><td></td><td>Less</td><td></td></tr>
<tr><td></td><td>12 Putwarees, at 5 each,... ... ...</td><td>720</td></tr>
<tr><td></td><td>And 10 per cent. to Mookuddums, ...</td><td>1,875</td></tr>
<tr><td></td><td>Net revenue, ...</td><td>16,155</td></tr>
</table>

Further details may be found in Major Young's report to Mr. Commissioner Ewer, dated the 28th November 1829. One very curious proposal was the abolition of five police
Abolition of police
chowkies. chowkies, which " he deemed perfectly useless, if not more than useless, for he was convinced that they gave more annoyance to the inhabitants than they afforded protection." With the saving of Rs. 1,884 thus effected, he suggested making an addition of $\frac{5}{100}$ to the mookuddums' *malikánah*. A still stranger thing is, that the whole scheme was unconditionally sanctioned by Resolution of Government, dated 16th March 1830.*

391. He accordingly proceeded to carry out his plans

* Forwarded on the 3rd April. The only modification introduced was, that the *mookuddums* were to be distinctly regarded as Officers of Government liable to removal for misconduct.

forthwith, and forwarded his report to the Commissioner on the 9th April 1831.   The settlement was made for ten ·years, from 1238 F. to 1247 F. inclusive. "The persons, at

Fourth settlement, for ten years, from 1238 F. to 1247 F.

whose charge and risk the land had been cultivated were recognized as proprietors of the same, and it was secured to them and their heirs for ever, subject to payment of rent.   The land belonging to each village, having been separately measured out to each zemindar, including land under cultivation, house, and garden, the whole was assessed at 3 annas per kutcha beegah of $1008\frac{1}{3}$ square yards, with a few exceptions, after which the zemindars were permitted to make a village distribution of the assessment agreeable to the quality of the land composing each estate."   Only the lands under cultivation were assessed.   The waste lands might be taken up by the nearest cultivating proprietor, on application through the mookuddum, at half an anna a beegah the first year; one anna the second; $1\frac{1}{2}$ anna the third; 2 annas the fourth; and 3 annas the fifth.   No village boundaries were marked off, each *mouzah* being left to extend itself as it could.   Copies of the returns forwarded with Major Young's report have not been kept among the Dehra Doon records.

392.   The grand defect of the old system had been, that

Defects of the fourth settlement.

the farmers had been subject to no restraint whatsoever, either in the management of their villages or the treatment of the cultivators.*   The

---

* Since the above was written, I have come across a letter, dated 9th April, 1831, from Major Young to Mr. W. Ewer, the Commissioner, clearly showing that the people themselves considered the Thekadars to be the real proprietors of the land (under Government), and fully acknowledged their seignioral rights by the payment

great error now made was, that prescriptive rights were summarily ignored wholesale. The consequent disadvantages have been pointed out and fully discussed in Mr. A. Ross' printed Report, No. 110, dated 12th June 1850. They consisted "chiefly in the minute subdivision of the zemindaree right, accompanied by equally minute subdivision of responsibility for the revenue." Each petty landholder naturally considered himself independent of the mookuddum, who, on his part, when in difficulties, screened himself from all responsibility with reference to the realization of the revenue, behind the acknowledged theory of the decennial settlement. The consequences of Major Young's mistake were not immediately felt, for the simple reason that the *parvenu* landholders, either not understanding or not appreciating the boon conferred upon them, in many instances never availed themselves of it, continuing to pay rent as cultivators to the *bonâ fide zemindars*. Besides, the abundance of good land without occupants generally rendered the payment of revenue easy.

of various exactions or cesses termed *mulbah*, which, not being under proper control, must have often pressed very heavily on the tenants.

The farmers collected

		R.	A.	P.		
On each oil-mill, loom, or buneea's shop, ...		1	0	0		
„ „ carpenter's, smith's, or other artificer's shop, ...		0	8	0		
„ „ water-mill, from		0	8	0	to Rs.	6
„ „ lime kiln, „		3	0	0	to „	7
„ „ boiler, „		0	2	6		

The owners of cattle brought into the Doon to graze, paid in milk or ghee at the rate of 4 annas a buffalo, and 2 annas a cow or bullock. Laborers, too, gave the Thekadar 10 or 12 days' labor in the year *gratis*. The farmer also levied a tax of Rs. 10 to Rs. 50 on the marriage of each widow. This, in Major Young's opinion, acted as a direct encouragement to *Sutee*. "Even superstition itself was taxed to fill the coffer of the Thekadar," for one farmer pocketed about Rs. 300 a year from the offerings made to the temple of Sitlá Devi at Raewálá.

393. But when, in 1837-38, the Government offered land to European grantees on much more favorable terms

Grants of 1837-38, their effect in raising the value of land.

than those of 1830, while Col. Young, acting under a misconception of the orders of the Board of Revenue, issued a proclamation* inviting natives to come forward and bid against the intruders, the value of land suddenly rose in the market, and the question of proprietary right became important. On the one hand, the imagination of European speculators was inflamed by an exaggerated idea of the advantages held out to them ; on the other, the ambiguous terms of Col. Young's proclamation induced natives to believe that they would obtain land on the same terms as their foreign competitors.

394. Col. Young, enamoured of his own theories, made

Fifth settlement, also ryotwaree, at the same rate, 1840-60.

another *ryotwaree* settlement for twenty years in 1840. The assessment remained as before, 3 annas per beegah, or 14 annas 6 *gundahs* per acre of cultivated land, of which 2 annas 6 *gundahs* went to the mookuddum, but the following modifications were introduced—(1), the Doon having been surveyed

Modifications introduced ; three in number.

by Capt. Brown in 1838-39, the boundaries of every village were determined; the cultivated, culturable, and barren land was measured off; and the survey became the standard of the assessable area instead of the *khusruh* measurement; (2), the assignment of one-fourth of the culturable land, free of assessment, to each village for grazing purposes ; (3), the offer of the remaining culturable land, first to the old cul-

---

* On the 1st March, 1838.

tivators, and next to other applicants on *indefinite* grant terms.

395. This settlement was never sanctioned. It lay open to the same general objections as the previous one, and also had other faults. The uniform rate of assessment on lands varying in quality, the redistribu-

Its defects; the same as in the previous one, besides certain special faults.

tion of which was left to the people themselves, an idea evidently suggested to Col. Young by his Jounsar Bawur experience, at length proved in many instances to be a great hardship. In the absence of joint responsibility, the re-distribution was nominal, the rate consequently pressed too heavily on some, and lay too lightly on others. Frequent remissions resulted. Again, the professional survey measurements exhibited much land as cultivated, that was neither cultivated nor occupied, but only culturable, yet the assessments were calculated according to the professional, not according to the khusrah measurement, which gave the area of each field. Thirdly, no rules were laid down for the disposal of that part of the culturable land devoted to grazing purposes; a fruitful source of wrangling. A fourth error was the omission to define the meaning of "grant terms," though, as Mr. A. Ross observes, the words certainly cannot have had reference to jungle grants on clearing leases, since the settlement was for 20 not 50 years.

396. Mr. F. Williams,* appointed Superintendent of Dehra Doon on the 16th January 1842,

Mr. F. Williams and Mr. H. Vansittart expose them.

commenced the exposure of these mistakes. Mr. H. Vansittart, who took office on the 7th February 1843, went to the root of the evil,

* Lately Commissioner of Meerut.

boldly questioning the justice, as well as the expediency, of the *Ryotwaree* system. His arguments, clinched by the notorious fact that a large number of the cultivators had never assumed the proprietary right conferred in the settlement of 1830, and that most expressed themselves perfectly contented with the position of *mouroosee* tenants, convinced Government of the correctness of his views, and a revision of Colonel Young's proceedings was decreed. Resolution No. 293, dated 22nd January, 1845, invested him with full powers as a Settlement Officer under Regulation VII. of 1822 and Regulation IX. of 1833, declaring his principal duty to be the determination and declaration of rights in each village.

397. He set to work in 1845, and concluded his operations before the end of the year. The assessments were lowered, tenures enquired into, and zemindaree rights conferred upon the old *malgoozars*, wherever their claims were proved to his satisfaction. His proceedings, however, seem to have been hurried, and in some respects defective, so a second revision was undertaken, and brought to a conclusion at the end of the year 1848, by his successor Mr. A. Ross, whose printed report is among the books of reference in every Collector's office, and it would be superfluous to do more than summarise the results of his labors, which included an entire re-measurement of each *mouzah*, according to the native method, and the demarcation of the village boundaries by means of pillars.

Revision of the fifth settlement, 1845-48.

398. An abstract from the general statement in acres (No. 1) attached to his report, compares the revised with past assessments.

Results of the revised settlement.

Abstract of General Statement in Acres (No. 1).

	Western Doon, 147 villages.			Eastern Doon, 36 villages.			Grand Total of Western and Eastern Doon, 183 villages.		
	R.	A.	P.	R.	A.	P.	R.	A.	P.
Highest jumma, 1st Settlement, ...	5,929	0	0	3,042	8	0	8,971	8	0
„ 2nd „	6,291	0	0	3,180	0	0	9,471	0	0
„ 3rd „	7,012	7	0	2,823	0	0	9,835	7	0
Average jumma of past 5 years, ...	15,857	6	0	2,767	4	2	18,624	10	2
Proposed jumma, ...	18,932	0	0	1,838	0	0	20,770	0	0
	ACRES.			ACRES.			ACRES.		
Area in acres, ...	1,72,793			35,422			208,215		
Deduct ⎰ Lákhiráj, ...	93			..			93		
Minhaee, ⎱ Barren, ...	92,978			26,917			119,895		
Malgoozaree ⎰ Culturable waste, ...	43,249			4,908			48,157		
Lately abandoned, ...	5,380			453			5,833		
Irrigated, ...	6,196			1,322			7,518		
Not irrigated, ...	24,894			1,822			26,716		
⎱ Total cultivation, ...	31,090			3,144			34,234		
	R.	A.	P.	R.	A.	P.	R.	A.	P.
Assessments on total area, per acre, ..	0	1	9	0	0	9¾	0	1	7$\frac{1}{10}$
Assessment on total malgoozaree land, cultivated and culturable, per acre, ..	0	3	9½	0	6	6	0	3	9$\frac{20}{1}$
Assessment on land under cultivation, per acre, ...	0	9	8$\frac{9}{10}$	0	9	3¾	0	9	8$\frac{4}{10}$

Statement No. 2 gives the Annual Jumma, from 1848-49 to 1860-61.

	Western Doon.			Eastern Doon.			Grand Total of Eastern and Western Doon.		
	R.	A.	P.	R.	A.	P.	R.	A.	P.
Jumma of 1847-48, the year previous to the revision of Settlement, ...	23,192	2	6	2,767	4	4	25,959	6	10
Proposed jumma ⎰ 1848-49, ...	18,932	0	0	1,838	0	0	20,770	0	0
1849-50, ...	19,389	0	0	1,846	0	0	21,235	0	0
1850-51, ...	19,925	0	0	1,857	0	0	21,782	0	0
1851-52, ...	20,483	0	0	1,871	0	0	22,354	0	0
1852-53, ...	21,063	0	0	1,887	0	0	22,950	0	0
1853-54, ...	21,662	0	0	1,906	0	0	23,568	0	0
1854-55, ...	22,283	0	0	1,928	0	0	24,211	0	0
1855-56, ...	22,911	0	0	1,950	0	0	24,861	0	0
1856-57, ...	23,535	0	0	1,972	0	0	25,507	0	0
1857-58, ...	24,168	0	0	1,994	0	0	26,162	0	0
1858-59, ...	24,796	0	0	2,016	0	0	26,812	0	0
1859-60, ...	25,427	0	0	2,038	0	0	27,465	0	0
1860-61, ...	26,056	0	0	2,060	0	0	28,116	0	0

2 E

A third (No. 6) gives the gross and net *jumma* of 1840-41, and of the Revised Settlement of 1848, exhibiting the net increase of the latter over the former throughout the whole Zillah.

	Western Doon.			Eastern Doon.			Total.		
	R.	A.	P.	R.	A.	P.	R.	A.	P.
Gross jumma assessed in 1840, ...	23,771	15	8	2,872	8	4	26,644	8	0
Deduct reductions granted at different times between 1840 and 1st May, 1848,	173	4	0		..		173	4	0
Remaining gross jumma previous to revision of 1848, ...	23,598	11	8	2,872	8	4	26,471	4	0
Deduct Minhaee. ⎰Huq Mookuddummee of 20 per cent.	4,640	10	8	562	7	4	5,203	2	0
Salary of 12 Putwaries at Rs. 63-8 per mensem, ..	571	8	0	190	8	0	762	0	0
Remission annually granted for several years prior to 1st May, 1848, ...	1,016	10	3	224	12	6	1,241	6	9
⎱Total Minhaee, ...	6,228	12	11	977	11	10	7,206	8	1
Net Jumma of 1840-41 actually collected, ...	17,369	14	17	1,894	12	14	19,264	11	11
		(sic)							
Proposed Jumma of 1848-49, ...	18,932	0	0	1,838	0	0	20,770	0	0
Decrease, ...		..		56	12	14	56	12	14
Increase, ...	1,562	1	3		..		1,562	1	3
Net increase, ...		..			..		1,505	4	9

Mr. Ross' Settlement[*] finally established the zemindaree system in the Doon. The tenures were thus classified :—

Zemindaree system finally established.

Pergunnah.	Zemindaree.	Puteedaree.	Bhyachárá.	Total.
Western Doon, ...	116	17	1	134
Eastern Doon, ...	35	...	...	35
Total, ...	151	17	1	169

Only six instances occurred in which the cultivators desired to be recorded as subordinate proprietors.

* In it the Eastern and Western Doon were separated by an imaginary line running about 8 miles east of Dehra. Cf. Mr. Daniell's Report of 22nd February 1864, para. 15. It cost Rs. 6,473-1-2.

399. In November 1860, Mr. Manderson commenced a

Seventh Settlement by Mr. C. A. Daniell, for thirty years, from 1863. His first report.

seventh, for thirty years, of which Mr. C. A. Daniell, took over charge in July 1862, and submitted his report to the Commissioner the 22nd February 1864. Copies of the statements attached to it are not forthcoming, but it appears from the report itself that the jumma of the ordinary *khálisah* villages, 352 in number, exclusive of grant lands, was raised from Rs. 20,520 in 1862-63 to Rs. 25,749 in 1863-64. "The area actually recorded as cultivation was 37,267 acres, the average rate per acre of cultivation by the new jummas was Rs. 0-10-10$\frac{2}{5}$. The whole malgoozaree area recorded was 75,514 acres, the average rate of jumma per acre malgoozaree was Rs. 0-5-4$\frac{3}{5}$. The actual area on which the cultivation of the classified rates was made was (cultivation and fallow) 42,093 acres, while the culturable waste area which did not come within the calculation was 33,421 acres* (paras. 53-54)."

400. The rates representing the rents realizable from

Rent rates.

the agricultural produce raised in kind or money (para. 50) were—

* A year after a different calculation was made, *vide* Census Report for 1865 :—

| | DEHRA. | | |
	Western Doon.	Eastern Doon.	Total.
Area in acres, ...	226,122	207,428	4,33,550
Malgoozaree or { Cultivated, acres, ...	33,918	10,982	44,900
assessed land, { Culturable, acres, ...	50,159	16,704	66,863
Minhaee or un- { Lákhiráj, acres, ...	11,362	8,771	20,133
assessed land, { Barren, acres, ...	1,30,683	1,70,971	3,01,654
Demand on account of land revenue for 1863-64 in rupees,	22,876	6,544	29,420
	RS A. P.	RS. A. P.	RS. A. P.
Rate per acre on total area, ...	0 1 7	0 0 6	0 1 1 0
Rate per acre on total malgoozaree, ...	0 4 9	0 3 9	0 4 2 6
Rate per acre on total cultivation, ...	0 10 9	0 9 6	0 10 5 8

		1st Class, per acre.			2nd Class, per acre.			3rd Class, per acre.			4th Class, per acre.		
		R.	A.	P.	R.	A.	P.	R.	A.	P.	R.	A.	P.
WESTERN DOOR.	Missun, ..	2	8	0	1	12	0	1	8	0	1	4	0
	Roslee, ..	1	12	0	1	6	0	1	0	0	0	12	0
	Dakhar, ..	1	8	0	1	2	0	0	14	0	0	12	0
	Sankra, ..	0	12	0	0	12	0	0	10	0	0	8	0
EASTERN DOOR.	Missun, ..	..	..	..	1	4	0	1	2	0	1	0	0
	Roslee, ..	..	..	..	1	2	0	1	0	0	0	12	0
	Dakhar, ..	..	..	..	1	2	0	0	14	0	0	12	0
	Sankra, ..	..	..	..	0	12	0	0	10	0	0	8	0

There were 39, 1st class; 99, 2nd class; 149, 3rd class; and 65, 4th class villages.

401. After the submission of Mr. Daniell's report, a revision was pronounced necessary (*vide* Memorandum by Senior Member, Board of Revenue, dated 20th June 1864), and he was directed—(1), to revise the assumed average rates with a view to the introduction of a permanent settlement, where practicable; (2), to examine all cases where any considerable tracts of waste lands or forest were included in village areas, and to assess the same wherever they proved to have been inadequately assessed.

Revision of seventh settlement: its object.

402. Owing to various interruptions, Mr. Daniell did not send up his second report,* till April 1867. Here again the usual tabular state-

Mr. Daniell's second report.

* No 133, dated 25th April, 1867.

'ments are wanting, but the most important points can
be mentioned. The following table shows the rates on which the revision took place (para. 21):—

Assumed rent rates.

Average Rent Rates per Acre under cultivation, including fallow.

	Class.	Missun, per acre.						Roslee and Dhakar, per acre.						Sankra, per acre.					
		Irrigable.			Unirrigable.			Irrigable.			Unirrigable.			Irrigable.			Unirrigable.		
		RS.	A.	P.	RS.	A.	P.	RS.	A.	P.	RS.	A.	P.	RS.	A.	P.	RS.	A.	P.
WESTERN DOON.	Class I., ..	3	8	0	2	0	0	2	4	0	1	4	0	1	4	0	0	12	0
	Class II., ..	3	0	0	1	8	0	1	12	0	1	2	0	1	2	0	0	12	0
	Class III., ..	2	8	0	1	4	0	1	8	0	0	14	6	1	0	0	0	12	0
EASTERN DOON.	Class II., ..	2	8	0	1	6	0	1	8	0	0	15	0	1	0	0	0	12	0
	Class III., ..	2	8	0	1	4	0	1	8	0	0	14	6	1	0	0	0	12	0

403. The estates recommended for permanent settlement as having reached 80 per cent. of their full cultivation, were 110; 73 in the Western Doon and 37 in the Eastern Doon, being, for the most part, supposed to be those beyond the reach of further improvement from the extention of canal irrigation (*vide* para. 40, *sq.*)

Estates reported for permanent settlement.

404. The revised jumma was to come into force from the 1st July 1866, commencing at Rs. 31,637, and the total number of *khálisah* mahals is stated to have then been 339, held in ordinary zemindaree or putteedaree tenures (*vide* para. 82, *sq.*)

Revised jumma commenced at Rs. 31,637, from 1st July, 1866.

	Western Doon.	Eastern Doon.	Total.
Estates,*	188	151	339
Total area in acres, ...	1,13,969	52,354	1,66,323
Barren and forest, ...	60,539	31,065	91,604
Culturable waste, ...	22,943	9,817	32,760
Cultivated including fallow, ...	30,425	11,434	41,859
Rent-free patches, ...	62	38	100
	RS.	RS.	RS.
Proposed Jumma, ...	24,887	6,750	31,637
	RS. A. P.	RS. A. P.	RS. R. P.
Rate on whole area, per acre, ...	0 3 6	0 2 0·75	0 3 0·521
Rate on Malgoozaree area, ...	0 7 4·86	0 5 0·983	0 6 9
Rate on cultivated area, ...	0 13 1	0 9 5·43	0 12 1

To this must be added the revenue from ten grant villages

* Classified thus by Mr. Daniell (para. 106) :—

Malgoozaree,	...	...	...	... 294
Putteedaree,	...	...	...	... 40
Bhyachárá, ...	...	...	...	... 5
			Total,	... 339

I cannot account for certain discrepancies in the various enumerations of khálisah mahals. The 388 estates given in the Census Report of 1865, were made up thus :—

Khálisah,... ... ... ⎫ 352
Rusudee grants, ... ⎪ Excluded from 11
Maafee estates, ... ⎬ statement in p. 47, 24
Tract given to Major Rind, ... ⎭ 1   388

Add

Fee simple estates under orders of 1861, 1358A., ... 12
„ by redemption of land revenue, ... 3
Good service grants, ... 3   18

406

Under the orders of 1861, waste land was to be sold in fee simple on payment of a price fixed by Government. Twelve tracts were so purchased. In the same orders holders of rusudee grants and of land under tea, &c., had the option of redeeming the land revenue. Two rusudee grants, and one tract paying land revenue as fixed at settlement, were so purchased. Cf. G.O., 4206, dated 15th August 1862 ; 1042A., dated the 17th September 1862. For further particulars, *vide* Appendix XII. For statement of annual jumma under current settlement, on which no orders have yet been passed, *vide* Appendix XIII.

(*vide* para. 93, *sq.*), yielding in 1866-67, Rs. 4,333.   The
land tax, therefore, really amounted to

Plus Rs. 4,333 from
grant villages, mak-
ing a total of Rs.
35,970.

a total of Rs. 35,970, while the actual
demand, which, according to the latest
official returns, has risen to Rs. 36,717,
was Rs. 35,687 for the current year (*vide* para. 116); of
this Europeans were responsible for Rs. 9,546.

405.   We thus see that, although the Doon yields a
respectable income from other sources, the

Comparatively
slight increase of
land revenue.

increase of the land revenue has not kept
pace with that of the population, having
little more than trebled since Mr. Cal-
vert's settlement, whereas the latter has more than quadrupled, nor is so large an increase as might be expected
from the apparent advantages of situation and climate,
ever likely to take place, except from the extension of tea
cultivation.   Large tracts are either irretrievably barren or
appropriated to the growth of timber, while elsewhere, the
more valuable crops, with the exception of rice and *paundá*,
will not thrive so well as in the plains, on account of the
excessive moisture.   There is also a deficiency of manure,
and much of the culturable soil is extremely poor, being
little better than sand and shingle.   In the midst of this
occur those fertile patches, the value of which has sometimes
given rise to expectations certainly not warranted by tradition, for when, in former days, every available square foot of
ground between the Ganges and the Jumna was, as is said,
under cultivation, the jumma is not alleged to have exceeded
Rs. 1,25,000.*   To all this may be added the fact that

---

* Mr. Daniell says—"in the Doon land even now is not so prolific as in the plains.
The heaviest cereal crops are scarcely high crops more than 3 to 5 of the plains."
Report of 1864, para. 102.

Mr. Daniell was unquestionably lenient in his assessments. The final orders of Government upon his report have not yet been received.*

406. A great deal of the improvement that *has* taken place, must be ascribed to canal irrigation, though it would be hard to say exactly how much. In his first settlement report (para. 63), Mr. Daniell attributes

Effect of Canal Irrigation, how much of the jumma may be attributed to it.

Rs. 4,160 of Rs. 7,941 assessed on an irrigable khusruh area of 8,143 acres, to the benefits of canal irrigation. He also gives a scale exhibiting the average difference in the growth of the several crops, both irrigated and unirrigated, adding that tea in the third or fourth year fails entirely without water, while sugar-cane, tobacco, and garden produce are, as a rule, entirely dependent on it (para. 64) :—

Irrigated, per acre.			Unirrigated, per acre.	
Rice, maunds, pucca,	...	16·18	6·10 maunds, pucca.	
Wheat, ,,	...	8·10	4·6	,,
Barley, ,,	...	6·7	4·5	,,
Gram, ,,	...	5·6	4·5	,,
Oats, ,,	...	7·8	5·6	,,
Mukka, ,,	...	8·10	5·6	,,

407. In his second report (para. 73), he makes another calculation, attributing a smaller proportion of the increase to canal irrigation :—

Calculations in Mr. Daniell's second report.

Total area of villages in which canal irrigation exists.	Actual area recorded as irrigable within those villages.	Proposed Jumma or demand of the above villages.	Portion of Jumma attributable to canal irrigation.
ACRES.	ACRES.	RS.	RS.
14,975	8,085	14,831	4,747

* *See,* however, Note at end of Section III. The cost of the settlement operations from first to last was Rs. 45,083. This included the expense of preparing entirely new field maps.

In all probability, neither of these estimates is sufficiently favorable to the canals.

408. Before concluding this section, I must make a few general observations on the effect of the last two settlements. Assuming my own statistics to be correct, or approximately so, I find the actual incidence of the land revenue cultivated, culturable, and total area of the District to be :—

Effect of the last two settlements upon the District.

Incidence of the Jumma.

Jumma.	Total area in acres.	Cultivated area.	Cultivable.	Incidence on total area.			Incidence on cultivated area.			Incidence on cultivable.		
RS.				RS.	A.	P.	RS.	A	P.	RS.	A.	P.
36,717	433,280	42,456	51,963	0	1	4	0	13	10	0	11	3

Frequent alienations of landed property followed the recognition of the zemindaree rights of the malgoozaree in the settlement of 1848. The statistics of transfers from that year to 1863 are :*—

Alienations.

Of whole estates, ... 60
Of portions of do., ... 81
Of biswah shares do., ... 118

Total, ... 259

These alienations all occurred in 131 States. Three only were by order of the Civil Court in execution of decrees; 244 were by private sale, 10 by free gift, and 2 through failure. In the forced sales the jumma was little more than 8 per cent. of the amount realized; in private sales, it

* *Vide* Mr. Daniell's second report, para. 109.

2 F

exceeded 10 per cent. of the purchase money.   This is hard
to understand, particularly as we learn from Mr. Daniell's
previous report * that the rates in each case were 8 per cent.
and 6 per cent., respectively ; in other words, the prices obtained in private sales bore, as one would naturally expect,
a *better* relative value than those of decree sales ; whereas,
the above statement is to the contrary effect.   The principal sellers were Rajpoots, 141 in number; and the principal
buyers, Europeans, no less than 91 ; the net result being,
that from 1848 to 1863 there has been an

Chiefly in favor of
Europeans.

increase of eighty-three Europeans to
thirty-seven Buneea landowners, with a
decrease of 110 Rajpoots, who form the majority of the
village proprietors.

409.   It is indeed a matter of congratulation that here
at least the Buneea monopoly over Civil

Progress of Euro-
pean enterprise.

Court sales has been broken through.
So far, the progress of European enterprise
in the Doon is extremely satisfactory, and its extent will be
better understood from a consideration of the fact that nearly
one-fourth of the whole demand of 1866-67 was collected
from Europeans.   They have, we may conclude, established
a firm footing among the landed proprietors of the District ;
and their speculations would have been more daring, had
not exaggerated expectations of the profits to be derived
from tea, in the minds of persons wanting the necessary
experience of its culture, re-acted in the shape of undue
despondency, but this feeling of discouragement is happily
beginning to wear away.

The Jounsar Bawur Settlements next claim attention.

* Para. 87.

SECTION II. FISCAL HISTORY OF THE DISTRICT (CONTINUED).

JOUNSAR BAWUR SETTLEMENTS.

410. In the first settlement from 1815-16 to 1817-18, Captain Birch, fixed the jumma at Rs. 16,247-8-0 a-year, or Rs. 18,000 inclusive of allowances and customs.*

First settlement, 1815-16 to 1817-18.

411. Capt. Ross, Capt. Birch's successor, made the second settlement, for a period of three years, from the 1st November 1818 to the 31st October 1821, at Rs. 17,001.

Second from 1818 to 1821.

412. Capt. Young took charge of the pergunnah on the 1st April 1819, and under orders from the Delhi Residency, dated 6th September 1821, made a third settlement for three years longer, from the 1st November 1821, to the 31st October 1824, at exactly the same rate as before. The summary nature of Capt. Young's operations may be judged from the fact that they only occupied five or six days. Then, as now, the number

Third from 1821 to 1824.

* Hamilton, Vol. II., p. 631, gives—

Jounsar,	..	..	..	..	15,600
Bawur,	..	..	..	..	1,100
Customs,	..	..	..	..	2,000
					18,700

of *Khuts* was 35. From the total of Rs. 17,001 must be deducted Rs. 1,501 on account of customs, leaving a balance of only Rs. 15,500 for land revenue. The vernacular records,* instead of two triennial settlements, treat the second and third as one sexennial. The stipend of the Chauntrás and Siánás amounted to Rs. 1,400 a year. The old system continued to work well, and up to July 1824, the collections were all made without the employment of a single coercive process, or even the deputation of a revenue officer to any of the villages.

413. The results of the fourth settlement, at first, also, Fourth, from 1824 to 1827. concluded for a term of three years, from the 1st November 1824, to the 31st October 1827, are thus summarised :—

Number of Khuts.	Number of villages.*	Total assessments.
35	445	RS. 18,701

This total includes Rs. 1,601 derived from the customs, and Rs. 1,485 more should be deducted on account of stipends to the Chauntrás and Siánás and other exactions made under the head of *mulba*. This makes the net land revenue Rs. 15,615. Other returns give Rs. 17,282 ; and, one, Rs. 19,000, including Lálá Deendyál's allowance. This settlement was almost immediately extended from a period of three to a term of five years, and seems Extended to a term of five years. to have been eminently satisfactory, for on the 8th March 1827, Major Young reported to Sir Charles Metcalfe, that all the collections had

---

* Evidently followed by Mr. Cornwall in his report, dated 18th March 1873. He gives the net jumma at Rs. 15,703.

† Number of zemindars, 2,469. *Vide* Young's Report, dated 12th Novr. 1824, &c.

been made up to date without any of the zemindars having been coerced, although the exactions of the Mahasoo Devtá caused some pressure in the Kándé division, where the god had, in a very short time, levied Rs. 588, besides the value of offerings, the amount of which could not be ascertained, on four *Khuts* paying a revenue of only Rs. 2,200.* Still, the country was generally prosperous, and the conduct of the Chauntrás, Siánás, &c., exemplary.

414. In this year the revenue received an accession of

Farm of the customs. Surplus; how utilised.

Rs. 750, by the farm of the customs to the highest bidder, and Major Young proposed that a third of the whole surplus income (about Rs. 12,000, without deducting the pay of European Officers), should be appropriated to making a road from Kálsee to Bástil, through the centre of Jounsar Bawur, 35 miles as the crow flies, with a branch line to meet Mr. Shore's road at Rajpore. On the 13th March 1828, the appropriation of Rs. 300 a month for the purpose in question was sanctioned, but the result of opening up the communications has fallen very far short of Major Young's sanguine anticipations.

415. He contemplated the immediate introduction of

Major Young's anticipations.

beasts of burden, the rapid increase of cultivation, and the expoliation of the other internal resources of the country; "the mines of Kandy which are now unknown except to those whose ignorance, poverty, and superstitious prejudices are a bar to improvement, would become objects of curiosi-

---

* The expenses of the village where the idol stayed (Kotee), and which paid a revenue of only Rs. 200, were Rs. 127-14-0. Besides the recognised means of extortion, the Mahasoo would often take a fancy to a house or other property, and appropriate it.

ty. Men of science and skill, capital, (*sic*) would be induced
to explore, and the result holds out a fair promise of remuneration. How gratifying it would be to see the iron
which abounds in these hills, superseding in the form of
chains manufactured on the banks of its rivers, (where the
mountain torrent would lend its powerful aid to the forge,)
those flimsy and expensive bridges formed of rope, and that
such a prospect is visible in the distance, I think may be
admitted. " We all know how little these expectations have

Not realised.

been realised. The revenue of Jounsar
Bawur has increased very slightly, and, in
spite of improved roads, the trade is unimportant, excepting
that carried on with Chukrata, which is solely dependent
upon the existence of the military cantonments.

416. On the 8th August 1829, Major Young, then

Fifth settlement ;
proposals for ; method
of assessment des-
cribed.

Superintendent of the Doon as well as of
Jounsar Bawur, submitted his proposals for
a new settlement, to the Commissioner, Mr.
W. Ewer. His policy was here conservative : " I think,"
he wrote, " the system which has prevailed for the last eight
years, is well suited to the genius of the people, and more
certain of giving satisfaction than if we were to assimilate
our proceedings more to the usage of the plains." I shall
allow him to describe the mode of assessment himself. " The
sum total which the country is capable of yielding is gather-

The land revenue
roughly estimated in
a lump sum

ed from the records in office, and a correct
knowledge of what these Districts have
been assessed at under former govern-
ments, as well as since they came under British authority,
taking into consideration the present circumstances of the
people, the nature of the past season, increase or otherwise,

population, and cultivation, the state of the market, and briskness of trade.* These when clearly ascertained are made known by the executive officer to the Chauntroo, or four representatives of the people, who from time immemorial have had the principal management of assessment and collection.

417. " When the agreement between the executive officer and the Chauntroo is concluded *and re-distributed by the Siánás, or headmen.* and registered, it is submitted to the Siánás or representatives of *Khuts* of which there are thirty-five, who have hitherto assembled at Kálsee for the purpose, and who being well acquainted with each other's resources, they soon agree to bear a certain portion of the tax which is to be levied. This agreement also having been registered, it is submitted to the Siánás of the villages composing the *Khuts*, who make a more minute division, there being 450 villages. Then the inhabitants of each village assemble, and a list of those who are to contribute having been made out, called a Gown Poorjee, the sum each man is to contribute is set down opposite his name and the name of his security also; this village agreement is read in presence of the subscribers, and when all have assented, it is signed by the executive officer and a copy lodged in the hands of the Sianas."

418. In proof of the excellence of the existing arrangement, he mentions that the whole of the *The system seems to have worked well.* revenue for the last five years had been paid up, yet " not even a chaprassie had been employed on revenue duties in the district, nor had

---

* The reader will notice that Major Young had rather a confused way of expressing himself.

there been a single complaint." The Chauntras and Sianas now spontaneously came forward with an offer of one thousand rupees, advance on the gross land revenue (Rs. 17,100) of the current settlement, and likewise volunteered to furnish 300 men daily for eight months in the year, in lieu of Rs. 3,000 of the Rs. 3,600 to be expended annually on the construction of the road through the centre of the District. The balance of Rs. 600 Major Young proposed appropria ting to the maintenance of overseers, the repair of tools, &c. The zemindars calculated upon completing the work within five years. This allowed only Rs. 1-4-0 a month for each laborer, whereas the laborers' wages on that part of the line lying between Mussooree and the Jumna had been from 4 to 5 Rs. a month, the year before.

Offer of Rs. 17,100 by the Chauntrás and Siánás.

419. The custom duties levied at Kálsee were regarded as a deduction from the assumed gross land revenue. They had been farmed to the malzamin* during the three last years of the current settlement, at rates ascending from Rs. 1,601 to Rs. 2,306. On this a decrease might be expected, because Mussooree and Landour already supplied a market for many articles which used formerly to find their way to the plains *via* Kalsee. The receipts being:—

Custom duties.

Estimate of revenue, net balance Rs. 14,965.	Land revenue,...	Rs. 18,100
	Kálsee duties (probably), ...	„ 2,000
	Total, ...	„ 20,100

The deductions would be :—

Half-yearly stipend to Chauntras and Siánás,	Rs. 1,535	
On account of road, ...	„ 3,600	
		„ 5,135
Balance, ...		„ 14,965

* *Vide* letter of 24th June, 1833.

420. The Government approving of Major Young's views,* he concluded a quinquennial settlement from the 1st November 1829, to the 31st October 1834, showing an increase of Rs. 1000 a-year in the land revenue, and a decrease of Rs. 505 per annum in the custom duties. In 1832-33, 1833-34, a slight remission of Rs. 329 a year seems to have been necessary in the Buntur Khut, immediately below Chakrata, owing to a partial inundation from the river Jumna,† but in other respects the fiscal management of the sub-division gave no trouble.

Quinquennial settlement on above data from 1829 to 1834.

421. The next settlement, also the work of Major (now Colonel) Young, was for fifteen years, from 1834-35 to 1848-49. His report is not at hand. By all accounts, however, the gross revenue, including customs and cesses, was Rs. 21,412-3-0 (Rs. 20,018-12-0 ?), and the net land tax, Rs. 16,280-0-0. Before the expiration of this settlement, unforeseen difficulties arose.‡

Sixth settlement, 1834-35 to 1848-49.

422. Previous to the annexation of Jounsar Bawur to the Doon, there had always been an official at the head of the native establishment, on a salary of Rs. 80 a-month, who, under the title of Dewan, performed the duties of Ameen, and Tuhseeldar, and generally assisted the Chauntras in the regulation of the Police and the decision of petty disputes. The last incumbent, Bakir Alee, appointed in the year

The Dewan. His duties.

---

* Order of Govt. 30th Sept. 1829 (forwarding letter, 3rd Oct.) Cf. Maj. Young's letter, dated 14th October 1830. In Mr. Cornwall's report and elsewhere, the net land revenue is stated to have been only Rs. 15,354 in this settlement.

† Young to Commissioner, 14th December 1832. Cf. 23rd of January 1833.

‡ Cf. Mr. A. Ross' report, dated 1st November 1848, and 30th April 1849.

2 G

1818, was unfortunately removed to Dehra as Tuhseeldar in 1830, and his place was not filled up. Now much of the success of Col. Young's administration must be attributed to this man's energy, and the Superintendent himself has emphatically recorded the fact.* Indeed it was the very satisfactory state of the country that induced Col. Young to propose the abolition of the Dewan's appointment, and his transfer to Dehra, in place of the actual Tuhseeldar, an arrangement designed to make a paltry saving of Rs. 50 a month! Hardly had this plan been suggested, than it was carried into execution. The result was, that the affairs of Jounsar Bawur soon became involved in hopeless confusion, for Colonel Young had quite enough to do in the Doon without attending to them, and things had hitherto gone on so smoothly that he was completely thrown off his guard.

Abolition of the office, detrimental to the District.

423. An unlucky co-incidence happened at the same period; the death† of Lala Deendyal, a man who, though highly esteemed, had incurred the enmity of the Putwaree, Shib Churun, a lowland *Buneea*, possibly also of the Chauntras, on whose rapacity, it is said, his influence used to act as a wholesome check. The old Malzamin's son, Kirpa Ram, was then a child only five or six years old, and his affairs consequently fell into helpless confusion under the venal management of goomashtas. Meanwhile the Chauntras, being in collusion with the Putwaree, availed themselves of the boy's minority to compass their own ends, so that,

Death of Lála Deendyál also unfortunate.

---

* "The flourishing and orderly state of these districts at present is the best proof I can offer of the probity and ability with which he executed the charge entrusted to him. Young 12th January, 1830. Cf Secy. Government 2nd February.

† In 1829.

notwithstanding the official recognition of the Málzámin's position at the commencement of the sixth settlement, he had really degenerated into a nonentity.

424. On reaching man's estate, Kirpá Rám resolved to assert himself, and, discovering that the Chauntroo had not only made an unfair distribution of the revenue, but also introduced the practice of levying unauthorised exactions, termed "necessary expenses" (*khurcha*), under such pretexts as journeys to Dehra or Meerut for the purpose of making appeals &c., and collected in the same manner as Government revenue, he positively refused to enter such items in the accounts. The other party, in turn, availed themselves of the establishment of strange mahajuns at Kálsee during his minority, and the peculiar method of calculating his profits,[*] to induce the Malzamin's clients to withdraw their custom from him, as well as to represent his fees in the light of an extortionate demand, the payment of which might be lawfully resisted. Kirpa Ram of course had his partisans, and Jounsar Bawur was thus divided between two factions, who contended for the mastery with alternating success.

Antagonism between his son and the Chauntrás.

425. In October 1844, the loud and persistent complaints about the usurious nature of the interest paid to the Malzamin, induced Mr. Vansittart to order that official's removal, on the strength of the Chauntroo's promise that they themselves would be responsible for the adjustment of the balances, and a settlement of accounts. The new system did not answer, and Mr. A. Ross, Mr. Vansittart's successor,

Mr. Vansittart orders the Málzámin's removal.

* In reality the Málzámin's method of calculating interest was *not* unique. As a general rule, *all mahajuns charge interest on loans, in advance, without exact reference to the time at which the debt may be repaid.*

finding that neither the claims of the Málzamin nor yet those
of Government had been satisfied, restored

*His reinstate-
ment.*　　　the former to his post in October 1846,

with the outward consent of the Chauntroo,
who merely made this concession with the object of avoiding a settlement of accounts, for when, owing to continued
complaints, Mr. Ross persuaded Kirpa Ram to forego his
hereditary emoluments, and agree to accept only six weeks'
interest on each quarterly instalment of revenue, his enemies, in defiance of the Superintendent's express orders,
had the audacity to set up one Mohun in his stead, and *for-
bade* any one to have dealings with him. The people suffered severely from this assumption of authority, because
Mohun was much more exorbitant in his demands than
Kirpa Ram, and the recognised claims* of the latter still
remained unsatisfied, nor did the exactions of the Chauntroo
themselves cease.

426.　Mr. Ross consequently suspended them in March
1848. They retaliated by authoritative-

*Suspension of the
Chauntroo, 1848.*　　ly declaring Kirpa Ram to be deposed,

and had the impudence to charge the
people with the expenses of a trip to Agra, undertaken
with the object of appealing against the Superintendent's
order—an item of Rs. 900. They proceeded, furthermore, to
collect this sum through some Government *chuprassees* they
had obtained a few months before, for the ostensible purpose
of collecting Kirpa Ram's balances. Indeed Mr. Ross's enquiries led him to the conclusion that their extortions amounted, in one shape or other, to several thousand rupees a year.

---

* The Local Government had sanctioned his receiving half the amount of interest
charged according to the old scale on the quarterly instalments.

427. Under these circumstances, he could expect no help from them in collecting *data* upon

Revulsion of popular feeling against the Chauntrás.

which to frame a new settlement. Their hostility was implacable, and the ignorant peasantry believed their calumnies, but his firm attitude at length broke down their popularity; the people's eyes, he says, were opened; they, all of a sudden, unanimously professed a sincere desire to get rid of their demagogues, whom they now affected to regard in the light of oppressors; in short, the power of the Chauntroo collapsed, and Karkoons (Putwarees), Siánás, cultivators, all, in fact, except the malcontents themselves, eagerly came forward with valuable information about the state of the country.

428. This sudden change in popular opinion is inexplicable. Mr. Ross tells us: "no sooner

Described by Mr. Ross.

did I make my appearance and converse with the people a little, than they confessed the error into which they had been led in siding even temporarily with the Chauntroo. They openly declared themselves incensed with the deception practised upon them—begged and prayed to be relieved from the oppresssions and extortions of the Chauntroo, admitted their ingratitude towards Kirpá Rám,* &c., &c." But ignorant people are not so easily convinced,

Probable explanation of it.

and, in the absence of some better explanation than that given by Mr. Ross, I venture to suggest that what really made them amenable to reason, was the prospect of the abolition of the Malzamin's fees† and of an increase in the Siánás' emoluments, under a new

---

* Report of 30th April, para. 34.

† *i.e.*, the interest in anticipation.

system of settlement. Except upon some such assumption, how can we understand that, even the refractory " Chauntroo seeing how completely they had committed themselves confessed their fault, and asked pardon for their offences, promising to be more obedient in future (!) " ?

429. His original proposals* were; *firstly*, the forma-

Mr. Ross's original proposals for a seventh settlement.

tion of a Khutwár settlement based upon careful local enquiries into the comparative resources of each *Khut* and each village ; *secondly*, the abolition of the Chauntrás and the management of each *Khut* through its own Siáná, who should receive $\frac{10}{100}$, instead of $\frac{5}{100}$, on the revenue, in accordance with the provisions of a regular Wajibulurz. To

Land revenue to be raised to Rs. 21,000. Deductions Rs. 4,536.

admit of this, the gross revenue was to be raised to Rs. 21,000, the settlement being for twenty years, from the 1st May 1848.

* *Vide* Report, 1st November, 1848. His account of the actual Receipts and Charges is as follows :—

Receipts.		R.	A.	P.	Charges.		R.	A.	P.
Gross revenue,	.. ..	20,000	0	0	Huq Busaunta, Syáná's salary, ...		1,000	0	0
					Chauntrás's salary,	..	400	0	0
					Road allowance, ..	..	1,000	0	0
					Establishment charged in monthly abstract,		894	0	0
					Salary of other officials, *e.g.*, Putwarees or Canoongo, ...		180	0	0
					Four Chuprassees to superintend repairs of roads,		192	0	0
					Barber !	..	18	0	0
					Furrash, ...	..	24	0	0
					Charitable and religious endowments, ..		152	0	0
					Stationery, ...	..	40	0	0
					Total, ..	..	3,900	0	0
	Total, ..	20,000	0	0	Balance, ..	..	16,100	0	0

The contemplated deductions were:—

Huq Busaunta,	... ...	Rs. 2,000	0 0
Road allowance,	... ...	,, 1,000	0 0
Peshkár, at Rs. 30,	...	,, 360	0 0
Mohurrur, at Rs. 15,	...	,, 180	0 0
Canoongo, at Rs. 15,	...	,, 180	0 0
Native Doctor, at Rs. 15,	...	,, 180	0 0
12 Chuprassees, at Rs. 48,		,, 576	0 0
Stationery, &c.,	... ...	,, 60	0 0

4,536 0 0

Gross Revenue, 21,000 0 0

Balance, 16,464 0 0

430. The main difficulty in the way, was the adjust-

Balances due to the Málzámin adjusted.

ment of the heavy balances standing against the Malgoozars in the Malzamin's books. These, on the 1st October 1848, amounted to no less than Rs. 10,560-13-0. However, six weeks apparently sufficed to adjust the accounts, which on the 15th November stood thus:—

Balances.			Realized.			Remitted.		
RS.	A.	P.	RS.	A.	P.	RS.	A.	P.
10,645	3	3	6,007	15	6	4,637	3	9

431. One arrangement made a radical change in the

Radical changes in the whole system; abolition of the Málzámin's and Chauntroo's offices.

whole system of the Jounsar Bawur settlements; the people were, with Kirpá Rám's consent, to be relieved of the interest in anticipation hitherto paid to the Málzámin, a boon equivalent to a reduction of Rs. 1,400 and upwards in the jumma. This measure involved the abolition of the Málzámin's office, and another equally important reform was the abolition of the Chauntroo, whose *Judicial* functions presented an irresistible temptation to corruption. A third change was the removal of the joint responsibility imposed on the whole pergunnah, one of less importance, because this joint responsibility had never been enforced. The fiscal duties of the Chauntroo were to devolve upon the Siana of each *Khut;* those of the Málzámin,* upon an official subordinate to the Dehra Tuhseeldar, and every *Khut* was to be a *bhyachara muhul,*† the shareholders in which would be jointly and severally responsible for the revenue assessed upon it.   Kirpa Ram's losses under the new scheme were calculated at Rs. 1,725 a year, or more, but the people themselves came forward and voluntarily signed an agreement to continue the payment of his *ghutkolaee* about Rs. 300 a year; strong testimony in favor of his probity. He, in return, offered to go security for the revenue assessed on each *Khut.*

432.   Mr. Ross‡ afterwards modified his views about the emoluments of the Siánás, considering five per cent. on the jumma a sufficient remuneration for their services, *plus* an allowance to defray necessary expenses, calculated in strict accordance with the record of rights, besides which, a general *dustoor-ul-umul,* or code of common law, was drawn up.   He finally fixed the gross jumma at Rs. 19,750, includ-

Final arrange-
ments. Jumma
fixed at Rs. 19,750.

---

* Who also appears to have had the powers of a Police officer.

† The *Khuts* only differ from the ordinary *bhyachárá muhuls* of the plains in that there is in each an ascendant family, one member of whom is appointed Siáná, and indeed this is elsewhere paralleled by the appointment of *lumberdars.*

‡ Report of 30th April, 1842.

ing Rs. 750 on account of the road allowance, and the *huq busaunta.* After deducting the latter item, Rs. 18,756 remained; after deducting both, the net balance was Rs. 18,006, a light assessment, compared with the great im-

Increase slight in proportion to improvement indicated by the Náhun Rájá's offer.

provement said to have taken place in the condition of the people and state of the country, indicated by the fact that the Nahun Raja offered to take a lease of the pergunnah at a rent of Rs. 27,000 a year. The Putwaree's fees came to Rs. 617-3-0, and the *ghutkolaee* to Rs. 293-2-6, so that the total charges of every description were Rs. 20,660-5-6. In the settlement just expired,* the gross jummas, inclusive of basaunta, had been Rs. 20,000; the Putwarees' fees, Rs. 614-8-6; the *ghutkolaee*

New settlement.

Rs. 313-13-6; and the interest paid in advance Rs. 1,412-3-0, so that these reforms relieved the people of Rs. 1,430-3-6 extra charges.

* *The totals of Statement No I. in Mr. Ross' Report of the 30th April 1849, are*

				Add duty on imports and exports.	Grand Total.
Number of Khuts,	..	..	35		
Number of Mouzahs,	..	..	377		
			RS. A.	RS. A.	RS. A.
Jumna, including Huq Basaunta of last years of each settlement.		1st Settlement,	16,708 8	1,992 8	18,700 0
		2nd Do.,	15,500 0	1,501 0	17,001 0
		3rd Do.,	17,100 0	2,305 0	19,405 0
		4th Do.,	15,100 0	1,800 0 } 3,000 0 }	19,900 0
		5th Do.,	20,000 0	..	20,000 0
Population in 1834.	Families.	Asamee zemindar,	2,421	..	..
		Do. Khoodkasht,	829	..	..
	Persons.	Asamee zemindar,	17,278	..	..
		Do. Khoodkasht,	..	..	..
Population in 1848.	Families.	Asamee zemindar,	2,529	..	..
		Do. Khoodkasht,	913	..	..
	Persons.	Asamee zemindar,	19,471	..	..
		Do. Khoodkasht,	5,755	..	..

2 H

The establishment consisted of :—

A Peshkár, ...	... Rs.	40 a month*
,, Putwaree or Canoongo,	... ,,	15 ,,
,, Persian Mohurrir, ...	... ,,	15 ,,
,, Native Doctor, ...	... ,,	15 ,,
,, Jummadar, ...	... ,,	8 ,,
12 Chuprassees,... ...	... ,,	48 ,,
Add for		
Stationery.	... ,,	3 ,,
And repairs of Tuhseel, ...	... ,,	4 ,,
		148 ,,

or Rs. 1,776 a year.

433. A settlement on the above principles was sanc-

Seventh settle- tioned on the 17th September 1849, for
ment from 1849 to ten years, with the single modification
1859, sanctioned. that the road allowance should be raised
to its original amount. In 1815, Mr. Ross submitted a

		Add duty on imports and export.	Grand Total.
	RS. A. P.		
Number of Cattle. { Large, ...	7,430 0 0	..	..
{ Small, ...	28,461 0 0	..	..
Number of Ploughs, ...	2,397 0 0	..	..
Málzámin's balance at close of settlement,	10,655 3 3	..	..
Proposed jumma, including Huq Ba- } saunta, ... }	19,750 0 0	Subsequently raised to ... ... Rs. 20,000 Deduct basaunta & roads allowance, ,, 2,000 Net. 18,000	

The actual establishment was :—

4	Chauntrás, ...	400		Brought forward, ..	1,630
	Putwarees, ...	180		Farrash, ...	24
2	Mohurrirs, ...	240		Malbuh, ...	54
9	Chuprassees, ...	432		Charitable allowances, ..	152
2	Native Doctors, ...	360*		Add for stationery, ..	40
	Barber, ...	18		Total, ...	1,900
	Carried forward, ..	1,630			

* One of these had been for years located at Debra.

* Kirpá Rám got the appointment. His brother Devee Dás succeeded him, and when Devee Dás died, Kirpá Rám's son, Shunkur Dás, was appointed Conoongo, an office which he still holds.

report upon the working of the new system, (dated 8th December.) The measures introduced had been completely

It works satisfactorily.

successful, and not one instance of permanent default had occurred. Not the least important and beneficial change was the preparation of a settlement *misl* for each *Khut*, corresponding generally to records in a regularly surveyed and settled district.

434. The patriarchal *regime* still survived to a certain extent. The Siana continued to settle

Remnants of the patriarchal system.

petty disputes arising within his own *Khut*, with the assistance of his brethren, while larger *punchayuts* elected by the parties concerned, decided those of a graver nature affecting two or more *Khuts*, subject to the general control of the Superintendent. So satisfactory did this judicial machinery prove, that even the *Buneeas* of Kálsee are said to have preferred it to the Civil

The dustoor-ul-umul.

Court of which the Superintendent himself was Judge. The *dustoor-ul-umul* guided the village courts. This Mr. Ross compiled himself

How compiled.

from popular tradition, only making alterations where local custom was directly opposed either to our own Criminal Law or to the dictates of common sense and morality. Provisions were, for example, inserted, prohibiting the practice of compounding felonies, or the disposal of such cases, more especially murder, by the Sianas, and also declaring the accusation of witchcraft to be a punishable offence, as well as the pernicious habit of cursing the ground from motives of vengeance. An anathema of the sort had the effect of throwing the land permanently out of cultivation.

435. Kirpa Ram, after having been appointed *Peshkár*,

resigned his post, and was consequently called upon to

Kirpá Rám appointed Peshkár; resigns his post.

enter into a security for the punctual payment of the revenue to the extent of his *malzaminee* allowance, under an order of Government, dated 17th September 1849.

436. The sole remaining point worthy of note in connection with this settlement is, that the total expenses incurred amounted to the very moderate sum of Rs. 178-5-0, divided thus—

Cost of the settlement; about Rs.178.

Salary of Amlah,	...	...	... Rs.	120 0 0
Stationery, ...	...	...	... ,,	45 3 0
Bookbinding,	...	...	... ,,	13 2 0
			Total ,,	178 5 0

437. The eighth, a decennial settlement, from 1860-61

Eighth settlement from 1860-61 to 1870-71.

to 1870-71, was the work of Mr. J. C. Robertson,[*] Assistant Superintendent, Dehra Doon. It is remarkable, because no attempt had ever been made before to measure the area of the sub-division. A plane table measurement gave the following figures :—

Total Area.	Cultivated Area.
2,16,925 acres, or 338 square miles.	21,603 acres, of which 164 were *maafee*.

The gross jumma was fixed at Rs. 21,525, from which certain cesses[†] had to be deducted,

* Cf. his report, dated 7th August 1860.

† The cesses are reported to have been more recently—

Putwaree's fees,	..	..	..	..	..	Rs.	788
Lumberdar's fees,	..	..	..	..	..	,,	1,200
District Dak at $\frac{4}{100}$,	..	..	..	..	..	,,	49
					Total ,,		2,037

Basaunta, ... Rs. 1,042
Takéena or Kárkoon's allowance, ... „ 788
                                      ——
                                      1,830
                       Balance, ... „ 19,695

and also Rs. 1,000 road allowance, so that the net balance
was Rs. 18,695. The malzamin's allowance was discontinued, and the last relic of his office abolished.

438. It would be difficult to reconcile the inelastic nature of the Jounsar Bawur land revenue

Inelastic nature of the Jounsar Bawur land revenue. with Col. Young's accounts of the improvement of the country and his consequent
great expectations, were it not that Mr. Robertson discloses
the unvarnished truth : " although the country is prosperous
enough near the Simla road, I had no idea of the miserable
state of Khuts more in the interior, as Lakkao, &c., until I
had seen them. One has also to bear in mind the fact, that
if the people consider that they have been over assessed,
they can easily cross over into Náhun or Gurhwal, where
they get land on more favorable terms. In fact under the
late settlement, several of the Zemindars of the Opurlee
Uthgaon Khut did so."

439. Mr. Robertson only met with one slight difficulty
in the course of his proceedings ; " some of

Difficulty about right of forests. the Siánás at first refused to sign the Dur-
ghwasts unless they had absolute control over the jungle
and waste land, but finding opposition useless gave in."

440. The cost of this settlement * was Rs. 4,771-14-1,
including Rs. 500 allowed for making

Cost of settlement. roads into the interior.

———

* All the revenue assessed was realised without the slightest difficulty, except in
one *Khut*, where the Siáná paid his own debts with the collections, *vide* Mr. Cornwall's report, dated 18th March 1873.

441.   Although the land tax had not proved susceptible
of any material increase, Mr. Robertson's
statistics tend to show that the resources of
the pergunnah were gradually developing.

Gradual develop-
ment of internal re-
sources.

NO. OF MOUZAHS		POPULATION IN 1849-50		POPULATION IN 1860-61		LARGE CATTLE		SMALL CATTLE		PLOUGHS	
1849-50	1860-61	Zemindars	Cultivating Proprietors	Zemindars	Cultivating Proprietors	1849-50	1860-61	1849-50	1860-61	1849-50	1860-61
377	385	19,512	5,700	23,835	6,750	10,870	32,304	27,227	50,105	2,488	4,589

442.   The last settlement, commenced by Mr. Cornwall,
Assistant Superintendent, Dehra Doon,
in the beginning of 1870, has not yet
received the sanction of Government. *
The separation of the Government forests
and the definition of their boundaries† preceded the regular operations. After this, the various *Khuts* were marked
off and their number‡ was increased to 37, of which 16
have been completely surveyed and the rest partially.

Ninth settlement,
has not yet received
the sanction of Gov-
ernment.

443.   The measurements were made without the aid of
the plane table, by the simple process of
multiplying the actual length of each field
into its average breadth.

Method of mea-
surement.

444.   The increase of cultivation proved so much less
than had been expected, that in some
cases land was at first supposed to have
escaped measurement altogether, but on

Increase of culti-
vation slight.

---

* But see note at end of Section III.

† *Vide* No. 434, dated 6th December 1872, to Commissioner.

‡ The Bawur *Khut* being separated into its five component *khags*, or subdivisions,
while two were too much intermixed with others to be marked separately.

second thoughts, Mr. Cornwall perceived the difference to be due to no allowance having been formerly made—" for the fact that, whereas the fields were horizontal or nearly so in most cases, the measurements had been hypothenusal." That is to say, in the previous settlement the hypothenuse had been measured, instead of the base of the triangle, as in the present instance. Unfortunately ill-health compelled Mr. Cornwall to go to England last March, leaving his work unfinished. Indeed the people had not up to date signed the engagements, refusing to do so, until the demarcation of the waste lands had been concluded.*

445. His observations confirm those of Mr. Robertson

His observations confirm Mr. Robertson's.

about the resources of the pergunnah; the *Khuts* situated on the road between Mussooree and Chukrata, and one large *Khut* close to Chukrata itself, proved to be the best; the second best are those situated at an average distance from Kálsee and Chukrata, and the worst, those away in the interior.

446. The proposed gross assessments give a total of

Proposed assessment Rs. 26,335.

Rs. 26,335, and the expenditure up to the end of March amounted to Rs. 24,455-8-7, an outlay arising principally from the cost of the *khusruh* survey. The settlement is to be decennial, but the people clamour for an extension of 20 years.

447. Mr. Cornwall calls attention to two points clearly

Points still needing reform.

needing reformation; *firstly*, there are only eight *putwarees* in the whole pergunnah, and it is ridiculous to expect them to do the work pro-

---

* Some difficulties also turned up about the forests.

perly; their number should be doubled; each ought to live in his own circle, keep a register of transfers, and record the decision, whenever the Sianas settle a dispute; *secondly*, the decision of cases by oath, allowed under the *dustoor-ul-amul*, when a dispute could be settled in no other way, is highly objectionable. This custom leads to such bitter feuds that the men of one *Khut* often refuse to eat or sleep in another, and will not allow their children to attend a school situated in an obnoxious village. Nor do these quarrels easily die out, being handed down from father to son, and breaking out afresh whenever any misfortune befalls the man who has taken the oath or his heirs, for the mishap is always attributed to the Nemesis of perjury.

SECTION III. FISCAL HISTORY OF THE DISTRICT, CONCLUDED.

448. The sole relic of the ancient canals remaining at the time of the conquest, was the Rajpore water-course,* which, though in a very dilapidated state, still supplied the people of Dehra with drinking water. Volunteers from the Sirmore Battalion used to repair it, until the Government sanctioned † the disbursement of Rs. 954 for that purpose, at Mr. Shore's recommendation, and also authorised the levy of an annual cess of one rupee on every mill driven by it, and three rupees per beegah of land irrigated from it; the proceeds to be devoted to repairs. Under this arrangement, some thirty pucca beegahs of land were irrigated in the year. Government disclaimed all idea of making profit from so petty a work. It was simply expected to pay its own expenses. The subsequent extension of the irrigation system has been already traced. Its results remain to be considered.

Canals; their origin.

449. Sixty-seven miles of miniature canals intersect the valley. In 1871-72 they irrigated an area of 10,734 acres, and yielded a revenue of about Rs. 43,800, which rose

Revenue from Canals.

* *Vide* Shore to W. Fraser, 2nd Member, Board of Revenue, 22nd December 1825, to Major Young, 17th April 1827 ; same to Secretary Government, dated 16th June, &c., &c.

† Order of the 25th May 1826.

last year some Rs. 6,000, with a proportional increase in the irrigated area.*

DOON CANALS.

Area irrigated and revenue from water-rates 1873.

	Area in acres.	Revenue.
		RS.
Beejapore Water-Course, ...	5,432	11,616
Rajpore do., ...	2,636	5,116
Kutha Puthur do., ...	2,788	4,615
Kalunga do., ...	2,050	2,880
Jakhun do., ...	1,096	1,435
Total, ...	14,002	25,662

Total Revenue for 1872-73—

	RS.	A.	P.
Water-rates, ...	25,662	7	11
Water sold for building, &c., ...	1,905	6	3
Mill-rents, ...	21,443	3	8
Sale of produce, ...	767	4	0
Fines and sundries, ...	36	4	0
	49,814	9	10
Revenue for 1871-72, which was higher than any preceding year, ...	43,854	5	7
Increase, ...	5,960	4	3

450. Captain Willcocks, Superintendent, Doon Canals, calculates the capital represented by these works at about Rs. 5,50,000, the interest on it being between Rs. 27,000 and Rs. 28,000. The same officer has been kind enough to prepare a series of tables giving all the available information on the subject of water-rates, area irrigated, and income yielded by the canals, from the year 1864-65 to the year 1871-72.

Capital represented by the canals.

* The average area irrigated from canals may be set down at 11,000 acres, and that irrigated from nuddies at 5,000 acres. Captain Willcocks calculates that there *ought* to be 20,000 acres of canal irrigation.

BEEJAPORE WATER-COURSE.

Dates.	Area irrigated, acres.	Revenue from irrigation.	Water sold by contract, revenue from mills and miscellaneous sources.	Total yearly revenue.	Length.	Remarks.
		RS.	RS.	RS.		
1864-65	3,677	2,867	7,187	10,054		*Opened on 8th January* 1841. The water rates were low, and continued so until 1864-65, when they were increased as follows :—
1865-66	2,016	2,842	7,467	10,309		
1866-67	2,842	5,109	6,578	11,685	11 Miles.	1st Class, per acre, ... Rs. 5 0 0
1867-68	3,275	5,882	6,902	12,784		2nd do. do., ... „ 3 0 0
1868-69	5,464	8,540	5,966	14,506		3rd do. do., ... „ 2 4 0
1869-70	4,068	7,931	6,141	14,072		4th do. do., ... „ 1 4 0
1870-71	4,411	9,153	7,091	16,244		These rates remain intact at the present time.
1871-72	4,440	8,773	8,508	17,381		

RAJPORE WATER-COURSE.

Dates.	Area irrigated, acres.	Revenue from irrigation.	Water sold by contract, revenue from mills and miscellaneous sources.	Total yearly revenue.	Length.	Remarks.
		RS.	RS.	RS.		
1864-65	2,485	2,321	8,692	11,013		Opened in 1844. Water-rates up to 1864-65 :—
1865-66	1,233	2,311	8,930	11,241		1st Class, per beegah, ... Rs. 0 12 6
1866-67	1,616	3,365	8,686	12,051		2nd do. do., ... „ 0 6 3
1867-68	2,133	4,148	9,889	14,037	12 Miles.	3rd do. do., ... „ 0 5 0
1868-69	2,040	3,861	7,253	11,114		When the rates were increased as follows :—
1869-70	1,353	3,457	8,937	12,494		1st Class, per acre, ... Rs. 5 0 0
1870-71	1,827	4,163	9,040	13,203		2nd do. do., ... „ 3 0 0
1871-72	1,815	4,118	10,350	16,478		3rd do. do., ... „ 2 4 0
						4th do. do., ... „ 1 4 0
						In 1871-72 the 4th Class rates were reduced to Rs. 0-12-0 per acre; the remaining classes remained as above noted.

KUTHA PUTHUR WATER-COURSE.

Dates.	Area irrigated acres.	Revenue from irrigation.	Water sold by contract, revenue from mills and miscellaneous sources.	Total yearly revenue.	Length.	Remarks.
		RS.	RS.	RS.		
1864-65	3,009	2,278	1,258	3,536		
1865-66	1,539	2,053	1,940	3,998		
1866-67	1,762	3,559	1,811	5,370	19 Miles.	Opened in 1854. Water-rates, former and present, the same as for the Rajpore Canal.
1867-68	2,125	4,207	1,190	5,397		
1868-69	3,157	5,470	1,064	6,534		
1869-70	2,426	5,162	1,101	6,263		
1870-71	2,971	6,026	1,226	7,352		
1871-72	1,624	3,018	1,253	4,271		

KALUNGA WATER-COURSE.

Dates.	Area irrigated, acres.	Revenue from irrigation.	Water sold by contract, revenue from mills and miscellaneous sources.	Total yearly revenue.	Length.	Remarks.
		RS.	RS.	RS.		
1864-65	1,754	1,233	470	1,703		Opened *in* 1859-60. The great drawback to this canal is, that the water at head dries up in the hottest months of the year. Works are now in progress to extend the pucca channel above a mile up the Song river bed, to where there is at all times a *full and constant* flow of water. Water-rates as for Kutha Puthur.
1865-66	1,080	1,310	563	1,873		
1866-67	1,690	2,849	425	3,374	13 Miles.	
1867-68	1,604	2,795	496	3,291		
1868-69	2,078	3,240	677	3,817		
1869-70	1,165	2,071	710	2,781		
1870-71	1,589	2,808	549	3,457		
1871-72	1,718	2,705	862	3,567		

JAKHUN WATER-COURSE.

Dates.	Area irrigated, acres.	Revenue from irrigation.	Water sold by contract, revenue from mills and miscellaneous sources.	Total yearly revenue.	Length.	Remarks.
		RS,	RS.	RS.		
1864-65	1,623	922	129	1,051		
1865-66	1,023	1,290	244	1,534		
1866-67	935	1,955	385	2,340		
1867-68	1,484	2,763	465	3,228	12 Miles.	
1868-69	1,380	2,348	385	2,733		
1869-70	1,188	2,162	408	2,670		
1870-71	1,285	2,358	500	2,858		
1871-72	1,137	1,747	418	2,165		

Remarks:

Opened in 1863-64. The water-rates were the same as for other Canals up to the Rubbee of 1871-72, when owing to the unproductiveness of the soil, the poverty of the people, and the distance from a good market, special rates for this water-course were fixed.

1st Class, per acre, ... Rs. 5 0 0
2nd   do.,   do., ... „ 2 4 0
3rd   do.,   do., ... „ 2 4 0
4th   do.,   do., ... „ 0 12 0

451.   Besides irrigation, the water-power has been, from

Water-mills.

time immemorial, applied to turning mills (*gurát* or *punchukkee*), in which nearly all the grain is ground.   These machines are of simple con-struction, consisting of two stones from two to three feet in diameter laid horizontally, the lower one being immovable, the upper revolving with a horizontal wheel fixed to it, and having floats arranged obliquely in a vertical axle passing through the lower mill-stone, so as to receive a stream of water from a shoot, or funnel, with a fall of 10 or 12 feet. A machine of this sort grinds from two to twenty-five maunds a day, according to its size and the fall of the water. The average is about ten maunds.   Such mills are found on the Asun, Tonse, Sooswa, Song, and some other smaller streams.   The millers pay a rent of Rs. 2 to 4 a year to the zemindar, and take a fee of two seers per maund of grain ground.   There are government mills along the Canals of superior construction, but built on the same plan.   These are let out to contractors, who are paid two annas a maund for grinding corn, except on the Rajpore and Beejapore Canals, where the rate has been raised to 4 annas.

452.   Irrigation from wells, it has been noticed, is

No irrigation from wells; effect of the Canals.

wholly unknown.*   That from Canals, though still capable of extension, has not only already been the means of increasing the land revenue immensely, but itself directly affords the State a larger income than can be expected from the land for many a long day.   Canals, again, have had a valuable moral effect.   The powerful stimulus they have given to

---

* There was once a little from two wells on the Mahobawálá tea plantation, when in the possession of Mr. Lemarchand.

agricultural enterprise has gone far towards rousing the natives from their once incorrigible apathy.

453.   A source of revenue even more important from a purely monetary point of view, is the Excise, which yields extraordinary returns in proportion to the small size of the population, a fact unhappily due, not so much to the general prosperity of the people, as to their intemperate habits.   The receipts under this head in 1872-73 were :—

Excise; a rich source of revenue.

License fees on sale of Country liquor,	Rs.	33,959 0 0
,, ,, European do.,	,,	1,490 0 0
Intoxicating drugs, ...	,,	7,145 0 0
Opium, ...	,,	5,948 0 0
Duty on *vend*, per gallon, ...	,,	270 0 0
Fines, ...	,,	35 0 0
	,,	48,847 0 0
Kalsee, ...	,,	1,102 0 0
Chukrata, ...	,,	3,168 0 0
Total	,,	53,117 0 0

454.   Yet the Doon Excise had a very humble origin ; viz., a shop established at Dehra by Mr. Calvert,* for the vend of spirituous liquors, at the rate of Rs. 1-4 a day, or Rs. 456-4 a year. This rose to upwards of Rs. 2,000 in 1825, when a shop for the sale of ganja, bhung and churus, was started at 5 annas a day, or Rs. 114-1 a year.†   In 1825-26 the Abkáree was farmed for Rs. 2,190, but the Abkár failed, and engagements were taken from him at Rs. 1,688-2 for the

Origin of the Doon excise,

* *Vide* Settlement Report of the 5th September 1817.
† Shore to 2nd Member Board of Revenue, dated 21st November 1825. He here states that the Abkáree at one time yielded only Rs. 136-14 a-year. Cf. letters of 20th October 1826 and 20th November 1828.

2 K

following year, from the 1st October 1826. In May 1827 Mr. Shore calculated the annual excise receipts at Rs. 1,802. From the 1st October 1827 to the end of September 1828, the Abkáree was farmed at Rs. 4 a day, or Rs. 1,460 a year, and the sale of intoxicating drugs at 6 annas a day, or Rs. 136-14-0 a year; total, 1,596-14-0. The year after, 1828-29, the Abkáree fetched Rs. 6 a day or Rs. 2,190 a year, and the intoxicating drugs, 14 annas a day, or 319-6-0 a year; total 2,509-6-0. It was at first intended that the engagement should be extended to three years, on Mr. Shore's recommendation, but Major Young, perceiving the real value of this source of revenue, objected to this arrangement,* and the sale of intoxicating drugs, being put up to open auction, brought in a return of Rs. 732 in 1829-30. The Abkáree receipts, however, seem to have remained in *statu quo* until the year 1239 F. 1831-32 A. D., when they rose to Rs. 3,660, while the sale of drugs was farmed for Rs. 1,006-8-0.

455. Merely judging from figures, we should conclude that the consumption of spirits and intoxicating drugs in the district had increased tenfold in fourteen years, and, even after making due allowance for European wants, that indulgence in stimulants has since progressed to a very surprising extent, by comparison with other parts of the country. But it is necessary to bear in mind that formerly the people freely used a home-made liquor inferior to that

Progress of intemperance.

* Letter of 23rd February 1829, answered 23rd March. Cf. his Settlement Report of 9th April 1831, *vide* also letter of 14th January 1833. *N.B.*—Mr. Shore was himself alive to the pecuniary importance of the Abkáree, but objected to it on moral grounds, and consequently avoided working it more than was absolutely necessary to avoid the charge of insubordination (*vide* his Notes, *passim*).

manufactured in the government distilleries. Much of the Doon spirits must also find its way into the neighbouring hill states. Drunkenness is certainly a popular vice, and has an undoubted tendency to increase. Still the evil has not taken root so deeply as a casual glance at statistics might induce one to suppose.

456. Jounsar Bawur contributes so little to the excise

Illicit distillation in Jounsar Bawur; income from Abkáree there small.

that illicit distillation and the sale of contraband opium, &c. is, we may be sure, extensively practised there. I append a

General returns for whole district for ten years; *see* Table.

Table showing the general returns for ten years, 1862-63 to 1871-72.

457. Another much older source of revenue used to be

Transit duties.

the transit duties collected on every article of commerce going to or coming from the hills or plains. The net sum realised, after the payment of expenses, was under Rs. 10,000 in 1222 F., and not quite Rs. 9,000 in 1223 F.; the gross collections being Rs. 16,000 and Rs. 15,200 in each year, respectively The same goods had constantly to pay twice or three times over, owing to the injudicious allocation of the collecting stations.

458. The consequent obstruction to commerce being

Their abolition.

great, and the income derived not large, Government abolished these duties in 1224 F. Mr. Moore soon afterwards represented that there were 106 estates in the Doon lying waste, yielding absolutely no income to Government, from which private individuals were making immense profits by appropriating the jungle produce. At least 50,000 pieces* of timber were, he reckoned, being annually cut down and exported, with-

---

* One calculation gave the number of carts laden with timber annually leaving the Doon at 5000 ; of bullocks bearing two kurries, each, 50,000.

out any acknowledgement of the right of Government to the forests.   He therefore recommended the imposition of a cess on such exports.

459. His views were approved of (30th January 1819), and the duties being held under direct management, produced during three years (1226-7-8 F.) an average of some Rs. 4,000. In 1822* they were farmed to Surjun Negee for Rs. 5,000 a year, from 1229 F. to 1232 F. inclusive.   In 1825 (28thOctober) they were farmed to various persons at a total of Rs. 8,500 a year, from 1233 F. to 1237 F. inclusive, with the exception of the Kheree pass,† yielding from Rs 150 to 200 a year, which was held *khám*.   In 1825-26 and 1826-27 balances‡ of Rs. 1,487 and Rs. 2,701 accrued on account of the Kansrao pass.   In the two last years of the settlement, the Kheree pass was farmed at the rate of only Rs. 91 a year (30th November 1828), for three months; of Rs. 300 per annum, for the remaining year and nine months (4th February 1829).

They are again introduced.

460. Major Young was justly of opinion that Mr. Shore had been too easy on the contractors, and thought the revenue from these customs was susceptible of a very great increase.   He also noticed that the effect of competition among the farmers at the various passes had been to lower the rates sanctioned by Government, and therefore recommended the introduction

Are raised from Rs. 4,000 to about Rs. 16,000 a year, under Major Young's management.

---

* *Vide* Order of Board of Commissioners, 15th March.

† Government had sanctioned Rs. 12,000 for the construction of a road through it by Lieut. De Bude, and the passage of bullocks dragging timber along the ground had to be stopped.

‡ Cf. Letter of 8th March 1828.   Altogether, the remissions amounted to Rs. 6,000, according to Major Young, 28th November 1829.

of the *ruwanah* system, except on the Ganges and Jumna *Ghats*. But such excellent terms were offered at the next auction sale, that the former arrangements seemed likely to be equally profitable, as well as simpler, if properly managed. The highest bids* were :—

Jumna and Ganges *Ghats*,	...	...	Rs.	6,425
The other Passes,	...	...	...	„	9,595
		Total,	...	„	16,020

giving an increase of Rs. 7,220 over 1829-30. The duties were accordingly farmed at this rate for a period of three years, from 1830-31. This settlement expired on the 1st December, and another auction sale† produced an annual income of Rs. 25,345 for three years longer, giving an annual increase of Rs. 9,325. Not having

Rise to upwards of Rs. 25,345.

had direct access to the Dehra records after 1833, I owe the rest of my information on this subject to the kindness of Mr. Brereton, the present Officiating Deputy Conservator of Forests, Dehra Doon.

461. From 1839 to 1844,‡ the right of collecting the duties of the timber exports was farmed

Increased income from 1839 to 1844 and subsequently; destruction of the forests.

to Atmágeer, Mohunt of Hurdwar, for Rs. 33,500 a year. Every one continued to hack and hew away at the trees, as he pleased, only paying certain dues to the farmer, in the event of the wood being exported. The latter made his own arrangements to secure the collections at the different passes. Reckless waste was inevitable, and the fine *sál* forests began to disappear rapidly. The absence of con-

---

* 25th September 1830. Cf. 8th December 1830. Cf. 28th November 1829.

† 30th September, 1833.

‡ *Vide.* Report of Captain Bailey R.E., Deputy Conservator of Forests Dehra Doon, to Conservator of Forests N. W. Provinces, dated 14th May 1872.

servancy was absolute. The district still abounded in fine
trees, 100 or 200 years old and upwards. All these fell
before the axe, and probably the rest would have gone with
them, had the roads been a little better. The consequences of this bad system are most perceptible in the Western
Doon. In 1844, Mr. Vansittart, having ascertained that

Which are kept
under direct manage-
ment from 1844 to
1855.

Atmágeer was in the receipt of about
Rs. 80,000 a year, discontinued the lease,
and kept the collections in his own hands.
This arrangement lasted till the year 1855,
when the Forest Department was established. In the

Forest Department
established in 1855.

interval, the revenue from this source
varied from Rs. 80,000 to Rs. 100,000,
an income dearly purchased, for the destruction was something incalculable. The system of con-
servancy is still very imperfect.

462. The jurisdiction of the Department extends be-

Its jurisdiction
extends over an area
of about 450 sq.
miles; produce from
1869-70 to 1871-72.

yond the boundaries of the Doon, including the whole of the Sewaliks, together
with a portion of Seharunpore, besides
tracts leased from the Teeree Rájá. Capt.
Bailey has calculated the Forest area, exclusive of the land
rented from the Rájá, at about 450 square miles, and the
amount of produce during the years 1869-70, 1870-71,
and 1871-72, to have been as follows :—

	1869-70.	1870-71.	1871-72.	Average.
	RS.	RS.	RS.	RS.
Timber, ...	21,143	6,923	55,837	27,968
Deodar from the Bhágeerathee,	42,023	1,805	...	14,609
Minor produce, &c., ...	20,121	23,463	40,982	28,189
	83,287	32,191	96,819	70,766

Forest Revenue; averages from Rs. 25,000 to Rs. 30,000 a year.

463. The income since 1859-60 has been :—

Year.							Amount.			Remarks.
							R.	A.	P.	
1859-60, from 1st Augt. 1859 to 1st Sept.						1860,	1,33,715	1	7	Not given separately for Seharunpore and Doon.
1860-61,	„	„	Sept. 1860	„	31st Augt.	1861,	64,870	2	4	
1861-62,	„	„	Sept. 1861	„	30th Sept.	1862,	34,622	4	11	
1862-63,	„	„	Oct. 1862	„	30th Sept.	1863,	22,647	6	0	
1863-64,	„	„	May 1863	„	30th April	1864,	22,201	13	1	
1864-65,	„	„	„ 1864	„	30th March	1865,	35,860	8	11	
1865-66,	„	„	April 1865	„	31st March	1866,	24,231	6	1	
1866-67,	„	„	„ 1866	„	„	1867,	26,772	9	8	
1867-68,	„	„	„ 1867	„	„	1868,	23,331	13	7	
1868-69,	„	„	„ 1868	„	„	1869,	26,045	2	1	
1869-70,	„	„	„ 1869	„	„	1870,	74,787	14	2	
1870-71,	„	„	„ 1870	„	„	1871,	32,191	8	6	Amalgamated with Seharunpore, and cannot be separated.
1871-72,	„	„	„ 1871	„	„	1872,	96,819	0	4	
1872-73,	„	„	„ 1872	„	„	1873,	90,332	8	3	

464. Among the trees of these forests are :—

Timber trees; most common list of.

The *Acacia katechu—khair—*formerly very common; an exceedingly hard and durable timber; yielding the " katechu " or *terra japonica.*

The *Acacia serissa—sirus—*a fine tree, abundant in Seharunpore.

The *Acacia stipulata—lájwuntá—*a very beautiful tree.

The Acacia elatior—kunghár. Also other acacias.

The *Ægle marmelos—*or *bel—*yielding a very hard useful timber of a yellow color; the fruit possesses valuable medicinal properties.

The *Butea frondosa—*or ordinary *dhák—*it flowers in March; the gum is called ' Indian kino.'

The *Buddlea neemdah—jilmala.*

The *Bergera Kœnigii—*a small tree with pinnate leaves and hard white wood.

*The Bauhinia purpurea—kachnár—*a handsome tree with white and pink flowers; the *Bauhinia* also grows in the form of an enormous creeper (*racemosa Vahlii* or *malghun*), one of the most remarkable features of the forest growth.

*The Buchanania latifolia—mooria piyal—*bearing a fruit called the *cherounjee.*

The *Cedrela toona*—or toon—scarce.

The *Careya arborea*—*khoombee*—very common. The wood is not very good, as it splits if exposed to the sun, and cannot resist damp, but was formerly used for making matchlock fuses.

The *Cochlospermum gossypium*—*gujra*—conspicuous on account of its large yellow flowers—yielding a gum called *kutteela*, supposed to have cooling properties.

The *Calcaria tomentosa*—*cheela*.

The *Cordia mixa*—*lusorah*—useless as a wood, but supposed to possess medicinal virtues.

The *Cathartocarpus* or *Cassia fistula*—*amultas*—the 'Indian laburnum;' the seed of the pod, which is remarkable for its length, and is called a 'monkey stick,' is a powerful purgative. It flowers in May, and its yellow blossoms are among the chief ornaments of the forest.

The *Calosanthes Indica*—*purloo* or *purkuth*—remarkable, like the *Cassia fistula*, for the length of its pods; the timber is worthless.

The *Diospyrus lanceolata*—*tendoo*—an ebony.

The *Chretia lœvis*—or *chumror*—common.

The *Erythrina stricta*—*dhol dhák*—ornamental owing to its beautiful scarlet blossoms, but worthless as timber.

The *Fiscus cunea*—a handsome tree, apparently more common than any other fig in the Sewaliks.

The *Grislea tomentosa*—*dhaee* or *dhoula*—the red petals of which are used for dyeing.

The *Kydia calycina*.

The *Melia azedarach*—*dek*—an excellent timber tree.

The *Murraya exotica*—*belghur*—a graceful shrub.

The *Nauclea cadamba*—*kudum*; *Nauclea parvifolia*—*kaim*; and *Nauclea cordifolia*—*huldoo*—the first is a fruit tree with yellowish wood used for making furniture; the wood of the second is in great request among the Seharunpore carvers; that of the third is also suitable for furniture making.

The *Pentaptera tomentosa*—*sain*—wood admirably adapted for building purposes, held in great request.

The *Pongamia globra*—*paphree*—a good road tree, from the seeds of which 'kurrunge' oil is made.

The *Phyllanthus emblica*—*aunlá*—a most majestic tree, bearing a bitter fruit, of which the natives make pickles, &c.

The *Rottlera tinctoria—kumbhul—*a shrub very abundant at the foot of the Sewaliks, bearing a red berry used as a vermifuge, from which a dye is also made.

The *Shorea robusta—sál—*well known.

The *Syzygium jambulanum—*or *jámun—*a good road tree.

The *Salvadora lanceolata—*or *jhal—*toothpicks are made of its wood.

The *Spondias mangifera—(aumbara)—*and *Semecarpus anacardium— bhiladur—*both worthless as timber trees, but deserving mention as characteristic of the Flora. The second produces an indelible marking ink.

The *Terminalia bellerica—*or *beehra—*a tree of striking appearance, with good wood.*

465. Higher up occurs a growth belonging to the Flora of Europe, the finest specimens of which are found in the Jounsar Bawur forests.

Jounsar Bawur Forests.

About these I can find out nothing anterior to November 1868, when they were placed under the management of a separate department, having been previously in charge of the Commissioner of the Meerut Division, the *ex-officio* Conservator. Mr. C. Bagshawe, Assistant Conservator, has kindly given me a sketch of their history from that date.

Revenue from Jounsar Bawur Forests.

466. Since then the income from them has been—

1869-70,	...	...	...	Rs.	93,754	0 0
1870-71,	...	...	...	,,	36,561	2 7
1871-72,	...	...	...	,,	84,399	7 1
1872-73,	...	...	...	,,	3,50,176	1 1
		Total,	,,		5,64,890	10 9

No revenue was credited to the year 1868, although about Rs. 75,000 were realized by the sale of timber for the Chukrata barracks. Any small income that may have

---

* The Doon is, I believe, the western boundary of the *Calamus;* a species called *Royleanus* (evidently after Dr. Royle) abounds there.

been previously derived from them was credited to the Dehra Doon Division.

467. A brief description of the forests within the *Their extent.* pergunnah itself, extracted from Major Pearson's Report, No 211A., dated 12th May 1869,* has been already given. But the division also includes a large tract producing *cheer*, silver fir, *cheel*, spruce fir, and *deodar*, at the head of the Jumna and Tonse rivers, leased from Busáhir and Gurhwál. In fact, the watersheds of these rivers define the forest boundary.

468. Major Pearson estimates the contents of the *Their contents.* Jounsar Bawur forests alone at,

1st class trees.	2nd class trees.
34,000	37,000

The principal trees are—

English Names.	Native Names.	Scientific Names.
Oak.	Bunj.	*Quercus incana.*
,,	Moroo.	,, *dilatata.*
,,	Kurzoo.	,, *semicarpifolia.*
,,	Tilunj or Banee.	,, *annulata.*
Silver fir.	Morinda.	*Picea Webbiana.*
Spruce fir.	Rál.	*Abies Smitheana.*
Cheel.		*Pinus excelsa.*
Cheer.		,, *longifolia.*
Cyprus.		,, *cypressus torolosa*
Deodar.		*Cedrus deodara.*
Maple.		*Acer.*

* Cf. Report of 5th December 1869.

469. The forests within the pergunnah have been divid-
Classification. ed into three classes :—

Class I. Reserved Forests, where no person or community has the right of grazing or cut-
Reserved Forests. ting timber.

Class II. Open Forests, where the village communities
possess limited rights of grazing and cut-
Open Forests. ting timber, but which they are bound
to protect from fire. Government has
the option of making parts of these forests first class
or reserved forests, provided that the village rights are left
intact.

Class III. Village Forests, in which the villagers have
full proprietary rights, save that of selling
Village Forests. timber or fuel from them, excepting trees
planted by the village community.

470. One item of revenue remains ; that derived from
the sale of stamps. The only information
Stamp Revenue, on the subject contained in the earlier
about Rs. 25,000. records is, that in 1826 the average sale of
stamp paper was forty sheets a month of 8 annas each, equivalent to Rs. 240 a year, and in 1831-32 the revenue from
the sale of stamps was Rs. 440-8-0.*

In 1872-73 the stamp revenue was—

Gross collections,	...	...	Rs.	26,438	0	0
Refunds,	...	...	,,	1,201	12	3
		Net, ...	... ,,	25,237	2	9

The returns for the ten preceding years were—

---

* Young, 14th January 1833.

DEHRA DOON STAMP REVENUE FROM 1862-63 TO 1871-72.*

Year.	Receipts.			Charges.				Net receipt.
	Total receipts.	Stamps sold.	Balance; penalties, &c.	Discount.	Refund.	Miscellaneous.	Total.	
	RS. A. P.	RS. A. P.	RS. A. P.	RS. A. P.	RS. A. P.	RS. A. P.	RS. A. P.	RS. A. P.
1862-63, ...	11,922 3 0	11,676 12 0	245 7 0	405 8 2	365 8 0	17 9 0	788 9 2	11,133 9 10
1863-64, ...	...	...	...	...	...	...	...	15,808 5 9
1864-65, ...	16,671 12 7	16,640 0 0	31 12 7	582 10 3	742 0 0	5 3 0	1,329 13 3	15,341 15 4
1865-66, ...	15,079 10 6	14,990 14 6	88 12 0	541 13 1	590 7 0	228 11 3	1,360 15 4	13,718 11 2
1866-67, ...	18,150 15 0	18,108 0 0	42 15 0	582 10 11	651 11 0	165 0 0	1,399 5 11	6,751 9 1
1867-68, ...	24,780 4 0	24,523 0 0	257 4 0	810 15 10	1,402 5 0	228 1 6	2,441 6 4	22,338 13 8
1868-69, ...	26,695 0 0	26,170 15 0	524 1 0	737 15 6	1,121 6 0	246 5 6	2,105 11 0	24,589 5 0
1869-70, ...	23,321 1 0	22,302 10 0	1,018 7 0	780 9 0	1,108 12 0	180 0 0	2,069 5 0	21,251 12 0
1870-71, ...	23,923 9 0	23,170 0 0	753 9 0	647 11 0	258 1 0	180 0 0	1,085 12 0	22,837 13 0
1871-72, ...	18,648 11 0	18,070 15 0	577 12 0	470 0 0	478 14 0	192 0 9	1,141 9 9	17,507 1 3

* The stamp income for Jounsar Bawur cannot be given separately.

471. A comparison of the fiscal statistics at three different periods shows that the revenue, albeit not very large, has increased immensely since the conquest.

Three periods compared; immense increase of revenue.

		RS.	A.	P.
Revenue in 1817-18,	From land,	11,244	12	0
	„ excise,	456	4	0
		11,701	0	0
Revenue in 1826-27,	Land, ...	13,570	0	0
	Excise, ...	2,000	0	0 (about).
	Customs, ...	8,700	0	0 („).
	Stamps, ...	240	0	0
		24,510	0	0
Revenue in 1872-73,	Land, ...	36,717	0	0
	Excise, ...	48,847	0	0
	Stamps, ...	25,237	2	9
	Canals, ...	49,814	9	10
		1,60,615	12	7

With the exception of the item under the head of stamps and excise in 1872-73, Jounsar Bawur has been left out of this calculation, because the increase in the revenue of the subdivision has not been so marked. The Forest income has also been excluded* from the returns of the last year, owing to the impossibility of distinguishing between items realized from the sale of timber cut within the District limits, and those belonging to the sale of timber cut beyond them, yet within the Forest boundary.

* Likewise the income-tax. The following Memo. shows its *actual proceeds* from 1860-61, to the present time :—

INCOME TAX.

1860-61,	..	Rs. 28,064	14	3	1868-69,	..	Rs. 2,782	0	0
1861-62,	..	„ 29,369	3	11	1869-70,	..	„ 9,123	0	0
1862-63,	..	„ 21,413	5	11	1870-71,	..	„ 21,667	0	0
1863-64,	..	„ 16,036	3	10	1871-72,	..	„ 6,884	0	0
1864-65,	..	„ 14,662	12	5	1872-73,	..	„ 4,742	0	0

During these years deductions from official salaries paid from Treasury were shown in the Treasury accounts, being excluded from the Income tax accounts rendered to the Board.

LICENSE TAX.

1867-68,	..	Rs. 5,996	0	0

CERTIFICATE TAX.

1868-69,	..	Rs. 3,057	8	0

Note.—The printed Report on the Settlement of Dehra Doon, published in the year 1871, containing the orders of Government on Mr. C. Daniell's proceedings, did not fall into my hands, before these sheets were actually going through the press. I am therefore compelled to consign the opinions of higher authority on the subject to a note.

Mr. F. Williams, the late Commissioner, defends Mr. Daniell's unquestionably light assessments on three grounds ;* *first*, that canal irrigation is not capable of any very great extension; *second*, that the country generally is still, as above noticed, in a backward state; and *third*, that the rates in the previous settlement had been remarkably low. The first assumption might be disputed fairly enough,† but the second point must be conceded, and the third is defensible on the score both of expediency and abstract justice. To it may now be added another consideration of no less weight, viz., that, even had Mr. Daniell's judgment not merited the confidence placed in it by the Commissioner, the disturbance of a decision, in the stability of which a lapse of seven years must be presumed to have strengthened the popular faith, would have been highly impolitic. The supposition that this may have influenced the final orders of Government is not improbable.

The Commissioner's preliminary observations, although so far favorable to the Settlement Officer's discrimination, prepare us for the inevitable conclusion,‡ that "the average rates, though fair and proper, under the present circumstances of this district, are very much too low for the basis of a Permanent Settlement. The highest rate for manured and irrigated land in the first class villages is only Rs. 3-8 per acre. Late enquiries in a district below, and information gained in other districts, show that a general average rate of Rs. 12 per acre, for such soil is too low. Mr. Daniell indicates that a rate approaching to this is not unknown in the Doon, where he states that short leases and contracts may be given for from Rs. 10 to 15 per acre.

"81. There is no reason why the rate of rent in the Doon should be one-third of the rates of other districts. I am aware that it is supposed that the produce in the Doon is one-third less than that of the soil beyond the Sewalik range; but that this is the case I doubt, and if it is, it can hardly be ascribed to want of fertility in the soil of the Doon.

"82. No one who compares the richness and strength of spontaneous vegetation in the Doon, the size of the trees and bamboos, the rank nature of the reeds and rushes and grasses with the stunted growth of spontaneous products in the adjoining district below, would readily admit that there can be any natural defect in the soil. No one who has seen the luxuriance of the Otaheite sugar-cane, to take a highly cultivated crop, or the great height to which the Rhea (the China grass plant) reaches in the Doon, or the height and dense growth of the Tor

---

* *Vide* His Report, pages 4, 5, paras. 43, 49.

† Cf. para. 87.

‡ Paras. 80, 81.

Dal (Cuterolia ?) in what is classed as inferior land, dependent only on the rain, can doubt the fertility of the soil.

" 83. In all tracts, as far as my experience goes, which have been unhealthy as the Doon has been, a slovenly style of tillage (the result originally of prostration from continued sickness) prevails for a long time.

" When man improves his work, it can hardly be doubted that the soil will respond, and as the population increases, rents will rise, if not to treble what they now are, which would be about the present standard of rents below, certainly to double the present rates. Probably the anticipation of this had some weight in the instructions given regarding Permanent Settlement in the Doon.

" 84. Finally, as far as this subject is concerned, Permanent Settlement surely should not be made in a district the rates of settlement of which are, on the total area, 3 annas 6 pie, *i. e.*, not sixpence per acre; on the productive area, 7 annas 4 pie and a fraction, not a shilling per acre; and on the cultivated area, 13 annas and 1 pie, a little over one shilling and sixpence per acre."

Beyond quoting these cogent arguments, I need not enlarge upon the question of a Permanent Settlement, one postponed indefinitely by the orders of 1870, rendering the adequacy of the prevalent rent-rates a condition indispensable to it.

The Board of Revenue endorsed Mr. Williams' views (2nd August 1871), only suggesting that, " taking into consideration the backwardness of the tract, and the transition state through which the Doon, in common with other parts of these provinces, is passing" a settlement for twenty years at Mr. Daniell's rates might be sufficient. The Government accordingly confirmed it up to the 30th June 1886, pronouncing, like the Commissioner and the Board, the settlement " to be light but not too light to warrant its being sanctioned.* There is much to be said in favor of low assessments in the Doon. The climate in most places is bad, and it is difficult to tempt cultivators to settle there. The soil is shallow and stony, and excepting. where irrigation from rivers or canals exists, it produces light returns. The backwardness of the valley is evidenced by the large proportion of holdings which pay rent in kind.† On these grounds the Lieutenant-Governor is prepared to confirm the settlement, but only for a period of 20 years. That period will be sufficient to allow for much development of agricultural means and wealth, and for extension of cultivation, while a longer term would involve an unnecessary sacrifice of the Government revenue. The settlement is accordingly confirmed till the 30th June 1886."

An increase of 9 pie per acre in the jumma has been attributed to the effects of irrigation, on the assumption of Mr. Daniell's data being correct. " The cultivated area of the 339 Khalsa villages in 1866 was 37,181 acres, and the incidence of the revenue on it was 11 annas 7 pie, which is a rise of 1 anna 1 pie over the

---

* *Vide* Resolution No. 1245A. 1873, para. 10. cf. para. 6.

† This is certainly true in the present instance, but the rule has its exceptions. An experienced settlement officer pointedly remarks : " Bundelkhund is not advanced because money rents are uni. versal, nor are Shamlee and Boorhanuh (zillah Moozuffernugger) backward because kind rents and crop rates are general."

revenue rate of 1848. Of these 37,181 acres, 12,663, or one-third, were irrigated. In 1848, 7,326 acres, or one-fourth of the cultivation, was irrigated. This increase (due to new canals) would alone account for a large part of the rise in the general revenue rate. Mr. Daniell calculates that, of the revenue as fixed by him, Rs. 4,747 are due to canals, which irrigate 8,085 acres. The irrigation rate is, therefore, 9 annas 4 pie, and this rate multiplied into the increased proportion of irrigation (one-twelfth* of the cultivated area) accounts for a rise of 9 pie per acre. The entire rise, therefore, attributable to improvement in the climate, increase of population, and rise on prices, is only 4 pie per acre."

As my own experience does not warrant my discussing the question of rent-rates, and it has nowhere been thoroughly gone into, either by the Government or the Board of Revenue, I may be permitted to quote the remarks of an anonymous writer on this subject, without, at the same time, committing myself unreservedly to his opinions.† "Mr. Daniell describes at some length his plan of operations. For purposes of assessment he distributed the soils of the district into three great classes—Meesun, Roslee and Dakur, and lastly Sankra—corresponding to manured land, loam, and light sandy land; and each of these again into irrigated and dry. According as villages contained the best lands in greater or less proportion and quality, he classed them as Nos. I., II., III. The rent-rates assumed on these soils are undoubtedly very low, even when the backwardness of the country has been taken into consideration. The highest rent-rate on the best irrigated meesun, apparently a sort of orchard land, is Rs 3-8-0 an acre, on the next Rs. 3-0-0, and on the last Rs. 2-8-0. The corresponding rent-rates assumed on the loam are Rs. 2-4-0, Rs. 1-12-0, and Rs. 1-8-0; and for the light soil Rs. 1-4-0, Rs. 1-2-0, and Rs. 1-0-0. By deducting some 40 or 50 per cent. from the irrigated rates we shall arrive at the respective dry rates for each acre. The proof Mr. Daniell gives of the adequacy and fairness of these rates is insufficient and unsatisfactory. In order to prove the rates applied to Class No. I of the villages, he takes a total area of 8,923 acres from among these villages, assumes their rental, by a mode of his own, to be Rs. 20,110, then applies his various soil rates to the net areas, and finds a total result of Rs. 30,162. He, therefore, concludes that his rates are fair and adequate as representatives of actual value; and that the ratio they bear one to the other accord with the varying qualities of the soils to which they apply. Now had the Rs. 20,110 been the actual rental of the area taken out, Mr. Daniell's conclusions might have been accepted. But his figures are partly assumptions. The Rs. 20,110, are made up of three items—(1), Rs. 3,178, which is described as the rental of 1,635 acres under *puttas* yielding an "average" rate of Rs. 1-15 an acre; (2), Rs. 10,500, which is described as the rental of 3,000 acres—" for which

---

* *i. e.*, the difference between the area irrigated in 1848, or one-fourth, and that irrigated in 1866, or one-third; the sum then stands thus :—

$$\frac{112 \text{ P} \times 3098}{37181} = 9 \text{ P.}$$

† *Vide* the *Pioneer* of October 14th 1873.

I estimate a rate of Rs. 3-8-0 "—and (3), Rs. 6,482, the rental of 4,288 acres, which are "estimated to yield throughout an average of Rs. 1-8-0." Now this is not a record of actuals with which an assumed rental should be compared. It is a rental assumed in one fashion to be compared with a rental assumed in another. The principal items of the Rs. 20,110 are the direct results of the application of *assumed* rates, so that the value of the process as an independent proof of the rates finally assumed is *nil*. In para. 26, Mr. Daniell tells us, that some of the lands included under item 2, rented at from Rs. 10 to Rs. 15 per acre. Why did he not let us have the actuals of some *one* year? These data may have been included in some statements referred to as not printed in the present report, but this is unfortunate, as we should have been in possession of some data by which to judge of the rates applied to Class No. 1.; so also for the *third* item which, it seems, includes merely lands paying rent in kind. But why did not the report give us the past ten years' average net produce? As the proof stands it is valueless; had the rates finally assumed been 50 per cent. higher the same proof could have been turned to account, &c., &c."

Indeed, Mr. Daniell's estimates have been pronounced even by Government to be mainly 'conjectural,' but, however unsatisfactory the process criticised may have been in theory, there can be little doubt as to the practical justice of his general conclusions, and it has, at any rate, been admitted by the highest revenue authorities in these provinces.

The same writer adds, "a rate of $4\frac{1}{2}d.$ an acre for a fertile and extensively cultivated country, and where not cultivated, covered with forest and rich vegetation is certainly a startling one." Not so startling as may appear at first sight— for the absolutely barren area has here been left out of the consideration altogether, the forests, which, having little or nothing to do with it, ought to have been , have not, and, lastly, the words "rich vegetation," when taken in connection with the context, hardly convey a correct idea of the capabilities of the balance. The pith of the statistics published with the Government report will be found in the additional Appendices to this compilation.*

Letter No. 1036a. of 1873, from the Officiating Secretary to the Government N. W. Provinces to the Officiating Secretary Board of Revenue, dated 16th May, contains the only orders that have, so far as I am aware, been hitherto passed on Mr. Cornwall's settlement report. It praises him for "the labor, intelligence and care" bestowed by him on the work; but postpones orders in confirmation of the assessments, "until the Superintendent of the Doon has reported the final adjustment of boundaries in connection with the forests, and until the question of the Siánás' agreement to the jummas has been settled;" declines to fetter the discretion of a future government by extending the settlement beyond a term of ten years; and refuses to interfere with the decision of cases by oath. It is silent on the subject of putwarries, and refers the educational question to the Director of Public Instruction.

* A, B, C.

SECTION IV. MISCELLANEOUS.

CONCLUSION.

472. Although the population of the Doon has more

Population of the Doon, although thin, has more than quadrupled in fifty-nine years. than quadrupled in fifty-nine years of British rule, the District is far from being densely inhabited, as the people number barely 76,413 souls to 673 square miles of country.

473. A rough census taken immediately after the con-

First and second Census. quest, set down the population at 17,000 or thereabouts. Another followed in the year 1823, giving*

Men,	... ...	7,465	
Boys,	... ...	4,309	Families,... ... 4,962
Women,	... ...	6,133	Houses, ... 8,188
Girls,	... ...	2,031	
?	... ...	241	

Total,   20,179,

to whom Mr. Shore, writing in 1827, added 4,100 persons belonging to the Sirmore Battalion, besides 250 attached to the Courts and Jail, in all 24,529; without counting about 1,000 hill men who came down every cold weather to seek employment, and as many more who came from the plains to

Effect of the Goorkha invasion on the proportion of children to adults. cut bamboos and timber, to make lime, or *khut,* and for other mercantile purposes. He attributed the paucity of children to the slaughter of the adult males during the Goorkha invasion,

---

* *Vide* Mr. Shore's Report of the 1st May.

and to the extensive practice of female infanticide, designed to save good looking girls from falling into the hands of the invaders. Hence the district was full of old widows and young unmarried men under thirty years of age. The only place then approaching to anything like a town was Dehra, containing 518 houses and 2,126 inhabitants. Gooroo Ram Ráe had, says tradition, raised it from the rank of a village, whereas Jakhun and Nuwada, once flourishing towns, had degenerated into mere hamlets.

474. In 1847-48 the population* is supposed to have

Calculations made by Mr. A. Ross in 1847-48. been—

Hindoos, ...	Agricultural,	...	18,534
	Non-Agricultural,	...	4,856
Mahommedans, ...	Agricultural,	...	4,783
	Non-Agricultural,	...	3,910
	Total,	...	32,083

475. No census was taken in 1853. That of 1865

Census of 1865. stands thus—

				Western Doon.	Eastern Doon.	Total.
POPULATION.	Hindoos,	Agricultural,	Males, { Adult, ..	4,751	2,369	7,120
			{ Children, ..	2,514	1,262	3,776
			Females, { Adult, ..	3,602	2,270	5,872
			{ Children, ..	1,806	979	2,785
		Non-Agricultural,	Males, { Adult, ..	13,245	2,869	16,114
			{ Children, ..	5,145	891	6,036
			Females, { Adult, ..	7,039	1,395	8,434
			{ Children, ..	3,940	754	4,694
	Mahomedans and others not Hindoos.	Agricultural,	Males, { Adult, ..	802	60	862
			{ Children, ..	451	30	481
			Females, { Adult, ..	578	46	624
			{ Children, ..	347	25	372
		Non-Agricultural,	Males, { Adult, ..	4,019	373	4,398
			{ Children, ..	1,421	107	1,528
			Females, { Adult, ..	1,936	110	2,046
			{ Children, ..	1,097	60	1,157
		Total, ...		52,693	13,606	66,299
No. of persons to each square British Statute mile of 640 acres each, ...				149	42	191

* Memo. on the Statistics of the N. W. P., p. 179½.

The total being 66,299, the population would therefore

Subsequent calcu-
lations. seem to have almost trebled in thirty-eight years, and has since increased by some 10,000. The large hill stations of Mussooree and Landour were, however, omitted from the above calculation, and Dehra is given as the only town in the district containing more than 2,000 inhabitants, viz., 6,847, although Rajpore is said to have had a population of 2,285 in December 1865, while Landour and Mussooree contained at the same period no fewer than 3,112 inhabitants; 311 Europeans, and 2,801 natives. Strange to say, in spite of increased traffic, Rajpore now appears with a population of only 1,959; Dehra numbering 7,316, and the two hill stations 3,048;

Mussooree,	... {	Europeans, ...	...	...	210	
		Natives,	...	...	1,464	1,674
Landour,...	... {	Europeans, ...	...	...	85	
		Natives,	...	...	1,289	1,374
						3,048*

476. The permanent European population of the Doon

Permanent Euro-
pean population up-
wards of 700. is—

Dehra Mu- nicipality,	{	Males,...	...	160	
		Females,	...	227	387
Mussooree, ...	{	Males,...	...	121	
		Females,	...	89	210
Landour, ...	{	Males,...	...	35	
		Females,	...	50	85
Dehra Cantonment,...	{	Males,...	...	8	
		Females,	...	17	25
		Total,	...		707†

* During the hot season, they have a large floating population, which does not enter into this calculation.

† This return includes only "European-born British subjects," but seems to be below the mark.

477. The official return of the Native Christian com-

Native Christians, 312?

munity differs with the figures extracted from the Mission reports, giving a much smaller total :—

Males,	...	...	...	...	126
Females,	...	...	...	...	186
					312

This must surely exclude the agricultural colony at Annfield.

478. In 1827 Major Young estimated the population

Population of Jounsar Bawur; Major Young's calculations in 1327; Mr. Ross' in 1848-49.

of Jounsar Bawur at 23,228 souls,* or about the same as that of the Doon. According to a statement quoted above, attached to Mr. A. Ross' report of the 30th April 1849, it fell to 17,278 in 1834, and rose to 19,471 in 1848, but the return published in the Statistics, N. W. Provinces, gives a higher estimate :—

Hindoos,	...	... {	Agricultural, ...	24,515
			Non-Agricultural,...	145
Mahomedans, &c.,	... {		Agricultural, ...	
			Non-Agricultural,...	24
			Total, ...	24,684

479. According to the Census Report of 1865, the

Census of 1865.

population had then risen to 36,532, made up as follows: —

* Jounsar,	...	... 17,983	Villages,	...	...	358
Kandé,	...	... 2,981	„	...	...	45
Bawur,	...	... 2,264	„	...	...	47
		23,228				450

							Jounsar Bawur.
POPULATION.	Hindoos,	Agricultural,	Males,	Adult,	..	..	8,324
				Children,	..	..	4,971
			Females,	Adult,	..	..	5,800
				Children,	..	..	3,944
		Non-Agricultural,	Males,	Adult,	..	..	1,366
				Children,	..	..	824
			Females,	Adult,	..	..	985
				Children,	..	..	598
	Mahomedans and others not Hindoos,	Agricultural,	Males,	Adult,	..	..	1,571
				Children,	..	..	1,106
			Females,	Adult,	..	..	1,156
				Children,	..	..	819
		Non-Agricultural,	Males,	Adult,	..	..	1,625
				Children,	..	..	1,186
			Females,	Adult,	..	..	1,339
				Children,	..	..	918
				Total,	..	..	36,532
No. of persons to each square British statute mile of 640 acres each,							109

480. It is now said to be 40,533, about 118 to the square mile, so that, unless the former calculations were erroneous, the rate of increase has been remarkably slow, a fact attributable to polyandry. The pergunnah contains no town with a population of above 2,000. A statement prepared in the Dehra Office represents the European element existing in connection with the Chukrata Cantonments to be much smaller than it really is:

Actual population of Jounsar Bawur.

European element.

Males, ... 315
Females, ... 172
                                                       ———
                                                       487,

for the actual strength of the 92nd Highlanders now quartered there is 884 men, without counting the miscellaneous European residents.*

* For the published returns of 1872, *see* additional Appendix D.

481.   The agricultural population of the district is that

Agricultural population; that of the Doon, how classified. which naturally claims the most atten-tion.   In the Doon, the cultivators are, as in the plains, distributed into three broad divisions; small proprietors cultivating their own land, cultivators with rights of occupancy, and tenants-at-will.   The following figures are supposed to give their numbers and the amount of land held by each class.*

TENANTS.				AREA IN ACRES.			
Former settlement.		Current settlement.		Former settlement.		Current settlement.	
Heredi-tary.	Non-heredi-tary.	Heridi-tary.	Non-heredi-tary.	Heredi-tary.	Non-heredi-tary.	Heredi-tary.	Non-heredi-tary.
2,478	2,384	3,083	4,734	12,771	8,924	12,482	17,305

* The total amount of land almost agrees with the cultivated area given higher up, p. 13, but these calculations can hardly be reconciled with those published in the Sudder Board's Report on Mr. Daniell's settlement, para. 30 :—

	Acres.	Per cent.
1. Cultivated by tenants paying in kind, ...	16,547	43·8
2. Cultivated by tenants with rights of occupancy paying in cash, ...	7,510	19·9
3. Cultivated by other tenants paying under terms of lease or contract in cash, ...	5,416	14·4
4. Cultivated by Proprietors, ...	8,254	21·9
	37,727	100

One peculiar sort of tenure, now obselete, was that called " Daeen." There were eight Daeens ; i. e., " village community talookas, extending over 109 villages, each talooka having an interest in some or all of the villages." Each used to be divided in 36 Jhoolahs. Mr. Ross did not materially interfere with them, making the settle-ment mahulwar. " In each village each Daeen estate was separately assessed." Mr. Daniell, on the contrary, settled them village by village. The old Daeens comprised " the land stretching from the vicinity of Dehra up the southern slope of the hills."

HEREDITARY TENANTS OF CURRENT SETTLEMENT.		NON-HEREDITARY TENANTS OF CURRENT SETTLEMENT.	
Number.	Area.	Number.	Area.
3,083	12,482, each 4 acres.	4,734	17,305, each 3 acres 2 roods.

Small proprietors cultivating their own land (*seer*).

Number.	Area.
749	12,067 acres, each about 16 acres.

482. The average holding of mere cultivators hence

Size of holdings, actual and hypothetical.

appears to be remarkably small; certainly not large enough to support a growing family, since five acres of ordinary land (or twenty-six local beegahs * five biswahs) are not admitted to yield the tenant a clear profit of more than Rs. 35 a year, and the estimate generally given of what is popularly considered a large, middling, or small holding, must be pronounced purely hypothetical;

Large holding.—38 acres, or about 200 *beegahs kutcha* (with four ploughs and sixteen bullocks).

Middling holding.—80 *beegahs kutcha* (with two ploughs and eight bullocks).

Small holding.—40 *beegahs kutcha* (with one plough and two bullocks).

483. It is indeed quite certain that tenants with more

---

* There being 5 beegahs, 5 biswahs *kham*, in one acre, and three kutcha beegahs in one pucca beegah, or 52½ yards square.

than forty kutcha beegahs under cultivation are seldom found, and few can gain a livelihood without having occasional recourse to other devices than tillage; petty trade, for instance, in goats and sheep, or hiring their services and those of their families at intervals between the seasons of sowing and reaping.

Few cultivators can support themselves solely by tillage.

484. It may be inferred that the peasantry are universally in debt; nothing more nor less, in fact, than bondsmen of the small Buneea money-lender, but in this respect they are no worse off than their brethren south of the Sewaliks. The interest on loans of course varies with the position of the creditor and the security offered. The lowest rate ever taken is 12 per cent. A well-to-do man pays 18 per cent. The average is about 24 per cent., though 37 per cent. is not uncommon, and an arrangement is almost always made by which the money lender secures from six to twelve months' interest, even if the debt be paid within twenty-four hours of the loan. The Doon Mahajun is, so far, not more grasping than his brother harpy of the plains.

Depressed condition of the peasantry; interest on loans.

485. But the agriculturist here labors under peculiar disadvantages. The breed of cattle, it has been remarked, is poor, and two bullocks cannot plough more than twenty-five *kutcha beegahs* in the year. Four bullocks generally keep forty beegahs under cultivation. A plough is called *kutcha* or *pucca* according as one pair of bullocks is yoked in it, or two. The amount of capital represented by each is thus made up—

Inferiority of the cattle prejudicial to agriculture; capital represented by one plough.

2 N

Bullocks (two, or four, as the case
may be,) ... ... Rs. 50   0   0 or Rs. 100-0-0
Plough, ... „   1   8   0
Muhruh, (clod-crusher,) ... ... „   2   4   0
Dundálee, (weeder or sort of harrow
with very long teeth,) ... ... „   0   4   0
Joolá, (yoke,) &c., ... „   0   7   C
Durántee, (sickle,) ... ... „   0   2   0
Khoorpá, ... „   0   3   0
Kootlá, (hoe,) ... ... „   0   4   0
Páthul, (a sort of billhook,) ... „   0   8   C
Kulháree, ... „   1   0   0
Jundrá, (the ordinary harrow, or *gáhin*,) „   0   4   0

Total, „   56 12   0 or Rs. 106-12-0.

486.   Considering their inferior character, the price of
Pasturage.   cattle is high.   An investment in live
stock, moreover, is very unsafe, foot and
mouth disease, &c., being endemic.   Yet there is no want
of good pasturage.   The Government forests, with their area
of nearly 200,000 acres, afforded the best, till lately.   The
rates charged were low, one anna a season per bullock or
cow; three, per buffalo; four, per camel, and 6 pie, per goat
or sheep.   In the Eastern Doon from Mohun to Hurdwar,
the people have been deprived of this boon, and at one time
an abortive attempt was made to stop grazing altogther.

487.   The relative proportions of tenants paying rent in
Tenants paying   money and kind approximately are—
rent in money and
kind; rent-rates.

	Cash.	Kind.
No. of tenants, ...	3,245	4,404
Area in acres, ...	10,365	17,618
Per beegah, annas, ...	7	8

In the immediate vicinity of Dehra, rents are usually paid in money, at the rate of from 3 annas to 8 annas a *kutcha beegah.* Generally speaking, the lowest rate is 3 annas, and the highest 12 annas, except in particular cases; for instance, 'kitchen gardens' in the possession of *Mális,* and yielding produce that bears a special value, such as potatoes, *paundá,* vegetables, &c. Land of this sort some-times fetches Rs. 2-8-0 a beegah.

488. Act X. of 1859 has had no time to affect the
Act X. has not had time to affect rent-rates. rent-rates in any way, having been in-troduced quite recently. Indeed hardly any one as yet understands the meaning of it, nor does the valley present a promising field of enter-prise for native *mukhtyars.*

489. Below the Himalaya, the agricultural process does
Method of cul-tivation. not differ essentially from that of the low-lands. The facilities for irrigation from canals and nuddees are, we have seen, great. Of manure, on the contrary, there is a great deficiency. One peculiarity, already noticed, is that, on the slopes of the hills and sides of ravines, the fields have to be cut in steps, one above another. Mr. Shore's des-cription of this contrivance, called "*kheel*" cultivation, is not quite correct; "it is made on the steep banks of
Kheel cultivation. ravines or hills which are covered with underwood, and is practicable in the same place once in from six to twelve years. The underwood is cut in January and left to dry. In the end of April it is burnt, and the ashes form the manure. The grain is then thrown on it, as the steepness of the ground would prevent any ploughing or harrowing. Mundooa, moonj, mash,

and some others are the grains thus sown; sometimes two or more are mixed together." He is decidedly mistaken in supposing that what is ordinarily understood by *kheel* cultivation is only practicable once every six or twelve years in the same place, and should have added, that, where ploughing is impossible, the land is prepared for the reception of the seed with a *koontlee* (*gaintlee*), a kind of pick. These terrace-like fields are also often skilfully irrigated from the mountain rills and bear first class rice.

490. According to the same authority, the usual rotation of crops in good land is: first, rice,

Rotation of crops; fallow land. second-class, sown in April and cut in August-September; next wheat, sown in October-November, and cut in April-May; then *til*, sown in June and cut in October-November; after which the land lies fallow till April, thus yielding three crops in two years. More recent enquiries give; first of all, wheat; then, rice; and, after that, *mundwá* and *tor*. The land where the latter has been reaped, ordinarily lies fallow, it is alleged, for a year; where the former, for six months, and then the sowing recommences in the same order. The richest soils alone yield two crops, and generally but one is annually sown in the same land. Not long ago, it was the custom, on account of the large quantity of land available in proportion to the demand, to cultivate a patch of jungle, and after reaping one crop, to immediately abandon it for another clearing. Now only the worst land is allowed to lie fallow any length of time, being meanwhile turned into grazing ground, so as to benefit from the manure of the cattle feeding upon it.

491. I append some calculations about the average out-

turn and value per acre of each crop, made by an intelligent Revenue officer, Kidár Narain,
Tuhseeldar of Dehra.*

Khureef crops; their yield, &c., per acre.

Average Out-turn and Value per acre of each crop.

Name of crop.	Average produce per acre, kutcha.	Value.	Season of sowing.	Season of reaping.	Cost of production per acre.
	MDS. SRS. C.	RS. A. P.			RS. A. P.
Dhán, chaitroo,	15 30 0	9 0 0	Chait.	Bhádon.	7 14 0
„ hultioo,	15 13 0	9 0 0	Jeth and Asárh.	Ditto.	7 14 0
„ kyáree,	31 20 0	21 0 0	Jeth.	Ditto.	13 2 0
Mundwá, ...	19 27 8	13 2 0			10 8 0
Til, ...	3 37 8	6 4 9	Asárh.	Mungsir.	
Oorud, ...	10 20 0	8 6 4			5 4 0
Lobya, koolhut,	7 35 0	7 14 0			
Mukkee, ...	10 20 0	7 0 0			
Sánwuk, ...	21 0 0	7 0 0	Asárh.	Bhádon.	5 4 0
Kungnee, ...	10 20 0	7 0 0			
Tuar, ...	10 20 0	7 0 0	Phágon.	Mungsir.	3 15 0
Arvee, ...	131 10 0	43 12 0	Jeth.	Bhadon to Mungsir.	32 2 6
Potatoes(*Deshee*),	157 20 0	157 8 0	Koár.	Mágh.	70 14 0
„ (*Puháree*),	105 0 0	78 13 11	Jeth.	Sáwun and Bhádon.	47 4 0
Paunda, ...	... ...	131 4 0	Chait and	Kuwár	63 0 0
Sugar-cane, ...	... ...	63 0 0	Baisákh.		31 8 0
Ginger,... ...	78 30 0	78 12 0	Jeth and Asárh.	Kátik and Mungsir.	26 4 0
Huldee, ...	19 27 8	39 6 0			26 4 0
Red peppre, ...	10 20 0	52 8 0			26 4 0

492. The calculation in the case of *chaitroo*, &c., is for
rice in the husk. *Arvee (caladium esculentum)* is princi-

* Now of Shamlee.

pally cultivated by Mális and Kunjras who begin dig-
ging it up in Bhadon. *Paunda,* sugar-
In what propor-
tions various khur-
reef crops are sown.
cane eaten in its natural state, is sown
only in the very best land, requiring plenty
of manure and artificial irrigation. The stumps are often
left standing and allowed to grow up again, under the
name of *moondá;* Rs. 131 would give, at one anna a stick,
2,096 sticks per acre. The sugar-cane, from which sugar
is made, *eekh,* is rarely sown; Rs. 63, at one pice a stick,
would give 4,032 sticks. The area under rice is said to
be 13,743 acres; under *mundwá,* 6,412; under *oorud,* 2,527;
under *tuar,* 2,401; under *til* and *torya,* 2,296; under *mukkee,*
1,135; under sugar-cane, 569; under vegetables, 599; while
miscellaneous khureef crops occupy 8,000 acres. The khureef is further characterised by a great scarcity of cotton,
juwar, and *bajra.* Ginger, turmeric, and red pepper, needing
a generous soil, abundant manuring, and liberal irrigation,
are only cultivated in small quantities, here and there.

493.   The area under wheat is said to be 12,890 acres;
Rubbee crops their
yield, &c.
under barley, 5,228; under *surson* and
alsee, 1,035; and under *mussoor,* 850.
Onions, garlic and tobacco, requiring a good soil and canal
In what propor-
tions cultivated.
irrigation, are only cultivated by Malies.
Oats and gram are scarce, being seldom
cultivated except by Europeans.

Name of Crop.	Average produce per acre, kutcha.	Value.	Season of sowing.	Season of reaping.	Cost of production per acre.
	MDS. SRS. C.	R A. P.			R. A. P.
Wheat, ...	15 30 0	12 9 6	} Kátik.	Jeth.	7 3 6
Barley, ...	21 0 0	10 8 0			6 14 3

Name of crop.	Average produce per acre, kutcha.	Value.	Time of sowing.	Time of reaping.	Cost of production.
	MDS. SRS. C.	RS. A. P			RS. A. P.
Jaí, ...	21 0 0	10 8 0 ⎫			7 3 6
Gram and peas, ...	10 20 0	5 4 0 ⎪			5 4 0*
Surson, ...	11 32 8	11 13 0 ⎬ Kátik.	Jeth.		6 9 0
Musoor, ...	10 20 0	5 4 0 ⎭			3 15 0
Onions, ...	204 30 0	51 3 0 ⎫			26 4 0
Garlic, ...	52 20 0	52 8 0 ⎬ Phágan and Chait.	Jeth.		26 4 0
Tobacco, ...	15 30 0	39 6 0 ⎭			31 8 0

494. The Hon'ble Mr. Shore's statistics on the same
Mr. Shore's calcu-   subject deserve to be reproduced.
lations on the same
subject.

Average Produce of different Grains, Khureef Crops.

Crops.	Seers of seed sown per beegah.	Seers of produce per beegah.	How many fold.	Average price per Rupee in pucca seers.
Rice, 1st quality, ∴	3	200	66?	35
„ 2nd „ ...	13	240	18	40
„ 3rd „ ...	5	160	32	35
Mundwá, ...	2	160	80	50
Oorud, ...	2	80	40	25
Koolhut or Gahut, ...	2	40	20	30
Jungoora or Sonk, ...	2	80	40	50
Oil seeds.				
Til, ...	½	40	80	30
Torya, ...	5	85	17	35

* The Tuhseeldar explains the equality of value and cost of production by the fact
that very little is sown, and, not to sell, but for the cultivator's own use.

Crops.			Seers of seed sown per beegah.	Seers of produce per beegah.	How many fold.	Average price per Rupee in pucca seers.
				Rubbee.		
Wheat,	...	...	13	120	$9\frac{1}{4}$	35
Barley,	...	...	10	240	24	40
Gram,	...	...	10	160	16	35
Gulda,	...	...	5	80	16	60
Musooree,	...	...	5	80	16	35
Oil seeds.						
Alsee,	...	...	5	40	8	30
Surson,	...	...	2	80	40	35

495. The grain produced is not nearly sufficient for

Famines unknown in spite of rise in prices.

home consumption ; prices, too, have risen, and still have a tendency to rise higher. Yet a famine has never occurred within the historic period, proof positive that the district cannot have been at any time very thickly populated. In 1861, the distress nowhere went beyond a scarcity, and the famine works* on the road through the Mohun Pass amply sufficed to meet the wants of all those needing relief. A tabular form prepared in the Superintendent's office, showing the prices current from 1861 to 1870 inclusive, is printed among the Appendices.†

496. One branch of agriculture peculiar to the Doon

Tea cultivation in the Doon ; its history.

is the culture of tea. A brief notice of its origin and progress is indispensable. Dr. Royle,‡ Superintendent of the Botanical Garden, Seharunpore, first recommended the experi-

---

* They were chiefly frequented by people from Seharunpore and other districts.
† Appendix XIV.
‡ Productive Resources of India, p. 258 *sq.*

ment of tea cultivation in our Himalayan possessions, to the Indian Government, in the year 1827, and again expressed his views in a report* to the Governor-General, Lord W. Bentinck, during the latter's visit to Seharunpore in 1831. About the same time, Dr. Wallich presented a paper to the Committtee of the House of Commons on the affairs of India, urging the cultivation of tea in the districts of Kumaon, Gurhwál, and Sirmore. Dr. Royle afterwards recurred to the subject in the introductory chapter to his illustrations of the Botany of the Himalayan mountains, in 1833.

497. Jurapanee, half way between Rajpore and Mussooree, was, he contended, one of the most favorable situations for an experiment of the kind (1834). Meanwhile, Lord W. Bentinck had, with the sanction of the Court of Directors, determined to give tea cultivation a fair trial, and a Committee was appointed to elaborate a plan for carrying out the design. The conclusion arrived at was, that "the proposed experiment might be made, with great probability of success, in the lower hills and vallies of the Himalayan range." To this they were, in a great measure, led by the fact, "that in the mountainous tracts of our northern and eastern frontier, several species of plants are found indigenous, which are also natives of China, and are not met with in other parts of the world." In 1835, tea plants reared from seeds of the Bohea tea were distributed to the most promising districts, and Dr. Falconer, Dr. Royle's successor, having chosen Gurhwál for the scene of his first

Sidenote: Jurápánee, the most eligible site for tea cultivation, according to Dr. Royle; Committee appointed.

Sidenote: Nurseries established in Gurhwál.

* Published in the Journal of the Asiatic Society of Calcutta, February 1832.

experiments, sent intelligence to his predecessor, in May 1838, that some plants, the produce of seeds from the Koth nursery in Gurhwál, were actually growing at Seharunpore itself. That they would flourish in the Doon seemed certain, but Dr. Royle remained constant to his original opinion in favor of Jurápánee.*

498.   Other counsels prevailed, and a Government plantation was started at Kowlageer near Dehra, under the management of Dr. Jameson, in the year 1844.   The farm covered 400 acres of good soil composed of clay and vegetable matter, with a slight mixture of sand, resting on the usual shingly subsoil of limestone, sandstone, clay slate, quartz, &c., &c., found in the surrounding mountains.   It was carried on with fluctuating success for twenty-three years.   In his report of 1850, Mr. Fortune,† a gentleman deputed by Government to visit the various plantations, stated, that "the plants, generally, did not appear to him to be in that fresh and vigorous condition which he had been accustomed to see in good Chinese plantations."   His report of 1856 was much more favorable, and he attributed the improvement to his own suggestions.   This elicited a rejoinder from the Superintendent of the Seharunpore gardens, who pointed out that, whereas Mr. Fortune now admitted the plants to be equal to any in China, he had previously condemned the Doon as unfitted for tea cultivation on insufficient data, and with regard to his *suggestions*, the improvement could hardly be attributed to them, because,

Marginal notes: Kowlageer tea plantation established, 1844.

Marginal notes: Controversy between Mr. Fortune and Dr. Jameson.

* *Vide* Productive Resources of India, pp. 279-303.   Published 1840.
† *Vide* Selections from the Records of the Government of India No. XXIII. Calcutta 1857.

far from being new, they were all contained in some notes prepared by Dr. Jameson himself, some years before, for the information and guidance of tea planters. It is impossible here to enter into a history of the controversy or to do justice to Dr. Jameson's efforts in the cause of tea culture. To them, suffice it to say, tea owes its position as the principal staple commodity of the district. The Kowlageer plantation was eventually sold to the Rájá of Sirmore for £20,000 in 1867. It repays the purchaser, and bids fair to afford handsome profits in process of time.

499. Dr. Jameson's calculations about the tea-bearing capabilities of the Doon in 1857 were *—

How much tea the Doon is capable of producing; ten million pounds per annum!

No. of acres capable of producing tea,	100,000
Yield per acre, ... lbs.	100
Total yield, ... ,,	10,000,000

(Besides 10,000 in Jounsar Bawur).

But, however satisfactory the prospects of tea cultivation may at present be, it is a safe prediction that the day at which the hypothetical total will be attained, or can possibly be attained, is still very far off.

500. In 1863-64,† the area under tea was only 1,700 acres, and a return prepared by the writer, at the request of the Secretary Board of Revenue, N. W. Provinces, after careful personal enquiry, two years ago, exhibited results falling very far short of Dr. Jameson's anticipations.‡

How much it really produces; about three hundred thousand.

* Vide Selections, ut supra, p. 39.

† Vide Mr. Daniell's first Settlement Report, para. 102.

‡ Vide Appendix XV. I have no hesitation in questioning the accuracy of the figures accepted by Government for 1872, viz. 1,801 acres, with an out-turn of 4,11,548 lbs., or 228·5 lbs. an acre! In his report for 1862-63, Dr. Jameson calculated the area under tea at 2,572 acres, and the out-turn at 56,540 lbs., the laborers employed on the plantations being 1,254.

Estimated area under tea cultivation in acres.	Estimated out-turn in lbs.	Estimated value of annual out-turn.		
A. R. P.		RS.	A.	P.
2,024 2 0	2,97,828	1,74,865	0	0

This certainly does not show any very striking increase in the area under tea cultivation, but it is satisfactory to observe that the average out-turn per acre exceeds even Dr. Jameson's assumed maximum. Experiments in this line have not proved prejudicial to agriculture of other kinds, for cereal cultivation has hitherto advanced side by side with tea culture, although in a few years the former will surely be left in the background, unless some unforeseen accident occurs to stay the progress of the latter.

501. The elements of success in such speculations are obviously capital and experience. Yet the failure of many planters has been solely due to a disregard of this patent truism.

Failures of tea speculators due to disregard of an obvious truth.

502. Mr. Fortune was of opinion that a capitalist with Rs. 2,00,000 might bring 1,800 acres of land under tea cultivation in eight years, and make a profit of at least Rs. 2,62,388 by the transaction!* Dr. Jameson's calculations are even more dazzling. He allows a profit of Rs. 1,67,972 on only 1000 acres of land in the same period!! Both statisticians, it is true, add, that from the gross profits should be deducted, "interest for capital invested, extra carriage, auctioneer's fees," and so forth, items which would make

How much might be made by tea cultivation.

* *Vide* Appendix XVI.

a serious alteration in the result, without taking accidental contingencies into account.

503. Government have always endeavoured to encour-

The liberality of Government towards planters.

age private enterprise in this direction, and offered land to planters on exceedingly favorable terms at an early date. The Kowlageer Tea Plantation was established with the same object, nor was it sold until tea culture had taken firm root in the district.

504. Dr. Jameson has accurately described the method of

Process of tea manufacture, where described.

cultivating and manufacturing the plant in a treatise published in the Selections from the Records of the Government of India.* The process is far too complicated to be explained here.

505. Another novel branch of agriculture, still in its

Rhea.

infancy, is that of Rhea, a plant growing wild in the valley, and yielding an excellent fibre when cultivated. Its manufacture, an art not yet perfected, requires large capital and expensive machinery. The only person who has hitherto ventured to speculate in this line of industry is Colonel Thelwall. Last May, he had 200 acres of land at Lucheewala actually under Rhea, 600 cleared, and stock ready for 2000 more. His machinery is worked by steam-engines, and a 12-horse-power water turbine having a fall of 27 feet. He employs on an average 300 laborers, and his crops are so valuable that it pays to wire fence them.†

506. The demand for labor on the Doon plantations is

* No. XXIII., p. 46 *sq.*

† This information, all that is at present available on the subject of Rhea, he has himself kindly given.

considerable. The number of laborers employed at Kowlageer alone in June 1872, was 250, and 213 (145 men;
68 women) were then working at Um-
baree. At the same time, some 55 were
working off and on, by contract, at the
small plantation of Goodrich, which, in the flush of the leaf,
employs 100 women and children, all working by contract, for twelve or fifteen days in each month, besides
ploughmen, gardeners, blacksmiths, &c. The West Hopetown establishment is 10 per cent. larger. There also the
contract system prevails. In June 1872, Colonel Thelwall
had about 300 souls in his employment.

Demand for labor on the plantations.

507. The rate of wages is so high that foreigners—Afghans, for example, and men from the
borders of Ladákh, called Aughanees, dispute the market with the Doonites. The
Afgháns, being excellent workmen, are paid 8 Rs. a month
on the Lacheewála estate; their tindals get 15 Rs; the
Aughanees, truculent, malingering fellows, exceedingly
hard to manage, used to get 8 Rs. a month; their tindals,
Rs 10. These men are usually employed on work requiring
a good deal of physical strength, such as quarrying stones
and constructing coarse masonry aqueducts. They are, in
fact, the "navvies" of the district. The rate of wages
for ordinary coolies from the Doon itself or Poorubeeas
from Oudh, Cawnpore, and Allahabad, is Rs. 5 a month;
a tindal getting Rs. 8. Although in 1852 they only
received Rs. 4 a month, they are not content now with Rs.
5—no deduction being made on account of a holiday every
Sunday. Their inclination to abscond without any apparent reason is extraordinary. On the tea plantations, the

Wages of labor on the plantations.

rates are not so high. The laborers chiefly employed
there are ordinary coolies, generally Chumars.

							Per month.	
							RS.	AS.
Beldars,	..	..	..	..	..	..	4	8
Tindals,	..	..	..	..	..	..	5	0
Chowdrees,	..	..	..	..	..	..	6 to 8	
Native tea-makers,		..	..	..	..	..	5	0

Such is the scale given by Mr. Mooney, the Manager of
of the Kowlageer estate, and it is believed to be that prevailing on all other tea plantations in the Doon, belonging
either to Europeans or rich natives, except of course where
work is done by contract, in which case wages depend upon
the terms of the agreement.

508. In the villages, quite a different system, much
less profitable to the agricultural laborer

*Wages of agricul-
tural laborers in the
villages generally
paid in kind.* (Dhoomra, Chumár, Kuhár, or Kolee), is
pursued. Payments are almost invaria-
bly made in kind. Reapers are always
so remunerated. The rates in kind are nominally five
pucca seers of grain a day, together with the straw, to each
man; three or four, to each woman. Ploughmen, weeders,
and perhaps some others, are occasionally paid in cash.
The money rates are said to be 2 annas a man; $1\frac{1}{2}$ annas, a
woman; and 1 anna, more or less, a child.

509. While on the topic of wages, I may as well
*Present and past
rates of wages.* here introduce a comparison between present and past rates of wages in general.
The records give the following scale from 1822 to 1824.*

* *Vide* Letter, of the 9th August 1824, and of the 4th December 1822. Cf. 14th
March 1829.

	Per month.			Per day.		
	RS.	AS.	P.	RS.	AS.	P.
Master mason, (*Ráj Mistree*), ...	6	0	0	0	3	0
Brick-layer, ...	5	0	0	0	2	8*
Adult coolie, ...	3	0	0	0	1	6 (about).
Boy, ...	1	14	0	0	1	0

In 1829, coolies' wages seem in particular cases to have risen to 2 annas a day, and carpenters' to 3 annas; black-smiths sometimes getting the same, but often less.

The present rates, compared with those of 1850, are—

1872.		1850.
Ordinary field laborers, ...	2 annas a day or the equivalent.	Five *kutcha* seers of grain.
Common coolies,	2 annas 6 pie.	2 annas.
Lohárs, brick-layers, and carpenters, ..	5 annas.	4 annas.

510. On the plantations, labor, it has been shown,
bears a special value, and the hill por-
The high rate of wages renders a fa-mine next to impos-sible. ters get from 3 annas to 4 or 5 annas
a day. The experience of 1861 proves
that among a people in this respect so
favorably circumstanced, absolute famine is a very remote
contingency.

* Sometimes Rs. 0-3-0 a day.

511. A remarkable absence of cultivating tenants characterises the agricultural population of
Jounsar Bawur. Nearly all the *zemindars*
either cultivate their own holdings. themselves, or do so through hired labor. Hureepore, Kotee,
and a few other places, form exceptions to this rule. The
Hureepore *zemindars* realise their rents in kind by *kun
butaes*, taking one-sixth of the whole produce. It is impossible to give an adequate idea of the condition of the
peasantry from the relative size of their farms. Produce
is the gauge of prosperity, and a farmer who turns out 50
maunds *pucca* of grain in the year, is considered to be very
well off indeed. The average size of the farms is perhaps
about two acres, but here a holding has a much greater
relative value than one of equal size elsewhere, often yielding turmeric, pepper, ginger, potatoes, opium and *gooyan*—
all valuable products; so that a man
with five acres of such land under cultivation is esteemed prosperous, and may
possibly clear Rs. 100 annual profits, or the equivalent.
Money again bears a greater relative value, and there are
extensive pastures which support flocks and herds without
expense to the owners. Goats and sheep, being abundant
and of good quality, are a source of considerable profit.
The breed of horned cattle, on the contrary, is wretched,
and where ploughing is practicable, a pair of bullocks cannot keep more than one acre under cultivation throughout
the year. *Kheel* cultivation is the rule,
the *koontlee* taking the place of the
plough. In general, the Jounsar Bawur
peasantry are well off, free from debt, and the rate of in-

*Hardly any cul-
tivating tenants in
Jounsar Bawur.*

*Comparatively
large value of the
holdings in propor-
tion to their size.*

*Method of culti-
vation; enviable po-
sition of the Jounsar
Bawur peasantry.*

2 P

terest on money lent is in consequence comparatively low, not more than 18 per cent. at the outside, usually less.

512. A cultivator is supposed to start with a capital of Rs. 56, thus calculated—

Capital of the ty-
pical cultivator.

Two pair of bullocks, ...	...	...	Rs.	50 0 0
Plough and appurtenances,	...	...	„	1 8 0
Merah, ...	...	...	„	0 8 0
Jundrah (of iron,)	...	...	„	2 2 0
Phaorah, ...	...	...	„	0 8 0
Axe, ...	...	...	„	0 12 0
Gaintee or Kuntlee,	...	...	„	0 4 0
Dànturuh, ...	..	...	„	0 4 0
Khoorpa, ...	...	...	„	0 2 0
		Total,	„	56 0 0

513. Potatoes, opium, rice, ginger and turmeric may be styled the staple commodities of the subdivision. The calculations made by the local officials regarding the out-turn value &c. of the principal products, are—

Staple commodities; potatoes, opium, ginger, &c.

Name of crops.	Average produce per acre.			Value.			Season of sowing.	Season of reaping.
	MDS.	SRS.	CH.	RS.	A.	P.		
Wheat, ..	5	0	0	10	0	0	Kartik and Mungsir,	Jeth and Baisákh.*
Barley, ..	7	0	0	7	0	0	Ditto, ..	Ditto.†
Rice, ..	8	0	0	12	0	0	Asárh-Chait, ..	Asanj and Kartik.
Mustard, ..	2	0	0	6	11	0	Asauj, ..	Chait and Baisákh.
Cheená, ..	4	0	0	3	0	0	Baisákh-Jeth, ..	Bhádon-Asanj.
Kungnee, ..	4	0	0	4	0	0	Chait, ..	Ditto.
Mundwá, ..	8	0	0	8	0	0	Asárh-Jeth, ..	Kártik.‡
Opium, ..	0	2	6	14	4	0	Phágun, ..	Asárh.
Ginger, ..	9	0	0	72	0	0	Asárh, ..	Mungsir.
Turmeric, ..	12	0	0	36	0	0		
Red pepper, ..	0	20	0	4	0	0	Asárh and Sáwun, ..	Mungsir, Asauj and Kartik.
Potatoes, ..	100	0	0	100	0	0		Mungsirand Asanj.
Chowlaee, ..	10	0	0	20	0	0	Jeth and Asárh, ..	Mungsir and Kartik
Oorud, ..	7	0	0	14	0	0		Kartik.
Gágtee, (arvee),	150	0	0	75	0	0	Asárh and Jeth, ..	Kartik and Mungsir.

* i. e., in Jounsar—in Kantah and Bawur it is sown in Bhádon-Asanj and reaped in Asárh.

† i. e., in Jounsar—in Kantah and Bawur it is sown in Mágh, and reaped in Jeth.

‡ Another product which cannot properly find a place in this list, is the walnut. **The trees blossom** in June, and the nuts are plucked in October. They fetch one rupee per thousand.

514. There are two inferior sorts of rice, called Gugan and Bugoee, sown in the month of Chait *Various sorts of rice.* in *baranee* land, and cut in Asauj. The former is white, the latter of a darkish hue; neither has a good flavor, and both are equally poor. The *kyaree* rice, which has to be transplanted, is sown in Asarh and Sawun, when there is heavy rain, and cut in Mungsir and Kartik. It is also called Chauhar, Gyasoo and Jhinjun. The variety known as Basmutee, likewise grown in *kyarees*, is not common. Another kind of rice named Chohurah, too, is produced. Ramjuwain is only found at Kálsee.

515. Jounsar Bawur resembles the Doon in the fact *Prices current; fluctuations in, comparatively slight.* that the fluctuations in the price current, excepting the item of fire-wood, are much less perceptible than in the other districts.* Prices have never either risen very high or fallen very low between 1861 and 1870. This must be in a great measure due to the immunity of the sub-division from absolute drought, an advantage which the Doon also enjoys, as well as to the sparseness of the population.

516. Landless, unskilled day laborers form a comparatively small section of the population, *Agricultural labor in Jounsar Bawur; relics of slavery.* because most families have a plot of land, which the various members, including women, help to till. The larger farmers alone employ Coolies, Chumárs, Doomras, &c., to plough, sow, and reap, giving them 'board wages' *(rotee kupra)* in return, or some land to live on rent-free. The latter method of payment is an interesting relic of the period when the laborers

---

* *Vide* Appendix XVII.

were slaves and serfs—*adscripti glebæ*.   Female labor is extensively employed; not, however, that of children.

517.   In the year 1830, or thereabouts, coolie labor

Wages in Jounsar Bawur. fetched the same price as in the Doon— Rs. 3 a month, and Rs. 4 for a tindal.   Artisans of a superior class, like carpenters and blacksmiths, being scarce, got better pay, from Rs. 7 to 9 a month.   We also learn from the records that the cost of constructing bridges across the Tonse and Jumna,

Curious items therein. included the extraordinary items of " sacrificial offerings to those rivers !*   These would hardly be now passed in a P. W. Department account, and might possibly lay the district officers open to the charge of idolatry.   From the year 1850 to 1867, wages remained stationery ; skilled artisans, *c. g.*, carpenters, *mistrees*, and blacksmiths, getting 4 annas a day, and common laborers only 1½ annas ; but the instant the Cantonments at Chukrata were established in 1869, the rates at once rose to 6 annas in the case of carpenters, 8 annas in that of *mistrees* and *lohárs*, and 3 annas in that of ordinary coolies, so that manual labor is still more profitable than in the Doon.

518.   In conclusion ; although the agricultural peasant-

Condition of the people generally. ry of the Doon itself are in a more or less depressed condition, the laboring classes proper throughout the whole district possess unusual advantages, and in some other respects the people are less deserving of commiseration than those in the rest of the province.   The intemperance and extravagance of the landowners has indeed caused the transfer of much proper-

---

* *Vide* Letters of the 25th October 1830, and 6th July 1830.

ty to Europeans and Máhajuns. At the same time, the very recent date of the acknowledgment of transferable proprietary rights, coupled with the total absence of a rural aristocracy, has retarded such changes, and rendered them less striking where they have taken place. Here, at least, we are spared the lamentable spectacle of good old families sinking into indigence and rotting miserably away.

519. The octroi system has been nowhere introduced.

Trade and traffic; receipts at the Asaroree and Mussooree toll bars.

It is therefore difficult to judge the exact extent and nature of the commerce. Some notion of the briskness of the traffic may be formed from the Asaroree toll receipts for 1870-71, viz., Rs. 11,180. In 1871-72, they were let out to a contractor for Rs. 14,000, and in 1872-73, they were again farmed for the same amount. The collections at the Mussooree toll bar last year were Rs. 5,252; expenses, Rs. 1,409-14-9. They have been since farmed for Rs. 6,500, clear profit.

520. The Doon trade naturally runs in two channels ;

The Doon trade takes two channels —the hills and the plains.

firstly, between the valley and the hills ; *secondly,* between it and the plains. The exports to the plains are principally timber, bamboo, lime, charcoal, catechu (*terra japonica*), rice, and, above all, tea. In return, the Doon receives, among other things, hardware of all sorts, cotton cloth, blankets, salt, sugar (*kand* and *goor*), grain, tobacco, dried fruits, and spices. All these again are sent on to the hills, whence come coarse blankets (*loee*), rice, ginger, turmeric, red pepper, pipe-stems made of a reed called *rungál*, birch bark, walnuts, honey, wax, lac, gum, resin, many kinds of roots and mosses, besides other coloring or medicinal substances.

521. Mr. Shore made the following estimate of the
Mr. Shore's estimate of the value of the annual imports and exports.
yearly value of the imports to the Doon and the hills, in his own time :—

Hardware (chiefly copper and brass pots),	...	...	...	...	Rs.	45,000
Salt, ...	...	...	...	...	,,	5,000
Cloth,	...	...	...	...	,,	50,000
Other articles,	...	...	...	...	,,	5,000
		Total,	...		,,	1,05,000

If any faith at all is to be placed in statistics, this should now be at least trebled on account of the increase in the population, independently of the large addition which ought to be made on account of the wants of Chukrata, Mussooree and Landour.   He reckoned the total value of the exports at about Rs. 45,000,[*] to which, after applying a similar process, we must add the value of the tea exported, for but a small portion of the two lakhs worth of tea annually made finds a market either here or in the hills.   Most of it is sold in the plains, and some of it has even found its way through Afghanistan to the Russian Army in Central Asia. Whether it will ever enter into competition with Chinese teas in the European market is extremely doubtful, because labor is so dear, and *it is absolutely impossible to foresee how far planters elsewhere could afford to underbid those of the Doon, were they ever seriously pressed by the latter.*

[*] When the transit duties existed, the exports were—

Ghee,	..	..	..	..	..	Rs.	12,000
Other articles,	..	..	..	..	..	,,	15,000
					Total,	,,	27,000

522. In Mr. Shore's day, the carrying trade was in the hands of Bunjaras, of whom about 1,500,

Carriage, rather scarce.

with 15,000 bullocks, lived at the foot of the Sewaliks. His rough estimate of all the cattle in the Doon was 33,000; of the carriage availble, one hundred carts. A few years before, there had been not more than 30 in the whole district. Now, the Doon is far from being wholly dependent on the Bunjaras, yet carriage is often difficult to obtain, although liberal rates of payment are offered.

523. The manufactures are of the very poorest description—coarse blankets, cotton cloth, mats,

Manufactures; of a poor description.

baskets, earthen pots and so forth. There is even a deficiency of common artisans, and good carpenters, blacksmiths, masons, &c., are not easily procured, unless hired from the plains. Formerly light boats were often built on the Ganges and Jumna, and floated down for sale below. Their manufacture has become rare. Attempts have been made to encourage that of silk, and mulberry trees are being planted out for the purpose in great numbers, but the success of the experiment is at present problematic.

524. With the exception of timber, the Jounsar Bawur exports are inconsiderable. They chiefly

Jounsar Bawur trade.

consist, besides timber, &c., of opium, turmeric, ginger, walnuts, red pepper, sheep, goats, and blankets. In 1827, Major Young calculated the profits on the sale of Bawur opium at Rs. 700 a year; on the sale of sheep, at about Rs. 200, and on that of blankets, at the insignificant sum of Rs. 80. The principal imports are—grain of every sort, perhaps 70,000 maunds a year;

salt, 8,000 maunds ; oil, 300 maunds ; sugar ; hardware ; and cloths. Kálsee is the great emporium, and the annual sale of grain there used to be at least 1,00,000 maunds. Of late years much of the trade has been diverted to Chukrata. When a Customs Department existed, the amount collected at Kálsee in three years during which the transit duties had been farmed at Rs. 1,800 a year, was*—

	1830.			1831.			1832.		
	RS.	AS.	P.	RS.	AS.	P.	RS.	AS.	P.
Imports, ...	1,136	2	9	830	5	6	956	3	9
Exports, ...	1,247	3	3	1,019	14	3	1,239	4	6
Total,... ...	2,383	6	0	1,850	3	9	2,195	8	3

and, as the population has since about doubled, the imports and exports have also probably increased proportionately. Most of the Jounsar Bawur opium finds its way into the Sikh States, particularly the Puteeálá territory.

525. The Doon has always enjoyed an enviable im-
Crime and Police   munity from heinous crime, and the po-
administration.   sition of the Police has ever been a com-
parative sinecure, except during the period of Mr. Shore's administration. He himself has recorded the criminal statistics of four years :—

	Year.	Highway robbery and dacoity.	Murder.	Theft above Rs. 100.	Theft above Rs. 50.	Theft below Rs. 50.
Criminal statistics of 1823-26.	1823,	4	...	2	4	32
	1824,	5	...	6	...	12
	1825,	4	1	4	...	9
	1826,	1	...	...	..	24

* Young to Secretary Government, dated 24th June 1833.   Cf. letter of the 3rd April, 1834

The value of the property stolen in each year was only Rs. 826; Rs. 2,926; Rs. 1,814; and Rs. 835; and the highway and gang robberies of 1823, 1824, and 1825 were the work of intruders from below, some of whose performances have been signalised in the historical part of this Memoir.

526. Female infanticide is believed to have been once *Female infanticide once common.* frequent, though nominally confined to the Rajpoots. It now is nearly, if not altogether, extinct.

527. *Suttees* used also to be common, but died out after *Also Suttee.* the British Conquest. The last, or one of the last, occurred in 1820.

528. Since the year 1826, crime has necessarily kept *Recent criminal statistics.* pace with the population and prosperity of the district. Nevertheless, it is not heavy, and many of the more heinous offences are to be laid to the charge of strangers, low Mahomedans and others from distant districts. The calendar for 11 years, from 1861 to 1871 inclusive, is as follows:—

Years.	Murders	Dacoities and robberies.	Lurking, house trespass and burglaries.	Thefts.	Robberies by administering poison.	Value of property stolen.	
						Total.	Recovered.
						RS.	RS.
1861,	...	...	15	57	...	744	76
1862,	2	...	36	221	...	8,368	3,001
1863,	4	2	61	282	1	10,367	1,909
1864,	...	7	112	374	...	17,188	3,157
1865,	1	1	94	267	...	10,864	3,209
1866,	...	...	40	220	1	7,468	3,136
1867,	...	3	55	336	2	14,438	5,634
1868,	2	2	38	283	2	8,562	2,048
1869,	2	1	134	328	1	14,506	5,465
1870,	...	...	60	212	...	8,902	4,247
1871,	1	1	74	152	...	13,986	3,275

The comparatively large amount of property stolen in 1824-25 was for the most part the booty of Kulwá's gang; the small amount stolen in 1861 may be fairly ascribed to the famine works. These then were exceptional years, and, putting them aside, I roughly estimate the annual proceeds of theft under Mr. Shore's administration at Rs. 850, in round numbers; at, say, Rs. 10,500 now-a-days; a calculation which makes ample allowance for the inclusion of Jounsar Bawur cases in the above returns. The true inference to be drawn from these figures is, not merely that petty felonies have multiplied about twelve times, while the population has been trebling, but *that the property worth stealing has increased in the ratio of* 12 *to* 1, whereas the population has only increased in the ratio of 3 to 1, within the space of half a century. In other words, the wealth of the district has grown very much faster than the population.

529. Attention has been drawn to the modest nature of the old Police establishment. The Police pay bill for November 1822 was :*—

Police establish-ments; old and new.

Thanah	Dehra,..	..	..	Rs. 105	0	0
,,	Kanhurwálá, ..	..		,, 91	0	0
,,	Suhnspoor,	..	..	,, 91	0	0
In all only		..	..	Rs. 287	0	0

This rose to Rs. 299 in January 1823, but Mr. Shore, notwithstanding the presence of armed banditti in the neighbourhood, found indigenous crime to be so slight, that, in the following June, he recommended the abolition of the Suhnspoor Thannah with a force of one darogha, one

---

* *Vide* Commissioner Glynn's letter, of the 8th March 1823. Cf. Shore's of the 7th June 1823. Cf. Glynn, 12th June.

mohurrir, one jummadar, and twelve burkundazes, and the substitution of an outpost dependent on Dehra, with one mohurrir and four burkundazes; an arrangement effecting a saving of Rs. 65 a month. It was sanctioned, one Jummadar, together with four burkundazes, being at the same time removed from Dehra to Asaroree, a new *chowkee*, for the purpose of protecting travellers. Village *chowkeedars* there were none; nor was there any need of them.* Next year further reductions took place. The Kanhurwala Thannah was abolished, and three chowkees were substituted in its stead :†—

		RS.	A.	P.	RS.	A.	P.
Lucheewálá,	1 Mohurrir, ...	8	0	0			
	4 Burkundazes, ...	16	0	0			
	Sundries,... ...	2	12	0	26	12	0
Khuruk,	1 Duffadar, ...	6	0	0			
	4 Burkundazes, ...	16	0	0			
	Repairs, ...	0	12	0	22	12	0
Puneealee,	1 Jummadar, ...	8	0	0			
	4 Burkundazes, ...	16	0	0			
	Repairs, ...	0	12	0	24	12	0
	Total Rupees, ...				74	4	0

Thus there remained only one Thannah and five out-posts in the whole district. Passing over the changes consequent upon the temporary connection of portions of Bijnour and Kumaon with the Doon, as foreign to the immediate subject of this Memoir, we come to the total abolition of the Police under Major Young's administra-

* Shore to Court of Circuit, dated 18th November 1823.
† *Vide* Shore, dated 24th April 1824. Ewer. 28th idem.

tion.   This turning point naturally leads us back to Jounsar Bawur.

530.   Most of the information obtainable about the Police administration of the subdivision in those halcyon days, is contained in a letter of Major Young to the Governor General's Agent at Delhi, without date,* but evidently written in the year 1824.   During the preceding six months only two cases of a serious nature had occurred; the first, a theft case, in which the culprit, after receiving thirty lashes, reluctantly consented to restore the stolen property, and was released on doing so; the second, one of quite a British character.   The inhabitants of two neighbouring villages assembled to celebrate a festival, and "as is frequent in similar occasions, the greater number of the assembly became intoxicated and then proceeded to fight without any previous dispute or enmity appearing to have existed."   In this drunken row several men were wounded, and one was unluckily killed.   The man who struck the fatal blow, was sentenced to suffer three months confinement, and two others were fined Rs. 20 each.†   No instances of misconduct on the part of the Sianas, the ex-officio Police officers, had hitherto come to light.   From that time down to the 8th March 1827, not a single capital offence was committed, and hardly any appeals were made to the Superintendent from the decisions of the Chauntroo in the exercise of their semi-judicial functions.

Jounsar Bawur Police administration.

* In his earlier correspondence Major Young equally disdained time and English grammar.

† During the same period thirty petty civil suits, generally about boundary marks or small debts, were disposed of by arbitration.

I can throw no light upon the working of the Jounsar Bawur Police, as distinct from that of the Doon, subsequently to 1827.

531. The original strength of the district police force organised under Act V. of 1861 was :*—

Police force organized under Act V. of 1861.

Sub-Inspectors.	Head Constables.	Foot Constables.
3	21	107

And the monthly cost of the whole subordinate police establishment, according to the Allocation Statement, was Rs. 1,768. The Allocation Statement of 1872 exhibits a slight reduction in the strength and cost of the force :†—

Sub-Inspectors.	Head Constables.	Foot Constables.
4	23	100

The cost of the establishment, including miscellaneous guards, is now Rs. 1,705-8 a month. Clearly, the progress of civilization has added to the expense of Government in a very remarkable manner, but no one who has had any official experience of the district can possibly say that the Police force is either too numerous or too costly.

* *Vide* Appendices XVIII.-XIX.

† Before the introduction of the 10 per cent. cess, there were 14 chowkeedars in the district, receiving Rs. 3 each a month. Under the new system, there are 300, paid at the same rate from the cess.

The same difference is perceptible in the cost of other branches of the administration.

532. Mr. Shore's *foujdaree, diwanee,* and jail establish-

Mr. Shore's judi-cial establishment. ments* originally cost Rs. 444 a month :—

Foujdáree.		Diwánce.		Jail.	
	rs.		rs.		rs.
Sherishtadar, ...	50	Sherishtadar, ...	50	Darogah, ...	30
Nazir, ...	15	Moonshee, ..	30	Jummadar, ...	10
Mohafiz duftur,...	15	Nazir, ...	15	4 Burkundazes, ...	16
Mohurrir, ...	15	Mohafiz duftur,...	15	Native doctor, ...	15
Purwanah Nuvees,	15	Mohurrir, ...	10	Bheestie, ...	4
6 Chuprassees and others, ...	50	English writer,...	50		
		Chaprassees, ..	24		
		Treasurer, ...	15		
	160		209		75

The order of Government sanctioning the above, dated the 29th March 1823, also authorised the entertainment of two sowars at Rs. 18 each, as well as the employment of the Civil Surgeon attached to the Goorkha battalion upon the medical duties of the Civil station, with an extra allowance of Rs. 100 a month.

533. The Tuhseelee establishment consisted of one

Tuhseelee estab-lishment. peshkar on Rs. 50, one mohurrir on Rs. 15, and 35 chuprassees at 4 Rs., each.† Soon after, a jummadar on 8 Rs. was substi-tuted to two of the latter, and a canoongo on 15 Rs.,

---

* *Vide* Letter of 11th February 1823.

† Letter of 6th June 1823. Cf. 15th July (Grindall to Shore).

with four mirdahs on 6 each, added; total Rs. 244. The
expenditure under the other headings for
April 1823 was—

		R.	A.	P.
Foujdáree, ...	160	0	0
Diwánee, ...	209	0	0
Jail, ...	75	0	0
Police, ...	308	0	0
Pay of Register (*sic*) and Joint Magistrate,	1,034	8	10
	1,786	8	10
Add Tuhseelee Establishment, ...	244	0	0
Total Rs., ...	2,030	8	10

In January 1824, Mr. Shore, finding himself in a position
to advocate reductions, gives the total monthly expenditure under every heading (exclusive of his own pay and
the Civil Surgeon's) at Rs. 970-8-0; that absolutely necessary, as only Rs. 628-12.*

534. From 1822, to 1827 a very moderate establishment sufficed to do the work of Jounsar
Bawur:—

Superintendent, ...	Rs.	313	8	0
Diwán and Mutusudees at Kálsee,	,,	120	0	0
Boatmen at Ghát over the river Tonse,	,,	4	8	0
Chauntroo and Siánás, ...	,,	116	10	8
Total per mensem,	,,	554	10	8

To this was added a native doctor,† stationed at Kálsee,
on Rs. 30 a month, in the year 1827.

---

* Letter 8th January 1824; answered 26th February.
† Commissioner's letter, dated 10th April 1827.

535   It would be useless, even were it possible, for me

Comparison be-
tween general ex-
penditure in 1853
and 1873.

to trace all the changes since rendered necessary by the growing requirements of the district, and the consequent introduction of a more complicated administrative machinery. It is enough to institute a comparison between the principle heads of expenditure in 1853 and 1873.

*Comparative Abstract of Dehra Doon Establishment.**

1853.		Per month.	1873.		Per month.
		RS. A. P.			RS. A. P.
Collector and Magistrate's			Collector's English-speaking		
English clerks,	.. ..	338 0 0	clerks, ...		190 0 0
Native clerks,..	.. ..	204 0 0	Native clerks,..		140 0 0
Civil Court, ..	.. ..	110 0 0	Miscellaneous employés, ..		74 0 0
Treasury, ..	.. ..	60 0 0			
Jail, ...	.. ..	296 0 0	*Treasury.*		
Police, ..	.. ..	252 0 0			
Personal guard,	.. ..	21 0 0	English-speaking clerks,	110	
		———	Native do., ..	125	235 0 0
		1,281 0 0			———
Tuhseels.			*Magistrate's office.*		
Dehra, ...	.. 308		English clerk, ..	30	
Kálsee, ...	.. 148	456 0 0	Native do., ..	96	126 0 0
		———			
			Abkaree department, ..		29 0 0
•			Stamp do., ...		15 0 0
			Canal do., ...		9 0 0
			TUHSEELS.		
			Dehra.		
			Revenue clerks, &c., &c.	328	
			Judicial do., ..	15	343 0 0
			Kálsee.		
			Revenue clerks, ..	205	
			Judicial do., ..	15	220 0 0
Carried forward, ..		1,737 0 0	Carried forward, ..		1,381 0 0

* *Vide* Appendices XX.-XXI.

1853.	Per month.	1873.	Per month.
Brought forward, ..	1,737 0 0	Brought forward, ..	1,381 0 0
		Chukrata.	
		Cantonment Magistrate's officer, ... 117 Treasury, ... 106 Abkaree, ... 76	299 0 0
		Office of Sub-Judge and Judge Small Cause Court, ..	220 0 0
		Total,..	1,900 0 0
		Add for police, ...	1,700 0 0
Total, ..	1,737 0 0	Total, ..	3,605 0 0

So that, even putting aside the pay of Covenanted European officials, the expense of general administration has very nearly quadrupled since 1823. If the items* excluded be taken into consideration, the difference will prove much more striking.

536. Under the old farming system, the management of the forests hypothetically cost the Government nothing. The Forest Department charges are now very large, and it is impossible to say exactly how much of them should be debited to the Doon. Some particulars will be found in Appendix XXII.

Forest Department establishment.

537. Like crime, litigation in the Civil Courts has in-

---

* Pay of Senior Assistant,	..	..	..	..	.. Rs.	833 per month
„ Junior,	..	..	..	..	„	500
„ Civil Surgeon,	..	..	..	..	„	550
„ Superintendent of Police,		..	..	..	„	400
„ Two Police Inspectors,	..	..	..	..	„	350
„ Cantonment Magistrate of Chukrata,		..	..	„	700

	Total,	.	„	3,333

2 R

creased immensely, and from similar causes. The number
of cases instituted in the years 1823, 1824,
Civil litigation.
1825, and 1826, were only 18, 14, 21, and
43, respectively; the total value of the causes of action
being Rs. 1,220, Rs. 734, Rs. 1,270 and Rs. 3,553, in each
year. The largest amount at stake in any one case was
Rs. 548. The returns of later years contrast strongly with
these : —

*List showing number and value of cases disposed of, in several Civil Courts
in Dehra Doon, during the last ten years.*

Year.	Sudder Sudoor's Court.		Sudder Ameen's Court.		Moonsiff's Court.		Small Cause Court.	
	No. of suits.	Total value.	No. of suits.	Total value.	No. of suits.	Total value.	No. of suits.	Total value.
		RS.		RS.		RS.		
1863, ...	4	6,786	35	16,892	518	33,048	...*	...
1864, ...	14	97,193	48	25,493	338	26,338	46	2,558
1865, ...	27	50,254	23	9,740	57	6,056	327	24,970
1866, ...	35	1,18,407	39	20,346	126	12,349	387	21,625
1867, ...	28	50,344	25	15,293	126	11,974	598	50,349
1868, ...	17	65,899	...	...†	151	26,135	705	26,047
1869, ...	14	1,05,659	...	...	162	25,494	839	37,593
1870, ...	19	51,171	...	...	136	24,319	641	27,818
1871, ...	25	48,575	...	...	127	18,481	331	17,950
1872, ...	20	94,992	...	...	111	27,167	261	14,496
1873, ...	95	1,54,770	...	...	31	5,572	381	28,419

* The Court of Small Causes was established in December 1864.
† The Sudder Ameen's Court was abolished in the year 1868.

Much of the modern litigation is due to the large number of Europeans either resident in the district or visiting the hills. Petty suits concerning master and servant, tradesman and customer, therefore mainly contribute to swell the list. Mussooree naturally presents the most encouraging field for displays of forensic talent, and helps to support more than one European pleader.

538. In education* the people are extremely backward, with the exception of those who have come under the beneficial influence of the Dehra American Mission. In the Doon, there is one solitary tuhseelee school, at Dehra, with an average daily attendance of about 30 scholars, and Jounsar Bawur boasts another at Kálsee, with a daily attendance of some 28 pupils. In the whole Doon there are but three village schools, with an attendance of about 78 boys; and Female Education, as reflected from the countenance of Government, has not more than 20 representatives at the outside. In Jounsar Bawur Proper, mental culture of the humblest description is merely nominal. No pretence of a thing so uncongenial to the temperament of the inhabitants was ever made before 1871-72. Mr. Robertson, having hinted at it in 1860, was compelled to report, "the Sianas set their faces so determinedly against having schools that it is useless to attempt to establish them." Subsequently the feuds between the villages were made an excuse for staving off the educational question. At last, three schools were established in 1871-72, to which five were added in 1872-73, and the sub-division can now, on a pinch, turn out no less than 112 professing scholars.

Marginal note: Education backward.

* Vide Appendix XXIII.

539.   The generally backward condition of the district has kept down the urban population, to which Dehra contributes about 7,300 souls.

Chief Towns; Dehra.

This town is situated in lat. 30° 18' 5S", long. 78° 4' 27", at an elevation of more than 2,300 feet above the level of the sea, on the road from the plains to the hills and, being the capital, distinguishes this tract as Dehra Doon, the Valley of Dehra.   Its foundation is commonly ascribed to Gooroo Ram Rae, who, we have already seen, settled there at the end of the seventeenth century.   His temple is the only edifice in the place with any pretentions to architectural beauty.   In the native city, which lies south of the European station, there are, besides a 1st class Police station, a Tuhseelee, and a small Jail, a tuhseelee school, and a Government girls' school, both thinly attended, for, as more than once remarked above, the American Mission almost wholly monopolises the educational work of the district.   It is divided into eight Mohullas; Dhamawala, Tcha (that of the well), Tuláb (of the tank), Jhunda (of the flag), Durshunee Durwaza, Khoorburah, Dandeepore, and Koomarhan.   The station contains a fixed Anglo-Indian population of about 400 persons, being one of the largest in the North-West Provinces.   To the west of it are the new cantonments of the 2nd Goorkha Rifles, or Sirmore Battalion.   Until a few years ago, Dehra used also to be the head-quarters of the Viceroy's Body Guard.   A church (St. Thomas') has been built there for the convenience of the residents who are members of the Anglican persuasion ; in addition to Catholic and Presbyterian places of worship, the former in connection with the Mussooree Convent, the latter with the American Mission.

The Dispensary, a most deserving charitable institution, had an attendance of—

In the Year.	In-Patients.	Out-Patients.	Total.
1870, ...	133	9,126	9,259
1871, ...	141	8,745	8,886
1872, ...	311	8,637	8,948
Total, ...	585	26,508	27,093

Dehra is one of the few post-towns*.north of the Sewaliks, a Municipality, and the head-quarters of the Great Trigonometrical Survey, as also of the administrative district staff; a place, in fact, of no small importance, and the station itself is certainly the prettiest, perhaps the healthiest, in these provinces. Except Suhnspore, where there is a district post office, the only other post-town is Rajpore, whose population hardly entitles it to be considered more than a big village, while it contains only one institution worth noticing, the Dispensary, which does good work in the way of out-door relief, as may be perceived from the following returns :†—

Rajpore.

Year.	In-Patients.	Out-Patients.	Total.
1870, ...	None.	4,063	4,063
1871, ...	1	3,678	3,679
1872, ...	17	5,027	5,044
Total, ...	18	12,768	12,786

* The post office is "non-disbursing," like that of Rajpore
† These statistics are Dr. MacLaren's.

540. The only other noteworthy places are the hill sanitaria of Mussooree and Landour, originally two separate stations, now grown into one, situated in latitude 30° 27′ 30″, longitude 78° 6′ 30″, and latitude 30° 27′ 30,″ longitude 78° 8′ 30″, respectively, partly in Dehra Doon, partly in Teeree, the crest of the Himalaya forming the boundary between British and independent territory. Bunog, the loftiest mountain on the Mussooree side of the Himalayan range, attains, according to the Great Trigonometrical Survey Map, an elevation of 7,433 feet above the level of the sea, the highest point of Landour being 7,459 feet. As early as the year 1826, the salubrity of the climate, which has a temperature ranging from 27° to 80°, attracted European residents, and the united stations at present have a permanent Anglo-Indian population of at least 300, which is increased enormously during the hot season by the influx of visitors from the plains. The permanent native population, upwards of 3,000, is subject to a similar increase at the same period. A convalescent depôt for European British soldiers was established at Landour in 1827. The average number of invalids is about 200, the depôt affording accommodation for 186 single men and 24 families.* The staff consists of one Commandant, one Surgeon, and one Station Staff Officer. This sanitarium contains three churches, one Roman Catholic and two Protestant, (St. Paul's and Mr. Taylor's Free Church,) besides two or three private schools, a disbursing post office and two

---

* Information supplied by Colonel Angelo, R.A., Commanding at Landour.

hotels. Mussooree has one Protestant Church* (Christ's), and one Roman Catholic Chapel. Among the educational establishments may be mentioned the Hampton Court and Diocesan Boys' Schools, and St. George's College (the Manor House), a Roman Catholic Institution of old standing. The principal girls' schools are—the Caineville House School and that connected with the Convent of Jesus and Mary at Waverley ;—the latter is always removed to Dehra in November, returning to Mussooree in March. This station also has a Public Library, a Masonic Lodge, a good Club, and, last not least, a Volunteer Corps. Furthermore, the existence of a brewery, three banks (one moves down to Dehra in the cold weather), and three hotels, not to speak of boarding-houses, sufficiently bespeaks the prosperity of the place, the local affairs of which are partly managed by a Municipal Committee. During the hot weather, the rush of visitors from below necessitates the constant presence of the Superintendent of the Doon, an Assistant with Civil Judicial powers, and the principal Police Officer, the management of the valley being left to a second Assistant. A local journal, of some little merit, has recently been started.

541. Mussooree and Landour are, many believe, the healthiest of the older hill stations, although
Climate; the Mussooree Nursery. in the rains, the climate is trying to most constitutions. The mildness of the tem-

---

* An attempt to get up a Union Church, common to both stations, and open to "Evangelical" Christians of all denominations seems not unlikely to be successful. The building is in process of construction, and on the 16th of September 1872, the Committee of Management had a balance in hand of Rs. 402-1-7 from a credit of Rs. 5,750-11-7. I need hardly add that the project has given rise to much dissension.

perature induced Dr. Royle, Superintendent of the Seharunpore Botanical Gardens, to select the former for the site of
a nursery in 1826. Since then, another nursery has been
established at Dehra, in connection with it, under the able
management of Dr. Jameson, the present Superintendent
of the Seharunpore Gardens. Although the natives of the
plains generally suffer from the effects of the cold, the attendance at the Mussooree Dispensary in the year 1872
was not large, amounting to only 2,450 (50 in-door and 2,400
out-door, patients), less than one-third of the attendance at
the Dehra Dispensary during the same period. It was
larger in the two previous years :—

Years.	In-door Patients.	Out-door Patients.	Total.
1870, ...	39	3,634	3,673
1871, ...	44	3,068	3,112
Total, ...	83	6,702	6,785

542. With the exception of Jurapanee, three miles
along the road up hill from Rajpore, and the
northern slopes descending into the Tee-
ree Raja's dominions, the Himalayan range here labors
under the disadvantage of being somewhat bare of vegetation. The principal trees that do occur, are the hill-oak
and the rhododendron. The rocks are chiefly clay slate,
magnesian limestone, and towards Landour, quartz. Water
is very scarce, and the scenery is lacking in Alpine bold-
ness, though it is difficult to imagine a more lovely
panorama than that presented by the Doon valley, when
viewed from the heights above, on a clear day, or immediately after a storm.

Scenery.

543. The urban population of Jounsar Bawur is still
Urban population of Jounsar Bawur. smaller in proportion than that of the Doon. Few of the villages have more than 400 inhabitants, none have 500; and of the towns, neither Chukrata nor Kálsee yet contains 2,000. The foundation of Chukrata
Chukrata. dates back to May 1866, but no troops arrived there before April 1869. The residents are, for the most part, military men, and the following estimate appears to under rate the purely military element:—*

Males,	...	...	...	...	...	1,137
Females,	...	...	...	...	...	142
						1,279

Belonging to the military community—

Males,	...	...	...	...	...	315
Females,	...	...	...	...	...	172
						487

544. Kálsee is an old town, having been long the chief
Kálsee. mart for all the hill country lying between the Sutlej and the Jumna.† The population is, however, quite insignificant, numbering only 883 :—

Males,..	...	...	...	...	621
Females	...	...	...	...	262
					883

It has completely yielded its former importance to its younger rival, but boasts the name of a Tuhseelee school, and a Dispensary, whose work for three years stands thus :—

Year.	In-door pátients.	Out-door patients.	Total.
1870, ...	33	1,831	1,864
1871, ...	42	1,912	1,954
1872, ...	36	2,503	2,539
Total, ..	111	6,246	6,357

* *Vide supra*, p. 270.
† *Vide* Hamilton's Description of India Vol., II., p. 631.

There is a non-disbursing post office at Chukᵣᵃᵗa and a branch post office at Kálsee.

545.   The strength of the fixed Anglo-Indian population,

Dehra Doon as a seat of European colonization in India.

at least seven hundred persons, of whom many are prosperous landowners, points to the Doon as a promising seat of European colonization in India, and I cannot conclude this Memoir more appropriately than by sketching the history of the older colonies alluded to in a former page.*   The contrast between their disasters and the most hopeful prospects of their successors may possibly reflect the destiny of the district.

546.   The original grants of 1838 were nine in number,

Grants of 1838; their size, situation, &c.

ber, and the *nominal* grantees, eleven; both covenanted civilians, soldiers, and merchants :†--

No.	Names of Grants.	Area in acres.	Names of Grantees.
1	Attica, ...	6,072	Mr. J. Athanas.
2	Arcadia,	} 11,360	⎧Captains H. Kirke and W. Barnett
3	Markham,		(he joined in 1840).
4	Innisfail, ...	7,462	Messrs. W. H. Taylor and A. Mac-Gregor. Major-General T. Newton (his interest in Innisfail was at first distinct from those of the others).
5	Endeavour, ...	977	Mr. C. Vaughan and Major E. Gwatkin (the latter seems to have afterwards withdrawn from this grant).
6	Hopetown ...	18,813	Messrs. G. H. Smith, and D. Maxwell, and Major E. Gwatkin.
7	Karjee Bughaut,	} 1,589	Mr. James Powell, Junior.
8	Bharroowálá,		
9	Nuglah,		

* *Vide supra*, p. 11.
† Return to an Address of the Honourable House of Commons, printed 3rd August 1859, pp. 3, 4, 54.

The progress and failure of the first four and the sixth will mainly occupy our attention. All of these, except Markham, were in the Western Doon; the Attic farm, almost in the centre of it, on the banks of the Sooarna Nuddee; Arcadia, having an area of 5,499 acres, about four miles west of Dehra; Innisfail, on the left banks of the Jumna; Hopetown, composed of three separate plantations, viz., East Hopetown, with an area of about 3,503 acres, immediately north of Arcadia, Centre Hopetown, with an area of 7,406 acres, just beyond the Attic farm, and West Hopetown, measuring 7,899 acres, southwest of Innisfail and close to the Jumna. The Markham grant appears to have covered 5,861 acres, but sometimes the united area of this farm and Arcadia is given as 13,360 acres, making a difference of 2,000 in the total.

547. The whole, then, occupied a large tract of from 46,000 to 48,000 acres; that is to say, from 72 to 75 square miles, about one-sixth of the valley, exclusive of the strips of highland that go towards making up the total area of the district. Under the warrants issued to the grantees in November 1840, they were bound to clear all within a period of twenty years, with the exception of the irremediably barren land, and one-fourth of the remainder deducted as approved of by Government. It is obvious that this condition would not have been easy to fulfil without an unusual combination of experience and capital, even had not an unforeseen accident occurred, in itself sufficient to have vitiated the most prudent calculations. The terms offered were favorable enough; the land was to be rent-free for the first three

They occupied an area of some 75 square miles.

Terms concluded in 1840.

years, after which rent was to be charged at gradually rising rates reaching a maximum of Rs. 12-0-6 per acre in the tenth year, the land being open to re-settlement at the expiration of fifty years. Government encouraged free competition among speculators,* and all were exceedingly sanguine about the result.

548.   At first things went on well.   Lord Auckland, visiting the Doon in March 1838, long be-
Their prospects in 1838; Lord Auck-land's visit to the Doon.   fore the confirmation of the grants, found upon one farm alone 600 acres already under the plough, and in a few months from 2,000 to 3,000 acres would, he expected, be under cul-tivation, where all had been a barren jungle, one short year before.   "The Otaheite and the Mauritius sugar-cane are the favorite objects of speculation, but cotton and indigo and almost very kind of produce, amongst others wool from the Bhootan sheep, are in contemplation; I objected to the distance from a market, and the answer was, 'we shall build boats from the timbers of the hills, and the sale of boats will fully pay the carriage.'"†   Unfortunately, his admira-tion for the energy of the colonists was tempered by the discovery that the best sites had been appropriated by the "public officers of the district, or persons nearly connected with them."   Colonel Young, who combined the offices of Civil Judge, Magistrate, and Collector, with that of Commandant of the Sirmore battalion, held
His comments.   10,000 or 15,000 acres in the name of Mr. M'Gregor, "a West Indian of excellent character and much experience."   His Captain and Joint Magistrate, Capt.

---

* Return, &c., *ut supra*, pp. 30, 47.

† Minute of the 23rd March. Return, *ut supra*, p. 6, *sq.*

Fisher, his Adjutant, Lieutenant Kirke, and Dr. Gray, his Assistant Surgeon, held about as much more in partnership with others; and " besides these were allotments, and applications for allotments, to the amount of from 70,000 to 80,000 acres, and amongst others, one from an engineer of two years standing in the army, now at Mussooree, for 4,000 acres." This Lord Auckland very properly held to be wrong, but, on the other hand, these transactions had been carried on with the knowledge, if not express sanction, of Sir Charles Metcalfe and the Sudder Board of Revenue, and the end in view rendered him averse to interference with the means. He therefore confined himself to calling for an exhaustive report on everything connected with the grants, and here the matter dropped for the present. After that we almost lose sight both of grants and grantees, until a blow smote them, to the profit of one unscrupulous individual, from a quarter whence it was least expected—so suddenly and at such a critical juncture as to render all speculations about the chances of ultimate success in most cases purely conjectural, and secondary to the consideration of the immediate cause of the wholesale smash which followed.

549. Shortly after the date of the grants, the grantees of six estates, Arcadia, East Hopetown, Attica Farm, Central Hopetown, West Hopetown, and Markham, united their interests in a Joint Stock Agricultural Company (called Maxwell, MacGregor and Co.), consisting of 40 shares with a paid up capital of £20,000, subsequently raised to upwards of £50,000 (?), when the grantees purchased Innisfail, besides a vast grant in the Seharunpore district, containing 20,000 acres, named Puttree Nuddee. The operations of the asso-

Maxwell, Mac-Gregor and Co.

ciation thus extended over an area of from 64,000 to 65,000 acres,—*one hundred square miles and more!* One of the principal shareholders was Mr. C. Lindsay of the Covenanted Civil Service, who bought up £3,400 worth of stock in 1841-42.

550. About the same ill-omened period, an official despatch† came from the Home Government, dated February 1842, animadverting, *firstly*, upon the special irregularity of allowing civilians to hold grants within their own jurisdictions; *secondly*, upon certain general irregularities, such as the grant of lands to non-resident and non-cultivating Europeans, in contravention of the instructions conveyed in a previous despatch of May 1838. The Court concluded " by desiring that all grants which had been in that, or in any other respect irregularly made, that is, made with an entire disregard of the rules which they had laid down in 1838, should, *as far as practicable*, be cancelled." On learning this, the persons whose interests seemed likely to be affected thereby, sent up a memorial, dated the 1st September 1842, through Mr. F. Williams, the Political Agent of Dehra Doon, replying to any reasonable objections apparent on the face of the despatch. To this document, no answer was received. However, the Lieutenant-Governor, N. W. Provinces, to whom a copy of the despatch had been sent by the Supreme Government, without any preliminary correspondence with them, issued a very judicious Notification, dated the 15th August 1843, to the effect that no Covenanted servant in the North West Provinces could *in future*

The Government order of the 17th April 1844; its history.

---

* Return, &c., *ut supra*, pp. 50, 54.

† *Vide* Return, p. 14 *sq.* Cf. pp. 35, 43, *sq.*

be permitted to engage in any such transactions within the limits of these provinces." No one was "required abruptly to close any engagement into which he might have entered; but....officers in civil employ were recommended by the Lieutenant-Governor to dispose of their interest in such concerns whenever an opportunity for their conveniently so doing might offer." This did not satisfy the Government of India, who, ruling that the injunction of May 1838, if taken in connection with the rule prohibiting officers in civil employ from holding lands in their own districts, practically precluded any of them from holding land in the Company's territories, peremptorily ordered the Lieutenant-Governor to intimate to all Covenanted servants that their tenure of the lands granted to them was conditional on their resigning the Company's service. Mr. Thomason made a vigorous remonstrance against this arbitrary decree, which completely ignored the fact that all the grantees had been not only permitted, but positively encouraged, to enter into the speculations now stigmatised as objectionable. Meantime, he suspended the issue of the new notification, pending further orders. But the Governor General, avoiding the question of justice or injustice, curtly replied that " he saw no reason to change the decision which had been already come to." Mr. Thomason was therefore compelled to issue a new proclamation, dated the 17th April 1844, requiring *all* covenanted officers who held, or were in any way concerned with the management of lands, to relinquish their interest by the 1st January 1845 at the latest, or to resign the service. The immediate responsibility for the effects of this order evidently rests with the Supreme Government of the day, not with the Home Government, as stated in a former page.* Its arbitrary nature is too palpable to need comment. It is not so clear from the published correspondence, how a rule originally applicable to civilians only, came to be turned against military men. The decree dealt a fatal blow to the firm of Maxwell, Mac-Gregor and Co.

551. The association was then thus represented :†—

Shareholders.	Shares.
Mr. G. H. Smith, C.S., ...	$7\frac{14}{24}$
Mr. C. Lindsay, C.S., ...	$7\frac{4}{24}$
Nuwáb Ahmed Alee Khán, ...	$5\frac{10}{24}$
Lieutènant H. Strachey, 66th N.I., ...	$4\frac{8}{24}$
Mr. W. H. Tyler, C.S., ...	3
Captain Barnett, Invalids, ...	3
Captain H. Kirke, 12th N.I., ...	3
Captain Fisher, 23rd N.I., ...	$2\frac{4}{24}$
Lieutenant Weller, Engineers, ...	$1\frac{2}{24}$
Major Swetenham, Invalids, (his shares in trust,)	$3\frac{6}{24}$
	40

The market value of each share was Rs. 5,000. As there

Its effect upon the firm of Maxwell, MacGregor and Co.

were only three of the shareholders, with a comparatively small interest in the concern, who did not belong to the proscribed classes, its total collapse appeared imminent. The seven others therefore memorialized the Court of Directors in July 1844, pointing out the hardship of their case, and, at the same time, expressing a hope that they might be allowed to continue their speculations " until the orders of the Court were received, or for such reasonable extension of the period as Government might see fit to allow."‡ No notice was taken of this special request, nor

* Page 11.
† Return, *ut supra*, pp. 18, 32, 39.
‡ Cf. Return, pp. 10, 13, 18, 43, 44. Cf. pp. 19, 25, 27, 32, 33, 51.

did any answer come to the memorial itself, till it was too late to mend the mischief, because the Court's Despatch of the 6th November 1844, extending the period fixed for the alternative of withdrawing from farming speculations or resigning the service to the 1st January 1846, only reached the

Notification of the 28th December 1844; sale of Arcadia, &c., &c.

Lieutenant-Governor on the 20th December 1844, and could not be officially promulgated before the 28th. Meanwhile, Mr. Smith being then absent in England, Mr. Lindsay is said to have availed himself of a panic among the other partners to force the sale of Arcadia, East Hopetown, Centre Hopetown, and West Hopetown, the head-quarters and backbone of the whole concern, which went for a mere song; the two first, for Rs. 20,500, the third and the fourth, for Rs. 5,000, on the 1st December 1844. The nominal purchaser of Arcadia and East Hopetown was Mr. Dallas, a Calcutta merchant; the real, Mr. Lindsay, who also purchased Attica for Rs. 1,000 in the name of Nubbee Buksh, a native shopkeeper, in the following March. Mr. Knyvett bought the other two. This was practically the end of a speculation which had involved an expenditure of four lacs and upwards. It is some satisfaction to know that Mr. Lindsay's shrewdness did not profit him quite as much as he expected.

552. The sequel must have been most provoking to the sufferers. Next came a despatch from the

Notification of the 3rd January 1846; fate of Markham and Innisfail grants.

Directors, dated the 23rd September 1845, distinctly recommending a course already suggested in the previous despatch, but not adopted; viz., that Government should use an intelligent discretion in granting special indulgences in cases where

2 T

people had, under the sanction of the local Government, become *bonâ fide* holders of lands not within the districts of their official employment. Another Notification to that effect was promulgated by the Lieut.-Governor on the 3rd January 1846. But, in the interim, Markham and Innisfail had been abandoned, while Puttree Nuddee passed into the hands of Mr. T. R. Richmond, who afterwards became a bankrupt, fetching only Rs. 11,000. Such was the untimely end of the firm. The difference between the market price of the shares in 1840-43, and that actually secured at the sales, was Rs. 1,63,000, after deducting commission. The greater part of this loss had ultimately to be borne *by the public*. One rarely meets with a more unfortunate instance of high-handed opposition by the Supreme Government to the wise recommendations of a Lieut.-Governor. I must now consider the much more difficult question of what might have been, but for the sudden interference of the Governor-General. This is a much more doubtful point than the immediate cause of failure, and I shall dispose of it by simply laying the facts bearing on it, before the reader, as I find them on record.

553. Lord Auckland's opinion was decidedly favorable to the success of the enterprise in 1838, and in the following year we find Arcadia thus described : " In 1839 about 700 acres of this land were in a healthy state of cultivation, and growing Bourbon, Egyptian and American cotton, Otaheite, Mauritius and native sugar-cane, besides wheat and other grains ; four villages had been built ; a sugar-mill, a threshing and winnowing machine were imported from

What were the actual prospects of the grantees? Evidence favorable to them.

England."* The famine of 1837 had placed an ample supply of labor at the command of the grantees. This advantage, however, was qualified by the fact of their having to feed a number of useless hands at their own cost, and when the scarcity ceased, the floating population that had drifted into the Doon in search of help, ebbed back to the plains. Elsewhere we read of clearances extending to 8,000 acres and upwards, maintaining a population of 4,200 souls—of 10,000 acres of cultivated lands and 3,888 bullocks—and we have some very precise statistics about the condition of the tract under consideration for the two years immediately preceding the collapse of Maxwell, MacGregor and Co.

Years.	Population.	Villages.	Ploughs.	Cultivated land.
				beegahs.
1842, ...	2,789	60	1,052	17,698
1843, ...	4,234	67	1,332	47,006

This shows a marked rate of progression at the critical period when the Supreme Government interposed to disturb all human calculations. The shares, too, were then selling at their full par value of Rs. 5,000 each. Again, the Lieutenant-Governor himself bore the following testimony in favor of the grantees in January 1844 : "Hopetown, Arcadia, and the Attica Farm, are well known to all who have visited the Doon, as interesting, and apparently thriving, establishments."

554. But he adds : "as a speculation the attempt has
Evidence unfavorable to them. failed, disease has carried off their laborers, murrain has destroyed their cattle, unthrifty and careless management by agents has disappointed their hopes. The persons who first engaged in

* Papers, *ut supra*, p. 34. Cf. pp. 12, 22, 23, 25, 26, 32, 35.

the undertaking are now on the point of withdrawing from it, owing to the disappointment of their expectations of profit," and Mr. G. H. Smith admitted in October 1843, that up to date, the undertaking, far from giving any return, had yearly swallowed up much more than it had yielded. Up to August 1843, more than four lacs had been spent upon it, of which his share was one lac, the hard earnings of twenty-two years' service. Indeed the speculators seem to have rather freely indulged in what the Sudder Board of Revenue styled, with a happy facility of expression, an "anticipative incubation of profits." They brought a threshing mill out from England at a cost of Rs. 7,000, and a sugar pressing mill, at a cost of Rs. 10,000 more, not to speak of Rs. 20,000 worth of buildings, stores, &c.

Mr. A. Ross' opinion.

Moreover we have Mr. A. Ross' word for it* that the failure was not consequent so much upon the orders of Government as upon natural causes, viz. :—

1st, The want of an indigenous or naturalized population ;

2nd, The extraordinary insalubrity of climate ; and

3rd, The deficiency of water.

He also mentions that the resignation of Attica was tendered in 1850, and only delayed because the agent had no power of attorney, and that, although Arcadia and East Hopetown were still in a comparatively flourishing condition, they did not "yield the returns expected or desired by their sanguine proprietor," Mr. Lindsay. The resignation of Markham and Innisfail, which he further insists on, does not seem to bear upon the question of potential success, having been an inevitable consequence of the disso-

---

* Papers, *ut supra*, p. 24. Cf. pp. 25, 26.

lution of the farming company, but the first and second difficulties pointed out by Mr. Ross were apparently acknowledged by some of the grantees themselves who, on one occasion, bitterly complained of the desertion of about two thousand of their cultivators and the death of many others from fever.

555. The fate of the Endeavour Farm lends an air of probability to his views so far, but how are we to account for his assertion about the deficiency of water in the Doon?

Circumstances casting doubt upon the correctness of his judgment.

Again, in proof of the correctness of his statements, he quoted the "fact" that the shares were going at half par in 1842. This of course enabled Mr. Smith and Captain Strachey to flatly deny Mr. Ross' "facts" altogether, and they offered to back their opinion by taking back land in the Doon, instead of pecuniary compensation for any losses they might have suffered.* In the face of such conflicting evidence, it is impossible to arrive at a conclusion in the matter with any degree of certainty. All that can be said is, that a costly system of management due to the inexperience of the grantees, added to the expenditure rendered inevitable, even with the greatest experience and economy, by the backward state of the district and the huge size of the grants, would have made success problematic under much

But success problematic under any circumstances.

more favorable circumstances, and, at all events, postponed the harvest of profit indefinitely. That money could have been speedily made from grants of moderate dimensions, managed with proper care and economy, was proved by the example of Mr. Powell's grants.

Papers, *ut supra*, pp. 21, 22.

556   The affair cost Government a pretty penny.*

Mr. Smith memorialised the Court of Directors about his grievances in 1847.

What the episode cost Government.

After some delay, his case was stated most fully and impartially in an able note by Mr. W. Grey, Under Secretary to the Government of India, dated the 29th November 1850. The pith of it is, that the arbitrary orders of 1844 were the immediate cause of the fiasco; they had forced the dissolution of the Association, at the same time narrowing the market and coming in a manner calculated to encourage swindling at the sales. Whether the concern would have died a natural death under àny circumstances, was purely a matter of conjecture, and Government being defendant in the case, as well as judge, should give the plaintiff the benefit of the doubt. Mr. Smith's claims were very moderate, either fresh grants in lieu of those of which he had been deprived, or the difference between the market price of his shares in 1843 and the price fetched in 1844. The Court of Directors approved of the latter arrangement and, ultimately, compensation was awarded to him and the other shareholders similarly situated as follows :†—

Name.	Share.	Proportion of 1,63,000 Rupees according to Share.	Interest on ditto at 4 per cent., from 1st Jan. to 1st Oct 1851.	Total compensation.
		RS.	RS.	RS.
Mr. G. H. Smith, ...	$7\frac{14}{24}$	30,902	8,344	39,246
Captain Strachey, ...	$4\frac{8}{24}$	17,658	4,767	22,425
Mr. W. H. Tyler, ...	3	12,225	3,301	15,526
Captain Kirke, ...	3	12,225	3,301	15,526
Estate of Captain Fisher (deceased),	$2\frac{4}{24}$	8,829	2,384	11,213
Captain Weller, ...	$1\frac{2}{24}$	4,415	1,192	5,607
Total, ...	$21\frac{4}{24}$	86,254	23,289	1,09,543

* *Vide* Papers, *ut supra*, p. 9, *sq.* 12, *sq.*
† December 1851, *vide* Papers, *ut supra*, p. 33.

Captain Barnett, Nuwáb Ahmed Allee Khan, and Major
Swetenham were afterwards pronounced to be entitled to
compensation at the same rates on the ground, that,
although the Notification of April 1844 was not directly
applicable to them, yet it practically affected them equally
with their partners, by narrowing the market, and so
depreciating the value of the property, and forcing them to
relinquish their lands, whether they liked it or not, in
consequence of the retirement of the other members of the
joint stock concern.* Captain Barnett estimated the total
losses of all at upwards of four lacs of rupees. I need
hardly add that Mr. Lindsay got nothing, except a re-
primand.

557. In spite of this rebuff, his admirable presence of
mind never failed him, and he presented
a very plausible petition to the Court of
Directors in September 1853, claiming
£2,750. His case is stated in a report by Mr. (now Sir
W.) Muir, Secretary to the Government N. W. P., dated
25th March 1854. The petitioner appears to have availed
himself of the agency of his own brother-in-law, among
other inferior agents, in getting possession of East Hopetown and Arcadia. On the 1st November 1846, he "vaca-
ted his appointment under circumstances not material to
the present case," and left the service in June 1847. Meanwhile, his obliging relative made over to him the proprietary right in both grants by a deed registered in the
Superintendent's office, wherein no price or consideration
for the transfer is mentioned. In May 1850, he sold half
of them to Major Thomas, a retired officer, for £3,350.

Mr. Lindsay's
case.

* Papers, *ut supra*, pp. 34-48. Cf. p. 48, *sq*

How Nubbee Buksh, the native shopkeeper, shuffled his acquisition into the hands of the real purchaser escaped Mr. Muir's scrutiny, but Mr. Lindsay resigned it, *under his own hand*, in May 1850.   The episode of his misconduct is a disagreeable one, and I should not recur to it, were it not that his proceedings added one to the many complications in the general case of the grantees : "the second cause to which the losses entailed on the firm by the sale of their property is attributed, is the absurd and ruinous measure adopted, for the sale was effected without notice or advertisement of any kind.   The partners present in the country appear, under the influence of panic, to have jumped at the first price offered and recommended to be accepted by one of their own number, who was the active agent for effecting the sale, and who, it is now generally understood, was also the actual purchaser, though his real character was veiled for some years under an ismfurzee. What but loss to the remaining members of the firm could be expected from a sale effected under such circumstances?"* The active agent was Mr. Lindsay, who, having obtained nearly double the price for which he had sold the East Hopetown and Arcadia grants *to himself* in the name of others, by the sale of one-half of them, now had the audacity to claim compensation, on account of the low price originally fetched !!   So Mr. Muir pointedly describes the nature of his claim, which was comtemptuously dismissed.

558.   Mr. Lindsay, unabashed, returned to the charge in March 1856, coupling a claim of some £10,000 on account of the enforced sale with another of £7,000, on account of timber, &c., cut

Claims on account of timber.

---

* Papers, *ut supra*, p. 52.

down and carried away from the grants by strangers, without the permission of the proprietors.* The reader may recollect that formerly every one was at liberty to cut timber as he pleased, paying the price of it in the shape of a toll to the contractors, who had the farm of the adjacent passes, at the time of exportation to the plains. In 1838-39, the grantees, then only "temporary squatters," holding their grants subject to any previous contract expressed or implied between Government and other parties, having no proprietary title to anything beyond the land cleared for cultivation, were, on attempting to enforce rights over the forests adverse to those of Government, enjoined to refrain from interference with that in which they merely had "an inchoate and imperfect" as opposed to an "absolute property." "The grantee has only a conditional and incomplete property in the waste portion of his grant until three-fourths shall have been cleared, ... and this incomplete property cannot nullify any rights of others which may exist in the subject matter."† The question became more complicated when the Sudder Board of Revenue, in paragraph 15 of their letter of the 27th September 1839, thus expressed themselves: "of course any portion of the forest which may fall within any grant will belong to the grantee," while the deeds of 1840, expressly reserving certain rights (e. g., to mineral products) to Government, tacitly left the absolute disposal of the spontaneous produce, which was beginning to rise immensely in value, to the grantee. Such was the view taken by Colonel Young in his letter

* *Vide* Papers, *ut supra*, p. 55 *sq.* Cf. Cases of Grantees *passim.*

† *Vide* Grantees' cases, p. 34, *sq* ; and letter from Secretary Sudder Board of Revenue, to Officiating Commissioner, Meerut Division, No. 189, dated 10th July 1838.

of the 12th March 1840, forwarding the form of engagement for the Hopetown Grants. Such, too, was the view
subsequently taken by more than one eminent counsel, and,
if the intention of the documents was something different,
it is strange that it was not precisely expressed, in the face
of the previous controversy. Disputes almost immediate·
ly broke out with greater violence than ever, because the
timber merchants and others continued their trespasses upon
the grants, and the authorities allowed duties to be levied
upon timber exported by the grantees themselves. At
last, Mr. MacGregor, the Manager and Attorney of Max·
well, MacGregor, and Co., memorialized the Lieutenant-
Governor* in the year 1846. The reply was a letter from
Mr. J. Thornton, Secretary to Government, N.W. Provinces, (No. 3915, dated the 12th September 1846), the
unsatisfactory nature of which cannot be denied by anyone
who examines the correspondence with candour. It simply begged the whole question in favor of Government,
conceding as a great boon, what has been termed, with
graceful ambiguity, " a *prospective memorial right* to what
stood on the grants;" the grantees might prevent any one
from trespassing upon their estates to cut wood, but if they
cut it themselves, and transmitted it to the plains they had
" to pay the regular tax upon it according to the tariff;" in
other words, they had literally to purchase their own property, since transit duties having been abolished by Act XIV.
of 1836, the dues levied were either a price or nothing ; they
were also debarred from appropriating timber previously cut
down by others and still lying within their boundaries.
Mr. Lindsay consequently memorialized the Court of Di-

* *Vide* Case of Grantees, p. 8. Cf. 27 to 34.

rectors in April 1849, but in vain. Again the Court was memorialized by the Hopetown grantees in January 1854, and, after some preliminary correspondence, the Court replied on the 13th February 1855, repudiating the theory that dues levied by the farmers were of the nature of a price paid and not a "tax or toll," but announcing that the Governor General had been pleased to gratuitously "direct the immediate discontinuance of this cess," except as regarded the timber from the Government forest lands. The indomitable Mr. Lindsay's men of business retorted by pointing triumphantly to Acts XIV. of 1836 and XIV. of 1843, and furthermore suggesting compensation for "past most serious injuries and losses." To this the Court apparently turned a deaf ear, so Mr. Lindsay encountered them again, single-handed, with a new memorial, in the following year. This elicited an advance of £200, to which a warrant for £300 was afterwards added on the condition of his giving a receipt in acquittance of all further demands. He had not accepted these terms on the 1st September 1858. Whether he ever did so, and whether any of his less enterprising companions received compensation, does not transpire from the correspondence before me.

559. Such is the *bathos* in which the history of the old grants ends. A repetition of the catastrophe signalised is impossible. Schooled by it the Government at once resolved that the size of future allotments should be limited to four thousand acres, a maximum since extended to five thousand, but likely to be reduced to five hundred.*

Present prospects of the European colonists.

---

* For Rules about Grants, *see* additional Appendix E.

Profiting by the misfortunes of their predecessors, settlers have learned that the production of tea or rhea is more remunerative than the cultivation of cereals, and to these two staples might perhaps be added coffee, besides indigo, the speculation most looked forward to in 1839.* The Anglo-Indian community already forms a comparatively strong element in the population. Not long ago, Mr. Daniell † judged it to consist of 990 persons, of whom 83 were land or householders, 41 being directly concerned in agriculture, and we may rest assured that accessions to their number will be henceforth solely dependent upon the stability of our rule.

560. My present undertaking has at last come to an end. The physical characteristics of a district about which wonderfully little is generally known, considering the interest attaching to it, has been described; its history, both ancient and modern, sketched; and the nature of its financial resources explained, together with their extent. Finally, I have endeavoured to give a notion of its natural capabilities for further improvement, and if I have any where failed in the execution of my design, the failure is not so much due to any want of conscientious research on my part, as to the disadvantages under which I have had to conduct the enquiry.

Retrospect.

* *Vide* Letter of Sudder Board of Revenue, dated the 16th July 1839, para. 26. A very unfavorable comparison between the Doon and Seharunpore, as regards certain products, has been instituted by an anonymous writer more than once quoted.

	Sugar per acre.	Rice per acre in Maunds.		Wheat Maunds.
		Irrigated.	Non-Irrigated.	
Zillah Dehra,	45 Rs. worth	15	10	7 or 8
Zillah Seharunpore,	90 to 100	25 to 50		15

† *Vide* his Second Report, para. 114.

APPENDICES.

Appendix I.

The District Engineer's account of materials for building and road making gives all the information available on that subject.

"Bricks in the Doon are generally made 6" × 3½" × 1¼" and are purchased as follows:—

1st Class (picked), ...	Rs.	3 8 0	per	1,000
2nd Class (take them as they come),	„	3 0 0	„	„
3rd Class, peela, ...	„	2 0 0	„	„

"English-sized bricks are made for the Chukrata road new works, and cost as near as possible, pucca, 9 Rs. per 1000.

"*Lime.*—Stone lime with the white stones picked out for *sufaidee* is sold unslacked at the kiln at Rs. 20 per 100 trade maunds; with the white stones left in, at Rs. 25 per 100 maunds. One hundred trade maunds will give about 120 maunds of lime, and 40 maunds of unburnt stone. One hundred maunds of slaked lime are equal to about 155 cubic feet.

"*Broken stone for metal* (which here takes the place of kunkur).—The cost varies with the distance the stone has to be carried. If broken on the spot, as near rivers and nuddees, the cost is from Rs. 2-8-0 to Rs. 3-0-0 per 100 cubic feet, according to the supply of labor attainable. The average for carriage is Rs 2-8 per 100 cubic feet, and for consolidating Rs. 2 per 100 cubic feet should be allowed, as water is scarce and labor dear. Contractors for this kind of work in the Doon cannot be depended on.

"The above gives Rs. 7-8-0 per 100 cubic feet for consolidated metalling, and the rate for one mile 12 feet wide and 6 inches deep, will be Rs. 2,376 "

The Tuhseelee rates for timber, &c., are—

Sál and Sain kurries,	best quality,	Rs.	50	0	0	a score.
„ „	2nd „	.. „	35	0	0	„
„ „	3rd „	.. „	20	0	0	„
(*Kokat*,*i.e.*, of other woods)	best „	.. „	25	0	0	„
„ „	2nd „	.. „	16	0	0	„
„ „	3rd „	.. „	10	0	0	„
Sál logs, 1st quality,	.. ..	.. „	2	0	0 per c. ft.
„ 2nd „ ..	.. ..	.. „	1	0	0 „
Phoolas, per thousand,	.. ..	.. „	4	to	5
Bamboos, per 100, ..	.. ..	.. „	4	to	5

Some of the Forest Department rates may be here quoted :—

Detail.	Length.	Thickness.	Per	Rate.
	feet.	inches.		RS.
Kurries, Sál, ..	15	6 × 5	Score.	45-0-0
„ „ ..	13	5 × 4	„	33-0-0
„ „ ..	12	5 × 4	„	32-0-0
„ Sain, ..	15	6 × 5	„	30-0-0
„ „ ..	13	5 × 4	„	22-8-0
„ „ ..	12	5 × 4	„	20-8-0
„ Jamun, ..	13	5 × 4	„	18-4-0
„ „ ..	12	5 × 4	„	17-4-0
Tors, dry Sál, ..	10½	14 to 18 round,	„	11-4-0
Bamboos, ..	From 6 to 15	From 4 to 9 girth.		0-2-0 to 0-4-6
Phoolas, ...			2 Bullock carts.	0 6-0
„ ..			100	0-2-0
Stones, Chuna, ..			2 Bullock carts.	0-6-0
„ „ ..			Buffalo.	0-1-6
„ „ ..			Mule, pony, donkey or bullock load.	0-1-0
Stones, Lime, ..			Maund.	0-1-0
Lime made with Government wood and stone, by the purchaser.			2-Bullock cart.	1-0-0
			Camel load.	0-8-0
			Buffalo „	0-3-0
			Mule „ &c.	0-2-0
			100 Maunds.	8-0-0

In Jounsar Bawur the Forest Department sells wood at the following rates :—

Deodar, (*Cedrus deodara*,) ... ... Rs. 1-0-0 per cubic foot.
Rai, (*Abies Webbiana*,) ... ... ,, 0-4-0 ,, ,,
Marinda, (*Abies Smithiana*,) ... .. ,, 0-4-0 ,, ,,
Cheer, (*Pinus longifolia*,) ... ... ,, 0-4-0 ,, ,,
Khail, (*Pinus excelsa*,) ... ... ,, 1-0-0 ,, ,,
Kursoo, (*Quercus semicarpifolia*,) ... ,, 0-4-0 ,, ,,
Bullies, ... ,, 1-0-0 each.
Small bullies for roofing, ... ,, 2-0·0 per score.
Ringáls, (small bamboos,) ... ... ,, 1-4-0 per 100.

Appendix II.

(No. 1955).

Extract from the Proceedings of his Excellency the Most Noble the Governor-General in Council in the Judicial Department, under date the 24th October 1822.

Extract from the Resolution of Government, dated the 24th October 1822.

1st. The period of Mr. Macsween's arrival at Agra being near, it becomes necessary to make provision for the execution of an arrangement heretofore in the contemplation of Government, but suspended until that event should relieve Mr. Graham, and enable him to supply the place of the Hon'ble Mr. Shore, Officiating Joint Magistrate at Boolundshuhr.

2nd. Mr. Shore stands appointed as Register at Seharunpore, and it was the intention of Government at the time of nominating him to that situation, to vest him with powers of Joint Magistrate, in the territory of Dehra Doon, and eventually to unite to his Judicial office the duty of Superintending the Revenue management of that tract of country.

3rd. It cannot be necessary to explain at length the motives which have induced the Governor-General in Council to desire to vest the Superintendence of the tract in question, in a single officer who shall reside on the spot for a considerable portion at least of every year.

4th. The policy of an arrangement of the kind in a territory very recently subjected to our dominion must be sufficiently obvious, so that it remains only to lay down the rules and principles which should guide Mr. Shore in his management of the tract.

5th. The Regulations of Government having been extended to the Dehra Doon, by Regulation IV. 1817, Mr. Shore's judicial functions will necessarily be those of Register (*sic*) and Joint Magistrate as defined in the Regulations, and his Lordship in Council resolved, that he shall be vested with the extra powers described in Sections IX., and XII. Regulation XXIV. 1814., Regulation II. 1815, and Section II., Regulation III., 1821.

6th. It is the intention of Government that Mr. Shore shall reside ordinarily at Dehra, or at such other place in the Doon as may seem to him best fitted to be his Sudder Station. During the rains, however, as well as when the Sessions for the Seharunpore Zillah may be holding by the Circuit Judge it will be convenient that he should come into Seharunpore, where he will still conduct the Revenue and Police duties of the tract especially placed under his management, though in other respects subject to the authority of the Judge and Magistrate, as Register and Assistant of the District.

Appendix III.

1817. A. D. *Regulation IV.*

A Regulation for annexing to the Zillah of Seharunpore, the tract of country called Dehra Doon, formerly composing a part of the territories of the Rájá of Nepál passed by the Governor-General in Council, on the 28th February 1817; corresponding with the 18th Phaugun 1223 Bengal era; the 26th Phaugun 1224 Fusly; the 19th Phaugun 1224 Willaity; the 12th Phaugun 1873 Sumbut; and the 11th Rubbee-us-sanee 1232 Hijeree.

Whereas the tract of country called Dehra Doon, heretofore forming a part of Gurhwál, has been ceded to the Honorable the East India Company, in full Sovereignty by the Rájá of Nepál, and whereas it has been judged advisable to annex that tract of country to the district of Seharunpore, the following rules have been enacted, to be in force from the period of their promulgation :—

Preamble.

II. The tract of country called Dehra Doon, heretofore forming part of Gurhwál, shall be annexed to the district of Seharunpore, and shall be considered subject in all matters of police and criminal jurisdiction to the Magistrate of the northern division of Seharunpore; and in all matters of a civil nature to the jurisdiction of the Dewanny Adawlut of that district.

The tract of country called Dehra Doon to be annexed to Seharunpore, and the existing laws and regulations extended to that tract of country.

The laws and regulations established for the internal administration of the ceded and conquered provinces, are hereby declared to be in full force and effect in the Dehra Doon, subject however, to the provisions contained in the following Sections.

Subject to the following provisions.

III. The Courts of Civil Judicature shall not be deemed competent to take cognizance of civil claims in the Dehra Doon, the cause of action in which may have originated previously to the 15th of May 1803, being a period of 12 years antecedent to the date of the convention, by which that tract of country was surrendered to the British Government.

Civil Courts prohibited from taking cognizance of suits if the cause of action shall have arisen previously to the 15th May 1803.

IV. *First.* The Court of Criminal Judicature are hereby prohibited from taking cognizance of any crime or offence, which may have been committed in any part of the Dehra Doon, previously to the 15th of May 1815, being the date of the convention by which the said tract of country was surrendered to the Honorable the East India Company.

Criminal Courts prohibited from taking cognizance of offences committed previously to the 15th May 1815.

Second. No part of the regulations in force, by which the punishment of any offence may be enhanced beyond the punishment prescribed for such offence according to the existing laws and usages of the territory in question, shall be considered applicable to any crime or offence committed within the Dehra Doon, between the 15th of May 1815, and the period of the promulgation of this Regulation.

Certain provisions of the regulations in force declared inapplicable to offences committed in the Dehra Doon between the 15th May 1815, and the promulgation of this Regulation.

Third. In cases, however, in which the penalties, established by the existing Regulations, may appear to be more lenient than those to which the offenders would have been subject under the pre-existing laws and usages of the Doon, such offenders shall nevertheless have the benefit of the provisions now established, supposing the offences to have been committed between the 15th of May 1815, and the period of the promulgation of this Regulation.

Provisions of the Criminal Regulations which may be favorable to the prisoner to be applicable to such cases.

V. The Governor-General in Council reserves to himself the power of fixing the periods, for which the settlement of the land revenue shall from time to time be formed in the Dehra Doon, according as local circumstances may appear to require, adhering however, as nearly as practicable, to the principles established for the settlement generally of the lands in the territories ordinarily denominated the ceded and conquered provinces.

Power reserved to the Governor-General in Council of fixing the periods for the formation of the Settlement of the land revenue.

APPENDIX IV.

1825 A. D. *Regulation XXI.*

A Regulation for annexing to the Jurisdiction of the Commissioner of Kumaon the tract of country called the Dehra Doon, and also the pergunnah of Chandee, heretofore forming part of the Districts of Seharunpore and Moradabad—passed by the Governor-General in Council on 8th December 1825.

I. By the provisions of Regulation IV. 1817, the tract of country denominated the Dehra Doon, was annexed to the district of Seharunpore, and the laws and regulations in force in that district were, with certain exceptions, extended to the Dehra Doon; local circumstances, however, have rendered it expedient to transfer the above-mentioned tract of country to the Jurisdiction of the Commissioner in Kumaon, and also to place under the same authority the whole of the Pergunnah of Chandee, part of which is now attached to the district of Moradabad, and part to the district of Seharunpore. The Governor-General in Council has accordingly been pleased to enact the following rules, to be in force from the date of their promulgation.

Preamble.

II. Section II. Regulation IV. 1817, which declared that the tract of country called the Dehra Doon, shall be annexed to the district of Seharunpore is hereby rescinded. The remaining Sections of that Regulation are to remain in force, but from and after the promulgation of this Regulation, the Dehra Doon shall be annexed to the jurisdiction of the Commissioner of the province of Kumaon.

Part of Regulation IV. 1817 rescinded, and Dehra Doon annexed to Kumaon.

III. In like manner the pergunnah of Chandee, partly situated in the District of Moradabad and partly in that of Seharunpore, is hereby separated from those districts, and declared subject to the authority of the Commissioner of Kumaon.

Also pergunnah Chandee.

IV. From and after the promulgation of this Regulation, the operation of all Regulations not expressly extended to the province hereinmentioned shall cease to have effect in the Dehra Doon, and in the pergunnah of Chandee; and the system of internal administration now established in the province of Kumaon, under the provisions of Regulation X. 1817, shall be considered applicable to those tracts of country subject to such modifications, as local circumstances, or other considerations, may hereafter render necessary or expedient.

Regulation X.1817. declared applicable to the Dehra Doon, and to pergunnah Chandee.

APPENDIX V.

(No. 65).

To

THE HON'BLE F. J. SHORE,
Dehra Doon.

SIR,—I am directed to acquaint you that the Right Hon'ble the Governor-General in Council has this day been pleased to remove you from the office of Register of Seharunpore and Joint Magistrate stationed in the Dehra Doon, and to appoint you to be Assistant to the Commissioner of Kumaon, with a salary of Rs. 1,500 per mensem.

Judicial Department.

2. As connected with your appointment, I am directed to transmit to you for your information, the accompanying copy of Resolutions this day passed by Government in the Judicial Department.

COUNCIL CHAMBER, }
The 8th December 1825. }

I am, &c., H. SHAKESPEAR,
Secy. to Government.

[*Copy*].

Letter from the Commissioner of Kumaon, dated 30th August 1825.

,, to ,, ,, ,, 29th September.

,, from ,, ,, ,, 30th October.

With reference to the documents above recorded, the Right Hon'ble the Governor-General in Council is of opinion, that the transfer of the Dehra Doon and the pergunnah of Chandee to the jurisdiction of the Commissioner of the Province of Kumaon, and the introduction into those tracts of country, of the system of internal administration now in force in that Province, will be far better adapted to the state of society, in those parts than to continue the enforcement of the general Regulations, and that the arrangements suggested by the Local Authorities of Kumaon and the Dehra Doon, are in a high degree calculated to promote the welfare and good Government of the people. His Lordship in Council is accordingly pleased to resolve that the Dehra Doon and the pergunnah of Chandee be separated from the district of Seharunpore and Moradabad, and be placed under the jurisdiction and authority of the Commissioner in the Province of Kumaon, and that a Regulation be enacted to that effect.

Judicial Depart-
ment Resolution's the
8th December 1825.

2. A Civil Officer will be appointed Assistant to the Commissioner of Kumaon, and will in that capacity conduct under his authority and instructions, the administration of Civil and Criminal Justice and the collection of the Land Revenue in the Dehra Doon, and in the pergunnah of Chandee, and also in the following pergunnahs of the Province of Kumaon, viz:—

> Gunga Sulan,
> Chound Kote,
> Baraseo,
> Dewulgurh.

and Nagpore.

3. The Assistant will exercise his discretion in visiting any part of the Jurisdiction committed to his charge that may appear to require his immediate presence, but it is desirable that his Sudder Cutcherry should be established in the Doon from May to October, and at Sreenuggur from the month of November to April. By this arrangement, as observed in a letter to the Commissioner under date the 12th of September last, the inhabitants of the Doon will have access to the Assistant throughout the

year, and the inhabitants of the hill pergunnahs during a large portion of the year, while the latter will have it in their power in cases of emergency to resort to the Commissioner's Court during the rainy season, when any difficulty of communication may exist between the hill pergunnahs and the Doon.

4. The Asssistant will exercise powers to the same extent as those vested by the General Regulations in a Zillah Judge and Magistrate and a Collector of Revenue, subject to the control and instructions of the Commissioner of Kumaon.

5. In all civil suits an appeal will lie to the Commissioner's Court from the decisions of the Assistant, under such rules as may from time to time be established for that purpose.

6. In the trial of criminal cases the Assistant will be guided by the spirit and principles of the General Regulations in force in the ceded and conquered provinces.

7. In cases of a heinous nature requiring a more severe punishment than a Magistrate is authorized to inflict by the General Regulations, but not coming within the description of crimes specified in Section 2, Regulation X. 1807, viz., murder or any species of homicide, not manifestly accidental or justifiable, robbery by open violence, as defined in Section 3, Regulation LIII. 1803, violent affrays attended with serious casualties or circumstances of aggravation, treason or rebellion againt the State, the Assistant shall, provided the person accused shall appear to have been guilty of the crime laid to his charge, forward the whole of his proceedings to the Local Commissioner (with a letter explanatory of his view of the case), who will pass such orders for the punishment or acquittal of the prisoner, as may be consistent with the general powers vested in him for the administration of criminal justice in the province of Kumaon.

8. If any person shall appear on due and careful investigation by the Assistant to have been concerned in any of the crimes specified in Section 2, Regulation X. 1807, it shall be competent to the Assistant without reference to the Civil Commissioner, to commit the offender to take his trial before the Judicial Commissioner, who may be appointed in conformity to the rule prescribed in Sections, 3 and 4 of the Regulation above cited. In making such commitment, the Assistant shall be guided by the rules contained in those Sections, and on the receipt of the report required to be made by Section 4, the Governor-General in Council will determine in

each instance, the time and place at which the prisoners shall be brought to trial.

9.   In sentences of temporary imprisonment, the Assistant and the Commissioner of Kumaon, respectively, will exercise their discretion in confining offenders either in the jail attached to the Court in the Dehra Doon, or in the jail at the station of Almorah, with reference to the place where the offence may have been committed, and with due regard to the health of the prisoner.

10.   The Assistant will furnish the Commissioner of Kumaon with monthly and other periodical returns of the Civil and Criminal business of his Court, in order that they may be incorporated in the annual report directed to be made by that officer to Government.

11.   In like manner the Assistant will forward to the Commissioner Monthly Statements of the collection of the Land Revenue in the territories committed to his charge, with a view to their being included in the accounts of the Province of Kumaon.

12.   The Sudder Tuhseeldar and Police Establishment of the Assistant will be entered in the monthly abstract of the Province of Kumaon, and an account of the contingent expenses incurred by the Assistant will be forwarded with those of the Commissioner for audit in the usual manner.

13.   The Governor-General in Council authorizes the following Establishments for the office of Assistant to the Commissioner of Kumaon, viz.:—

JUDICIAL ESTABLISHMENT.

1 English writer, ... Rs.		100
1 Serishtadar, ... „		50
1 Hindeenuvees, ... „		15
2 Mohafiz Duftars, @ Rs. 15, ... „		30
1 Nazir,.. .. .. „		15
8 Chuprassies, @ Rs. 4, ... „		32
1 Treasurer, ... „		15
1 Furash, ... „		4
1 Gunga Jullee,.. .. .. „		4

JAIL ESTABLISHMENT.

1 Darogah, ... „		30
1 Jummadar, ... „		10
1 Native Doctor, ... „		15
4 Burkundazes, @ Rs. 4, ... „		16
2 Bhistees, @ Rs. 4, ... „		8
1 Mehtre, ... „		3

Total per month, Rs.,   ..   347

POLICE ESTABLISHMENT.

		RS.	RS.
1. *Chokee at Kotdewara.*			
1 Jummadar,	... ...	10	
1 Duffadar,	... ...	5	
4 Burkundazes,	... ...	16	
Contingencies,	... ...	2	33
2. *Chokee Shorepore*, ditto,...	... ...		33
3. *Chokee Luchewala.*			
1 Jummadar,	... ...	8	
1 Duffadar,	... ...	5	
4 Burkundazes,	... ...	16	
Contingencies,	... ...	2	31
4. *Chokee, at Khurruck*, ditto,	... ...		31
5. *Chokee, Khansrao*, ditto,	... ...		31
6. *Chokee, Mohusa.*			
1 Jummadar,	... ...	8	
1 Duffadar,	... ...	5	
4 Burkundazes,	... ...	16	
Contingencies,	... ...	2	31
7. *Chokee Suhnspore*, ditto,	... ...		31
	Per month, ...		221

ESTABLISHMENT FOR THE COLLECTION OF REVENUE.

		RS.
1 Peshkár,	... ...	50
1 Mohurrir,	... ...	15
1 Jummadar,	... ...	8
20 Peons, @ Rs. 4,	... ...	80
3 Mirdahs, @ Rs. 6,	... ...	18
2 Suwars, @ Rs. 18,	... ...	36
Stationery and Purkhye,	... ...	9
Contingencies,	... ...	4
1 Canoongo,	... ...	15
	Per month, ...	235

ESTABLISHMENT FOR COLLECTION OF REVENUE AT SREENUGGUR.

		RS.	A.
1	Tuhseeldar, ...	50	0
2	Hindee writers, ...	20	0
1	Jummadar, ...	8	0
22	Peons, @ Rs. 3-8, ...	77	0
	Stationery, &c., ...	9	0
2	Canoongoes, ...	62	8
3	Putwarees, ...	15	0
	Per month, ...	241	8

14. The Dehra Doon and pergunnah Chandee will form the Hoozooree Tuhseel under the management of the Peshkár, and the collections of the Revenues of the pergunnahs of Gunga Sulan, Baraseo, Chaund Kote, Dewalgurh and Nagpore, will be entrusted to a Tuhseeldar stationed at Sreenuggur.

15. The Peshkár and Tuhseeldar will be entrusted with the management of the Police in their respective Provinces, subject of course to the immediate orders and control of the Commissioner's Assistant.

16. The Assistant is authorized to correspond directly with all public officers on points of current business relating to the tract of country placed under his immediate charge, but all references and reports of a general nature to Government, or to the Board of Commissioners, should be made through the Commissioner, in order that they may be submitted with the sentiments of that officer.

17. The Governor-General in Council is pleased to appoint the Hon'ble Mr. Shore to be Assistant to the Commissioner of Kumaon on a salary of Rs. 1,500 per mensem.

(*A true copy.*)

H. Shakespear,

Secretary to Government.

Appendix VI.

1829 A.D. *Regulation* V.

A Regulation for rescinding part of Regulation X. 1817, and parts of Regulation XXI. 1825—passed by the Governor-General in Council on the 12th May 1829.

Regulation V. 1829.

1. Whereas local circumstances have rendered it necessary and expedient that the tract of country denominated the Dehra Doon should be separated from the jurisdiction of the Commissioner for the province of Kumaon, and that the rules prescribed by Regulation X. 1817, for the trial of persons charged with the commission of heinous offences in the Dehra Doon, or in Jounsar Bawur, Poondur, and Sundokh, and other small tracts of country situated be-

Preamble.

tween the rivers Jumna and Sutlej, should be rescinded, the Governor-General in Council has been pleased to enact the following Regulation, to be in force from the date of its promulgation.

Parts of Regulation XXI. 1825, as declare Dehra Doon annexed to the jurisdiction of the Commissioner of Kumaon, and the provisions of Regulation X. 1817, as are considered applicable to Dehra Doon, rescinded.

II. Such parts of Regulation XXI. 1825, as declare the Dehra Doon to be annexed to the jurisdiction of the Commissioner for the province of Kumaon, and that the provisions of Regulation X. 1817, shall be considered applicable to that tract of country rescinded.

III. *First,* such parts of Regulation X.* 1817, as provide for the appointment, by the Governor-General in Council, of a special Commissioner for the trial of persons charged with the commission of heinous offences in Dehra Doon, or in the several reserved tracts of territory situated between the Jumna and Sutlej, and require that in certain cases the trial shall be referred for the final sentence of the Court of Nizamut Adawlut, are hereby rescinded.

Parts of Regulation X. 1817, as provide for the appointment of a special Commissioner for the trial of persons for heinous offences in the Dehra Doon, and the reserved tracts of territory between the Jumna and Sutlej and as require that certain trials be referred to the Court of Nizamut Adawlut rescinded.

Second. The administration of criminal justice in the Dehra Doon, and in the reserved tracts between the Jumna and Sutlej above-mentioned, shall hereafter be conducted under such rules and instructions as the Governor-General in Council may please to issue for the guidance of the Officers to whom it may be entrusted.

Criminal justice how to be administered in future in the Dehra Doon, and in the reserved tracts between the Jumna and Sutlej.

Extract from the Proceedings of the Right Hon'ble the Governor-General in Council, Judicial Department, under date, 12th May, 1829.

To—W. EWER, *Commissioner of Revenue and Circuit, 1st Division, Meerut.*

SIR,—I am directed to transmit to you the accompanying extracts from a correspondence with the Commissioner of Kumaon relative to the boundary between that Province and the Dehra Doon and its dependencies, and to communicate to you as follows regarding the arrangements

* Regulation X. 1817 was rescinded *in toto* by Act X. 1838.

that have been made for the future management of the latter tract of country.

2. Pergunnah Chandee, as well as the Tuhseeldaree of Sreenuggur, is to be placed under the authority of the Commissioner in Kumaon.

3. That part of Section 2, Regulation XXI. 1825, by which the Dehra Doon was annexed to the jurisdiction of the Commissioner for the province of Kumaon has been rescinded.

4. The river Ganges is to constitute the boundary between the province of Kumaon and the Dehra Doon and its dependencies.

5. The officer appointed to superintend the affairs of the Dehra Doon and its dependencies will be subject to your authority as Commissioner for the districts of the Northern Doab, in the same manner as the Local officers of those districts. And the Resident at Delhi will possess and exercise the powers of the Courts of Sudder Dewany and Nizamut Adawlut, and of the Sudder Board, in regard to the Dehra Doon, in like manner as the Resident is vested with those powers in regard to the districts of the Northern Doab, under the provisions of Clause 2, Section 9, Regulation I. of 1829.

6. In the administration of the Revenue, and of Civil and Criminal Justice, and of the Police, the Superintendent will exercise powers to the same extent as those vested by the general regulations in a Zillah Judge and Magistrate, and a Collector of Revenue, subject to your control and instructions.

7. In Civil suits, an appeal will lie to you in your capacity of Commissioner.

8. In the trial of Criminal cases, the Superintendent will be guided by the spirit and principles of the General Regulations in force in the ceded and conquered provinces.

9. In cases of a heinous nature requiring a more severe punishment than a Magistrate is authorized to inflict, the Superintendent shall commit the offender to take his trial before the Commissioner at the next sessions to be held in the Dehra Doon; provided always, that, if the sessions are not likely to be held within reasonable period, and the crime shall not be of such a description as to render the prisoner liable to suffer death or imprisonment for life, the Superintendent shall forward the whole of his proceedings to the Commissioner (with a letter explanatory of the case), who will pass such orders for the punishment or acquittal of the pris-

oner as may be consistent with the general powers vested in him for the adminstration of Criminal justice.

10. So much of Regulation X. 1817, as provides for the commitment and trial of persons charged with heinous crimes committed in the Dehra Doon, and in Jounsar Bawur, Poondar, and Sundokh, and other small tracts of country situated between the rivers Jumna and Sutlej, and requires that a report shall be made to Government in each case of commitment, has been rescinded.

11. Sessions of jail delivery shall be regularly held at least once a year in the Dehra Doon, by the Commissioner of the 1st Division, appointed under Regulation I. of 1829 for the trial of prisoners committed by the Superintendent of the Dehra Doon and its dependencies; and if the Commissioner shall consider the crime charged against a prisoner to be established, he shall either refer the case for the final sentence of the Resident at Delhi, or if the case be within the competence of the Judges of Circuit, under the regulations in force in the ceded and conquered provinces, he shall issue his warrant for the punishment of the criminal.

12. If the case shall be referred to the Resident at Delhi, it will of course be the duty of the Commissioner to forward a full report of the circumstances attending it, together with his own proceedings and those of the Superintendent or other officer making the commitment, for the final orders of the Resident.

13. The sentence of the Resident, whether for the release or punishment of the prisoner, shall be issued through the channel of the Commissioner, and shall be duly enforced by the Superintendent or other officer above-mentioned.

14. It will be the duty of the Superintendent of the Dehra Doon and its dependencies to furnish the Commissioner with periodical returns of the civil and criminal business of his Court, and with statements in regard to the collection and management of the revenues as may be required from him.

15. The foregoing orders of Government will be communicated to the Commissioner of Kumaon and to the Superintendent of the Dehra Doon and its dependencies, with instructions to make the necessary arrangements relative to the disposition of the Revenue and Judicial Establishments of the Dehra Doon, which have hitherto been included in those of Kumaon, but which it will now be necessary to bring under separate account.

16. Mr. Shore having embarked for England, I am directed to acquaint you that the Governor-General in Council has been pleased to appoint Major F. Young, of the 68th Regiment Native Infantry, Commanding the Sirmore Battalion, to be Superintendent for the affairs of the Dehra Doon and its dependencies, with a consolidated salary of Rs. 500 Sonat per month, including the allowance now drawn by him in the Political Department as Superintendent of Jounsar and Bawur.

Appendix VII.

Act No. XXI. of 1871.

Passed by the Governor-General of India in Council. Received the assent of His Excellency the Governor-General on the 11th July 1871.

An Act to give validity to the operation of the General Regulations and Acts within the Dehra Doon.

Whereas it is necessary to give validity to the operation of the General Regulations and Acts within the district under the Superintendent of the Dehra Doon, and to indemnify all officers and other persons who have acted in the said district under the said Regulations and Acts; it is hereby enacted as follows:—

Preamble.

1. The Regulations and Acts now in force in the district of Seharunpore are hereby declared to extend to the said district of Dehra Doon, and no judgment heretofore given, order passed, or proceeding had in the said district, shall be deemed to have been or to be invalid, merely because any Regulation or Act, under or in reference to which such judgment, ordered, or proceeding was given, passed, or had, was not in force at the time of such judgment, order, or proceeding, or on the ground of a defect of jurisdiction in any Court or Officer.

Confirmation of the Regulations and Acts in force in the Dehra Doon.

2. The High Court and the Board of Revenue of the North-Western Provinces shall exercise, and shall be deemed to have been heretofore authorized to exercise respectively in the said district, all the powers which the said High Court or Board of Revenue are at present, respectively, authorized to exercise in any part of the North-Western Provinces.

Jurisdiction of the High Court and Board of Revenue North-Western Provinces, over the Dehra Doon.

3. The District Court of Seharunpore shall be deemed to have been heretofore the District Court of the said District of Dehra Doon, and shall be the District Court of such District until the Local Government otherwise directs; and may, subject to the provisions of Act VI. of 1871, hear appeals from decisions given in the said district before the passing of this Act.

District Court of Seharunpore to be deemed the District Court of the Dehra Doon.

4. Nothing in this Act shall apply to that portion of the Dehra Doon District called Jounsar Bawur, and referred to in Section XI. of Act XXIV. of 1864.

Saving of Jounsar Bawur from the operation of this Act.

APPENDIX VIII.

Dustur-ool-umul of Jounsar Bawur, as drawn up by MR. A. Ross, with proposed additions and amendments by MR. J. C. ROBERTSON.

Mr. A. Ross.	*Mr. J. C. Robertson.*

Whereas the revenue is fixed on the general resources of the Zemindars as well as upon the lands actually under cultivation and not as in the Doon and plains, it is necessary to have knowledge of the capabilities of the people as regards quantity of sheep, goats, plough-cattle, laborers, and quantity of land; and of its produce, viz., walnut-trees, apricots, &c., cabbages, honey. All this is referred to as, on account of the frequent changes or distribution of shares, a frequent change of the revenue is necessary.

2. In this pergunnah, land is not measured in beegahs and biswas in the usual manner; there is only the measurement of the beegah, that is

Mr. A. Ross.   *Mr. J. C. Robertson.*

to say, as many pathas of seed as
they sow in their lands the measurement of that land is called so many
pathas, namely such and such a field
is four-pathas or five-pathas. The
patha is one kind of measurement, of
which mention is made in paragraph
3. In the new measurement, according to the orders of Government,
each piece of cultivated land has
been measured in blocks by acres—
one acre four beegahs, or one beegah
one rood.

3. The weight is according to
paemane, viz., the kutcha seer is called
a seer, and the pucca seer is called two
seers and a half, and four kutcha
seers make one patha (of rice or *oorud*), sixteen pathas make one doon,
and twenty doons make one khar,
and twenty seers kutcha make an
adhooue, forty seers kutcha make sixteen pucca seers; the chittack, and
adhpou are not used here, but the
quarter-seer and half seer are.

4. 1*st.*—There are two kinds of
cultivators, one *mouroosee* and the
other *gair mouroosee.* Cultivators
are of the Brahmin and Rajpoot caste,
and have the power to sell or otherwise dispose of their lands. They
have in every way a right and title
to their villages, but the *gair mouroosee* cultivators have no right to
sell or otherwise dispose of their
lands; but to the Zemindar, whose

Mr. A. Ross. *Mr. J. C. Robertson.*

land they cultivate, they pay rent in money ; this payment is called *kara*.

2nd. If any *mouroosee* cultivator removes or runs away from his villages the land in the first place should be made over to his brother, nephew, or any other nearest relation he may have ; if he have no relations, the Siáná of the *Khut* distributes the land among the *mouroosee* cultivators of the village. But if they do not agree to such an arrangement the Siáná gives it to some other person on a *gair mouroosee* tenure, and settles the quota of revenue payable by him. And if any such land cannot be settled in the above manner it'lies fallow, and the Siáná distributes the amount due from it over the whole *Khut*, according to the capabilities of each person : but no Dome, Bajgie, or any such castes can get possession of such land ; only Brahmins and Rajpoots can, and they can only hold it on a *gair mouroosee* tenure.

3rd. As regards a runaway cultivator, it was always the custom that, without any limitation as to time, whenever he chose to re-settle and ake possession of his land, whatever Government revenue was due could e collected from him, and he not rego his claim to his land unless

Mr. A. Ross.   *Mr. J. C. Robertson.*

he became a *mouroosee* cultivator in another place, or resigned his claim by writing a *baznama*. As this causes confusion, and loss of revenue to Government, we have, with the permission of Government, ordained that a runaway cultivator can reclaim his right to his land within five years, after which time the new cultivator can lay claim to the land, no matter if the former cultivator has or has not become a *mouroosee* of any other place.

4th. If the Siáná should make a *jair mouroosee* a *mouroosee* cultivator, he should give such person or persons a bond : the candidate must give Rs. 2 to the Siáná, Rs. 4 and a goat to the *puncháyut*, and Rs. 2 to the residents of the village of which he is made a *mouroosee* cultivator.

5th. When the tenant of any *Khut* or *Mehal* settled in another, the practice was that there was still a claim upon him for the revenue of his former tenures, and in his new *Khut* he gave *kara*. Now we have to ordain that in such a case there be no claim upon him for his tenures in his former *Khut*, and he will only pay the revenue in his new *Khut*.

6th. If a cultivator dies, leaving a widow and young children, and the widow takes to herself another husband, the husband can claim the tenures of the former one as *gair mouroosee*, but in any such case it is custo-

Mr. A. Ross.

Mr. J. C. Robertson.

mary to take a written document from
the new husband that the claim to any
such tenures (as he may have got by
marriage of the widow) of the children
of the former husband, and any that
might be born of him shall be as
follows :—Two-thirds are claimable
by the children of the former husband, and one-third by any children
that might be born of him; if, however, a cultivator should at his death
be in debt and have no heirs, then
whoever takes possession of his effects is liable for and must pay his
debts.

5. When land that has been lying fallow is taken possession of for
cultivation, the natural boundaries of
the village should be looked to, such
as trees, khuds, water-courses. Land
for grazing goats and sheep can be
taken without reference to boundaries.

All trees are the property of Government, except a few near villages
which were included in the *chuks*,
and were planted by the Zemindars.
The Zemindars have, however, permission to cut wood for making
ploughs, houses, or for their own
private use as fire-wood, but are not
allowed to sell it; and those in
whose *Khuts* there is no deodar, are
allowed to bring them from the
Khuts they have been accustomed,
subject to the above conditions. And

Mr. A. Ross.   *Mr. J. C. Robertson.*

the persons from whose *Khuts* the wood is cut are not allowed to charge for it. They have a complete right to all *bansie* jungle, and to medicines, such as *kakua, singhie;* and as they pay revenue on those, they also possess the right of grazing cattle. But other rights, such as mines, belong to Government, and no Zemindars can cultivate any barren land which has not been included in any *chuk*, without permission of the Collector. And Government has the right of selling and letting that land to whomsoever it chooses.

6. If there should be a quarrel with any other *Khut* about boundaries, it is settled either by *puncháyut* or by making oath, but it is settled by oath only where it cannot be settled by *puncháyut*. The person in possession should take the oath, and if the Siáná is interested he must take the oath, and in case he should refuse, the opposite party should be given the oath. Any quarrel about the lands in each *Khut* is settled in the same way.

Measurements having been made, and boundary-pillars erected to avoid future disputes, a report is to be made within fifteen days after a case has been decided, stating what decision has been arrived at, and what objections either of the parties make to the decision ; if no proper objec-

Mr. A. Ross. *Mr. J. C. Robertson.*

tion is filed within fifteen days, the decision of the arbitrators will be confirmed.

7. The customs of the puncháyuts are, that when a case has been settled by puncháyut, the puncháyut can claim a rupee from both sides, and and as regards the claim of the puncháyut in heavy cases of quarrel about boundaries, as described in para. 6, or regarding abductions of females, *vide* para. 15, the puncháyut can claim two rupees from each side.

8. *1st.*—In the whole pergunnah there are thirty-five *Khuts*. Each *Khut* contains several villages. The head man of the *Khut* is called Siáná. The duties of the Siáná are as follows:—To keep the Zemindars contented, to collect the dues of Government according to custom only, equal shares according to the capabilities of each one; to settle all quarrels; and look after the welfare of new ryots; and obey the orders of Government. The Siáná and Zemindars of *Khuts* are of the same caste and parentage, but the title of Siáná is hereditary. In some *Khuts* there is a difference of caste between the Siáná and the Zemindar.

One *Khut* constitutes a *Mehal.*

If any ryot does not pay his dues, the Siáná can sue him in court for the amount, and if a cultivator should run away, he can distrain his effects,

Mr. A. Ross.

Mr. J. C. Robertson.

through the Tuhseeldar, that they may be forthcoming when called for by the authorities, in order that Government may not be a loser; and if he cannot by any means in his power collect the Government revenue he must re-arrange the *phant* over his *Khut.* The *phant bundee* must be filed in the tuhseel in December: if the Siáná should fail to do this, he makes himself liable for such arrears. But even if no alteration is made, the *phant bundee* must be filed, in order that the arrangements for the following year may be looked into, and may be settled by the end of April.

2nd. The Siáná is appointed in the following way:—On the death of a Siáná his eldest son succeeds; but if he should be under age, or otherwise unfit, the title of Siáná still continues in his name. His brother or any other son of the deceased, does the work for him as his deputy, or *naib;* and if the Siáná wishes, he can make his eldest son Siáná during his lifetime; but his brothers have no claim to the Siáná because they are Zemindars: the Siáná can, if he chooses, allow them to receive a portion of the *bisouta.* In case of division of property, the Siáná *charee* is not distributed, though all other property is. A younger son cannot take the title of Siáná. If the eldest son

Mr. A. Ross.   *Mr. J. C. Robertson.*

should die, and have children, such children can claim the title, no one else can claim it.

3rd. When a Siáná dies without issue, his wife cannot claim the title of Siáná; deceased's brother succeeds to the post.

4th. In each *Khut* there are several Siánás, but that person is considered the head Siáná whose orders and power extend throughout the *Khuts.* In this pergunnah the village of such a Siáná is called " *khoond.*"

5th. If the Siáná should in any way injure the Government revenue, or act contrary to the Government orders, or injure the ryots by harsh measures, or wrongfully levy fines from the ryots of Government, or should be remiss in obeying the orders of his superiors (or Government), he may, according to the orders of Government, be dismissed. In such a case the person who has the next claim, and is capable, will succeed to the *Siáná-charee,* if approved by the district office. If he should wish, for any particular reason, to give up his claim, to the Siáná *charee,* it is customary to do it in the following manner:— First, he resigns his claim to his brother, then to any other person; but the rightful owner cannot sell it to destroy the rights of the next person.

Mr. A. Ross.   *Mr. J. C. Robertson.*

9. In many *Khuts* in each of the villages there is an officer of lower rank than the Siáná, who is called in the language of the district, " *chuckroutta.*" There is this difference between him and the Zemindar, that in some *Khuts* the Siáná from his own share gives the one or two rupees each, and in some *Khuts* the Siáná at the termination of any suit makes the Zemindars give him something. These *chukrait* do all the work of the *Khut* under the guidance of the Siáná, but if he should disobey the orders of the Siáná, the Siáná can dismiss him and appoint another person (*chukrait*) in his place.

10. If a Siáná should have to attend kutcherry or the district officer on his tour, he is entitled to a coolie as a servant, and another to carry a load; he also receives one seer of *atta* from each Zemindar. Formerly Siánás were in the habit of distributing any heavy expenses incurred by them over the whole pergunnah. On account of the great injury done to the Zemindars by this, that custom is abolished, and in future a Siáná will be entitled, once a year, to levy from each Zemindar at the rate of one-half anna per rupee of jumma payable by him, to cover his expenses when employed on business in the *Khut*; but he can claim no

Mr. A. Ross.   *Mr. J. C. Robertson.*

other fees except small perquisites that he is entitled to from his office.

11.   *1st.*—If a Zemindar wishes to sell any portion of the land he has under cultivation, he must first through the Siáná get the permission of the shareholders of his village, and also of the Zemindars of the *Khuts.* When a person of that *Khut* wishes to buy it, he cannot sell or mortgage it to a resident of another *Khut.*

2nd.—It was formerly usual that a purchaser of land was responsible for the revenue, and a mortgager was not responsible.   Not approving of this we have changed it as follows, viz. :—in either case—viz., either of a mortgage or sale—the person in possession is responsible for the revenue.

But the deed of mortgage must contain a condition that only the Zemindaree rights are mortgaged, not the land itself ; but when the mortgagee takes possession, he is only entitled to it till his claim has been paid, or till the expiry of any period agreed on at the time of the mortgage. The mortgager is also responsible for the revenue. All charges of possession must be entered in the *phant bundee.*

3rd.—Formerly, in case of sales, if the purchaser and seller lived in

Mr. A. Ross.   *Mr. J. C. Robertson.*

the same *Khut*, the purchaser gave a
dinner to the relatives of the seller,
and four annas for their having been
witnesses. All the other witnesses
of the sale received one anna per
rupee on the value of the sale. Besides the price of the land, he gave
one rupee (*khurtawun*), or gave a dinner to the relatives of the seller. The
Siáná of the *Khut*, the relatives of
the seller, and other residents, attest
the deed of sale; if the purchaser belong to another *Khut* his relatives
should be witnesses, but receive nothing for it.

4th.—With regard to mortgage.
It can only be completed by permission of the Siáná. No period is fixed
for the duration of the mortgage,
and no fees are paid; and the Siáná
receives four annas for writing the
deed, the mortgage must be recorded
by the *karkoon*.

5th.—If any one sells or mort-
gages any thing to two people, and
the first purchaser takes possession,
and the money is returned to the
second, the seller is considered dis-
honest.

12. *1st.*—If, according to custom,
four brothers have two, or perhaps one,
wife between them, and four or five
daughters are born, and one of the
brothers marries again, the children
are not shared between them, but

Mr. A. Ross.   *Mr. J. C. Robertson.*

remain with the woman; and the woman cannot go to the younger brothers, but must live with the elder; but the children are entitled to equal shares from the four brothers, which are paid to the elder. If they separate, the elder brother bears expenses of the marriages.

2nd.—Goods are divided in the following manner, viz.:—After deducting one thing of each kind, and one field for *pitans*, viz., rights on account of seniority, and half of that field, viz., *kanchoo*—for the youngest, all the rest are divided equally among them; but if there should be any bought land, viz., by mortgage or sale, or if there is any of their own land mortgaged in another place, that is also divided among them.

The Siáná distributes the shares, and receives one sheep, one goat, one dish, one weapon and five rupees. The puncháyuts receive five rupees, and the villagers two rupees; but if they are poor, no one receives anything in the shape of fees: no fees are paid in cattle.

3rd.—If the mother or father should be alive, the brothers with whom they live must provide them with a cow, plate, clothes, *budlen* currie; but if there are two fathers and mothers the second receive nothing.

4th.—If any man have three wives,

Mr. A. Ross.   *Mr. J. C. Robertson.*

and they have children in unequal numbers, viz., one have two, another three — at the time of sharing, the children all receive equal shares, except that the son with whom the first mother is to live will receive a little more.

5th.—If two brothers have one wife, and have two children at the death of the wife, and both brothers marry again, and after the marriage the elder brother dies, leaving four sons at the time of sharing, after deducting half the whole property for the children by the first marriage, the remainder is divided into six equal shares: from those six shares two more besides the half previously deducted, are given to the children by the first marriage.

6th.—Daughters can claim no shares in the paternal property; only the following is the custom—that the father should provide whatever is necessary for marriage ceremonies; and ·if he have any grown-up brothers, he should get them married.

13. The following are the customs as regard marriages. That only the Mia and Rawuth castes intermarry with the Kunnaith and Bhat castes, Brahmins and Rajpoots; in this district the marriage ceremony is called " *jhajerae*."

1st.—The bridegroom's f a t h e r gives the father of the bride one

Mr. A. Ross.

Mr. J. C. Robertson.

rupee as earnest money; the father of the young woman will give him a feast (dinner) of *pourees;* this makes the betrothal binding. The bride's father having dressed the young woman in a *chola,* a *damun,* and a *dhatou* (head-dress), and having given her as many dishes, &c., as in his power, goes with all his relatives to the bridegroom's father's house, and the bridegroom's father gives them one or two dinners.

2nd.—If the bridegroom's father should decline to fulfil the contract of marriage after the betrothal has taken place, he must not take back the earnest money he has given; but if the bride's father should give her in marriage to another party without the permission of the young man's father to whom she is betrothed, the girl's father will pay the young man's father sixty rupees.

14. When a son and heir is born, alms are distributed according to the means of the parents; and if any one be in great sorrow, their relatives give them a he-goat and a rupee, to try and dispel their sorrow.

15. If any person of low caste should run away with the wife of a respectable man, then, either the person who runs away with her, or any person who allows them to remain in the district, must pay one hundred

Mr. A. Ross.   *Mr. J. C. Robertson.*

and twenty-five rupees; or else the woman, together with the person who ran away with her, should go out of the country. If it be proved that intimacy has previously existed, the man should be made to pay twenty-five rupees through the Siáná. If any person of respectable caste seduces a woman of respectable caste, he is made to pay a fine of sixty rupees.

16. The following is the custom in this district as regard bargains :—There are no written documents taken; everything is done verbably; if any person knows how to write, he will write it down. If any quarrel arise on this account, it is settled in the following way :—If a debtor denies his entire debt, the *sahokar* has to swear to it in the name of his deity, but if a debtor denies a part of his debt and acknowledges a part, the *sahokar* gets that portion of the money which the debtor acknowledges, and for the remaining he must make the usual oath.

2*nd.*—As regards interest, the following is the custom.—The debtor has to give the *sahokar* eight pucca seers of corn at each harvest for each rupee, until the original sum is paid up, and if any one is unable to pay interest, and becomes insolvent, the *sahokar* takes his original amount in

Mr. A. Ross.   *Mr. J. C. Roberton.*

the presence of four arbitrators, and if
the *kooth* (viz., the eight seers paid
annually) remain due, he foregoes it.
If a debtor cannot pay his interest to
the *sahokar*, and has to give much
grain, then the *sohokar* makes him
pay double the original debt.

3rd.—The following is the custom
with regard to debts of grain :—That
for the space of one year the original
quantity is increased 50 per cent.,
and in the second year the accumula-
ted amount, or that which remains
after a part being paid back, is again
increased 50 per cent. If the debtor
has not paid any interest, and becomes poor and insolvent, then the
sahokar takes three times the original amount of his debt.

17. *1st*—In this district the most
binding oath is by the Deity Muka-
soon (sic). To swear by, especially
the one in Kally Bole, viz., Benoli, is
more particularly binding.

2nd.—There was also the following custom prevalent in this district:
—Often in cases of quarrels amongst
themselves, people used to offer up
at the temple of their deity stones
from the *Khuts* and mud from their
houses ; and that house having become the residence of their deity, fell
to ruins—no person could take possession of it. In several cases deities
were in the habit of ordering " land
or house be freed ! " and this order

Mr. A. Ross.   *Mr. J. C. Robertson.*

of the deity was made known by the
Mallees, who come from Gurhwál.
The Government having thought this
custom wrong, did away with it.

18.   Besides persons of high caste,
there are other people of low caste,
such as carpenters, bajgies, kolies,
blacksmiths, goldsmiths, chumars,
&c., but these attend to their own
trades and get pay for the work they
each perform.   Every Zemindar gives
to the blacksmith, bajgie, and carpenters only four pathas of corn; the
chumar does the work of the master
in whose service he is, if he gives
him food and clothing, and gives a
little land to his family.

2.   All disputes between servants
and masters to be referred to arbitrators.

20.   If any person steal sheep,
goats, &c., and eat them or sell them,
if the theft of one of these be proved,
seven will be taken from him in exchange for each one he has stolen;
and if the person will not give them,
then he will be forwarded to the kutcherry and punished as a thief.

21.   If any serious case of murder,
&c., occurs, it was the custom to decide such case by puncháyut.   It is
now no longer in the power of the
people to interfere in such cases; the
cases must be decided by the District Officer.

Mr. A. Ross.   *Mr. J. C. Robertson.*

22. If there is any quarrel among the people, generally they settle it themselves, or the Siáná settles it, and if the Siáná even, should not be able to settle it, the case is brought before the Magistrate to be settled.

23. Besides the above-mentioned customs, some of the customs of the under-mentioned *Khuts*, viz., Churtharee, Malaitha, Kothai, Rungao, Hurreepore Beas, differ somewhat from the customs of the other *Khuts* in the district of Jounsar Bawur.

2nd.—For in these *Khuts* the entire family of the Siáná are entitled to receive *bisouta*. One person from amongst them is made the Sudder Siáná, and whatever power the Sudder Siáná has in other *Khuts* is given to the whole of the Siáná's family in these. After the Sudder Siáná, the eldest son becomes Sudder Siáná.

3rd.—All the cultivators of these *Khuts* are *gair mouroosee*; none of them have power to sell their cultivated lands. The Siáná has power to make them cultivate the lands, or to take away the land from them.

4th.—In the *Khuts* of Kálsee, viz., Hurreepore Beas, there is one custom quite different from the rest of Jounsar, that is to say, the revenue in this *Khut* is not taken upon the capabilities of each one. There is plenty of cultivable land; the Siánás take the

Mr. A. Ross.   *Mr. J. C. Robertson.*

rest in *bhutaee ;* and all the remaining customs of the whole pergunnah
are the same.

[NOTE.—The " *Dustoor-ool-umul,*" as it stands above, was drawn up by Mr. Ross
in 1851. The alterations and modifications proposed by Mr. J. C. Robertson are
shown in the second column. These were afterwards incorporated in the original
rules, and the whole accepted and signed by the Siánás of each *Khut.*]

APPENDIX IX.

1817 A.D. *Regulation X.*

A Regulation for the trial of persons charged with the commission of
certain heinous offences in Kumaon and other tracts of territory ceded to
the Honorable the East India Company by the Rájá of Nepál, and subject to the British Government, passed by the Vice-President in Council
on the 22nd July 1817.

Of the territories ceded to the British Government by the Rájá of
Nepál, under the treaty of peace concluded on the 2nd day of December
1815, many portions have been since restored to the Native chiefs, to
whose authority they were formerly subject, or have been transferred to
the independent authority of other Native chieftains or powers.

The portions of territory ceded to the Rájá of Nepál which have
been retained under the authority and dominion of the British Government
are as follows, viz. :—

1*st.*—The tract of country called Dehra Doon, heretofore forming a
part of Gurhwál.

2*nd.*—The province of Kumaon.

3*rd.*—Jounsar Bawur, Poondur, and Sundokh, and other small tracts
of country situated between the rivers Jumna and Sutlej.

By the provisions of Regulation IV. 1817, the tract of country denominated Dehra Doon, has been formally annexed to the district of
Seharunpore, and the laws and regulations in force in the latter district,
have, with certain exceptions, been extended to the Dehra Doon. Local
circumstances, however, have rendered it inexpedient that a similar ar-

rangement should at present be adopted in the province of Kumaon, or in the reserved tracts of country situated between the rivers Jumna and Sutlej.

The administration of the police and of civil and criminal justice, with the management of the revenues, as well in Kumaon as in the several places last mentioned, is conducted by British officers, under instructions issued for their guidance by the Governor-General in Council.

Embarrassment, however, having been experienced in the several places above-mentioned, from the want of a suitable tribunal for the trial of prisoners charged with offences of a heinous nature, the Vice-President in Council, with a view to provide for the due and deliberate investigation of charges of that nature, has been pleased to enact the following rules, to be in force from the period of their promulgation.

2. The British officers who now are, or hereafter may be invested with the charge and Superintendence of the Police, and with the administration of criminal justice in the province of Kumaon, or in the several reserved tracts of territory situated betweeen the rivers Jumna and Sutlej, are hereby prohibited from awarding punishment against any persons charged before them with having been concerned, either as principals or as accomplices, in the commission of the following offences, viz., murder, or any species of homicide not manifestly accidental or justifiable, robbery by open violence, as defined in Section 3, Regulation LIII. 1803 ; violent affrays attended with serious casualties or circumstances of aggravation ; treason or rebellion against the State.

British officers in charge of Kumaon, &c., not to award punishment against offenders charged with certain crimes of a heinous nature.

3. If any person subject to the jurisdiction of the British officers above alluded to, whether from local residence or from the perpetration of a criminal act within the limits of the British territory under their respective superintendence, shall, on due and careful investigation, appear to have been concerned, either as a principal or as an accomplice, in the commission of any of the crimes above-mentioned, such person shall be kept in close custody, and shall be committed to take his trial before a Commissioner to be nominated and appointed for that purpose by the Governor-General in Council.

Such offenders, how to be proceeded against.

4. It shall be the duty of the local officer immediately on making the

commitment, to report the case to the Governor-General in Council, who will take the necessary measures for nominating an experienced judicial officer as Commissioner to hold trials of this nature, at such time and place as may appear proper in each instance, or at such stated periods as may be found convenient.

Commissioners to be appointed by Government.

5. In the conduct of the trial, the Commissioner will exercise the same powers as are vested in Judges of Circuit, and will be guided by the spirit and principles of the regulations in force in the ceded and conquered provinces ; provided, however, that it shall not be necessary that any law officer should attend the trial, or any *futwa* should be required in such cases.

Powers vested in the Commissioner.

6. If the Commissioner should be of opinion that the crime charged against the prisoner is not established by the evidence, he shall issue his warrant for the release of the prisoner.

Commissioner may release prisoner if not convicted.

7. If Commissioner shall consider the crime charged against the prisoner to be established, he shall either refer the case for the final sentence of the Court of Nizamut Adawlut, or if the case be within the competence of Judges of Circuit, under the regulations in force in the ceded and conquered provinces, he shall issue his warrant for the punishment of the criminal.

Commissioner to refer case to Nizamut Adawlut if charge be proved.

8. If the case shall be referred to Nizamut Adawlut, it shall be the duty of the Commissioner to forward to that Court a full report of the case, together with his own proceedings and those of the officer by whom the commitment may have been made.

With a report and the proceedings on the case.

9. On receipt of the proceedings, the court of Nizamut Adawlut will, without requiring any *futwa* from their law officers, pass such sentence or order as on due consideration they may deem proper and consistent with the spirit and principles of the Regulations in force in the ceded and conquered provinces.

Nizamut Adawlut to pass final sentence.

10. The sentence of the Nizamut Adawlut, whether for the release or punishment of the prisoners, shall be issued through the channel of the Commissioner who may have held the trial, and shall be duly enforced by

the local British officers by whom the commitment may have been

Sentence, how to be carried into effect.

made, or who may at the time be entrusted with the management of the local police.

11. *1st.*—Whenever a native subject of the British Government charged with having been concerned in the commis-

In what cases the local officers may take cognizance of crimes committed within the territories of i n d e-p e n d e n t States or chieftains.

sion of a criminal offence within the territories of any independent State or Chieftain situated in the vicinity of Kumaon, or of the reserved tracts of country be-tween the Jumna and Sutlej rivers, shall be appre-hended by, or shall be delivered up to, the British officers invested with the charge of the police in those places, respectively, the officers in question shall be deemed competent to investigate the charge, and to release or punish the accused, under the general powers vested in them by the Governor-General in Council.

2nd.—Provided, however, that if the charge shall be of the nature of any of those described in Section 2 of this Regulation, the local officer shall proceed in the manner directed in Sections 3 and 4 of this Regula-tion; and the Commissioner who may be appointed to hold the trial, as well as the Court of Nizamut Adawlut, shall in such cases be guided by the provisions of Sections 5, 6, 7, 8, 9, and 10 of this Regulation.

12. It shall not be competent to the local officers intrusted with the administration of Criminal Justice in Kumaon, and in the several reserve

Crimes committed b e f o r e 15th May 1815, not cognizable by British officers.

tracts of territory situated between the rivers Jumna and Sutlej, or to any Commissioners who may be ap-pointed under this Regulation or to the Nizamut Adawlut to take cognizance of any crime or offence which may have been committed in any part of the tracts of country above adverted to, previously to the 15th May 1815, being the date of the conven-tion by which they were surrendered to the Hon'ble the East India Company.

13. No part of the Regulations in force in the ceded and conquered

Sentence, how to be regulated with regard to offences committed between 15th M a y 1815, and t h e pro-mulgation of this Re-gulation.

provinces by which the punishment of the crimes specified in Section 2 of this Regulation may be en-hanced beyond the punishment ordinarily inflicted for such crimes according to the former laws and usages in force in those tracts of country, shall be considered applicable to persons convicted of having committed those crimes previously to the promulgation of this Regulation.

14. In cases, however, in which the penalties established by the Regulations in force in the ceded and conquered provinces

Same subject.

for murder or other species of homicide, robbery by open violence, violent affrays attended with serious casualties or circumstances of aggravation or for treason and rebellion against the State, may appear to be more lenient than those to which the offenders would have been subjected under the pre-existing laws and usages of Kumaon, and of the reserved tracts of territory situated between the rivers Jumna and Sutlej, such offenders shall, nevertheless, have the benefit of the provisions now established, supposing the offences to have been committed between the 15th May 1815, and the period of the promulgation of this Regulation.

Appendix X.

Act No. XXIV. of 1864.

Section XI. The administration of Civil and Criminal Justice, and the

Administration of justice and collection of Revenue in tract known as Jounsar Bawur in whom to be vested.

superintendence of the settlement and realization of the public revenue, and of all matters relative to rent, within the tract of country in the Dehra Doon called Jounsar Bawur, are hereby vested in such Officer or Officers as the Lieutenant-Governor of the North-Western Provinces may, for the purpose of tribunals of first instance, or of reference and appeal, appoint.

XII. The Officer or Officers so appointed shall be guided by the

Rules for administration.

Rules made before the date fixed for this Act to come into operation by the Lieutenant-Governor of the North-Western Provinces under the authority of Act XIV. of 1861 (*to remove certain tracts of country in the Rohilcund Division from the jurisdiction of the tribunals established under the General Regulations and Acts*), for the guidance of the Officers appointed to administer the tracts of country described in the said Act.

XIII. The Lieutenant-Governor of the North-Western Provinces

Code of Civil Procedure may be extended to certain tracts.

may, by notification in the Official Gazette, extend the Code of Civil Procedure to the said tract of country known as Jounsar Bawur and the tracts of country described in the said Act XIV. of 1861.

XIV. Nothing in this Act, or in the said Act, XIV. of 1861,
Such tracts not to be held excluded by this Act or Act XIV. of 1861, from the operation of the Indian Penal Code. shall be held to exclude the said tract of country known as Jounsar Bawur, or the tracts of country described in the said Act XIV. of 1861, from the operation of the Indian Penal Code.

XV. This Act shall come into operation on the first day of May 1864.
Operation of Act.

The nature of the Terai Rules has been so fully explained in the text, that it is quite unnecessary to reprint them *in extenso*, and Section XII. of Act XXIV. of 1864 gives all that need be known about Act XIV. of 1861, with reference to Jounsar Bawur.

Appendix XI.

Synopsis of Regulation XX. of 1817.

A brief explanation of the substance of this Regulation is quite sufficient for all practical purposes.

The Preamble states its general object; viz., to define the duties and powers of all Police Officers, as well as the responsibilities of proprietors or farmers of land with reference to Police Administration.

Section II. details the sections and provisions of former Regulations hereby rescinded.

Section III. is very important, vesting the appointment and removal of Police Officers almost absolutely in the District Magistrate. Herein lies the main distinction between the old and new system. Section IV. explains the relative rank and general functions of Officers on the Thannah establishments. Sections V. to XI. treat of Badges, Arms and Accoutrements; powers and duties of Police Officers employed at out-posts; leave of absence, &c.; Thannah Records; Returns, &c., to Magistrates; *daks* and so forth; and irregular practices. The rest of the Regulation (Sections XII. to XXXV.) is occupied with rules of procedure superceded by the new Code. Among the distinctive points may be noted; the swearing of witnesses by police darogahs in certain special cases laid down in other regulations; absolute freedom in the manner of recording confessions; the use of the stocks; the detention of prisoners up to 48 hours; and interference by Police Officers, under certain conditions, in cases of distraint for arrears of rent, with a view to assist the distrainer.

6

Appendix XII.

Fee Simple Grants under Lord Canning's Rules of 1861. Notification, Govt. N. W. P., No. 1358a., dated 11th December 1861.

No.	Name of Grant.	Name of Proprietor.	Area in acres.			Amount of purchase money.			Remarks.
			A.	R.	P.	rs.	A.	P.	
1	Chunderbunee, ...	Col. Barlow, ...	635	0	0	1,595	0	0	Paid.
2	Annville, ...	Mrs. Carberry, ...	754	0	0	3,255	0	0	1/10 purchase money paid only.
3	Chunderbunee, ...	Kadir Khan and Koora,	312	3	12	1,177	8	0	Do.
4	Attic farm, east of the Sooarna	Mrs. Mackinnon, ...	1,010	0	0	4,050	0	0	Do.
5	Attic farm west of ,,	,,	1,113	0	0	3,795	0	0	Do.
6	East Hopetown, ...	Dehra Doon Tea Company	3,503	0	0	14,285	0	0	Do.
7	Arcadia, ...	,, ,,	5,499	0	0	23,730	0	0	Do.
8	Central Hopetown, ...	Mrs. Vansittart, ...	3,327	0	0	7,702	0	0	Rs. 6000 paid.
9	Pirtheepore, ...	Mr. Charles Swetenham,	2,513	0	0	9,887	8	0	1/10 purchase money paid.
10	Dhoocota, ...	Mrs. General Dick, ...	252	0	9	1,250	0	0	Paid.
11	Umbaree, ...	Col. H. T. Macpherson,	520	0	7	1,300	0	0	1/10 paid.
12	Lyster grant, ...	Col. H. H. Lyster, ...	1,022	0	0	4,985	0	0	Paid.
			20,460	3	21	77,021	0	0	

(Remarks for rows 4–7:) Those who have not paid up the price, pay interest at 10 per cent. per annum.

Note.—According to Mr. Daniell the totals are—acres 20, 801 ; Rs. 79,423.

Grants purchased on redeeming the land Revenue.

Area in acres.		Proprietor.
492	1. Dalunwálá.	Mrs. General Dick.
264	2. Bukhtawarpore. ...	Mrs. Mackinnon.
213	3. Koloopanee.... ...	Hafiz Ahmud Hussein.

Good Service Grants Revenue Free.

Area in acres.		Proprietor.
2,090	1. Balawálá.	Capt. Forest's children—lately purchased by Rájá of Nahun.
2,002	2. Raynor Grant. ...	Mrs. Raynor's husband for service in Mutiny.
544-2-5.	3. Burasee.	Soobedar Singheer Thappa, 2nd Goorkha Regiment.

Lease or Russudee Grants.

Area in acres.	Revenue.	Proprietor.
3,950	1. Annfield.	Mrs. Rind.
Tract of forest.	2. Land attached to above, ...	Do. { Pays Rs. 5 per annum, and is not strictly speaking a Russudee Grant.
217	3. Talepoorah.	Brothers Powell.
960	4. Jeewungurh.... ...	Goolab Singh.
213	5. Koloopanee.	Kunhya Singh.
1,589	6. Koonja-Karghi. ...	Brothers Powell.
599	7. Mirzapore.	Ditto.
608	8. Chuktunwálá. ...	Rana Petumber Singh.
930	9. Ranee-pokri. ...	Luchmanpoorie and others.
4,961	10. Markham.	Colonel T. W. Thelwall.
7,894	11. West Hopetown. ...	Mrs. Vansittart.

Note.—No. 2, a bit of forest land near Annfield made over to Major Rind, at a nominal rent is generally put down as a Russudee Grant, making eleven in all, but this is really incorrect. The first seven and the last are in the Western Doon; the rest in the Eastern Doon.

APPENDIX XIII.

Land Revenue for each year of Mr. Daniell's Revised Settlement.

Years.			Western Doon.	Jumma of grants in Western Doon.	Eastern Doon.	Jumma of grants Eastern Doon.	Total.
			RS.	RS.	RS.	RS.	RS.
1863-64,	...	...	...	19,836	2,936	5,913	631	29,316
1864-65,	...	...	...	19,836	3,162	5,193	664	29,575
1865-66,	...	...	..	19,836	3,338	5.913	812	29,899
1866-67,	...	...	...	24,871	3,566	6,747	845	36,029
1867-68,	...	...	...	24,871	3,762	6,747	868	36,248
1868-69,	...	...	...	24,871	3,938	6,747	889	36,445
1869-70,	...	...	...	24,871	4,047	6,747	1,344	37,009
1870-71,	...	...	...	24,871	4.083	6,747	1,354	37,055
1871-72,	...	...	...	24,871	4,119	6,747	1,361	37,098
1872-73,	...	...	...	24,871	4,144	6,747	1,366	37,128
1873-74,	...	...	...	24,871	4,169	3,747	1,367	37,154
1874-75,	...	...	...	24,871	4,181	6,747	1,957	37,756
1875-76,	...	...	...	24,871	4,194	6,747	1,957	37,769
1876-77,	..	...	...	24,871	4,202	6,747	1,957	37,777
1877-78,	...	...	...	24,871	4,209	6,747	1,957	37,784
1878-79,	...	...	...	24,871	4,215	6,747	1,957	37,790
1879-80,	...	...	...	24,871	4,216	6,747	2,546	38,380
1880-81,	...	...	...	24,871	4,216	6,747	2,546	38,380
1881-82,	...	...	...	24,871	4,216	6,747	2,546	38,380
1882-83,	...	...	...	24,871	4,216	6,747	2,546	38,380
1883-84,	...	...	...	24,871	4,216	6,747	2,546	38,380
1884-85,	...	...	...	24,871	4,216	6,747	2,988	38,822
1885-86,	...	...	...	24,871	4,216	6,747	2,988	38,822
1886-87,	...	...	...	24,871	4,216	6,747	2,988	38,822
1887-88,	...	...	...	24,871	4,216	6,747	2,988	38,822
1888-89,	...	...	...	24,871	4,216	6,747	2,988	38,822
1889-90,	...	...	...	24,871	4,216	6,747	2,988	38,822
1890-91,	...	...	...	24,371	4,216	6,747	2,988	38,822
1891-92,	...	...	...	24,871	4,216	6,747	2,988	38,822
1892-93,	...	...	...	24,871*	4,216†	6,747	2,988‡	38,822

The totals here differ from those in Annual Jumma Statement, Appendix B., but I have no means of explaining discrepancies satisfactorily, and they are so slight as to be practically immaterial.

* After the settlement was over, Rs. 292 were remitted for ever on account of Daneewálá village, the same having been purchased by Mrs. Dick in 1869-70.

† Deduct jumma of the Bukhtawarpur Grant by Mr. Mackinnon ; redeemed in.

Year, 1867-68, 1868-69, 1869-70, 1870-71, 1871-72, 1872-73, 1873-74, 1874-75, 1885-76, 1876-77, 1877-78, 1878-79 to 1892-93.
Jumma, 86   92   100   108   115   ;122   129   133   139J   141   143   146

‡ The jumma of half of Kolhoopanee Grant was remitted from 1871-72, when redeemed by Ahmud Hussein. The jumma was :—

Year, 1871-72, 1872-73, 1873-74, 1874-75, 1875-76, 1876-77, 1877-78, 1878-79, 1879-80 to 1892-93.
Jumma, 108   114   121   126   129   132   135   136   137

APPENDIX XIV.

Statement showing the comparative price of Agricultural Produce and Provisions in Dehra during the last 10 years.

	Number of seers sold per rupee (1 seer = $2\frac{1}{16}$ English pounds.										Averaeg of the 10 years.
	1861.	1862.	1863.	1864.	1865.	1866.	1867.	1868.	1869.	1870.	
Paddy (*dhán*), ...	18¾	35½	39½	28½	24½	25¾	26	28	15¾	26½	26¾
Common rice (husked), ...	11	17½	20¼	15½	12½	13¼	14½	14¼	8½	12¾	14
Best rice (husked),	6½	7½	9¼	8	7	7	7¼	7	6	6¼	7¼
Wheat, ...	12	23½	28¾	23¼	19½	19½	19½	18	11½	13¾	19
Barley, ...	14¼	34¾	43¼	33	26¾	28½	27¾	27½	15½	22¾	27¼
Til, ...	15	9	10	12	11	...	...	10¼	9	10½	10¾
Mustard (*surson*),	10	13	11	16	16	...	...	15½	12	15¼	13½
Mundooa, ...	18¾	26¾	50	31½	25½	26	...	17¾	15	25¾	23¾
Lentils (*mussoor*),	10	27¾	31¼	28¼	21¾	26	21½	22	12	16¾	21¾
Tuar, ...	11¾	26½	...	...	18	27	...	...	...	17½	20
Cleaned cotton, ...	3¾	3¼	1¾	1½	2¾	2	3½	...	1¾	1¾	2¼
Sugar, refined, ...	2¾	2¾	3	3	3½	3¼	2¾	2¾	2¾	2½	3
Salt, ...	8¼	8	7	6¾	7¼	7¼	7¼	7½	6¾	7	7¼
Ghee, ...	2¼	2	2	2	1¾	2	1¾	1½	1¾	1¼	1¾
Milk, ...	16¾ qts.	16 qts.	17 qts.	17 qts.	16 qts.	14½ qts.	14½ qts.	14 qts.	11 qts.	16 qts.	15¼ qts.
Spirits (25° below proof),	1⅓	1⅓	$1\frac{1}{15}$	$1\frac{1}{15}$	$1\frac{1}{15}$	$1\frac{1}{15}$	$\frac{8}{9}$	$1\frac{1}{15}$	$\frac{8}{9}$	$1\frac{1}{15}$	$1\frac{19}{225}$
Shira, ...	13½	20¼	33	27	28	30	30	19	11	16	23
Goor, ...	8½	10	11½	9½	11¼	14¾	7½	8¼	7	9¾	9¾
Gágla, ...	...	...	...	...	...	...	...	16	21¼	12	16½
Zaminkand, ...	...	...	...	...	...	...	...	16	12	21¼	16½
Potatoes, ...	...	...	...	...	...	...	...	21¼	16	12	16½
Onions, ...	...	...	...	...	...	...	...	16	12	21¼	16½
Garlic	...	...	...	...	...	...	...	8	9	7	8
Peas (European),	...	...	...	...	...	...	...	8	9	7	8
Turnips, ...	...	...	...	...	...	...	...	32	21¼	16	23
Carrots, ...	...	...	...	...	...	...	...	32	21¼	16	23

A second Statement slightly differing from the former is added.

Years.	Wheat.	Barley	Gram.	Rice.	Bajra.	Oorud.	Indian corn.
	seers.	md. srs.	seers.	md. srs.	seers.	seers.	md. srs.
1858, ...	27	1 5	35	0 30	35	28	1 0
1863, ...	30½	1 6½	31	1 0	35	24	1 10
1870, ...	14	0 23	13½	0 20	14	16	0 20

APPENDIX XV.

No.	Name of plantation.	Name of owner, &c.	Estimated area under cultivation in acres. Acres. Rds.	Estimated annual out-turn in ℔s. ℔s.	Estimated value of annual out-turn. RS. A. P.	Remarks.
1	Arcadia, ...	Dehra Doon Tea Co., "Limited." Manager, Mr. Minto, ...	220 0	50,000	70,000 0 0	This calculation is for the current year, 1871. The manager says, that allowing the possible out-turn to be 15,000 ℔s., and making deductions for loss, he considers 125,000 ℔s. only as the amount which would actually reach the market. He has also made allowances for the fact that the class of tea made by him (green) has fallen 3 annas or 4 annas a pound since February.
2	Hurbunswálá,	... ...	330 0	80,000		
3	Annfield, ...	Annfield Tea Company. Manager, Mr. Watson,	300 0	50,000	37,500 0 0	
4	Bunjarawálá,	Mrs. Knyvett, ...	100 0	5,264	2,632 0 0	This calculation is for 1870. The concern being a private one, and badly managed, like all of the same sort in the Doon, it is hard to obtain exact statistics, but those given are pretty correct.
5	Luckunwálá,	Ditto,	50 0	1,048	655 0 0	The same remarks apply here also. Moreover this was a jungle in 1869, and not more than 400 ℔s. of tea have been sold as yet.

No.	Garden	Proprietor or Manager							Remarks
6	Kowlaghir,	Nahun Rájá. Manager, Mr. Mooney,	250	0	54,026	0	27,013	0	
7	Goodrich,	Mrs. Vansittart,	80	0	6,200	0	3,900	0	The out-turn in 1869 was 400 lbs.; in 1870, 5000; that given is the estimated out-turn for the current year. The value of the 1869 out-turn was Rs. 2,200, which in 1870 increased to Rs. 3,300. Mrs. Vansittart considers that this may possibly rise to Rs. 4,000 in 1871.
8	New Goodrich,	Ditto,	2	1	40	0	28	0	A very young plantation tried experimentally in other soil.
9	West Hopetown,	Company, "Limited,"	68	0	10,000	0	6,250	0	The Company has been kept going by contributions among the Shareholders, but its prospects are improving. Col. Macpherson. the resident shareholder, to whom the accounts are rendered, has furnished this return.
10	Nirunjunpore,	Col. Macpherson,	80	0	4,800	0	3,000	0	This calculation is for 1870. The plantation in that year did not pay its working expenses in spite of facilities for canal irrigation.
11	Ambaree,	Ambaree Tea Co, Manager, Mr. Barnard,	170	0	13,000	0	10,000	0	This calculation is also for 1870.
12	Rosevilla,	Capt. Swetenham,	48	0	3,000	0	2,000	0	
		Carried forward,	1,698	1	2,77,378	1	1,62,978	0	

APPENDIX XV.—(*Continued*).

	Name of plantation.	Name of owner, &c.	Estimated area under cultivation in acres.		Estimated annual out-turn in lbs.	Estimated value of annual out-turn.			Remarks.
			Acres.	Rds.	lbs.	Rs.	A.	P.	
13	Charleville,	Brought forward, ...	1,698	1	2,77,378	1,62,978	0	0	The returns for 1869, when the estate was in Mrs. Dick's hands are as follows:—
		Mrs. Dick, let to Mrs. Reily, ...	76	0	4,000	2,500	0	0	Acres. lbs. Rs. 60 3,000 1,800 In 1870, the estate was under the management of a native agent who is said to have rendered no accounts. The calculation given for the present year is a rough estimate by Mrs. Reily's son.
14	Hurbhujwálá,	Lala Rám Nath, ...	110	0	9,000	5,344	0	0	
15	Gurhee, ...	Lala Rám nath, ...	30	0	2,200	1,362	0	0	
16	Durtáwálá and Ambeewálá,	Mohunt Preetum Dass, ...	17	0	800	300	0	0	
17	Nuthunpoor,	Myan Rubere Singh, son of Rájá Lal Singh,	15	1	450	281	0	0	
18	Dhoom Singh's Plantation,	Dhoom Singh, ...	59	0	3,000	1,500	0	0	
19	Nirunjunpore,	Kunhya Lal, ...	19	0	1,000	600	0	0	
		Total, ...	2,024	2	2,97,828	1,74,865	0	0	

APPENDIX XVI.

Rough Sketch of the quantity of land which could be brought under Tea cultivation, with a capital of Rupees 2,00,000, and also intended to show the probable amount of expenditure and profits spread over a space of six and eight years.

1,800 ACRES OF LAND.

Expenditure from 1st to 6th year, inclusive.

	Rupees
Factory and houses for Tea makers,	6,000
Bungalow for Overseer,	1,400
Pay of Overseer, at Rs. 100 per month, for 6 years,	7,200
,, of 500 men, at Rs 4. per month, for 6 years,	1,44,000
,, of 10 Chowdries, at Rs. 8 per month, for 6 years,	5,760
,, of 1 Moonshee, at Rs. 12 per month, and 2 Chupprassees, at Rs. 5 per month, for 6 years,	1,584
Rent of land for 6 years, at Rs. 1,350 per annum,	8,100
Expense of preparing tea, in 3rd, 4th, 5th and 6th years, say 20 men, at Rs. 5 per month,	4,800
Four Chinese tea manufacturers, at Rs. 34 per month, for 4 years,	6,528
Implements, passage money for manufacturers, carriage, &c., say,	8,628
Contingencies for 6 years, say Rs. 1,000 per annum,	6,000
Total,	2,00,000

Income from 3rd to 8th year, inclusive.

	Rupees.
Tea manufactured in the 3rd year, say 10 ℔s. per acre, at 8 annas per ℔.,	9,000
Tea manufactured in the 4th year, say 30 ℔s. per acre, at 8 annas per ℔.,	27,000
Tea manufactured in the 5th year, say 80 ℔s. per acre, at 8 annas per ℔.,	72,000
Tea manufactured in the 6th year, say 120 ℔s. per acre, at 8 annas per ℔.,	1,08,000
Tea manufactured in the 7th year, say 150 ℔s. per acre, at 8 annas per ℔.,	1,35,000
Tea manufactured in the 8th year, say 200 ℔s. per acre, at 8 annas per ℔.,	1,80,000
Total in the 8th year,	5,31,000
Deduct amount supposed to be expended in 8 years,	2,68,612
Profits Rupees,*	2,62,388

Working expenses in the 7th and 8th year.

	RS.
Overseer's pay for 2 years,	2,400
500 men for 2 years,	48,000
10 Chowdries for 2 years,	1,920
1 Moonshee and 2 Chuprassees for 2 years,	528
Rent of land for 2 years,	2,700
Expense of preparing tea doubled, say,	4,800
Wages of four Chinese for 2 years,	3,264
Contingencies for wear and tear of implements, boxes, &c., in 2 years,	5,000
Total Rupees,	68,612
	2,68,612

* There would be sundry expenses deducted from this sum, such, for example, as interest of capital for the first six years, auctioneers' fees, carriage, &c., if the Teas were sold in India ; and carriage, freight, and other shipping charges if exported to Europe and America, or the Colonies. I have put down the pay of the Overseer at Rupees 100 per mensem, as that is the sum at present paid by Government ; but it would probably be necessary to raise that to Rupees 300 if a good man could be procured. I have supposed the whole of the 1,800 acres to be planted in one year ; but this would probably be impossible, as it would take some time to select the land, and the requisite number of plants might not be procurable at once. In this case, however, the expense for labor would be proportionably less.

R. FORTUNE.

Dr. Jameson makes the following calculation for 1,000 Acres during the same period.

INCOME.	RS.	EXPENDITURE.	RS.	RS.	RS.
3rd Year.		**1st Year.**			
		To Plantation Establishment.			
By tea prepared in 3rd year, from 400 acres, at ℔s. 20 per acre, 400 × 20 = ℔s. 8,000, at 1 rupee per pound, ...	8,000	Moonshie, Chuprassees, &c., ...	600		
		120 Mallies at Rs. 4 each, ...	5,760	6,360	
4th Year.		*To extra Establishment.*			
By tea prepared in 4th year, from 400 acres, at ℔s. 40 per acre, 400 × 40 = ℔s. 16,000; and ℔s. 40 from 400 acres, at ℔s. 20 per acre, 400 × 20 = ℔s. 8,000. In all ℔s. 24,000, at 12 annas per pound, ...	18,000	1 Carpenter, at Rs. 8 per month, ...	96		
		1 Smith, ,, ,, ...	96	192	
		To Extraordinary expenses.			8,852
5th Year.		**2nd Year.**			
By tea prepared in 5th year, from 400 acres, at ℔s. 80 per acre, 400 × 80 = ℔s. 32,000; and do. from 400 acres, at ℔s. 40 per acre, 400 × 40 = ℔s. 16,000; and from 2,000 acres, at ℔s. 20 per acre, 200 × 20 = ℔s. 4,000. In all ℔s. 52,000, at 8 annas per pound, ...	26,000	House for Planter, ...	1,600		
		Implements, bullock, &c., ...	700	2,300	
		To Plantation establishment, ...		6,360	
		,, Extra establishment, ...		192	
		,, Extraordinary expenses, implements, &c., ...		800	7,352

3rd Year.

To Plantation establishment, ...		6,360	
" Extra ...		384	
" Native tea-maker's establishment			
1 Jummadar, at Rs. 10 per month, ...	120		
12 Native tea-makers, at Rs. 5 each, ...	720	840	
" Extraordinary expenses, wood for boxes, &c., ...		800	
" Building a factory, ...		2,000	
50,000			10,384

4th Year.

To Plantation establishment, ...	6,360	
" 30 Extra málies, at Rs. 4 each for 3 months,	600	
" Tea-maker's Establishment, ...	840	
" Carpenters, &c., planking teas, ...	800	
" Extraordinary expenses, land rent, wood for boxes, making ditto, ...	1,800	
78,000		10,400

5th Year.

To Plantation establishment, ...	6,360	
" 40 Extra málies, at Rs. 4 each for 5 months,	800	
" Tea-maker's establishment, ...	900	
" Tea-packing " ...	900	
" Extraordinary expenses, carriage of tea, land rent, extra coolies, &c., ...	3,000	11,960
95,000		
Carried forward, ... 2,75,000		48,948

6th Year.

By tea prepared in 6th year, from 400 acres, at ℔s.150 per acre, 400 × 150 = ℔s. 60,000; and from 400 acres, at ℔s. 80 per acre, 400 × 80 = 32,000; and from 200 acres, at ℔s. 40 per acre, 200 × 40 = ℔s. 8,000. In all ℔s. 100,000, at 8 annas per pound, ... 50,000

7th Year.

By tea prepared in 7th year, from 400 acres, at ℔s. 200 per acre, 400 × 200 = ℔s. 80,000; and do. from 400 acres, at ℔s. 150 per acre, 400 × 150 = 60,000; and from 200 acres, at ℔s. 80 per acre, 200 × 80 = ℔s. 16,000. In all ℔s. 1,56,000, at 8 annas per pound, ... 78,000

8th Year.

By tea prepared in 8th year, from 800 acres, at ℔s. 200 per acre, 800 × 200 = ℔s. 160,000; and from 200 acres, at ℔s.150 per acre, 200 × 150 = ℔s. 30,000. In all ℔s. 1,90,000, at 8 annas per pound, ... 95,000

Carried forward, ... 2,75,000

APPENDICES.

INCOME.	RS.	EXPENDITURE.	RS.	RS.	RS.
Brought forward,	... 2,75,000	Brought forward, ...	...	...	48,948
		6th Year.			
		To Plantation establishment, ...		6,360	
		„ 60 Extra málies, at Rs. 4 each for 5 months,		1,000	
		„ Tea-maker's establishment, ...		1,200	
		„ Tea-packing establishment, carpenters, &c., ...		1,200	
		„ Extraordinary expenses, carriage of teas, land rent, wood for box-making, extra coolies, &c., ...		4,600	14,360
		7th Year.			
		To Plantation establishment, ...		6,360	
		„ 150 Extra málies, at Rs. 4 each for 5 months, ...		3,000	
		„ Tea-maker's establishment, ...		2,000	
		„ Tea-packing establishment, carpenters, &c.,		1,800	
		„ Extraordinary expenses, carriage of teas, land rent, wood and lead for boxes, extra coolies, &c., ...		6,500	19,660

8th Year.

To Plantation establishment,	...	6,360
" 250 Extra málies, at Rs. 4 each for 5 months,	...	5,000
" Tea-maker's establishment,	...	2,500
" Tea-packing establishment, carpenters, &c.,	...	2,200
" Extraordinary expenses, carriage of teas, land rent, wood and lead for boxes, extra coolies, &c.,	...	3,000
		24,060
By remaining in hand as profit,	...	1,67,972
Total Rupees,		2,75,000

Total Rupees, ... 2,75,000

I append a calculation made by a Native Planter.
One Beegah (kutcha) of land.

(First year).

	RS.	A.	P.	RS.	A.	P.
Cost of :—						
Ploughing, ...	0	4	0			
Making holes to plant in, ...	4	0	0			
Manure and cart hire, ...	3	0	0			
10 seers of seed, ...	5	0	0			
Wages of 8 men for digging up plants, ...	1	4	0			
Carriage of pindee or earth round plants, 8 men, ..	1	0	0			
Putting in pindee, 8 men, ...	1	4	0			
Dowl-pindee, ...	0	5	0			
Digging *thaonla* (trough) round plants, 8 men, ..	1	4	0	17	5	0

(No yield in 2nd year).

	RS.	A.	P.	RS.	A.	P.
Further cost :—						
1st year, digging and repairing, ...				2	0	0
2nd „ „				4	0	0
Land revenue, 1st year, ...	2	0	0			
„ 2nd year, ...	2	0	0	4	0	0
Canal water rent, 1st year, ...	0	8	0			
„ 2nd year, ...	0	8	0	1	0	0
Sundries and Tools, ...				2	10	0
Total cost, ...				13	10	0

Yield in 3rd year :—

Green leaves, ...	2 maunds, }	kutcha.
Equal to dry leaves, ...	20 seers, }	

Expense in 3rd year :—	RS.	A.	P.	RS.	A.	P.
Land revenue, ...	2	0	0			
Canal „	0	8	0			
Digging and repairing, ...	6	0	0			
Picking leaves, ...	2	8	0			
Making tea, ...	3	2	0			
Fire-wood, ...	1	0	0			
Baskets and tools, ...	1	14	0	17	0	0

Yield in 4th and 5th years :—

Green leaves, ...	3 maunds, }	kutcha.
Equal to dry leaves, ...	30 seers, }	

Expense in 4th and 5th years :—

	RS.	A.	P.	RS.	A.	P.
Land revenue, ...	.. 2	0	0			
Canal „	.. 0	8	0			
Digging and repairing, ...	.. 6	0	0			
Picking leaves, ...	.. 3	12	0			
Making tea, ...	.. 4	11	0			
Fire-wood, ...	.. 1	3	0			
Baskets and tools.	.. 1	14	0	20	0	0

Average yield, 25 seers kutcha, at Re. 1 per seer kutcha, Rs. 25-0-0.
Average cost, Rs. 18-8-0.

Appendix XVII.

Statement showing the comparative prices of Agricultural Produce and of Provisions in Kálsee during the last 10 years.

	Number of seers sold per rupee (1 seer = 2 1/16 English pounds.)										Average.
	1861.	1862.	1863.	1864.	1865.	1866.	1867.	1868.	1869.	1870.	
Paddy, ..	25	25	30	30	30	30	30	30	30	32	29
Common rice (husked),	10½	14	18¼	14	11¼	9½	11½	11½	7¼	10½	11¾
Bets rice, (husked),	9¼	12	12¾	11½	9½	8	9¼	8½	5¾	6¾	9¼
Wheat, ..	12¾	20¼	29¾	22¾	18¼	16	17	16	10½	12	17½
Barley, ...	17½	28¾	39	31¼	24¼	24	26¼	30½	14½	21¼	25¾
Lentils, (mussoor,)	12½	17½	25	20½	19¼	15¾	18	16½	11¾	13	17
Cleaned cotton,	...	...	...	...	...	...	...	...	...	...	...
Sugar (raw),..	6	6½	8	7¾	8¾	9	7½	6¾	5½	7	7¼
Sugar (refined,)	2¾	2¾	3¼	3¼	3¼	3¼	2¼	2½	2½	2¾	2¾
Salt, ...	8	7¾	6¾	7	7	6¾	6¼	7¼	6½	6¾	7
Ghee, ...	2¼	2	2	2	2	1½	1¼	1½	1¼	1¾	1¾
Milk, ...	10¼	16½	16	16	15	17	15½	13¼	12¾	10¾	14¼
Tobacco, ..	10	8	8	8	7¾	7½	6½	7¾	7¼	6	7½
	qts.	qts.	qts.	qts.	qts.	qts.	qts.	qts.	qts.	qts.	pt. gils.
Spirits 25° below proof,	1⅓	1⅓	8/9	8/9	8/9	8/9	8/9	8/9	8/9	8/9	13 37/45
	seers.	seers.	seers.	seers.	seers.	seers.	seers.	seers.	seers.	seers.	seers.
Goor, ...	7½	8	9	9	10¼	11½	8¾	7½	7½	9¼	8¾
Sheera, ..	11	14	11	17¼	23	...	...	20	...	...	16
Potatoe, ..	26	26	26½	25	27½	19¾	19	19	19	23	23
Gagla, ..	60	70	50	50	45	60	50	40	45	38	50¾
Firewood, ..	240	240	200	200	200	200	160	155	150	150	190
Wages of unskilled laborers, per rupee.	men. 8	men. 8	men. 8	men. 8	men. 6	men. 6	men. 5	men. 5	men. 5	men. 5	men. 6½

APPENDIX XVIII.

ALLOCATION STATEMENT OF THE DISTRICT OF DEHRA DOON 1861.

Detail of A. D. and Tuhseel Guards, with names of Stations and Outposts.

Stations.	A. District Police.				D. Municipal Police.				Tuhseel Guards.		Total of each Station.				Remarks.
	Sub-Inspector.	Head Constables.	Mounted Constables.	Foot Constables.	Sub-Inspectors.	Head Constables.	Mounted Constables.	Foot Constables.	Head Constables.	Foot Constables.	Sub-Inspectors.	Head Constables.	Mounted Constables.	Foot Constables.	
Dehra, ...	1	2	..	12	..	1	..	12	1	4	1	4	..	28	
Mussooree, ...	1	2	..	12	..	..	..	..	..	..	1	2	..	12	
Suhnspore, ...	1	2	..	12	..	..	..	..	..	..	1	2	..	12	
Rajpore,..	..	2	..	6	..	..	..	3	..	..	..	2	..	9	
Kansrao, ...	..	2	..	6	..	..	..	..	..	..	..	2	..	6	
Landour, ...	..	..	..	..	..	1	..	8	..	..	..	1	..	8	
Rajghat, ...	..	1	..	4	..	..	..	..	..	..	..	1	..	4	
Jeewun Gurh, ..	..	1	..	4	..	..	..	..	1	4	..	2	..	8	{ Tuhseel Kálsee.
Timlee Pass,.. ..	..	1	..	4	..	..	..	..	..	..	..	1	..	4	
Khujnawer Pass,..	..	1	..	4	..	..	..	..	..	..	..	1	..	4	
Shorepore Pass, ..	..	1	..	4	..	..	..	..	..	..	..	1	..	4	
Lucheewala, ...	..	1	..	4	..	..	..	..	..	..	..	1	..	4	
Khurkuree, ...	..	1	..	4	..	..	..	..	..	..	..	1	..	4	
Total, ...	3	17	..	76	..	2	..	23	2	8	3	21	..	107	

Return of Police Establishment, Dehra.

Nature of duties on which employed.	Sub-Inspectors. No.	Cost.	Head Constables. No.	Cost.	Mounted Constables. No.	Cost.	Foot Constables. No.	Cost.	Grand Total. No.	Cost.	Remarks.
		RS. A.		RS. A.		R. A.		RS. A.		RS. A.	
A.											
Qr. Guard & Magazine,	...	...	1	10	...	...	4	24	5	34	
Orderlies of P. Hospital,	...	...	...	...	...	...	2	12	2	12	
Orderlies of P. Officers,	...	...	...	...	...	...	2	12	2	12	
Drill Instructor, ...	...	...	...	...	...	...	...	...	...	...	
School Master, ...	...	...	...	...	...	...	...	...	...	...	
Total, ...	...	...	1	10	...	...	8	48	9	58	
B.											
On duty in Mgt.'s Court,	...	...	3	30	...	...	6	36	9	66	
City Police Station,	1	70									
Police station, 1st class,			2	50							
„ „ 2nd class,	1	50	2	40	...	...	76	456	96	846	
Out-posts,			4	60							
Road Patrols,	1	30	9	90							
Total, ...	3	150	20	270	...	...	82	492	105	912	
C.											
Jail Guard, ...	...	...	1	12 8	...	...	6	36	7	48 8	
Lock up Guard, ...	...	...	2	20	...	...	12	72	14	92	
Treasury Guard, {	...	...	1	20	} ...	...	12	72	14	102	
			1	10							
Tuhseel Guard, ...	...	...	2	20	...	...	8	48	10	68	
Personal Guards, ...	...	...	1	10	...	...	4	24	5	35	
Total, ...	...	...	8	92 8	...	...	42	252	50	344 8	
D.											
			1	20							
Reserve, ...	2	60	1	15	} ...	...	28	168	35	293	
			3	30							
	2	60	5	65	...	...	28	168	35	293	
Total of A., ...	...	...	1	10	...	...	8	48	9	58	
Total of B., ...	3	150	20	270	...	...	82	492	105	912	
Total of C., ...	...	...	8	92 8	...	...	42	252	50	344 8	
Total of D., ...	2	60	5	65	...	...	28	168	35	293	
Total, ...	5	210	34	431 8	...	...	160	960	199	1,607 8	
Municipal Police, ...	...	...	2	20	...	...	23	138	25	158	
	5	210	36	457 8	...	...	183	1098	224	1,768	(sic)

Division of Armed and Civil Police.

	Sub-Inspectors.	Head Constables.	Foot Constables.	Mounted Constables.	Total.	Remarks.
Armed Police.						
Jail Guard, ...	...	1	6	...	7	
Hawalat Guard, ...	...	2	12	...	14	
Treasury Guard, ...	...	2	12	...	14	
Tuhseel Guard, ...	...	2	8	...	10	
Quarter & Magazine Guard,	...	1	4	...	5	
Drill Instructor, ...	...	...	...	...	...	
Personal Guard, ...	...	...	...	...	...	
Station and Out-posts, ...	...	...	12	..	12	
Reserve, ...	...	2	16	...	18	
Total, ...	...	10	70	...	80	
Civil Police.						
Hospital Orderlies, ...	...	...	2	...	2	
Superintendent's do., ...	...	...	2	...	2	
School Master, ...	...	...	...	...	...	
Magistrate's Court, ...	...	3	6	...	9	
Personal Guards, ...	...	1	4	...	5	
Stations and Out-posts. ...	3	17	64	...	84	
Reserve, ...	2	3	12	...	17	
Total, ...	5	24	90	...	119	
Total of Armed Police, ...	...	10	70	...	80	
Total of Civil Police, ...	5	24	90	...	119	
Total of Muncipal Police, ...	...	2	23	...	25	
Grand Total, ...	5	36	183	...	224	

Sanctioned Armament of District.

	Fire-arms.	Swords.
Stations and Out-posts, ...	...	52
Mounted Constables, ...	...	...
Reserve, ...	80	31
Municipal, ...	...	14
Others, ...	...	5
Total, ...	80	102

(By Order). CHARLES DODD, *Lieut.*,

Personal Asst. to Inspector Genl., Police, N. W. P.

APPENDIX XIX.

ALLOCATION STATEMENT OF THE DEHRA DOON DISTRICT, 1872.

Dehra Doon Division of Armed and Civil Police.

	Sub-Inspectors.	Head Constables.	Foot Constables.	Total.	Fire-arms.	Swords.	Remarks.
Armed Police.							
Jail Guard, ...	...	1	6	7	7	...	
Hawalat Guard, ...	...	2	12	14	14	...	
Treasury Guard, ...	...	2	12	14	14	...	
Tuhseel Guards, ...	...	2	8	10	10	...	
Quarter Guard and Magazine Guard, ...	...	1	3	4	4	...	
Drill Instructor, ...	...	...	...	...	...	...	
Stations and Outposts, ...	...	...	12	12	12	...	
Reserve, ...	..	2	14	16	16	...	
Total, ...	...	10	67	77	77	...	
Civil Police.							
School Master, ...	...	...	...	...	...	...	
Magistrate's Court, ...	...	3	6	9	...	6	
Stations and Outposts, ...	4	20	69	93	...	59	
Reserve, ...	2	3	10	15	...	20	
Total, ...	6	26	85	117	...	85	
Total of Armed Police, ...	...	10	67	77	77	...	
Total of Civil Police, ...	6	26	85	117	...	85	
Total of Municipal Police, ...	...	1	11	12	...	6	
Grand Total, ...	6	37	163	206	77	91	

Note.—One Sword allowed for each mounted Constable, in addition to the number of Swords specified in allocation.

(By order, &c). CHARLES DODD, *Capt.*,
Personal Asst. to Inspt. Genl. of Police.

ALLAHABAD, }
The 1st Feby., 1870. }

Detail of Police Establishment Dehra Doon.

Nature of duties on which employed.	Sub-Inspectors.		Head Constables.		Foot Constables.		Grand Total.		Remarks.
	No.	Cost.	No.	Cost.	No.	Cost.	No.	Cost	
A.		RS.		'RS. A.		RS.		RS. A.	
Quarter and Magazine,	...	...	1	10	3	18	4	28 0	
Drill Instructor,	...	...	...	...	...	...	...	...	
School Master.	...	...	...	...	...	...	...	...	
Reserve,	2	60	1 / 1 / 3	20 / 15 / 30	24	144	31	269 0	
Total,	2	60	6	75	27	162	35	297 0	
B.									
Magistrate's Court,	...	...	3	30	6	36	9	66 0	
Stations and Outposts,	1 / 1 / 2	70 / 50 / 60	2 / 3 / 6 / 9	50 / 60 / 90 / 90	81	486	105	956 0	
Total,	4	180	23	320	87	522	114	1,022 0	
C.									
Jail Guard,	...	...	1	12 8	6	36	7	48 8	
Lock-up Guard,	...	...	2	20	12	72	14	92 0	
Treasure Guard,	...	...	1 / 1	20 / 10	12	72	14	102 0	
Tuhseel Guard,	...	...	2	20	8	48	10	68 0	
Total,	...		7	82 8	38	228	45	310 8	
Total A.,	2	60	6	75	27	162	35	297 0	
Total B.,	4	180	23	32	87	522	114	1,022 0	
Total C.,	...	...	7	82 8	38	228	45	310 8	
Total,	6	240	36	477 8	152	912	194	1,629 8	
Muncipal Police,	...	...	1	10	11	66	12	76 0	
Grand Total,	6	240	37	487 8	169	978	296	1,705 8	

Detail of Tuhseel Guards, Stations and Outposts.

Stations.	District Police.			Municipal Police.			Tuhseel Guards.		Total of each Station.			Remarks.
Dehra, ...	1	2	12	...	...	...	1	4	...	1	3	16	
Mussooree, ...	1	2	12	...	...	...	...	...	...	1	2	12	
Suhnspore, ...	1	2	9	...	...	...	...	...	...	1	2	9	
Kálsee, ...	...	1	6	...	...	...	1	4	...	...	2	10	
Chukrata, ...	1	2	9	...	...	...	...	...	...	1	2	9	
Rajpore, ...	...	2	6	...	...	3	...	...	...	...	2	9	
Kansrao, ...	...	2	6	...	...	...	...	...	...	...	2	6	
Landour, ...	...	...	...	...	1	8	...	...	...	...	1	8	
Rajghat, ...	...	1	3	...	...	...	...	...	...	...	1	3	
Jeewun Gurh, ...	...	1	3	...	...	...	...	...	...	...	1	3	
Khujnawur, ...	...	1	3	...	...	...	...	...	...	...	1	3	
Asaroree, ...	...	1	3	...	...	...	...	...	...	...	1	3	
Lucheenalair Bhogpore,	...	1	3	...	...	...	...	...	...	...	1	3	
Khurkhuree, ...	...	1	3	...	...	...	...	...	...	...	1	3	
Total, ...	4	20	81	...	...	1	11	2	8	...	4	23	100

APPENDIX XX.

Dehra Doon Establishment on 1st April, 1853.

Description of Service.	Amount of pay.	Remarks.
English Office.	RS.	
Head Clerk, ...	150	
2nd Do., ...	80	
Clerk,...	40	
Do., ...	40	
Do., ...	20	
Duftry, ...	8	
Total, ...	338	
Amlah.		
Sherishtadar,...	60	
Naib do., ...	25	
Wasil Bakee Navis, ...	20	
Nazir, ...	15	
Mahafiz Duftar, ...	15	
Mohurrir, ...	10	
Jumma Khurch Navis, ...	15	
Duftry, ...	6	
1 Jummadar,...	6	
8 Chuprassees, @ Rs. 4, ...	32	
Total,	204	
Superintendent's Personal Guard.		
1 Duffadar, ...	5	
4 Burkundazes, @ Rs. 4, ...	16	
Total, ...	21	
Civil Establishment.		
Sherishtadar, ...	40	
Naib do., ...	20	
Mohurrir, ...	15	
Do., ...	15	
5 Chuprassees, @ Rs. 4, ...	20	
Total, ...	110	
Carried forward, ...	673	

Dehra Doon Establishment on 1st April, 1853—(Continued).

Description of Service.	Amount of Pay.	Remarks.
	RS.	
Brought forward, ...	673	
Treasury.		
Treasurer, ...	50	
Asst. Do., ...	10	
Total, ...	60	
Jail Establishment.		
Darogah, ...	30	
Naib do., ...	15	
Blacksmith, ...	7	
Native Doctor, ...	20	
Compounder, ...	6	
Jummadar, ...	16	
Duffadar, ...	8	
Do., ...	8	
Naick, ...	6	
36 Sepoys, @ Rs. 5, ...	180	
Total, ...	296	
Police Establishment.		
Chokee, Mussooree.		
Jummadar, ...	15	
Mohurrir, ...	10	
10 Burkundazes, @ Rs. 4, ...	40	
Total, ...	65	
Chokee, Rajpore.		
Jummadar, ...	15	
Mohurrir, ...	8	
5 Chuprassees, @ Rs. 4,... ...	20	
Total, ...	43	
Chokee, Khurkhuree.		
Jummadar, ...	12	
9 Burkundazes, @ Rs. 4, ...	36	
Total, ...	48	
Carried forward, ...	1,185	

Dehra Doon Establishment on 1st April 1853—(Continued.)

Description of Service.				Amount of Pay.	Remarks.
				RS.	
Brought forward,			...	1,185	
Chokee, Rut.					
Jummadar,	...	...	...	12	
9 Burkundazes, @ Rs. 4,	...	...		36	
		Total,	...	48	
Chokee, Shorepore.					
Jummadar,	...	...	...	12	
9 Burkundazes, @ Rs. 4,	...			36	
		Total,	...	48	
		Total,	...	1,281	
Tehseel, Dehra.					
Tuhseeldar,	...	...	...	80	
Mohurrir,	...	...	...	15	
Wasil Bakee Nuvees,		...	...	15	
Canoongo,	...	...	...	15	
Sowar,	...	...	...	18	
Do.,	...	...	...	18	
Native Doctor,	...	...	...	15	
Mirda,	...	...	...	6	
Do., ...	...	...	...	6	
Jummadar,	...	...	...	10	
24 Chuprassees, @ Rs. 4,	...	...		96	
Stationery,	...	...	...	14	
		Total,	...	308	
Jounsar Bawur.					
Peshkár,	...	...	...	40	
Mohurrir,	...	...	...	15	
Canoongo,	...	...	...	15	
Native Doctor,	...	...	...	15	
Jummadar,	...	...	...	8	
12 Chuprassees, @ Rs. 4,	...	...		48	
Stationery,	...	...	...	3	
Repair to Tuhseel,	...	...	...	4	
		Total,	...	148	
Total Tuhseelee Establishment,			...	456	
Superintendent's ditto,			...	1,281	
		Grand Total,	...	1,737	

9

Appendix XXI.

Dehra Doon Establishments on 1st April 1873.

Description of Office.	Amount of Pay.	Remarks.
	RS.	
English Office.		
Head Clerk, ...	150	
Clerk, ...	40	
Acting do., ...	...	
Total, ...	190	
Native.		
Sherishtadar, ...	60	
Naib do., ...	25	
Ruobukar Nuvees, ...	20	
Izhar Nuvees, ...	10	
Total, ...	115	
Treasury.		
Treasury Clerk, ...	70	
Clerk, ...	40	
Treasurer, ...	80	
Naib do., ...	15	
Potdar, ...	5	
Jumma Kurch Nuvees, ...	25	
Total, ...	235	
Record Office.		
Mohafiz Duftur, ...	25	
Total, ...	25	
Miscellaneous.		
1 Dufturee, ...	7	
1 Sweeper, ...	4	
1 Khulassie, ...	5	
6 Chuprassees, @ Rs. 5-8,	33	
5 Do., @ Rs. 5, ...	25	
Total, ...	74	
Carried forward, ...	639	

Dehra Doon Establishments on 1*st April* 1873—(Continued).

Description of Office.	Amount of Pay.	Remarks.
	RS.	
Brought forward, ...	639	
Huzoor Tuhseel.		
Tuhseeldar,...	150	
Sub-Deputy Collector, ...	40	
Revenue Accountant, ...	20	
Seea Nuvees, ...	15	
Tuhveeldar, ...	10	
1 Canoongo, ...	20	
Total, ...	255	
Miscellaneous, Huzoor Tuhseel.		
2 Land Measurers, ...	12	
10 Messengers, @ Rs. 5, ...	50	
Stationery Allowance, ...	11	
Total, ...	73	
Tuhseel Kálsee.		
Sub-Deputy Collector, ...	100	
Seea Nuvees, ...	15	
Cashier, ...	10	
1 Canoongo, ...	20	
Total, ...	145	
Miscellaneous, Kálsee Tuhseel.		
2 Land Measurers, ...	12	
8 Messengers, @ Rs. 5, ...	40	
Stationery Allowance, ...	8	
Total, ..	60	
Carried forward, ...	1,172	

Dehra Doon Establishments on 1st April 1873—(Continued).

Description of Office.	Amount of Pay.	Remarks.
	RS.	
Brought forward, ...	1,172	
English Office.		
Judicial Clerk, ...	30	
Native.		
Sherishtadar, ...	40	
Naib do., ...	20	
Mohurrir, ...	15	
Do., ...	15	
1 Dufturee, ...	6	
Total, ...	126	
Judicial Clerk, Dehra Tuhseel,	15	
Do. Kálsee do.,	15	
Total, ...	30	
Abkaree Department.		
Mohurrir, ...	20	
1 Chuprassee, @ Rs. 5, ...	5	
1 Do., @ Rs. 4, ...	4	
Total, ...	29	
Stamp Department.		
Mohurrir, ...	15	
Total, ...	15	
Canal Department.		
2 Chuprassees, @ Rs. 4, ...	8	
Stationery allowance, ...	1	
Total, ...	9	
Grand Total, ...	1,381	

Establishments of the Chukrata Offices, 1st April 1873.

Cantonment Magistrate's.

			RS.	RS.
1 Sherishtadar,	...	...	45	
1 Nazir, ...	...	...	20	
1 Mohurrir, ...	...	...	20	
1 Dufturee, ...	...	...	8	
4 Chuprassees, @ Rs. 6,		...	24	117

Treasury Office.

1 Clerk, ...	...	...	75	
1 Treasurer, ...	...	...	25	
1 Chuprassee,...	...	...	6	106

Abkaree Department.

1 Darogha, ...	...	...	25	
1 English Clerk,	...	...	15	
6 Chuprassees, @ Rs. 6,		...	36	76

		Total, ...	... 299

Civil Courts Establishment, Dehra Doon, 1st April 1873.

Designation.			Salary.	Remarks.
			RS.	
Clerk of Court, ...	...	...	80	
Bailiff, ...	...	...	50	
Mohurrir, ...	...	...	25	
Do., ...	...	...	20	
Do., ...	...	...	15	
Do., ...	...	...	15	
Contingencies, including Stationery, ...			10	
Dufturee, ...	...	...	5	
		Total, ...	220	

Officers who have held Office of Superintendent Dehra Doon.

Name of Officers.	Appointment.	Date of Appointment.
T. P. Calvert, ...	Asst. Collector of Seharunpore, in Charge of Dehra Doon, ...	29th March 1816.
A. Murray, ...	Ditto,	11th November 1817.
M. Moore, ...	Ditto,	10th July 1818.
Hon'ble F. J. Shore,	Joint Magistrate of Dehra Doon, (took charge on 21st Jany. 1823),	24th October 1822.
Do., do., ...	Asst. to Comr., Kumaon, at Dehra Doon, ...	8th December 1825.
Col. F. Young, ...	Joint Magistrate, Asst. Commr. of Kumaon, Offg. appd. 17th July 1828. Decr. 10th 15th August 1828.	
Ditto, ...		
Ditto, ...	Called Superintendant, Dehra Doon and Political Agent,	5th June 1829.
F. O. Wells, ...	Superintendent and Pòlical Agent,	30th Decr. 1841.
F. Williams, ...	Ditto,	16th January. 1842.
H. M. Lawrence, ...	Ditto,	14th January 1843.
H. Vansittart, ...	Ditto,	7th January 1843.
A. Ross, ...	Ditto, (20th January?)	16th March 1846.
M. B. Thornhill, ...	Ditto, (1st Dec. 1852?)	11th March 1853.
R. H. Dunlop, ...	Ditto,	1st April 1854.
H. G. Keene, ...	Ditto,	1st March 1856.
R. Manderson, ...	Ditto,	18th April 1860.
S. S. Melville, ...	Ditto,	1st July 1862.
R. Manderson, ...	Ditto,	1st February 1864.
S. S. Melville, ...	(22nd March ?)	May 1864.
C. A. Daniell, ...		May 1866.
J. Sladen, ...		3rd May 1867
W. W. G. Cornwall,	Offg. from Decr. 1868 to	25th August 1869.
H. G. Ross,... ...		11th November 1869.

Appendix XXII.

Statement of Expenditure from 1859 to 1873; Forest Department, Dehra Doon and Seharunpore.

Dehra.	Amount.			Seharunpore.	Amount.			Total.		
	RS.	A.	P.		RS.	A.	P.	RS.	AS.	P.
1859-60.										
Establishment pay, ...	4,515	9	0							
General expenditure, ...	43,777	10	10							
	48,293	3	10					48,293	3	10
1860-61.										
Establishment pay, including allowances, ...	5,365	8	5							
General pay, including allowances, ...	24,060	14	11							
	29,426	7	4					29,426	7	4
1861-62.										
Establishment pay, including allowances, ...	6,093	15	4							
Extra pay, including allowances,	844	12	1							
General expenditure, ..	11,754	9	4							
	18,693	4	9					18,693	4	9
1862-63.				**1862-63.**						
Establishment pay, ...	5,332	3	3	Establishment pay, ..	910	11	2			
Extra pay, ...	1,967	6	2	General expenditure, ..	2,219	14	7			
General expenditure, ..	10,876	9	8							
	18,176	3			3,202	9	9	21,378	12	10
1863-64.				**1863-64.**						
Establishment pay, ...	4,136	14	8	Establishment pay, ..	3,578	5	11			
General expenditure, ...	8,494	11	11	General expenditure, ..	1,758	14	3			
	12,631	10	7		5,337	4	2	17,968	14	9

Statement of Expenditure from 1859 to 1873; Forest Department, Dehra and Seharunpore—(Continued).

Dehra.	Amount.			Seharunpore.				Amount.			Total.		
	Rs.	A.	P.		Rs.	A.	P.	Rs.	A.	P.	Rs.	A.	P.
1864-65.				**1864-65.**									
Establishment pay, .. 4,886 13 11				Establishment pay, .. 4,861	12	9							
General expenditure, .. 7,471 9 11	12,358	7	10	General expenditure, .. 7,814	15	7		12,676	12	4	25,035	4	2
1865-66.				**1865-66.**									
Establishment pay, .. 12,198 4 6				Establishment pay, .. 9,178	7	0							
Extra pay, .. 567 3 9				Extra pay, .. 93	6	7							
General expenditure, .. 10,886 13 6	23,652	5		General expenditure, .. 8,033	2	3		17,304	15	10	40,957	5	7
1866-67.				**1866-67.**									
Establishment pay, .. 8,637 7 4				Establishment pay, .. 5,029	8	1							
Extra pay, .. 1,062 13 4				Extra pay, .. 166	13	6							
General expenditure, .. 6,645 5 4	16,347	10		General expenditure, .. 6,579	1	11		11,775	7	6	28,123	1	6
1867-68.				**1867-68.**									
Establishment pay, .. 5,620 2 9				Establishment pay, .. 5,782	15	2							
Extra pay, .. 335 1 10				Extra pay, .. 34	10	2							
General expenditure, .. 4,830 11 7	10,786		2	General expenditure, .. 4,086	5	2		9,903	14	6	20,689	14	8
1868-69.				**1868-69.**									
Establishment pay, .. 19,159 5 2													
Extra pay, .. 949 8 4				The revenue of these two years is given separately in the cash-book, but the expenditure is mixed up, and therefore cannot be ascertained separately.									
General expenditure, .. 25,971 10 10	46,080	8	4										
1869-70.													
Establishment pay, .. 21,250 7 0													
Extra pay, .. 846 9 10													
General expenditure, .. 50,230 9 10	72,327	10	8								72,327	10	8

1870-71.								
Establishment pay, ..	22,446	14	6	44,616	11	2	44,616	11	2
Conservancy and working, ..	22,169	12	8						
1871-72.									
Establishment pay, ..	19,501	1	7	58,555	2	1	58,555	2	1
Conservancy and working, ..	39,054	0	6						
1872-73.									
Estsblishment pay, ..	24,334	13	3	46,948	9	11	46,941	9	11
Conservancy and working, ..	22,613	12	8						

Amalgamated.

Appendix XXIII.

Schools, Dehra Doon District.

Name of Schools.	1870-71.		1871-72.		1872-73.		Remarks.
	Admission.	Attendance.	Admission.	Attendance.	Admission.	Attendance.	
Tuhseelee.							
Dehra, ...	38	32	34	29	34	31	
Kálsee, ...	32	27	34	28	35	30	
Hulkabundee, Dehra Doon.							
Bhogpore, ...	33	24	32	25	37	28	
Lukhond, ...	32	28	37	27	42	34	
Ranghurwálá, ...	37	24	25	19	26	18	
Jounsar Bawur.							
Bastil, ...	...	...	21	21	19	13	
Naraya, ...	...	...	18	17	14	12	
Nugtoo, ...	...	...	20	16	23	16	
Oodpulta, ...	...	...	...	...	25	21	
Bhumarie, ...	...	...	...	...	14	11	
Mundhanee, ...	...	...	...	...	15	14	
Khadee, ...	...	...	...	...	20	17	
Laoree, ...	...	...	...	...	10	8	
Girls School.							
Dehra, ...	16	11	19	13	13	10	
Ladpore, ...	12	10	11	10	9	5	

For facility of reference, I reprint some statements which have already appeared in the published report on the last settlement of Dehra Doon.

Appendix to Statement No. IV., or the General Statement of Maafee Villages in Dehra Doon.

Pergunnah.	Number of Villages.	Name of Village.	Full area.	MINHAEE.		Culturable waste.	CULTIVATED, INCLUDING FALLOW.			Total.	Nominal Jumma.
				Lákhiráj.	Barren.		Judeed or fallow.	Irrigated.	Unirrigated.		
1	2	3	4	5	6	7	8	9	10	11	12
											RS.
WESTERN DOON.	1	Banjerawálá, ..	503	..	60	153	2	133	155	290	175
	2	Chamasaraee, ..	6,563	4	6,288	3	34	8	226	268	300
	3	Dehrakhas, ..	1,902	19	436	94	6	977	370	1,353	1,500
	4	Dhurtawálá, ..	304	14	54	27	5	199	5	209	220
	5	Dobhalwala, ..	147	13	26	20	10	..	78	88	80
	6	Goruckpoor, ..	26	..	..	..	..	3	12	15	20
	7	Jakun, ..	19	..	11	:	..	..	19	19	10
	8	Meonwálé, ..	975	..	80	381	25	..	489	514	320
	9	Mulhawala, ..	227	..	13	..	2	202	10	214	160
	10	Prempore, ..	129	..	15	..	..	78	36	114	75
	11	Punditwaree, ..	367	,,	57	49	17	238	6	261	250
	12	Rajpore, ..	56	11	29	5	3	..	8	11	60
		Total Western Doon, ..	11,218	61	7,069	732	104	1,838	1,414	3,356	3,170
EASTERN DOON	1	Bungayn, .;	50	..	11	2	2	..	35	37	35
	2	Burkote, ..	839	19	211	204	21	..	384	405	150
	3	Byragra, ,,	29	2	9	..	..	17	1	18	20
	4	Gohree, ..	766	..	231	497	13	25	..	38	40
	5	Jogeewálá, ..	129	..	1	80	5	43	..	48	40
	6	Khurkurree, ..	129	..	35	50	11	33	..	44	40
	7	Khuruk, ..	955	..	192	7 05	52	6	..	58	40
		Carried forward,	2,897	21	690	1,538	104	124	420	648	365

Appendix to Statement No. IV., or the General Statement Maafee Villages in Dehra Doon.—(Continued).

Pergunnah.	Number of Villages.	Name of Village.	Full area.	MINHAEE.			CULTIVATED, INCLUDING FALLOW.				Nominal Jumma.
				Lákhiráj.	Barren.	Culturable waste.	Judeed or fallow.	Irrigated.	Unirrigated.	Total.	
1	2	3	4	5	6	7	8	9	10	11	12
											Rs.
		Broughtforward,	2,897	21	690	1,538	104	124	420	648	365
Eastern Doon.	8	Khyreekhord, ..	227	3	25	142	2	55	..	57	40
	9	Majree, ..	252	..	71	1	..	..	180	180	90
	10	Purteednugger,	810	..	102	570	6	120	12	138	100
	11	Rikikase, ..	1,908	3	1,085	820	..	..	..	..	50
	12	Tupobun, ..	123	..	9	66	6	40	2	48	40
		Total of Eastern Doon, ..	6,217	27	1,982	3,137	118	339	614	1,071	685
		Total of Western Doon, ..	11,218	61	7,069	732	104	1,838	1,414	3,356	3,170
		Grand Total of Maafee Villages, ..	17,435	88	9,051	3,869	222	2,177	2,028	4,427	3,855

(Signed).   C. A. DANIELL,

Superintendent.

APPENDIX C.

DOON CANALS.

RETURN of Areas and Classes Irrigated, Revenue realized for the same, and Miscellaneous Revenue during the past seven Official Years.

Invested Capital up to the end of 1871-72, Rs. 5,57,860.

Seasons.	1st Class. Sugar-cane and land requiring water all the year round, at Rs. 5 per acre. (Acres.)	2nd Class. 1st class rice, tobacco, and gardens, per fusl, at Rs. 3 per acre. (Acres.)	4th Class. 2nd class rice, wheat, and all other crops, at Rs. 1-4 per acre. (Acres.)	Total area irrigated. (Acres.)	Revenue from assessed area. (Rs. A. P.)	Water sold by contract. (Rs. A. P.)	Manufacture, &c., &c. (Rs. A. P.)	Mill-rents. (Rs. A. P.)	Sale of produce. (Rs. A. P.)	Fines and sundries. (Rs. A. P.)	Total Revenue from all sources. (Rs. A. P.)	Total annual expenditure, repairs, plantations, contingencies, &c., &c. (Rs. A. P.)
1865-66	896	3,467	2,626	6,989	9,462 . 3	4,428 8 0	1,938 4 7	12,788 1 8	314 9 10	24 0 0	28,955 8 4	19,289 1 0
1866-67	1,815	1,862	5,175	8,852	16,599 4 3	4,426 4 0	1,920 14 3	11,485 12 11	374 12 0	12 4 0	34,818 11 9	18,946 5 9
1867-68	1,105	2,922	6,667	10,694	19,673 8 1	3,505 0 0	1,487 12 7	13,623 7 5	444 4 0	4 0 0	38,737 11 1	19,634 9 1
1868-69	677	2,832	10,508	14,017	23,335 11 7	1,795 11 0	1,084 6 2	11,946 4 10	517 10 0	25 8 3	38,704 8 7	21,360 8 13
1869-70	723	3,130	6,448	10,301	20,570 5 5	2,147 0 0	1,416 6 6	13,783 6 3	301 10 0	62 8 4	38,281 8 3	19,935 13 9
1870-71	856	3,814	7,522	12,192	24,507 12 7	2,432 0 0	1,304 5 7	14,604 15 9	208 11 0	54 9 11	43,112 14 10	20,650 10 3
1871-72	649	3,587	6,502	10,736	20,361 13 6	2,331 8 1	1,238 5 1	19,358 4 9	575 8 3	9 5 0	43,854 5 7	20,913 10 11
Total for seven years,	6,719	21,614	45,448	73,781	1,34,510 2 8	21,065 9	10,390 6 7	97,570 5 7	2,737 1 1	191 15	2,66,465 4 5	1,40,730 2 10
Mean annual total,	960	3,088	6,493	10,540	19,216 0 0	3,009 0 0	1,484 0 0	13,940 0 0	391 0 0	27 0 0	38,066 0 0	20,104 0 0

The totals will be found to differ slightly from those of the items given in pp. 243-6 of the text.

APPENDIX C.—(Continued).

Statement showing the Total Area Irrigated by Canals, and Income from Irrigation, for 1865-66.

Name of Canal.	IN KHUREEF (1865).								IN RUBBEE (1865).								IN WHOLE YEAR.				
	By measurement.				By contract.				By measurement.				By contract.				Area in acres.			Income.	
	Area in acres.		Income.		Approximate area in acres.		Income.		Area in acres		Income.		Approximate area in acres.		Income.						
	AC. R. P.	RS. A. P.			AC. R. P.	RS. A. P.			AC. R. P.	RS. A. P.			AC. R. P.	RS A. P.			AC. R. P.		RS. A. P.		
Beejapore,	1,105 3 0	1,310 12 3			1,266 1 0	1,492 12 0			828 2 0	1,531 5 3			860 0 0	1,589 1 11			4,060 2 0		5,923 15 3		
Rajpore,	587 3 0	786 15 11			721 3 0	966 4 0			540 0 0	1,174 0 11			469 2 0	1,021 4 10			2,319 0 0		3,948 9 8		
Kutta Puthur,	831 0 0	851 13 0			478 2 0	489 11 2			574 2 0	1,206 9 7			370 2 0	778 3 1			2,254 2 0		3,326 4 10		
Kalunga,	570 0 0	664 5 8			2 0 0	2 7 4			418 0 0	645 15 11			13 0 0	20 11 9			1,003 0 0		1,333 8 8		
Jákhun,	381 2 0	500 7 0			4 2 0	6 4 6			554 0 0	789 10 9			... ...	... ...			940 0 0		1,296 6 3		
Total,	3,476 0 0	4,114 5 10			2,473 0 0	2,957 7 0			2,915 0 0	5,347 10 5			1,713 0 0	3,409 5 7			10,577 0 0		15,828 12 10		

I am quite unable to reconcile these figures with those of pp. 243-6 for same year.

Appendix D.

Extract from published Report of Census of the N. W. P., 1872.

Abstract of the Total Population (Vol. I., pp. viii, ix).

Particulars.	Male.	Female.	Total.
Non-Asiatics, ...	577	484	1,061
Mixed Races, ...	83	107	190
Native Christians, ...	201	259	460
Hindoos, ...	59,998	42,816	102,814
Mahomedans, ...	7,832	4,588	12,420
Total, ...	68,691	48,254	116,945
Number per square mile, ...	67	47	114

It will be observed that the total here given almost exactly agrees with the sum of the items in pages 266 and 270 ; viz., 76,413 + 40,533 = 1,16,946.

Table showing Density of Population (Vol. I., p. xiii).

Particulars.	1872.		1865.
Number of persons per square mile, ...	114		101
Percentage of cultivation on area, ...	125		...
	Miles.	Acres.	Miles.
Area in square miles, ...	1,020	471	1,020·74
Cultivation do., ...	128	328	103·67

Proportion of Mahomedans to Hindoos, and percentage on Total (p. **xxi**).

Particulars.	1872.	1865.
Proportion of Mahomedans to Hindoos, ...	10 to 82	...
Percentage of Mahomedans on Total Population,	10·7	20·6

Agricultural Population distinguishing (p. **xxv**).

Particulars.	Males.	Females.	Total.
Hindoos, ...	29,310	23,402	52,712
Mahomedans, ...	1,680	1,292	2,972
Total of agricultural population, ...	...	...	55,918
Percentage of Hindoos,...	...	...	45·6
,, Mahomedans, ...	...	...	2·6
Percentage of all Creeds, ...	...	...	48·3

Details of Agricultural Population (p. **xxvii**).

Particulars.	Males.	Females.
Landowners, { Hindoos, ...	10,472	8,001
Landowners, { Mahomedans, ...	16	7
Total, including Christians and others, ...	10,489*	8,011
Cultivators, { Hindoos, ...	18,838	15,401
Cultivators, { Mahomedans, ...	1,664	1,285
Total, including Christians and others, ...	20,615	16,803

* This is evidently incorrect, but I must let it stand.

Number of Children under 12 ; Adults and Percentages for the same
(p. xli).

Particulars.	Males.		Females.	
	Under 12.	All ages.	Under 12.	All ages.
Hindoos, ...	18,281	59,998	15,581	42,816
Mahomedans, ...	1,891	7,832	1,600	4,588
Percentage of Hindoos, ...	30·5	...	36·4	...
„ Mahomedans, ...	24·1	...	34·9	...

Table M. II. (pp. xlii, xliii).

Particulars.	1872.	1865.
Male, { Adults, ...	47,692	41,380
{ Children under 12, ...	20,264	19,908
Female, { Adults, ...	30,319	26,256
{ Children under 12, ...	17,306	15,287
Total population, ...	1,15,581*	
Total of minors, ...	37,570	
Rates per 1,000 of boys and girls under 12, percentages :—		
Males, ...	...	324·8
Females, ...	...	367·1
Both Sexes, ...	...	342·3
Hindoos, { Males, ...	304·9	
{ Females, ...	364·1	
Mahomedans, { Males, ...	242·7	
{ Females, ...	350·1	
Total, { Males, ...	298·1	
{ Females, ...	363·3	

* This total disagrees with that of Table I., apparently owing to the exclusion of Europeans, &c., for 1,16,945——1,061 =1,15,884.

11

Quinquennial Terms of Age up to 15 *for Total Population,* (p. xlv).

Particulars.			Number.			Percentage.		
			0 to 5.	5 to 10.	10 to 15.	0 to 5.	5 to 10.	10 to 15.
Males, ...			8,844	8,067	6,758	13·0	11·9	9·9
Females, ...			8,737	6,493	4,223	18·5	13·6	9·3
Both Sexes, ...			17,581	14,560	10,981	15·2	12·6	9·5
Hindoo.	Males, ..		7,985	7,324	5,980	13·3	12·2	10·0
	Females, ..		7,897	5,819	3,766	18·5	13·6	8·8
	Both Sexes,		15,882	13,143	9,746	15·5	12·8	9·5
Mahome-dan.	Males, ..		811	710	767	10·4	9·1	9·7
	Females, ..		786	624	411	17·1	13·6	9·0
	Both Sexes,		1,597	1,334	1,168	12·9	10·8	9·4

Percentage of Total Population showing sex and religion, (p. lv.).

Particulars.			Between 10 to 13.		Between 10 to 20.		Between 13 to 20.	
			Males.	Females.	Males.	Females.	Males.	Females.
Hindoos, ...			6·1	5·3	20·0	19·2	13·9	13·9
Mahomedans, ...			5·5	5·2	20·0	20·9	14·5	15·7

Statement showing the area and Percentage on Total area, (p. lxxvi.)

Particulars.	Miles.	Acres.
Cultivable Area,...	100	510
Cultivated ,, ...	128	328
Total, ...	229	198
Total Area, ...	1,020	471
Percentages of cultivable area, ...	22·4	
,, ,, cultivated ,, ...	12·5	

Table P. (p. lxxxviii).

PERCENTAGE ON TOTAL HINDOO POPULATION.

Brahmans.	Rajpoots.	Buniyas.	Others Castes of Hindoos.
10·0	32·2	2·6	55·2

General Statement of area and Population (pp. 1, 2.)

Abstract.

Area in square miles.		Number of villages, mouzahs or townships.	Number of enclosures.	Number of houses.	Total Population.
Miles.	Acres.				
1,020	471	965	15,592	24,744	116,945

Average calculated from preceding Columns.

Persons per square mile.	Villages, mouzahs or townships per square mile.	Persons per village, mouzah or township.	Enclosures per square mile.	Persons per enclosure.	Houses per square mile.	Persons per house.
114	·9	121	15	7	24	4·6

Details of Population (p. 3, 4, 5, 6.)

Particulars.	Houses.	Males.	Females.	Total.
Number of superior sort, ..	5,142	..	..	..
„ their inhabitants, ..	..	..	..	30,376
„ inferior sort, ..	19,602	..	..	..
„ their inhabitants, ..	..	..	..	85,335
Total, ..	..	..	..	1,15,711
Hindoos, ...	..	59,998	42,816	1,02,814
Mahomedans, ...	..	7,832	4,588	12,420
Christians and others, ..	..	214	263	477
Total, ..	..	68,044	47,667*	..

Percentage on above.

Particulars.	Houses.		Hindoos	Mahomedans.	Christians and others.	Total.	
	Superior.	Inferior.				Males.	Females.
Inhabitants of houses,	26·3	73·7	88·9	10·7	0·4	58·8	41·2
Males, ...	...	...	58·4	63·1	44·9	...	...
Females, ...	...	...	41·6	36·9	55·1	...	...

* Probably owing to exclusion of Europeans, &c., the total here given differs from those of the earlier tables.

Statement showing nationalities (p. 36 *sq.*)

I omit the Tables which distribute the population according to infirmities, ages, sex, education, land, and land revenue, as being far too elaborate to serve any practical purpose.

Particulars.		Males.	Females.	Total.
Non-Asiatics.				
Europeans, United Kingdom { English,	...	152	210	362
Irish, ...	...	92	85	177
Scotch,	...	45	27	72
French,	...	7	6	13
Germans, ...	...	1	1	2
Italians,	...	5	...	5
Unspecified, ...	...	275	155	430
Total, ...	...	577	484	1,061
Americans, ...	...	1	2	3
Mixed Races, Eurasians, ...	...	83	107	190
Asiatics.				
Chinese, ...	...	7	2	9
Hindoos, ...	...	59,998	42,816	102,814
Mahomedans, ...	...	7,832	4,588	12,420
Native Christians, ...	...	201	259	460
Total, ...	...	68,038	47,665	115,703

The total number of Hindoos is made up thus—

Brahmans, ...	10,279
Rajpoots, ...	33,125
Buniyas, ...	2,664
Miscellaneous, ...	56,746
	102,814
Add for Mahomedans, ...	12,420
Do. Native Chirstians, ...	406
Do. Chinese, ...	9
	115,649

which disagrees with the total number of Asiatics above given. The total of all, including Europeans, will be thus either 116,957 or 116,903, *i. e.*, slightly in excess, or slightly below previous returns. The minute details of Asiatic castes, clans, and races are left out, because they are to my certain knowledge perfectly worthless. Some are omitted, which ought to be entered, *e. g.*, Bajgi, Khasia, Mhair, Heree, Negee, and even Ranghar (!!); while others are entered, which ought to have been omitted, *e. g.*, Syuds and Moghuls, of whom there are absolutely none in the Doon, though a few stray Sheikhs and Pathans may be found. No confidence can, in my opinion, be placed in such statistics. The Native Christian Census is, however, nearer the truth than that given in p. 269 (*vide supra*).

I pass over the Statistics from page 147 to page 200, inclusive, as being not likely to be of much use.

Statement showing the Number of Villages and Towns according as they contain (p. 201).

	INHABITANTS.										Total number of towns and villages.
Less than 200.	From 200 to 500.	From 500 to 1,000.	From 1,000 to 2,000.	From 2,000 to 3,000.	From 3,000 to 5,000.	From 5,000 to 10,000.	From 10,000 to 15,000.	From 15,000 to 20,000.	From 20,000 to 50,000.	Above 50,000.	
854	85	16	9	...	...	1	...	...	...	...	965

Area and population of Pergunnahs and Tuhseels (p. 218).

		PERGUNNAH.				
		Western Doon.	Eastern Doon.	Total.	Jounsar Bawur.	District.
		Mls. Acs.	Mls. Acs.	Mls. Acs.	Mls. Acs.	Mls Acs.
Area in Square miles and acres,	Total, ..	343 39	334 231	677 270	343 201	1,020 471
	Cultivated,	74 399	24 405	99 164	29 164	128 328
Area of land charged with Government Revenue in square miles and acres,	Total,	202 269	89 418	292 47	343 201	635 248
	Unculturable, ..	96 488	47 20	143 508	304 236	448 101
	Culturable,	44 190	20 581	65 131	9 445	74 576
	Cultivated,	61 231	21 456	83 47	29 164	112 211
Number of Villages, ...		No. 279	No. 199	No. 478	No. 487	No. 965
Population, ..	Males, ..	35,438	9,492	44,930	23,114	68,044
	Females,	23,955	6,780	30,735	16,932	47,667
	Both Sexes, ..	59,393	16,272	75,665	40,046	115,711*
Number of persons per square mile,..		173	48	111	116	113
„ males „		103	28	66	67	66
„ females „		70	20	45	49	47
		Rs.	Rs.	Rs.	Rs.	Rs.
Amount of payment to Government whether as land revenue, quit-rent, or Peshcush, ...		28,587	8,121	36,708	19,695	56,403
Amount of payment to Government including land revenue, quit-rent, Peshcush, local rates, and cesses,		32,284	9,123	41,407	21,655	63,062
Amount of rent, including local cesses paid by cultivators, ..		74,578	15,598	90,176	21,655	111,831
		A. R. P.	A. R. P.	A. R. P.	A. R. P.	A. R. P.
Rate of incidence of Government revenue per acre of,	Total area, ..	0 2 1	0 0 7	0 1 4	0 1 5	0 1 5
	Area paying Govt. revenue,	0 3 6	0 2 3	0 3 2	0 1 5	0 2 3
	Total cultivated area, ..	0 9 7	0 8 3	0 9 .3	1 0 10	0 11 0

With reference to Table No. 11, page 246, I would only remark that it seems incredible that there should be not a single idiot in the Kálsee Tuhseel, while the number of lepers there has been probably unduly swollen by recruits from the surrounding native hill states. This is ac-

* I do not understand how this total has been arrived at, unless it has been obtained by *re-adding* the nine Chinese mentioned in a former Table, to the sum total of Asiatics entered in the same statement and then subtracting !!

tually the case in the Doon, where, in all probability, far more than 70 are to be found.   I pass on to

Table No. V. (p. 288), *showing the distribution of the great Castes.*

Castes.		Western Doon.	Eastern Doon.	Jounsar Bawur.
Brahmans, ... {	Males, ...	2,032	1,383	2,500
	Females, ...	1,438	1,055	1,871
	Total, ...	3,470	2,438	4,371
Rajpoots, ... {	Males, ...	4,765	3,233	10,734
	Females, ...	3,476	2,666	8,251
	Total, ...	8,241	5,899	18,985
Buniyas, ... {	Males, ...	1,247	246	282
	Females, ...	634	182	73
	Total, ...	1,881	428	355
Other Castes, {	Males, ...	20,736	3,906	8,934
	Females, ...	14,048	2,479	6,643
	Total, ...	34,784	6,385	15,577
Mahomedans, {	Males, ...	6,446	723	663
	Females, ...	4,096	398	94
	Total, ...	10,542	1,128	757

The totals, if added up, will be found to be at variance with all the earlier Statistics, giving 1,15,241, but if to this 406 Native Christians be added, the total comes within 2 of my own previous calculation under the head of Nationalities, based on Mr. Plowden's figures, in page lxxxvi.

The following Statement showing the number of Non-Asiatic residents, whose occupations have been recorded, may not be devoid of interest, though the sixth column might mislead, without reference to the text.

Government employés.	Military.	Scholars.	Librarian.	Pensioners.	Landholder, agriculturist.	Photographers.	Tailor.	Bankers.	Brewers.	Bailiff.	Managers.	Merchants.	Apothecaries.	Hotel-keepers.	Tea-planters.	Barrister.	Pleaders.	Priests, Clergymen, &c.	Chemists.	Confectioner.	Farrier.
62	224	185	1	18	4	3	1	4	2	1	3	2	8	5	3	1	2	8	2	1	1

Two noteworthy points remain. Of the 9,720 Mahomedans and others, not Hindoos, entered in the 1865 Census Report, (vide supra, p. 270) it would appear from a report by my successor, Mr. Donovan, that only 41 were Mahomedans, the majority being Kolies, 3,192 ; Dooms, 3,033 ; and Chumars, 2,916 ;* and Mr. Ross rightly attributes the actual increase in the Mussulman element to the requirements of the Chukrata cantonments. He also explains the remarkable disproportion between the male and female population of the Doon by the fact that it mainly consists of immigrants of whom most are men.

Appendix E.

Grant Rules, 1848–1862.

The rules for the grant of waste lands passed soon after the failure described in the text, will be found in Appendix No. XXI. of the Directions to Revenue Officers, p. 451. A Notification of the Government N. W. Provinces, dated the 28th November 1848, limited the size of each grant to 4,000 acres, expressly withholding the right of property in the spontaneous products of the land from the grantee, who was not to interfere with any one accustomed to use or consume them, and also reserving

* Vide present Census Report, Vol. I., p. 462.

the right over running streams of water, as well as mineral products, to Government. The leases were to be for fifty years, as in 1840, and the rates per acre remained the same, being *nil* in the first year, and then rising from As. 3 in the fourth, to Rs. 0-12-6 in the tenth year. It is unnecessary to give further details.

Notification, No. 2109 of the 26th September 1855, advertised grants *for tea cultivation* in Kumaon and Gurhwal, each of which was not to fall short of 200, or exceed 2,000 acres, one-fourth being rent-free in perpetuity. Nothing was to be charged for the first four years, after which the rate per acre would rise by arithmetical progression from one anna to one rupee at the end of twenty years. The full assessment on a grant of 2,000 acres could not therefore exceed Rs. 1,500. The lease then expired. The public were encouraged to apply for seeds and plants to the Superintendent, Botanical Gardens, N. W. Provinces, to whose influence the Notification may be traced.

Notification No. 1340A., dated 29th September 1860, modified the rules of 1848, extending the area of the grants to 5,000 acres each, and in 1861 another, several times alluded to in the above pages, No. 1358A., dated the 11th September, was issued by the Lieut.-Governor, N. W. Provinces, for the purpose of giving effect to a Resolution of the Governor-General, Lord Canning; No. 3264, dated the 17th October 1861, "regarding the sale of waste lands in fee simple, and the redemption of existing land revenue." Rules of procedure were thereby laid down for the guidance of Collectors, which I give *in extenso* as they have a special reference to the Doon (*vide supra*, p. xlii.)

(COPY).

Notification Revenue Department.—No. 1358A.

Dated Camp, Jhansie, the 11th December 1861.

With reference to paragraphs 8 to 37 of the Resolution of His Excellency the Viceroy and Governor-General in Council, No. 3264, dated the 17th October 1861, relative to the sale of waste lands, the Hon'ble the Lieut.-Governor is pleased to publish, for the information of all concerned, the following rules of procedure which have been prepared by the Sudder Board of Revenue, N. W. Provinces, and have received the approval of the Government of the N. W. Provinces :—

Rules of Procedure.

The attention of all Officers in charge of Districts containing unassigned waste lands, is directed to the first portion of the Revenue Resolution of the Viceroy in Council, No. 3264, dated the 17th October, to the provisions of which they are required to give full and immediate effect.

2. The Collector should at once proceed to prepare a statement of all special tracts reserved from the operation of this Circular under paragraphs 23 and 24 of the above orders, as being required for forest purposes, for grazing or firewood preserves, for building sites or for any other public object. This statement should be exposed in his office, and facilities should be given to intending applicants to make themselves aware of its contents.

3. When an application for the assignment of a specific tract of waste land is received, the Collector will first consider whether any objection or special limitation is required by reason of the land being required for any of the above-named purposes, and in the event of such being the case and the applicant still prosecuting his demand, the Collector will report the matter for the information of the Commissioner.

4. In other cases, he will at once proceed to enquire whether the land applied for is encumbered by any prior claim of property or occupancy.

5. Where it is evident that there exist rights of property or of exclusive occupancy, either active or latent, the applicant will be informed that the case cannot be taken up under the Grant Rules, excepting in favor of the party originally possessed of those rights, or who has purchased them from such party. " It will be an important part of the Collector's duty to make certain that any transfer of such rights shall have been made with a complete and fair understanding on the part of all concerned."

6. In case of there being any doubt as to whether existing rights are of the exclusive character necessary to bar alienation, the Collector will report the case to the Commissioner.

7. Where no claims of the nature supposed are known to exist, the Collector will advertise the application for a term of thirty days, by an Ishtahar to be stuck up in his office, and in the Police and Revenue Posts nearest to the property, as well as in any villages on the land or adjoining thereto. He will also, where he deems it advisable, have the purport of the application verbally explained to the inhabitants of those villages, and to any other parties likely to be interested in the grant.

8. Objections to the grant will be carefully considerd and disposed of on their merits.

9. Where no objections are brought forward within the period specified, or when they have been decided to be invalid, a Memorandum will be forthwith given in the Form A. to the applicant, intimating that the land has been allotted to him, subject to fulfilment of the Rules laid down by the Supreme Government. Great care will be necessary in defining the land thus allotted in such manner as that no possibility of misunderstanding may exist as to its position and extent, and especially as to its not infringing on the boundaries of adjoining lands held under anterior claims of proprietorship or exclusive occupancy.

10. No allotment, as above, will be made exceeding 3,000 acres; and in the Hill Districts no grant of tea lands shall exceed 2,000 acres. Where any special reason may exist against the assignment of so large an area, such as proximity to a station, &c., and the grantee may not be content with a smaller area, the Collector will report the case for orders, with his opinion as to the degree of further limitation which is called for.

11. The Collector will next calculate the cost of surveying the grant, and of erecting durable pillars of demarcation. This will be at the lowest rate for which land of the nature applied for is ordinarily surveyed in the district. But provision must be made for the measurement being accurately conducted, on the plane table system, and in such wise that a correct estimate may be formed of the amount of land "uncleared," and of the amount "unencumbered with jungle," as also of the portion which may fairly be held to be unculturable. A scale of charges of survey should be prepared and hung up in the same way as the statement referred to in paragraph 2. The Collector will submit a copy of this scale to the Commissioner for the approval of the Board.

12. When the cost of survey has been paid in, the Collector will intimate to the applicant that he is at liberty to take possession of the land.

13. The survey will be proceeded with forthwith, and no time should be lost in the erection of the boundary pillars.

14. Where an estate has been already surveyed and marked off this portion of the operations will, of course, be dispensed with, and no charge will be made against the applicant further than is necessary to secure an accurate plan of the new estate with the requisite boundary marks.

15. Immediately on completion of the survey, or, where a fresh survey is not required, immediately on the allotment having been definitely concluded, the Collector will calculate the purchase money on the amount of culturable land in the grant at the rates of Rs. 2-8-0 per acre for uncleared land, and Rs. 5 for land unencumbered with jungle.

16. He will then invite the grantee to pay in the full amount, or at his option any portion of it, being not less than one-tenth. One-tenth must be paid down at once, to warrant the grantee remaining in continued occupation. Immediately on its payment, the Collector will deliver the Deed of Grant (Form B.), with plan of the estate, to the grantee, and will enter his name provisionally in the district records as proprietor of the grant.

17. Wherever it may seem necessary to make any reservation of the rights of Government, under paragraphs 12 and 13 of the Resolution, the Collector will report the circumstances for the orders of the Commissioner.

18. In any case in which prior to the delivery of the Memorandum of assignment (Form A.), more than one application has been received for the same land, the Collector will, after the necessary survey, advertise the grant for sale, and proceed under ordinary rules for such sales. He will fix the upset price according to the rule laid down in paragraph 15 of the Resolution, including in the same the cost of survey.

19. The sale will be concluded in favor of the highest bidder on his paying down one-tenth of the sale price. The Deed of Grant (Form B.) and plan of the estate will then be made over to him, and possession be immediately given, subject to the conditions laid down in paragraph 27 of the Resolution and paragraph 25 of this Circular.

20. So soon as the grantee's name has been provisionally entered in the proprietary register, he is entitled to apply for the reservation of any adjoining plot, not exceeding the previous grant in area, that is available and has not been already applied for, which can then be surveyed at his expense, and reserved for him; he will in such be at liberty to obtain possession of the additional tract under the same procedure and conditions as the original grant; " but subject to the obligations that within 5 years from the date of his previous grant, he shall fulfil the conditions necessary to his being recorded as proprietor of this further grant, and that two-thirds of the previous grant, that is, of its culturable area, shall within the same time have been brought under cultivation. If he should fail in either

obligation, the reservation of the plot will cease. There need be no limit to the number of further grants which·may be successively taken up in fulfilment of the obligations."

21. Holders of grants under former rules, " who have not yet completed the purchase of their grants," may commute them under the new rules without limitation of area. The purchase money will be calculated at Rs. 2-8-0 per acre on any portion of the culturable area at the time being "uncleared;" and at Rs. 5-0-0 on all that is at the same time "unencumbered with jungle." Ten per cent. of this sum must be paid down at once, and the balance treated as directed in the present rules for any new grants. Grantees shall have the option of redeeming the Land Revenue under paragraph 50 of the Resolution by payment of twenty years' purchase of the maximum yearly assessment of their existing grant, provided that they will not be required to pay more than the maximum rates specified in paragraph 29, that is to say $2\frac{1}{2}$ rupees an acre for uncleared, and 5 rupees an acre for cleared, land, as existing at the time at which application is made for redemption.

22. The foregoing rules will not apply to any grants re-settled, or otherwise concluded on a Zemindaree footing, at a fixed assessment.

23. Wherever the permission is applicable, it must be acted upon at once, but a period of six months may be allowed for the grantee to make his election between the old and new rules. An intimation should be served on each existing grantee, entitled to the option, to the above effect. After expiry of the term it will not be open to him to apply for commutation under this Circular.

24. It will be observed that an existing grantee can purchase, under the new rules, any portion of his grant, retaining, if he pleases, the remainder upon the terms of the original grant. It must not, however, be permitted to a grantee to break up his grant into many minute portions under this concession, rejecting, or retaining under different titles, such scattered portions. The tracts selected for purchase must be compact, continuous, and well defined.

25. From the date of the Deed (Form B.) three months will be calculated; and whatever balance of purchase money is found to be then unpaid, will be entered as an arrear against the grantee, who is to be charged with 70 per cent. per annum on such arrear. This

charge should be treated in the same manner as a demand of Land Revenue liable on default to the same measures for recovery of arrears.* The amount should be demanded twice a year, with the May and November instalments, and should be entered at the foot of the Pergunnah Towzee in the same manner as Land Revenue, though the amount (being subject to diminution on each further payment) will not be added to the rent roll of the district.

* "The land will be held liable to resale in default of the regular payment of such interest, should there be no crop or other moveable property on the land from which the claim of Government can be satisfied."

26. Every grant will be reported through the usual channel for the information of Government immediately on the Deed of Grant being delivered to the grantee.

27. Every six months a report will be submitted of any sums that may have been realized within that period as purchase money. This must be carefully drawn up, in order that the provisions of paragraph 56 of the Resolution may be carried into effect. A copy of the six monthly report will be simultaneously sent to the Deputy Auditor and Accountant General.

28. In the Annual Administration Report, the amount so realized within the year, and the total amount from the commencement of the system up to date, will be noted ; and also the sum realized as interest on unpaid balances of purchase money.

29. The rules for compensation of any rights which may subsequently come to light as having existed on the grants are given in paragraph 19 of the Resolution. All such cases will be reported to the Commissioner.

30. The title conveyed by the Deed of Grant is a full and complete title, which the Government guarantees against all other claims. The grantees and their heirs or representatives are to be regarded the sole legal owners of the land, and no transfer of property in it will be recognized by the Courts or Revenue Officers unless duly registered. A separate register of all grants made under these rules will be carefully maintained in the following form in the Collector's Office, both in English and in the Vernacular.

Number.	No. of grant.	Name of grantee.	Purchase money.	Payment of instalments with date of each.	Date of Deed of Grant.	Subsequent registered transfer or successions.

The maps or plans of all grants sold under these rules will be kept in a series corresponding with the numbers in this Register. All previous Circular Orders on the subject of Grants of Waste Land are hereby cancelled. Future applications will be disposed of under the present orders.

A.

MEMORANDUM.

.... having made application for assignment to him of a grant of land in the .... pergunnah, and no right of proprietorship or of exclusive occupancy having, after the prescribed advertisement, been found to exist therein, notice is hereby given that the land specified below has been allotted to .... as a grant, subject to fulfilment of the prescribed rules.

(Here is to follow a description of the situation of the land, its extent, and the boundaries with which it is to be granted).

Dated,.......................

Collector.

B.

FORM OF GRANTS.

Know all men, by these presents, that the Government North Western Provinces has conferred on................his heirs, executors, administrators, and assigns, the grant of a tract of land measuring British Statute acres .... situate in .... to be holden by him in full proprietary right, subject to the following condition:—

I. The purchase money for this grant is Rupees ...., of which Rupees .... have been already paid. On the* ...., if the entire purchase money has not been paid up, interest at 10 per cent. per annum will be charged on the balance, and thereafter, until the entire purchase money be paid up, such interest will be chargeable on all unpaid arrears of the purchase moneys; and all payments by the grantee shall be first carried to the credit of any outstanding arrear of interest due on such purchase money.

* Enter the date calculated three months from date of this Deed.

II. Arrears of interest shall be treated in the same manner as arrears of Land Revenue, and shall be subject to the same measures of realization.

III.   No transfer of proprietary right will be recognized by the Civil Courts, or by the Revenue Officers of Government, unless duly registered.

IV.   The right of the public to roads in the grant is not to be interfered with.   The grantee is to pay a contribution of one rupee per annum for every 1,000 rupees of purchase money in lieu of the demands of the State for aid in repairing the high roads ; which payment is commutable at 20 years' purchase.   The grantee will have no claim on Government for making or repairing private roads.

V   The grantee is to erect permanent boundary marks round his grant, and to keep them in a state of repair.

This will ordinarily be done at the time of survey.

VI.   The grant conveys the plenary rights to all products both above the surface and below the same.   (Here any exceptions which may have been approved by superior authority to be noted).   But wherever any persons have been accustomed to use or consume the spontaneous products of the soil, the grantee shall not interfere with them so long as they do not trespass upon or otherwise injure the cultivated portion of the land.

VII.   For the preservation of the public peace, the grantee shall, at the requisition of the Magistrate maintain a chowkeedar for every sixty houses or families resident in the grant.   The chowkeedar shall receive Rs. 3 per mensem.   For every three chowkeedars there shall also be maintained by the grantee a *goryt* or reporter, at a salary of Rs. 2 per mensem.

VIII.   Arrears on account of road fund, or chowkeedar's salary, may be realized by distraint of the crops or other property of the grantee.

IX.   The prescriptive rights of other proprietors in streams running through or bounding the estate will be maintained for purposes of irrigation or navigation, and for the transport of timber or other property, and for other purposes of general utility.   The Government reserves to itself the right which it everywhere possesses over all such streams, whether for purposes of irrigation or navigation, and, whenever it sees fit, can assume the control of the waters, and distribute them in such manner and on such conditions as may seem most conducive to the public good.

13

X. The lands included in this grant are shown in the subjoined table:—

No. of map.	No. of grant.	Name of grant.	Name of grantee.	Area in acres.	Deduct irremediately barren acres.	Remaining culturable acres.	Area unencumbered with jungle.	Uncleared area.	Purchase money.

$$\text{Boundaries,} \begin{cases} \text{North,} \\ \text{East,} \\ \text{South,} \\ \text{West,} \end{cases}$$

XI. On the payment of the purchase money in full with all arrears of interest, the grant will belong to the grantee free for ever from all demand for Land Revenue.

By order of His Honor the Lieutenant-Governor, North Western Provinces.

(Signed.) G. COUPER,

Secy. to Govt. N. W. P.

Then followed Despatch No. 14 of the 9th July 1862, from the Secretary of State, which it is needless to analyse. The main point in it is, that it indicated the absurdity of fixing an uniform price for land, without regard to situation or capabilities. Fresh orders were consequently issued by the Supreme Government.

No. 4206.—Revenue.

To—The Secretary to the Government of Bengal, N. W. Provinces, Punjab, and its Dependencies.

15th August 1862.

Sir,—With reference to the correspondence noted on the margin, I am desired to transmit, for the information and guidance of the Lieutenant Governor, copy of a Despatch* received from the Secretary of State, regarding the sale of waste lands and the redemption of the existing Land Revenue.

* Revenue, No. 14, dated 9th July, 1862.

2. It is desirable that rules for regulating the sale of waste lands should be prepared, with as little delay as possible, in conformity with the modified provisions now prescribed by Her Majesty's Government; but it will be observed that all arrangements which have been already completed under the terms of the Resolution promulgated by the Government of India last October, in regard either to the purchase of waste lands or the redemption of the Land Revenue, are to be maintained, the present Despatch not being intended to have retrospective effect.

Referring to the concluding words of the 76th paragraph of the Secretary of State's Despatch, I am desired to request that a report showing the extent to which any such arrangements have been made may be furnished as soon as possible.

As regards the sale of waste lands, the principle points upon which the provisions of the Resolution of October last, must be modified, in conformity with the instructions now received, are as follows :—

4. Paragraph 29 of the Resolution which fixed a uniform price throughout India of Rs. $2\frac{1}{2}$ per acre for uncleared land, and of Rs. 5 per acre for land unencumbered with jungle, is cancelled, and it is ordered that the several Governments and Lieutenant-Governors shall fix, after communication with the Chief Local Authorities, a minimum price, suited to the circumstances of the various descriptions of land which they may find to be at their disposal in each District of their Presidency or Province.

5. In modification of paragraph 30 of the Resolution, which prescribed the sale of the land by auction, in the event of more purchasers than one being desirous to buy the same tract, it is ordered that in every case the land shall be put up to auction at an upset price, and sold to the highest bidder.

6. The provision contained in paragraph 25 of the Resolution, admitting of possession being given to an applicant for land in anticipation of survey, will be modified as directed in paragraph 11 of the accompanying Despatch. In conformity with these directions the land applied for must, in every instance, be surveyed, and the boundaries marked out before it is advertised for sale. The applicant for the grant, it will be observed, is to be required to deposit the estimated cost of the survey, which will of course be restored to him if he should be eventually out-bid for the land. It is of great importance that a ready agency should be provided for effecting the preliminary survey and marking out boundaries, so that applicants for land may be subjected to no unnecessary delay.

7. The provision which is made in paragraph 31 of the Resolution for reserving adjoining lands at the requisition of those who take grants must be regarded as withdrawn, it being inconsistent with the general injunction for resort to sale by auction.

8. In the 21st paragraph of the Despatch, herewith enclosed, it is ordered that the provision in paragraph 50 of the Resolution, which limits the price to be paid in the commutation of a grant under terms of that paragraph to Rs. 5 an acre, shall be withdrawn. It is also observed by the Secretary of State that the provisions generally which relate to the commutation of existing grants under the new rules contained in paragraphs 33 and 50 of the Resolution require revision.

9. As it has already been found that some misunderstanding prevails in regard to the intention and scope of these paragraphs—it seems desirable that the present opportunity should be taken of stating what the Governor-General in Council understands to have been their purpose. It appears to the Governor-General in Council that it cannot reasonably be maintained that parageaph 33 of the Resolution was intended to include land the absolute sale of which has already been effected, but for which the purchase money has not been wholly been paid up, being by the terms of sale, payable by instalments. It is obvious that in such a case there could be no question of the applicability or the inapplicability of the limitation of the new rules as to area, inasmuch as the owner has already purchased absolutely the whole area in his possession whatever it may be, and, therefore, though he may not have paid the whole of the purchase money, it is manifest that the permission accorded by the concluding words of the paragraph to purchase absolutely as much or as

little of the area as may suit him, has no application to and could not possibly have contemplated any such case. The 33r1 paragraph of the Resolution can, therefore, in the opinion of the Governor-General in Council, be held applicable only to the case of those grantees who hold their lands on terms which do not comprise the right of acquiring an absolute ownership in fee simple. Such grantees, it is the object of the 33rd paragraph to declare, may obtain that right by commuting their grants under the rules for the sale of land in fee simple.

10. Paragraph 50 of the Resolution declares the terms upon which communication may be made in the case of one, and that a very large class of existing grants. This paragraph, when modified according to the instructions of Her Majesty's Government, will stand as in the margin.

Grants which have already been given for a term of years at progressively increasing rents, such as those in the Soondurbuns, will be treated as if the land were permanently settled, if the holder wishes to redeem the future Land Revenue at the highest rate fixed for any year during the currency of the grant, provided there is no right of occupancy other than that of the lessee, or that derived from him.

11. In the case of existing grants, which do not fall under the terms of paragraph 50, the conditions on which commutation under the new rules will be allowed may be settled with reference to the average value obtainable for waste lands of the same description in the District when sold by auction.

12. As it is highly desirable that persons who wish to avail themselves of the Resolution come to by the Government to dispose of waste lands by sale in fee simple should be enabled to carry their intentions into effect with the least avoidable delay, and as the directions now received from Her Majesty's Government are on most points clear and specific, the Governor General in Council will not require that the detailed rules to be framed by the several Local Governments should be submitted for the sanction of the Government of India before they are acted on. A copy of the rules should however, be forwarded as soon as they are finally approved by the Lieutenant-Governor, and if on any point the intention of Her Majesty's Government should seem to the Lieutenant-Governor to be doubtful, the question should be referred to the Governor-General in Council for determination. As legislation will be necessary to give legal effect to the provisions of paragraph 19 of the Resolution, a bill for that object will be introduced, on the meeting of the Governor-General in Council, for legislative purposes.

13. With respect to that part of the Secretary of State's Despatch which discusses the important questions of a redemption of the land revenue and of a permanent settlement, the Governor-General in Council thinks it unnecessary at present to do more than point special attention to the conclusion which is announced in the 26th and the 63rd paragraphs as to the extent to which redemption of the existing Land Revenue is to be permitted, and to the 72nd paragraph, in which the conditions are finally stated, which, in the opinion of Her Majesty's Government, should be attained before a permanent settlement is conceded. It will be observed that this paragraph contemplates that the previous sanction of Her Majesty's Government should be obtained to the introduction of a permanent settlement in any district. Early steps should, therefore, be taken to obtain the information which will be required to enable the Local Government to submit the Report referred to in the 73rd paragraph as to the extent to which it may now be expedient to give effect to this important measure.

The following Resolution was consequently passed by the Local Government:—

No. 1042A.—REVENUE DEPARTMENT.

Dated 17th December 1862.

With reference to paragraphs 8 to 37 of the Resolution of His Excellency the Viceroy and Governor General in Council, No. 3264, dated 17th October 1861, relative to the sale of waste lands in fee simple, as modified by the Despatch of the Right Hon'ble the Secretary of State, No. 14, (Revenue,) dated 9th July 1862, the Hon'ble the Lieutenant-Governor is pleased to publish for the information of all concerned, the following revised Rules of Procedure, which have been prepared by the Sudder Board of Revenue, N. W. Provinces, and have received the approval of this Government.

Rules of Procedure.

1 to 5. Same as in pages xci, xcii.

6. In case of there being any doubt as to whether existing rights are of the exclusive character necessary to bar alienation, the Collector will report the case, through the Commissioner, to the Sudder Board of Revenue. If the rights claimed though not exclusive, should appear to the Sudder Board of Revenue to be such rights of pasturage, wood cutting, &c., as commonly obtain in the hill districts and are entitled as " existing rights in a rude form" to protection under paragraph 6 of the Resolution of the Governor General in Council. No. 3264, dated the 17th of October 1861, the Board will instruct the Collector to endeavour to bring the applicant for the grant and the parties who possess a right to use the spontaneous products of the soil within the tract applied for, to a mutual agreement as to the terms upon which (if any) an hereditary and transferable property in the soil may be given to the former subject to the exercise of their customary rights by the latter. If an amicable arrangement become so, the Collector will report the particulars for the information and sanction of the Sudder Board of Revenue. Otherwise the Collector will proceed to estimate the value of the prescriptive rights, as above, on a liberal basis, and will submit the case, through the Sudder Board of Revenue, to the Government in view to the payment of full compensation.

7. Where no claims of the nature supposed are known to exist, the Collector will calculate the cost of surveying the grant, and of erecting durable pillars of demarcation. This will be at the lowest rate for which land of the nature applied for is ordinarily surveyed in the district. (*The rest is the same as in para.* 11 *of former Rules.)*

8. No allotment as above will be made exceeding 5,000 acres; and in the hill districts no grant of tea lands shall exceed 2,000 acres, &c., *as in para.* 10 *of former Rules.*

9. When the cost of survey has been paid in, the survey will be proceeded with forthwith, and no time should be lost in the erection of the boundary pillars.

10. Where an estate has been already surveyed and marked off, this portion of the operations will, of course, be dispensed with, and no charge will be made against the applicant further than is necessary to secure an accurate plan of the new estate with the requisite boundary marks.

11. On the completion of the demarcation and survey, or, in the

case of surveyed land, immediately on the boundaries of the proposed grant being marked by substantial pillars, the Collector will issue an advertisement, describing the land to be sold, stating the upset price, and specifying the place and date of sale. The period of the advertisement will be for not less than thirty days. The upset price will be fixed at five rupees for cultivated, and two rupees eight annas for uncultivated land, unless for some special reason (such as proximity to a station, valuable timber being on the land, &c.,) that rate be held to be inadequate; in the latter case the Collector will report what upset prices he thinks proper, and on its being confirmed by the Board, he will prepare his advertisement accordingly.

12. The advertisement will be published in the Official Gazette and in two up country newspapers, and the Collector will also cause an Ishtahar to be stuck up in his office, &c., *as in para. 7 of previous Rules.*

13. Any objections to the grant will be carefully considered and disposed of on their merits. If they are held to be valid, the sale will be stayed, and the circumstances reported through the Commissioner to the Board.

14. At the sale, which will be conducted on the usual footing of an auction sale, the land will be assigned to the person offering the highest price, or in the event of no competitors, to the applicant at the upset price, the cost of survey (if made) being added in both cases. In case the applicant is not the purchaser, all monies paid by him on account of survey will be forthwith refunded to him.

15. Immediately on conclusion of the sale, the purchaser will pay down one-tenth of the sale price. On this payment being made, the Collector will at once deliver the Deed of Grant (Form A.) with plan of the estate to the grantee, and will enter his name in the District Records as proprietor of the grant. Possession will at the same time be given.

16. Same as para. 17 of former Rules.

17. Grants which have already been given for a term of years at progressively increasing rent, will be treated as if the land were permanently settled, if the holder wishes to redeem the future land revenue at the highest rate fixed for any year during the currency of the grant, provided there is no right of occupancy other than that of the lessee, or that derived from him. The rates for redemption will be calculated according to the market rate of 4 per cent. Government Securities at the time being,

as directed in paragraph 75 of the Despatch of Her Majesty's Secretary of State.

18. As laid down in paragraph 11 of the same Despatch, the title acquired by sale under the rules now promulgated is to be held subject to the provisions of any legislative enactment, which may hereafter be passed for disposing of the claims of third persons subsequently preferred.

19, 20, 21, and 22. Same as in page xciv.

23. A separate Register of all Grants made under these rules will be carefully maintained in the following form in the Collectors Office, both in English and in the Vernacular. No transfer of proprietary right will be recognized by the Revenue Officers of Government unless duly registered, after having been acknowledged by the transferee in person, or by duly authorized Agent, before the District Officer, or one of his Assistants.

See Table, page xcv.

The maps or plans of all grants, sold under these Rules, will be kept in a series corresponding with the numbers in the Register.

24. All previous Circular Orders on the subject of grants of waste Land are hereby cancelled. Future applications will be disposed of under the present orders.

A.

FORM OF GRANT.

Know all men by these presents that, &c., as before, page xcvi.

I. and II. Same as before, page xcvi.

III. No transfer of proprietary right will be recognized by the Revenue Officers of Government; unless duty registered; and no transfer of interest, or creation of new interest in the grant, beyond a lease of three years, without an acknowledgment by the transferee in person, or by authorized Agent, before the District Officer, or one of his assistants.

IV. As before, except that payment is no longer commutable.

V. As before.

VI. As before, but is silent about spontaneous products.

VII., VIII., IX., X., and XI. As before.

XII. The title conferred by this grant will not exempt the proprietor

14

from any taxes, cesses or liabilities (other than liability for the Land Revenue) which may hereafter be imposed by law.

I may conclude this Appendix by mentioning an enterprise which deserves to be signalised on account of its daring, if for no other reason ; the
purchase of nearly 8,000 acres of land, forming a part of the Old Hopetown grant (*vide supra*, p 314,) at an upset price of Rs. 2,00,000, by the
Rev. Mr. Woodside, from the Dehra Doon Tea Company · · the purpose of
founding a Native Christian Colony. His plan was to · · · the whole
into 1,600 shares of 5 acres each. The value of one ac · · · · tion
under Rs. 24, a five-acre-share would therefore be Rs. 1 · · · · ·rties
contributing one share would secure the *support of a family.*"* The
word share, however, is calculated to mislead, because, the project not
being a commercial, but a charitable, one, each shareholder merely has the
right to nominate a Christian family to reside in the Colony, so that the
money invested is, properly speaking, a *donation* held in trust by the
American Mission. The contributions had reached Rs. 15,595 on the
1st March 1873, but Mr. Woodside took leave to England not long after,
and, it is to be feared, not much has been done since in the way of collecting subscriptions, nor do Christian colonists seem over-anxious to
occupy the land. In February 1873, three families were located there,
and subsequently some others "calling themselves Christian.," strangers
to the Doon, accepted employment. Unfortunately, most of these turned
out to be really vagrants, and took the first opportunity of absconding.
One of the most earnest advocates of the scheme is Mr. Login, C.E.,
F.R.S.E., &c., &c., who has written a very enthusiastic letter on the subject. The marked success of his own experiments in cotton farming
renders him sanguine about the future of the Colony, to the practical
working of which he generously offers the aid of his own experience. I
myself. on the other hand, am of opinion that Mr. Login's engineering
and agricultural skill, even when backed up by Mr. Woodside's indomitable energy can never make such a project succeed, and I should not be
surprised to see the land again in the market before long.

* *Vide* Prospectus published in February 1873.

The following are the villages included in the proposed Colony :—

Number.	Name of Village.	Acres.	Roods.	Poles.	Tenure.	Descriptive Remarks.
		AREA.				
1	Kharakpúr, ...	349	1	3	Rent free.	In the valley of the Asun at the foot of the Sewalik range, the greater portion watered by the Asun, and Manuksid spring.
2	Manúkpúr, ...	444	1	30	„	
3	Ratanpúr, ...	313	1	39	„	
4	Mansadevi Oghi, ...	1,145	3	0	„	
5	„ Bhir ngh,	698	1	23	„	
6	Devipúr, ...	185	1	29	„	
7	Umedpúr. ...	481	2	33	„	Lying on the plateau between the Tonse and Asun rivers, and all irrigable.
8	Hopet·· ..	355	1	20	„	
9	r .	221	2	23	„	
10	.. ...	354	3	18	„	
11	... ...	245	3	5	„	
12	_nakarpur, ...	342	0	0	„	On plateau between Asun and Tonse.
					Govt. rent.	
					RS. A. P.	
13	Shisham Bári, ...	1,488	2	30	209 9 9	Irrigable from Asun to junction of Asun and Tonse. Also on north side of the Asun: good road through the lands.
14	Siduwála, ...	470	3	25	51 2 0	
15	Jhajra, ...	395	0	22	61 6 6	
16	Bansiwála, ...	152	2	2	19 7 0	
17	Dholkot, ...	66	1	33	8 4 0	
	Total, ...	7,718	3	15	349 13 3	